CHALLENGING GENDER INEQUALITY IN TAX POLICY MAKING

This volume takes a critical look at the gender of tax policy around the world. Contributors based in eight different countries examine the profound effects that gender norms and practices have had in shaping tax law and policy, and how taxation in turn impacts upon the possibilities for equality along gender, race, class, sexuality and other lines. Chapters explore how the gendered fiscal state might be theorized; how structural choices about rates and bases in tax policy design contribute to gender inequality; how tax policy affects family configurations and perceptions of what constitutes family; how fiscal systems impact on savings and wealth accumulation by women and men; and the role of different policy-making processes and institutions in occluding and sometimes challenging these patterns. Most significantly, perhaps, the book explores these questions in an international frame, traversing countries and continents. The conclusion: fiscal policy has deep-rooted, long-standing gender implications that affect virtually every aspect of our social, political and economic lives whether we live in Canada, Australia or Kenya.

Oñati International Series in Law and Society

A SERIES PUBLISHED FOR THE OÑATI INSTITUTE
FOR THE SOCIOLOGY OF LAW

Recent titles in this series

Changing Contours of Domestic Life, Family and Law: Caring and Sharing edited by Anne Bottomley and Simone Wong

Criminology and Archaeology: Studies in Looted Antiquities edited by Simon Mackenzie and Penny Green

The Legal Tender of Gender: Welfare Law and the Regulation of Women's Poverty edited by Shelley Gavigan and Dorothy Chunn

Human Rights at Work edited by Colin Fenwick and Tonia Novitz

Travels of the Criminal Question: Cultural Embeddedness and Diffusion edited by Dario Melossi, Máximo Sozzo and Richard Sparks

Feminist Perspectives on Contemporary International Law: Between Resistance and Compliance? edited by Sari Kouvo and Zoe Pearson

Challenging Gender Inequality in Tax Policy Making: Comparative Perspectives edited by Kim Brooks, Åsa Gunnarsson, Lisa Philipps and Maria Wersig

For the complete list of titles in this series, see 'Oñati International Series in Law and Society' link at www.hartpub.co.uk/books/series.asp

Challenging Gender Inequality in Tax Policy Making

Comparative Perspectives

Edited by
Kim Brooks
Åsa Gunnarsson
Lisa Philipps
and
Maria Wersig

Oñati International Series in Law and Society

A SERIES PUBLISHED FOR THE OÑATI INSTITUTE
FOR THE SOCIOLOGY OF LAW

•HART•
PUBLISHING
OXFORD AND PORTLAND, OREGON
2011

Published in the United Kingdom by Hart Publishing Ltd
16C Worcester Place, Oxford, OX1 2JW
Telephone: +44 (0)1865 517530
Fax: +44 (0)1865 510710
E-mail: mail@hartpub.co.uk
Website: http://www.hartpub.co.uk

Published in North America (US and Canada) by
Hart Publishing
c/o International Specialized Book Services
920 NE 58th Avenue, Suite 300
Portland, OR 97213-3786
USA
Tel: +1 503 287 3093 or toll-free: (1) 800 944 6190
Fax: +1 503 280 8832
E-mail: orders@isbs.com
Website: http://www.isbs.com

British Library Cataloguing in Publication Data
Data Available

ISBN: 978-1-84946-123-8

Typeset by Compuscript Ltd, Shannon
Printed and bound in Great Britain by
Lightning Source UK Ltd

Acknowledgements

This collection springs from a workshop held in May 2009 at the International Institute for the Sociology of Law (IISL) in Onati, Spain, the first we believe, ever to have brought together such an internationally diverse group of researchers working on issues related to tax policy and gender equality. The editors are grateful to the IISL for hosting that workshop and to all its participants, most especially those who contributed to this collection of original essays.

Contents

List of Contributors

Kim Brooks was appointed Dean of the Schulich School of Law in July 2010. She formerly held the H Heward Stikeman Chair in the Law of Taxation at McGill's Faculty of Law. Professor Brooks' primary research interests lie in the areas of corporate and international tax, and tax policy.

Bridget Crawford is a Professor of Law at Pace University School of Law in White Plains, New York. She teaches courses in Taxation; Wills, Trusts and Estates; and Feminist Legal Theory. She is the editor, with Anthony Infanti, of *Critical Tax Theory: An Introduction* (Cambridge, 2009). She can be reached at bcrawford@law.pace.edu. You can follow her on Twitter at @ ProfBCrawford.

Paloma de Villota is Professor Doctor of Applied Economy at Universidad Complutense de Madrid. Her research interests include labour market, fiscal and social policies and gender budgeting. She writes reports for the European Commission and Spanish institutions. She has collaborated with UNIFEM, ILPES, CEPAL and the Council of Europe. She has worked with many European Universities in different projects and with American institutions such as FLACSO, UNAM (México). She is a member of the International Association of Feminist Economics and member of the board of the Instituto de Investigaciones Feministas (Spain).

Åsa Gunnarsson is Professor of Jurisprudence and Tax Law at the Department of Law, Umeå University. Her research covers a wide range of issues on law and the gendered fiscal state. She currently leads a research programme funded by the Bank of Sweden Tercentenary Foundation, titled Feminist Studies on Taxation and Budgeting (FemTax).

Anthony C Infanti is a Professor of Law at the University of Pittsburgh School of Law. His research focuses particularly upon the intersection of tax law with sexual orientation and gender identity. He is co-editor of *Critical Tax Theory: An Introduction* (Cambridge University Press, 2009). Professor Infanti is an elected member of the American Law Institute and the American Bar Foundation.

Marjorie E Kornhauser is Professor of Law at Arizona State University College of Law where she teaches tax and tax policy. Her research focuses on the intersection of tax and society, including political, historical and gendered aspects of taxation. Among her recent publications is a chapter in another Hart publication: 'Remembering the "Forgotten Man" (and Woman): Hidden Taxes and the 1936 Election' in J Tiley (ed), *Studies in the History of Tax Law: Volume 4* (Hart Publishing, 2010).

Kathleen A Lahey is Professor of Law and Queen's National Scholar, Faculty of Law, Queen's University, and co-director, Feminist Legal Studies Queen's. Her research includes corporate, personal, international, and comparative taxation and policy, property law, gender budgeting, women, sexualities, and race in fiscal policy and human rights. Recent publications include *Women and Fiscal Equality* (special edition, *Canadian Journal of Women and the Law*, 2010), 'Women, Substantive Equality, and Fiscal Policy' (*CJWL*, 2010), and 'International Transactions, Taxation, and Women: The Critical Role of Gender Analysis' (*UBCLRev*, 2010). She frequently advises parliamentary committees, policy units, and the media on tax/budget issues. Email: kal2@queensu.ca.

Dr Ann Mumford is a Senior Lecturer in the School of Law at Queen Mary, University of London. Ann's research interests are in the fields of fiscal sociology, budgetary processes, and the intersections of law, gender and equality. She has written two monographs, *Taxing Culture* (Ashgate, 2002); and *Tax Policy, Women and the Law* (Cambridge University Press, 2010).

Lisa Philipps is a Professor at Osgoode Hall Law School of York University in Toronto, Canada. She is co-editor of *Tax Expenditures: State of the Art*, ed Lisa Philipps, Neil Brooks and Jinyan Li (Toronto, Canadian Tax Foundation, 2011), and co-author of David G Duff, Kim Brooks, Benjamin Alarie and Lisa Philipps, *Canadian Income Tax Law*, 3rd edn (Markham, Ontario, LexisNexis, 2009).

Kirsten Scheiwe is Professor of Law at Hildesheim University, Germany since 2000. She works mainly in the areas of family law, social law and legal comparison and investigates law in social context from the perspectives of interdisciplinary and comparative legal analysis and gender studies. She received her PhD from the European University Institute, Florence and her habilitation from Frankfurt University.

Ulrike Spangenberg is a Berlin-based independent consultant who has worked with clients in government, trade unions and a variety of other organisations. A lawyer by training, she has specialized in Gender and Fiscal policy. She is the author and co-author of several key studies on the intersection of taxation and gender in Germany. Contact: spangenberg@gleichstellungsinstitut.de.

Miranda Stewart is an Associate Professor at Melbourne Law School, University of Melbourne. She recently edited *Housing and Tax Policy* (Australian Tax Research Foundation, 2010) and is a co-author of *Death and Taxes* (Thomson, 2009) and *Income Taxation: Commentary and Materials* (Thomson, 2009). She is currently researching taxation of the not-for-profit-sector and issues in tax and development.

Bernadette Wanjala is a PhD Fellow in Economics at the Development Research Institute, Tilburg University, the Netherlands. She has wide research experience and publications in macroeconomics, macro modelling, development economics and gender aware macroeconomics. She has previously worked as an Assistant Policy Analyst in Macroeconomics Division, The Kenya Institute for Public Policy Research and Analysis (KIPPRA).

Casey Warman received his PhD in Economics from Carleton University in 2006. He teaches in the Economics Department at Queen's University. His research interests primarily involve empirical issues in the areas of immigration, gender differentials, labour market, and health economics. His research has been published in the *Canadian Journal of Economics*, *Labour Economics* and the *American Economic Journal: Economic Policy.*

Maureen Were is a researcher at the Research and Policy Analysis Department of the Central Bank of Kenya. She holds a PhD in economics, with wide experience in economic research and the field of macroeconomic modelling. She has written a number of papers on pertinent macro and socio-economic issues relating to Kenya.

Maria Wersig studied law and gender equality at the Freie Universität Berlin. She has worked as a policy adviser within the Parliament of the Federal Republic of Germany and is currently a doctoral candidate at the Otto-Suhr-Institute of Political Science (Berlin). Her research interests include family law and policy, taxation, legal gender studies and comparative constitutional studies.

Frances Woolley is a Professor in the Department of Economics at Carleton University. Her area of expertise is the economics of the family and public policy, particularly with respect to the tax treatment of families. She blogs regularly at Worthwhile Canadian Initiative, http://worthwhile.typepad.com and for the Globe and Mail newspaper.

Introduction

LISA PHILIPPS, KIM BROOKS, ÅSA GUNNARSSON AND MARIA WERSIG

THE GENDERED DESIGN and implications of many areas of law, economics and political science have been subject to robust, thoughtful, detailed analysis and critique. While a gender analysis of tax policy exists, its contours have not been explored with the same degree of scrutiny and a gender analysis of much public policy in the tax area is missing altogether. This book begins to fill a critical gap by focusing on the profound effects that gender norms and practices have had in shaping tax law and policy in different countries, and how taxation in turn impacts upon the possibilities for equality along gender, race, class, sexuality and other lines. The chapters explore questions about how the gendered fiscal state might be theorized, how structural choices in tax policy design contribute to gender inequality, how tax policy affects family configurations and perceptions of what constitutes family, and how fiscal systems impact savings and wealth accumulation by women and men. Most significantly, perhaps, the book explores these questions in an international frame, traversing countries and continents. The conclusion: fiscal policy has deep-rooted, long-standing gender implications that affect virtually every aspect of our social, political and economic lives whether we live in Canada, Australia or Kenya.

Tax policy research in general must increasingly contend with the intertwining of national and international norms and institutions in fiscal governance (Avi-Yonah 2007; Christians 2009; Christians et al 2008; Cockfield 2005 and 2006; Stewart 2003). The power to raise and spend public revenues remains fundamentally associated with the nation state and the research in this volume illustrates the diversity of tax policy choices made historically by different countries. At the same time, states increasingly set their fiscal directions in response to pressures associated with global economic integration, capital mobility and market deregulation. The transnational quality of fiscal policy became even more apparent after 2008 when the worldwide financial crisis led to new multinational commitments to engage in stimulus budgeting and to cooperate in preventing tax evasion. The crisis has also exposed the massive (and massively gendered) social risks that populations face in a world of unstable markets and limited welfare state safety nets, often comprised largely of tax-based programmes. These risks are magnified in many countries by demographic ageing which puts additional pressure on the organizing and financing of care work and reproduction, with enormous implications for the gendered division of paid and unpaid labour. The fiscal deficits resulting from the combination of these pressures will need to be addressed in some fashion. As governments and international bodies grapple with these challenges, tax policy will play a central role both as a means of financing public action, and as a powerful instrument for delivering programmes, distributing resources and incentivizing behavioural changes. Thus, it is not surprising that in the wake of the crisis, scholars and policy makers have begun to analyze how tax systems may have contributed to past problems and how they might be redesigned to foster economic growth, discourage excessive risk taking by market actors and shore up the economic security of vulnerable individuals (Edgar 2010; International Monetary Fund 2009; Shaviro 2009). Yet new tax measures are unlikely to achieve their goals unless the policy makers who design them are attuned to gender differences in income, wealth, opportunities, and responsibilities.

The authors in this book draw on a variety of intellectual frameworks to analyze the gender saturated character of tax policy choices. Indeed, the collection demonstrates that gender analysis of tax law can proceed from a range of different theoretical and political perspectives. Most of the contributors make their disciplinary home in law and hence one focus of the book is on feminist legal and socio-legal analyses of specific rules, procedures and institutions of tax law. Many of the chapters shed light on assumptions about gender or sexuality that are embedded in the design of legal norms, or on the differential effect of tax laws when applied to women and men who occupy different positions in markets and households. Others approach the subject from a more economic perspective that analyzes the way taxes incentivize the behavioural choices of men and women as individuals and in various household forms (see especially Paloma de Villota, chapter six; and Casey Warman and Frances Woolley, chapter nine). Other important intellectual backdrops include feminist scholarship on welfare states and on the gendered implications of neoliberal economic policy. For example, some chapters investigate the tax dimensions of a broad shift away from policies that assume two-parent households supported by a primary breadwinner, towards a system modelled on universal market engagement by self-reliant individuals (see, for example Ulrike Spangenburg, chapter thirteen; Kirsten Scheiwe, chapter ten). Finally, this volume adds to a growing academic and policy literature on gender budgeting, most of which has focused on the spending side of fiscal policy (as discussed by Bernadette Wanjala and Maureen Were in chapter seven). One of its important contributions is to illustrate how gender analysis can be applied more systematically to the revenue side of budgets.

Fortunately, we were not required to start our analysis from scratch. While there is much to be added to the gender analysis of fiscal policy, the authors in this collection were able to build on earlier path-breaking work by feminist scholars. In some countries more than others, a feminist tax policy literature is rich and deep, although far from complete (Alstott 1996; Brown 1997; Dulude 1985; Fellows 1998; Kahng 2004; Lahey 1985; Lipman 2003; Mennel 1986; Mückenberger et al 2007; Philipps 1996; Shurtz 1998; Staudt 1996; Stewart 1998; Young 1995). Although some jurisdictions have been fortunate to have several scholars working in the area, no jurisdiction has policy makers that have fully engaged with their suggestions.

Each of the four chapters included in Part I: Gendering the Fiscal State offers a perspective on the role of gender in defining the overall frame within which tax policy debates are played out. Though anchored by case studies of tax reform in particular locations and at particular times, their purpose is not to develop detailed policy prescriptions. Rather, they serve to enable critical analysis by revealing how apparently gender neutral tax regimes can be implicated in the production and reproduction of unequal gender relations. The first chapter, by Kathleen Lahey, places the subject matter of this book squarely in historical context. Lahey argues that the fundamental source of women's inequality in tax law is their continuing absence as true subjects of fiscal policy independent of their relationships with men. Indeed, in her view the 'basic nature and function of the state, of taxation, and of fiscal policy remain grounded in preoccupation with male control over women' (14). Lahey excavates the profoundly gendered ontology of tax law from pre-Roman times and traces this history to the unstated assumptions that frame contemporary tax policy debate.

Ann Mumford and Miranda Stewart (chapters two and three) examine recent processes of tax reform in England and Australia, respectively. Both point out the limited interest that policy makers have demonstrated in gender issues, apart from using taxes to encourage women's participation in paid labour or to deliver baseline welfare. Other dimensions of gender inequality tend to drop out of the picture, as Stewart discusses in relation to the distribution of opportunities to accumulate capital. A further theme connecting these two chapters is the continued pressure exerted by a market-oriented economic policy paradigm in contemporary tax policy making. Each turns to a broader theoretical approach (new institutionalism for Mumford, development theory on capabilities for Stewart) to open up the analysis of tax systems to a fuller consideration of the issues and constraints that women face as economic actors.

The final chapter in Part I by Åsa Gunnarsson (chapter four) emphasizes the pivotal role of the public/private divide in structuring the tax treatment of women as compared with men. Comparing German, French and Swedish approaches to the tax unit, she finds that they offer opposing visions of gender equality as a function of either promoting sameness (universal market participation) or accommodating difference (women as primary carers), with neither fostering the integration of these activities.

Gunnarsson also critiques the Swedish tax reforms of 1991 as poorly designed from the perspective of both economic growth and women's equality. She argues that the concentration of tax cuts on high income men ignored the efficiency gains that could have been reaped by reducing taxes for more women, whose paid labour supply is more responsive to changes in the after-tax wage. Instead, reformers relied on welfare measures to address gender equality concerns, leaving women exposed to welfare walls in the form of high tax back rates on benefits when they start to earn income. On this level, Gunnarsson echoes Stewart's concern with an exclusive focus on baseline economic security for poor women, as opposed to their broader inclusion in the full range of market opportunities.

Following Part I, the book shifts from macro level analysis to closer studies of specific tax policy problems. Many of the remaining chapters address subject matters that have not frequently, or have never, been considered from a feminist perspective. The contributors to Part II on Bases and Rates all provide examples of how gender equality is impacted by decisions about the basic structural design of tax systems. Bridget Crawford's study (chapter five) probes the meaning of income and considers how taxation of earnings from surrogacy contracts would impact women's equality. The current IRS practice of loose enforcement in this area appears in an immediate sense to be better for women undertaking an inherently gendered form of economic activity. Yet Crawford argues that taxation is the preferred option, both from the symbolic perspective of validating women's reproductive activities as 'work', and because of the potential indirect benefits that surrogates will obtain by becoming taxpayers.

Paloma de Villota (chapter six) widens the analysis of structural tax design by demonstrating the complex interaction of base, rates and tax unit in shaping the gender distribution of personal income taxes in Spain following successive rounds of tax reform. She identifies several potential sources of gender bias because of the different earning profiles of men and women, the differential tax rates applied to wages and capital gains, and the continued option for married persons to file individually or jointly. Similar themes are pursued by Bernadette Wanjala and Maureen Were (chapter seven) in the context of Kenya. Both of these chapters point out the difficulty of thoroughly understanding or explaining the gender impact of tax policies in the absence of fully gender disaggregated tax and economic data. This barrier is particularly acute in countries that use a joint tax return. Nonetheless, both Villota and Wanjala and Were located sufficient data to conduct a partial analysis that provides at least a window onto the gendered impact of tax policies. Wanjala and Were add a further dimension to the picture by studying the incidence of Value Added Tax in Kenya, demonstrating the sometimes surprising effects of decisions to exempt a particular good or service from the tax. Their contribution bears on the question of tax mix and is important not least because many countries outside North America rely so heavily on VATs or other consumption taxes to raise a large share of revenues. Wanjala and Were's study especially illustrates the differences that lie between tax systems in rich and poor countries, and the way gender interacts with other key socio-economic characteristics of Kenyans, such as the divide between urban and rural populations and between owners and non-owners of land. This opens a very large question that should be on the agenda for future research in this field, that is, how gender analysis of tax policy in individual countries connects to issues of global inequality among more and less wealthy countries.

The need for careful attention to demographic diversity is brought into the foreground by Part III on Tax and the Family. These chapters not only interrogate the consequences of fiscal policy for different kinds of families, but question the degree to which fiscal policy constructs the normative family. Anthony Infanti (chapter eight) focuses on the design and effect of the medical expenses deduction in the United States comparing so-called traditional and non-traditional families, but more fundamentally his chapter probes the constitutive nature of taxing legislation using the medical expenses deduction as a foil. Infanti's chapter throws into relief the ways in which tax policy design can take for granted stereotypes about gender. For example, he demonstrates that the design of the medical expense deduction elides questions about the identity of the recipient of the medical treatment and presupposes particular family configurations, most notably reflecting the view that only heterosexual families procreate.

The second chapter in Part III, by Casey Warman and Frances Woolley (chapter nine), turns to the implications of tax policy for same-sex couples. State recognition of same-sex relationships has been a hot button issue in many parts of the world in the last decade: naturally, given that all income tax legislation takes spousal relationships into account in at least some of its provisions, one consequence of legal recognition for same-sex couples is a change in the tax treatment of the individuals in the relationship. Warman and Woolley rely on Canadian data to build a demographic profile of self-identified gays and lesbians in Canada. They conclude, in contrast to studies undertaken in other jurisdictions, that legal recognition of same-sex marriage has had few tax advantages for working-age gays and lesbians; nevertheless, for single parents, the legal recognition of relationships can lead to a substantial loss of benefits delivered through Canada's tax legislation.

The final two chapters in Part III turn to the gendered consequences of tax design for 'traditional' families employing Germany as a case study. Kirsten Scheiwe (chapter ten) details the impact of child benefits and deductions for expenses related to child rearing. The gendered division of work in the home, particularly around the raising of children, is one of the most palpable illustrations of gender inequality, so it is perhaps shocking that this has not been taken into account in any adequate way by fiscal policy makers around the globe. One of the most important contributions

Scheiwe's chapter makes is her insistence that taxation, social security and direct benefits must be analyzed together to present a sophisticated view of the state's role in providing particular incentives and disincentives for child care work. Scheiwe concludes that Germany's approach to this area results in highly uneven consequences, some intended and some unintended, across families depending on the family's form and its income class.

Maria Wersig (chapter eleven) concludes Part III of the collection. Wersig's chapter complements the others in this section—her review of the German system of joint taxation reveals the dominance of the bias toward traditional families identified also in Infanti's chapter. The chapter includes a historical review of the basis for joint taxation of spouses and she critiques its gendered repercussions. Germany's constitutional constraints present yet another layer to the complicated story of why Germany continues to tolerate joint taxation when it unequivocally constitutes bad gender politics. Wersig's appeal for reform might be echoed in other countries where joint taxation and income splitting continue to hold sway in fiscal policy.

An area that has been desperately lacking in gender analysis is the consequences of fiscal policy for women's saving and capital investment; therefore, the collection concludes with Part IV which turns the analytical focus to Savings, Wealth and Capital Gains. Part IV opens with a contribution from Lisa Philipps (chapter twelve). Philipps complicates the narrative that income splitting is always bad for women by focusing on the possibilities for women if income splitting were coupled with a legal requirement that the split income (or the underlying assets) actually be transferred to the lower-income spouse. At its core, Philipps' argument demands that feminist scholars and policy makers consider whether there are autonomy enhancing moves that could be made in tax policy design if we were serious about wanting to redistribute wealth intra-family.

If intra-family transfers present one means of supporting saving and wealth accumulation by women, another mechanism is to offer government support for employer-provided pensions. Ulrike Spangenberg (chapter thirteen) takes on the difficult question of whether tax regulations actually violate constitutional prohibitions against discrimination. She argues that the fact that many vulnerable groups are under-compensated or not covered by government-subsidized employer-provided pensions requires at least some additional compensation for these excluded or under-subsidized groups, otherwise the tax system results in indefensible indirect discrimination.

Finally, the collection includes a groundbreaking chapter by Marjorie Kornhauser (chapter fourteen) on the gendered implications of capital gains taxation. Of all forms of income, capital gains receive some of the most favourable tax treatment worldwide. A standard narrative (and an important one) would explore the degree to which that preference benefits primarily men. But Kornhauser goes much beyond that narrative, looking also at the explanatory rationale for the dominance of men as investors in capital assets. Kornhauser delves into the behavioural investment tendencies of men and women and queries whether those investment practices exacerbate the gender inequality inherent in the capital gains preference. She provides a more nuanced story about the policy moves governments should make in designing the rules governing capital gains taxation.

An active engagement with policy immediately raises the question of which institutions and processes can best be mobilized to challenge and change the status quo, and which may represent barriers which themselves need to be reformed. Read as a group, the chapters in this volume show why legal instruments are essential, yet also limited in their ability to bring about meaningful change on the ground, and this is true even when law makers collaborate through international institutions to create norms such as tax treaties or conventions to eliminate discrimination against women. The book reveals the complementary roles played by different branches of the state, such as treasury officials and women's bureaus, legislatures and courts, revenue administrators and statistical agencies. It also raises persistent questions about how feminist researchers and civil society advocates can best engage with these institutions and processes to achieve thoughtful policy changes and to evaluate both successes and failures. The collection contributes to the emerging literature that takes seriously the impact of policy making on women. It does not, by any stretch, canvass all of the issues or provide definitive solutions. Instead, we hope it serves as a call for other researchers and policy makers to grapple with the questions it raises, pursuing new lines of inquiry and interrogating fiscal policy for all its consequences, particularly the consequences for those most exposed to market discrimination.

REFERENCES

Alstott, A (1996) 'Tax Policy and Feminism: Competing Goals and Institutional Choices' 96 *Columbia Law Review* 2001.

Avi-Yonah, RS (2007) *International Tax as International Law* (New York, Cambridge University Press).

Brown, DA (1997) 'Race, Class, and Gender Essentialism in Tax Literature: The Joint Return' 54(4) *Washington and Lee Law Review* 1469.

Christians, A (2009) 'Sovereignty, Taxation, and Social Contract' 18(1) *Minnesota Journal of International Law* 99.

Christians, A, Dean, SA, Ring, D and Rosenzweig, A (2008) 'Taxation as a Global Socio-Legal Phenomenon' 14 *ILSA Journal of International and Comparative Law.*

Cockfield, AJ (2005) *NAFTA Tax Law and Policy: Resolving the Clash Between Economic and Sovereignty Interests* (Toronto, University of Toronto Press).

—— (2006) 'The Rise of the OECD as Informal "World Tax Organization" through National Responses to E-Commerce Tax Challenges' 9 *Yale Journal of Law and Technology* 59.

Dulude, L (1985) 'Taxation of the Spouses: A Comparison of Canadian, American, British, French and Swedish Law' 23 *Osgoode Hall Law Journal* 1.

Edgar, T (2010) 'Financial Instability, Tax Policy, and the Tax Expenditure Concept 63 *Southern Methodist University Law Review* 969.

Fellows, ML (1998) 'Rocking the Tax Code: A Case Study of the Tax Treatment of Work-Related Child-Care Expenditures' 10 *Yale Journal of Law and Feminism* 307.

International Monetary Fund (2009) *Debt-Bias and Other Distortions: Crisis-Related Issues in Tax Policy*. Available online at: www.imf.org/external/np/pp/eng/2009/061209.pdf).

Kahng, L (2004) 'Innocent Spouses: A Critique of the New Tax Laws Governing Joint and Several Tax Liability' 49 *Villanova Law Review* 261.

Lahey, K (1985) 'The Tax Unit in Income Tax Theory' in ED Pask et al (eds), *Women, the Law, and the Economy* (Toronto, Butterworths) 277.

Lipman, FJ (2003) 'Enabling Work for People with Disabilities: A Post-Integrationist Revision of Underutilized Tax Incentives' 53 *American University Law Review* 393.

Mennel, A (1986) 'Frauen Steuern Staatsfinanzen' *Feministische Studien* 71.

Mückenberger, U, Spangenberg, U and Warncke, K (2007) *Familienförderung und Gender Mainstreaming im Steuerrecht* (Baden-Baden, Nomos).

Philipps, L (1996) 'Discursive Deficits: A Feminist Perspective on the Power of Technical Knowledge in Fiscal Law and Policy' 11 *Canadian Journal of Law and Society* 141.

Shaviro, D (2009) 'The 2008–09 Financial Crisis: Implications for Income Tax Reform', NYU Law and Economics Research Paper No 09-35. Available online at: papers.ssrn.com/sol3/papers.cfm?abstract_id=1442089.

Shurtz, N (1998) 'Critical Tax Theory: Still Not Taken Seriously' 76 *University of North Carolina Law Review* 1837.

Staudt, NC (1996) 'Taxing Housework' 84 *Georgetown Law Journal* 1571.

Stewart, M (2003) 'Global Trajectories of Tax Reform: The Discourse of Tax Reform in Developing and Transition Countries' 44 *Harvard International Law Journal* 139.

Woodman, FL (1998) 'Women and Children in the Economy: Reflections from the Income Tax System' 47 *University of New Brunswick Law Journal* 311.

Young, CFL (1995) '(In)visible Inequalities: Women, Tax and Poverty' 27 *Ottawa Law Review* 99–127.

Part I

Gendering the Fiscal State

1

The 'Capture' of Women in Law and Fiscal Policy: The Tax/Benefit Unit, Gender Equality and Feminist Ontologies

KATHLEEN A LAHEY

IT IS WELL known that the movement towards gender equality has been contested and slow, and that in no country have women yet attained genuine and full equality with men. Less visible is the fact that equality gains are not just difficult to achieve, but are extremely fragile and can be reversed quickly when the impact of law and policy on women as a sex/gender class is not kept at the forefront of the agenda.

Over the last ten years, women in Canada have learned this hard fact. This chapter connects the dramatic erosion of women's status in Canada in recent years with tax and fiscal policies that reinforce women's traditional lack of social, economic and political power and disproportionate responsibilities for unpaid and underpaid work. Instead of simply looking for specific policy alternatives to those that currently shape the new status quo, however, this chapter examines how 'masculine capture' of governance, revenue and social resources in longer-term processes of state-building has made it possible for women to become formal 'legal persons' in some types of legal, social and economic situations, but has continued to prevent women from acting as true and equal 'subjects' of the state in the same way that men do. This inquiry traces the 'capture' of women reflected in the first recorded law codes and tax practices (from the ancient Middle East and Rome) through the development of continental and English taxation, colonial exportations and contemporary tax policies and posits that until fundamental concepts like value and work are re-visioned around women as equal subjects, women's equality will remain elusive.

THE FRAGILITY OF WOMEN'S EQUALITY: CANADA, 1985–2009

Women's equality in Canada received a huge boost when the new Charter of Rights and Freedoms prohibited sex discrimination effective in 1985. This constitutional development was accompanied by tremendous social interest and a huge number of studies, policies and laws enacted to support the promise of equality. The rapid improvement in the status of women was reflected in the UN Human Development Index (HDI) and Gender-related Development Index (GDI) (UNDP). In 1995, Canada was ranked only ninth in the UN's GDI (HDI: 1990–93 data), but within a few short years rose to first for four years in a row. During this time, Canada adopted the UN Platform for Action at the 1995 Beijing world conference and began actively implementing gender mainstreaming and gender-based analysis.

This commitment was short lived. By 2000, budgetary, tax and spending changes had begun to undercut women's economic equality in Canada. These changes included tightened eligibility for unemployment insurance benefits, maternity leave and parental leave (all implemented in the mid-1990s); spending cuts for childcare, privatization of government services, making low-income benefits more 'target efficient' by reverting to the 'male breadwinner' model of tax and benefit assistance and the shift from social assistance to 'workfare'. At the same time, tax cuts for high-income business owners and corporations were implemented and, most recently (since 2006), a minority conservative government has expanded the use of joint tax and benefit measures while doing nothing to redress disproportionately high tax rates for those with low incomes.

The impact of these changes has been dramatic and highly visible. By 2001, Canada had dropped to third in the UN GDI (reporting on 1999 data) and to seventh in the 2006 GDI (reporting on 2004 data). Newer indices that place less emphasis on general development levels in order to isolate changes in the status of women reveal that this trend has accelerated rapidly since then. The new World Economic Forum Gender Gap Index ranked Canada fourteenth in 2006, eighteenth in 2007 and thirty-first in 2008 (World Economic Forum 2008). In 2009, the UN ranked Canada seventy-fourth in its new gender disparity measure, which ranks countries by the size of the gaps between their general human development index (HDI) and GDI scores (UNDP 2009).

On every measure, the deterioration of women's equality in Canada is shocking. At base, however, the problem is that despite earlier gains in gender equality, the fundamental economic disadvantages of women were never meaningfully addressed nor changed. Figure 1 reveals that even now, men's and women's incomes in Canada continue to be markedly gender segmented, reflecting women's continuing lack of equal access to income equality and their disproportionate relegation to unpaid and poorly-paid work.

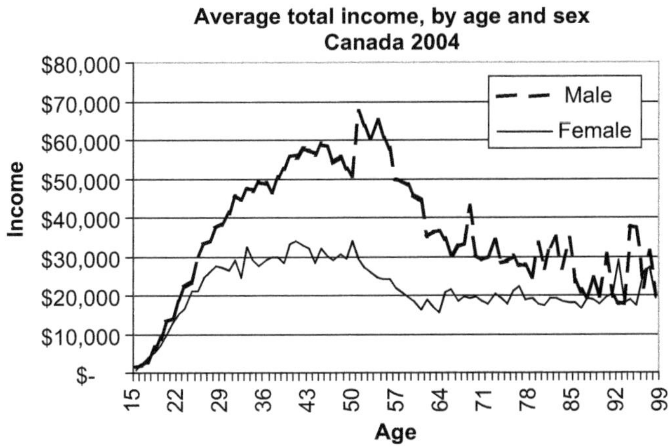

Figure 1: Average Total Income by Age and Sex, Canada 2004
Source: Statistics Canada, SPSD/M, v. 8.

These are, of course, aggregate figures. But hidden within these averages are the numerous tax and spending decisions that negatively affect women, and the continuing reluctance to design fiscal policies to redress women's inequalities. To provide one example, in 2004, only 31.5 per cent of workers receiving 'regular' employment insurance benefits were women, while 68.5 per cent were men. This is because since the mid-1990s, Canadian employment insurance coverage and eligibility criteria have made it difficult for women to qualify for regular benefits unless they fit a standard 'breadwinner' model and tie women's benefits to their lower average incomes even when they do qualify (Lahey 2009a). To give another example, high educational or professional attainment does not insulate women in Canada from excess workloads. A recent study of the Ontario legal profession found that women lawyers perform an average of 35 hours of unpaid work each week (care of children, elders, other family members and home) while men lawyers doing the same paid work reported only 13 hours of unpaid work each week. Women lawyers also worked slightly reduced hours of paid work per week until their children reached the age of 16—not just while they were younger (Kay et al 2004).

Obviously, the rapid deterioration of women's equality in Canada is not due only to changes in fiscal policy. However, the failure of the Canadian state to use its governance and regulatory powers to eradicate longstanding disparities in resources and opportunities available to men and women, especially when combined with fiscal policy that only 'sees' women in their relations to other entities yet 'sees' men as 'subjects' to whom the state is accountable, has powerfully perpetuated the conditions that constitute women's inequality.

This chapter suggests that such ontological challenges cannot be met by finding the 'right' equality claim or by constructing 'better' arguments to persuade governments to root out gender-based hierarchies. Rather, they require policy analysts to identify how the basic nature and function of the state, of taxation and of fiscal policy remain grounded in preoccupation with male control over women. The rest of this chapter examines this preoccupation as reflected in the texts of some of the oldest recorded tax laws, in the use of taxation to reinforce gendered, heterosexist, racist, classist and pro-natalist legal hierarchies and, finally, in the continued use of 'tax unit' rules to concentrate ownership of incomes and wealth in male hands. When viewed from the standpoint of institutional histories of law and taxation, the links between the 'capture' of women in law and taxation and the ongoing use of various forms of the 'marital unit' or the 'family unit' in fiscal policy can be discerned behind the screen of relentlessly gender-neutral language used by contemporary states to inscribe their policy choices.

This chapter also invites readers to imagine how, when women are not ontologically perceived as being 'subjects' in the same way that men are, women's identities can be made visible and compelling to policy makers (Hekman 2007: 36–37). With male-centred perspectives on the nature of women's existence already deeply embedded in law, governance, accounting concepts and fiscal policy, the process of imagining how women can define and gain respect for their 'possible lives' in legal and fiscal policy is the ultimate ontological challenge.

MASCULINE 'CAPTURE' IN EARLY LAW AND HIERARCHIZING TAXATION

Taxation is a core governance function. Tax systems clearly predated the emergence of recorded laws and the administrative state, and even early forms of state organization could not have emerged unless viable tax systems had already been put into place (Levi 1989: 1–2). Thus, taxation can be thought of as being both constitutive of the state and integral to the basic mechanisms of social and economic control that make it possible for states to grow in power (Levi 1989; Bräutigam 2002).

The constitutive nature of taxation is reflected in early law codes of emerging states. When these codes were first developed, they were not about tax rules; the texts of the codes themselves make it clear that taxation pre-existed the codes as prior manifestations of sovereignty, and was not constituted by law codes (Steele 1948: 17). While ancient Middle Eastern rulers made surprisingly modern statements on tax policy when taking power—promising lower taxes, social justice, economic growth and help for the weak and vulnerable—early law codes were clearly not tax instruments (Cooper 1986; Black et al 1997–2006).

The 'Capture' of Women in Roman Tax Law

Judging by the actual content of Babylonian, Sumerian and then Roman law codes, the 'capture' of women was a high priority during the ancient era. Legal texts of these early states were concerned not with governance, but with constituting the family unit and placing it under the direct control of husbands. Over time, male heads of household gained control over women's productive and reproductive capacities and over property ownership (Goetz 2006: 2; *cf* Eisenstein 1986, 1979; Delphy 1984). Being placed under the direct control of male heads of households did not just deprive women of the right to own and accumulate property; it literally prevented them from acting outside the domestic sphere to establish direct relationships with the state and to be 'seen' as citizens of the state.

Roman law played a key role in this process as it incorporated its own earlier law codes into the formal law of persons. This system prohibited women, slaves, children and aliens from exercising any legal powers concerning property, business, governance and politics, while 'citizens'—men of the property-owning and ruling classes—were deemed to hold those powers in their stead. This was accomplished through the legal fiction of the *unitas personae* ('one person' or 'unitary person') that was used to merge women, children and slaves with the 'person' of the husband/father/owner in the eyes of the law. All their 'powers' were said to flow into the legal personality of the husband/father/owner, leaving him as the sole legal representation of all those married, fathered or owned by him. In turn, this legal fiction denied to all but citizen males the capacity to engage in acts recognized and enforceable in law. (For example, the capacity to engage in property transactions, contracts, employment, litigation, or legal proceedings, to consent to marriage, to hold custody of their own children, to vote/speak in the forum or to hold public office (Scott 1932: 1, 64; Watson 1970: 32–39).)

Because early legal systems did not recognize women as legal persons or as subjects, they consequently did not recognize women as owners of property or as producers of wealth for purposes of tax laws. Instead, women's productive activities (and those of slaves and other workers) were completely subsumed within the original units of taxation used to collect revenues. For example, assessments of the value of a farm, a garden or a house for taxation purposes considered the productivity of the land, the skill and knowledge of the actual workers and the production record of the unit—but women's contributions to that production were completely ignored as the male head was treated as owning the property and income, and was made liable for taxation. Women were thus several steps removed from direct contact with the state and its agents. Only husbands had direct and immediate contact with the state (Levi 1989: 79–84).

The Use of Taxation to Regulate Gender, Sexuality, Race and Class

Although privileged Roman women gradually gained some access to property (Miles and Driver 1960; Watson 1970) women were initially considered to be exempt from taxation precisely because they had no economic or political power. However, as rulers discovered how taxation could be use for purposes of social control, tax measures were gradually devised to regulate gender, sexual, race and class hierarchies. The first reported use of taxation to control women's behaviour is found in the Oppian laws (215 BCE) prohibiting women from wearing gold ornaments or multicoloured dresses and from using chariots. When Cato found himself unable to quell women's huge public protests over these laws, he hit upon the strategy of replacing them with heavy taxes on the forbidden items (Durant 1944: 89).

Augustus pursued similar goals through a combination of direct family law and tax law, although his objective was not to regulate women's dress and means of transport, but to promote heterosexual marriage and reproduction. His Julian Laws (18 BCE) required all men under the age of 60 and all women under 50 to be married, voided bequests prohibiting remarriage and prohibited childless women from inheriting (Coffield 1970: 25–26; Lefkowitz and Fant 1982: 181). He then reinforced these rules with tax penalties: men's estates paid heavy inheritance taxes on bequests made to anyone other than their children, and both married women with fewer than three children and unmarried women paid heavy wealth taxes each year (Durant 1944: 224).

Later rulers attempted to expand the taxation of women despite earlier exemptions, and as the Empire deteriorated, direct taxation of women began in lower classes as prostitutes and 'slave girls' were taxed heavily. Growing poverty and child abandonment resulted in the introduction of the *alimenta* (family child allowances) and in the late Empire, women were counted as half a *caput* for the poll tax (Coffield 1970: 43–55).

The structures of Roman law left women economically, legally and politically disenfranchised, dependent on men for support (whether as wives, prostitutes or welfare recipients) and singled out along with men in same-sex relationships, free women and slaves for punitive action in property and tax law if they failed to actively meet the state's requirements for heterosexual marriage, reproduction and property relations. The Emperor's official title (*Pater Patriae* or 'father of the fatherland') paralleled the legal concepts of *pater familias* and *patriae potestas*, which condensed all legal capacities within households into the hands of the chief male in the household and constructed the married couple as the basic unit of legal policy. At the same time, the ruler's superior powers permitted him to reach into the household to directly regulate all the individuals and property within it (Severy 2003: 192). The stringent denial of women's legal capacities within this system was integral to this system.

THE MARITAL UNIT BECOMES THE BASIC UNIT OF TAXATION

The Roman law of persons played a crucial role in defining the tax/benefit unit as later societies developed national tax systems. Although England and Europe appeared to develop two distinct legal traditions—English common law and European civil law—both traditions incorporated Roman laws incapacitating women. Not surprisingly, both also adopted the married couple as the basic unit of taxation.

In England, the Roman law of persons survived centuries of disuse as small-scale political units developed localized feudal revenue systems to meet their needs for political cohesion and revenues. As national-level governance was re-established after the Norman Conquest, Roman images of men as holding all familial powers and of women as lacking virtually all civil and political capacities were grafted onto military tenures to maintain clear man-to-man bonds of fealty by lord to king. England's common law courts adopted the Roman legal doctrine of *unitas personae* to fashion the common law doctrine of coverture, which dictated that women merged with their husbands on marriage to become 'one person'—the husband. The doctrine of coverture or 'civil death' suspended women's legal capacities during marriage and prevented them from acquiring direct interests in property (Baker, 1971: 144–49, 258–66; Blackstone, 1765: 1: 442–45).

In Europe, political fragmentation of the former Roman Empire created scope for the emergence of customary property laws in Europe, including Germanic community property systems. The Roman doctrines of *pater familias* and *patria potestas* persisted in varying degrees in Europe, but localized and regional community property systems—particularly in northern Europe—came to permit married women to own anything they acquired by gift or inheritance as their own separate property, considered them to be equal owners of property acquired by the married couple during their cohabitation and empowered them to inherit and deal with up to half or even the whole of their deceased husbands' estates (De Funiak and Vaughn 1971: 21–22, 31–35). This was radically different from the status of women in England, where widows were only allowed to use a small portion of their husband's property, and then only for her life (dower). Women also had more legal capacities in medieval cities in Europe, where they took on increasing roles in market production during the same period that the doctrine of coverture continued to be applied rigidly in England (Howell 1988: 177).

However, by the early modern period, neither the spread of community property regimes nor bourgeois liberal ideologies of property rights and political representation were able to free women from their by then ancient marital disabilities. In fact, just the opposite seems to have occurred. Throughout Europe, even civil codes that had given equal property interests to both spouses (Howell 1998: 115–20) came to assign full management power over community property to the husband during marriage, effectively erasing women's exercise of ownership rights during marriage and excluding women from trades and businesses they had carried on during the medieval period (Howell 1998: 177, 183, 259–60). In England, which had expunged most traces of customary community property systems after 1100 CE, the political rationale for private property was reconceptualized during the bourgeois period as one of the 'natural rights of man'. Despite the emergence of liberal rights discourse, the doctrine of coverture remained unchanged. For example, John Locke's labour theory of property clearly assigned ownership of everything produced in the 'household' as belonging to the male head, and seemed to treat women as important primarily because they guaranteed paternity through which property ownership could be 'completed' by transmitting it through inheritance to children (Locke 1824: 145–59, 175–77).

The Married Couple is the 'Tax Unit'

As income taxation evolved in the 1700s, both the English common law doctrine of coverture and the continental civil code rules regarding management and control of community property were taken as defining the economic realities of the husband-wife relationship. Whether the marital estate was deemed by common law doctrine to be owned by 'one person'—the husband—or was directed by civil codes to be managed and controlled by the husband, women continued to be viewed as lacking capacity to be taxed directly as individuals, and instead the marital unit was treated as the 'tax unit'. This is illustrated quite clearly in the two first income tax systems adopted in the early modern period: when Sweden enacted its first income tax statute in 1710, it was a community property state; when England enacted its income tax statute in 1799, it remained a common law/coverture state. Despite this significant difference, however, both countries adopted the married couple as the legal tax unit, and both treated the husband as representing the interests of that entity (Barner 1959; Björne 1972; Marshall and Walsh 1970).

In the 1800s and 1900s, married women's property laws and then family property law reforms in England, the rest of Europe and many of their former colonies (most of which had in the meantime adopted the legal regimes of their parent countries) began to undo the doctrines of coverture and management. Despite the erosion of these doctrines, however, the married couple continued to be used as the basic tax unit in most jurisdictions, and thus truly individualized tax systems continued to be rare for some time. As a result, the assumptions of ancient laws were effectively translated into modern tax statutes, which continued to depict men as owning women's production and property, women as 'persons' in law but not as true 'subjects' and women's interests in taxation as subjugated to the state's view of marriage and the family. Simply removing women's many legal disabilities in common law and civil law did not, on its own, result in re-imagining women as having the political or legal capacities of individuals for fiscal purposes.

Marital Aggregation Overtaxes Married Women

On a technical level, the use of the married couple as the basic unit of tax policy aggregates couple incomes in the hands of husbands. This can be seen in the income tax statutes enacted in both England and Sweden, despite their differing legal regimes. In England, the first permanent English income tax statute incorporated the common law of coverture into the Finance Act by providing that 'profits of any married woman living with her husband shall be deemed the profits of her husband' (Marshall and Walsh 1970). In Sweden, and later in other European community property countries, male control and management of community property was treated as assigning all spousal income to the husband for tax purposes, despite the fact that community property laws were considered to give both spouses immediate ownership interests in each other's assets and incomes (Malmström 1955: 411–12).

So long as incomes are all taxed at the same rate, which was the case for many years in Sweden, marital aggregation by itself does not tax married and single women differently. However, the immediate use of graduated income tax rates in England in the 1800s and the eventual increase in Swedish tax rates after the Second World War (Barner 1959; Lindencrona 1979) imposed tax penalties from over-taxation on married women, when the income tax attributable to their earnings was compared with that of either their husbands or single women. Long after married women in England and Sweden gained legal control over their own incomes and property in the 1880s, married women's incomes were still deemed to belong to their husbands, 'stacking' the wife's income on top of her husband's income in the calculation of the married couple's income tax liability. Unless the combined incomes are so small that all income is still taxed at the lowest income tax rate, marital aggregation will always overtax married women's incomes because it pushes wives' incomes into higher tax rate brackets than if they were single (or if they were husbands).

CHALLENGING 'FISCAL COVERTURE' WITH INDIVIDUAL TAXATION

From a policy perspective, it is extremely easy to eliminate the over-taxation of women that arises from marital aggregation: all over-taxation disappears when each spouse is treated as a separate individual. Using the individual as the basic tax unit ensures that each spouse is able to take full advantage of his or her own lowest income bracket. It also satisfies horizontal equity by imposing the same amount of tax on all taxpayers with the same incomes, regardless of whether they are married, single, male or female.

Indeed, one view of the evolution of the tax/benefit unit since the early 1900s posits that the marital unit has largely been replaced with individual taxation, and that continued use of the marital unit by a small minority of countries is outmoded and destined to repeal (CBO 1997). However, this is a simplistic view, because merely declaring the 'individual' or 'every person' to be the legal taxpayer will not automatically insulate married women from over-taxation through marital aggregation. Detailed examination of most income tax systems reveals that even when the marital unit has been replaced by individual taxation, the resulting tax system can still contain marriage-based provisions that perpetuate fiscal coverture and marital aggregation. These dynamics are illustrated by the transition from marital to individual taxation in the UK and Sweden.

Individualizing Income Taxation in the UK

It took some 190 years from the time the first national income tax was introduced in England in 1799 for the UK to replace marital aggregation with individual taxation. Women had begun protesting the over-taxation caused by marital aggregation in the late 1800s, but with little effect (Barr 1980; Knowles 1920: 151–60; Marshall and Walsh 1970; Royal Commission 1920). Married women's property legislation, anti-discrimination legislation and even citation by the European Union failed to bring about timely change. During that period, married men remained the sole point of contact between the married couple and the revenue agency, women had to reveal all of their income to their husbands, but had no right to examine or sign their husband's tax returns and even tax benefits designed to ameliorate the over-taxation of women could be claimed by and paid to husbands only.

The UK eliminated marital aggregation in 1990 (except for older couples) (Chan 1999). Shortly after that, however, marital aggregation emerged anew in the Working Family Tax Credit, which uses the married couple's total income to determine eligibility for earned income tax credits and directs the most generous benefits to workers who can obtain 'standard' full-time employment. This formula, which is becoming typical of earned income tax credits adopted in other countries, reinstates male capture within low-income couples by reinforcing the 'male-breadwinner' model of the family in tax/benefit policy (Chan 1999; Millar 2003).

Sweden's Individualized Tax System

Even Sweden, which now has one of the most individualized tax systems in the world, and has even devised tax policies that encourage women's paid work and fiscal equality, took a profound detour as successive governments moved from marital aggregation to individual taxation. Despite women's protests against over-taxation in the post Second World War period (Magnusson 2000: 188, 221) the government decided to adopt US-style marital aggregation (joint filing, described in the next section of this chapter) instead of individual taxation. It took another 20 years of criticism and protest before joint filing was finally replaced with individual taxation.

When Sweden did move to individual taxation, it did not immediately drop all marital provisions. At the time, the government bowed to political pressures to offer single-income couples a 'housewife deduction' to compensate for the loss of the large tax benefits of US-style joint filing (Sundberg 1975; Gustafsson and Bruyn-Hundt 1991: 32–33). Until the wealth tax was abolished, preferential brackets for married couples gave them lower effective tax rates than those for single persons. And as in the UK, even the strongly individualized Swedish fiscal system treats social assistance as subsidiary to other sources of income for a growing range of family members, including married spouses and, more recently, cohabitants, children with occasional earnings, adult children living at home and students (Wennberg 2008: 72–76).

Although England and Sweden represent two distinctively different legal traditions—common law and civilian—neither state has completely freed women from fiscal coverture (Chan 1999; Wennberg 2008). Particularly for those with low incomes and single mothers, discourses of 'the family' and dependency undercut what would be individualized claims to social support if made by unmarried women. Even when freed from marital aggregation in income taxation, such individualized systems covertly reinforce the capture of women through social support measures, regardless of whether these benefits are structured as tax provisions or as direct spending.

US JOINT FILING: MARITAL AGGREGATION WITHIN INDIVIDUAL TAXATION

The US has historically been very influential in matters of tax policy. In particular, after the Second World War, many other countries adopted the United States' new form of marital aggregation, now known as joint filing. Indeed, the influence of US joint filing continues, with the former Howard government in Australia making strenuous efforts to adopt it (but failing) and Canada enacting targeted joint filing in the form of pension income splitting in 2006 (discussed below) and in some registered investments in 2009. Because of its global impact, the dynamics leading to the adoption of marital aggregation/income splitting in the US are outlined here to highlight how the 'capture' of women in fiscal policy resulting from this transition was made to seem not just reasonable, but imperative, and how, in the end, lack of regard for women helped sell this policy proposal.

Individual Income Taxation in the US

Although the 1913 US income tax system used the individual as the tax unit from the beginning, it was never administered as a strictly individual system. The government permitted spouses to transfer their own personal exemptions to each other, let married men to claim double (and later, enhanced double) exemptions unless their wives had significant incomes and accepted 'individual' returns filed in the same 'joint' tax return instead of in two separate returns. All these practices legitimized marital pooling of incomes and exemptions from the outset (Treasury Decisions 1914: 2090; 1915: 2137).

Although these administrative practices made the original US individual system functionally similar to the UK marital aggregation model, that was not a concern; most incomes were too low to attract any income tax liability in any event (Byrd and Wolff 2003; Treasury Decisions 1914: 2090; 1915: 2137). As average incomes rose, however, the practice of permitting couples to aggregate their incomes and transfer their exemptions to each other (including any special marital exemptions) injected the 'stacking' effect of marital aggregation into an otherwise individualized income tax system. This is because if all spousal exemptions are transferred to one spouse (usually the husband) the second spouse will receive no tax relief on a second income. As in UK-style marital aggregation, this stacking effect then pushes second incomes into higher income brackets than if the second earner were unmarried, and that higher tax burden cannot be reduced by any exemptions (Bittker and Stone 1972: 340).

Although more limited than the stacking and over-taxation effects of full marital aggregation, the tax effects of transferable exemptions are not trivial. When the US government decided that recruiting women to paid work was a national priority during the Second World War, it reduced the size of the spousal exemptions with breathtaking speed. This, in turn, reduced the amount of over-taxation wives experienced when they entered into paid work. Shortly afterwards, the 'Victory Tax', a separate supplementary income tax, was actually structured as a true individual tax, in that it did not permit spousal exemptions to be transferred or shared at all (IRC 1939, section 25(b)(1); Victory Tax 1942, section 452).

Despite these effects, however, the US individual tax unit, even when hybridized by transferable exemptions and income pooling, did not penalize women to the same extent as full marital aggregation systems did (in the UK, for instance). Because the US system did use the individual as the legal taxpaying unit, dual-income couples whose incomes exceeded the tax-free zone could still calculate each spouse's tax liability separately, enabling each spouse to take individual advantage of the progressive rate structure. (This was the result whether they opted to file their physical tax forms on one joint form or separately.)

The US Debate: Individual Taxation versus Marital Aggregation with Income Splitting

Despite generous enhanced and transferable marital exemptions, high-income taxpayers quickly exploited the vulnerability of the early US income tax system to business and family income splitting. Instead of enacting general anti-avoidance rules to block income splitting, the government initially agreed that spouses in community property states could split their incomes by virtue of their state property law regimes (Opinions of the Attorney General 1920: 298; Treasury Decision 1914: 2090; 1915: 2137; Treasury Decision 1921: 3138). The availability of income splitting in community property states fuelled efforts in common law states to obtain similar outcomes. The government having approved income splitting, court decisions tended to favour taxpayers, and the legal complexities and indeterminacy surrounding income splitting defeated efforts to rein it in with litigation (Lyon and Eustice 1962; Rice 1955). During this time, the Treasury countered with proposals to Congress for UK-style marital aggregation (without any income splitting features), which fuelled political controversy (Lahey 2009b).

The debate over the individual tax unit in the US became a 30-year struggle over whether married couples should be subject to UK-style marital aggregation (without splitting) or whether community property-style marital aggregation (with splitting) should be available. Failing to obtain adoption of the UK aggregation model, in 1947 the Treasury finally proposed that all married couples be permitted to aggregate and split their combined incomes as if everyone lived in community property states. This new joint tax system conferred significant tax benefits on higher income spouses (usually husbands) and was wildly popular with all taxpayers, even though few realized that only high-income taxpayers received significant benefits from income splitting.

Joint Filing Overtaxes Married Women

The tax benefits of joint filing came at a high price for women in the United States. As a modified form of marital aggregation, the large tax benefits available to husbands through 'joint filing' required that lower-income spouses (usually wives) be overtaxed. Single-income couples treated half of that income as belonging to the non-earning spouse. If the second spouse also had income, however, the two halves of the second income would, in effect, be 'stacked' on top of the first income. This stacking meant that the second income would receive little or no benefit from any tax exemptions, deductions or credits usually available, and thus that the second earner would bear a higher tax as a married person than as a single person.

Women in the US were aware that joint filing would have a negative impact on them. Indeed, this had even been recognized by the US Supreme Court in 1930 (*Poe v Seaborn* 1930: 117). Yet women's efforts to speak out politically had little effect on the outcome of the political debate over the tax unit, because complex political forces either drowned out women's voices altogether, or put the words of others in women's mouths as the debate unfolded.

The adoption of the US form of marital aggregation/income splitting did not appear to be about how to make good policy choices, but was driven by envy, anger, sexism and postwar politics. As early as 1939, four states had replaced their common law property laws with new community property law, and by 1948, when the crucial vote on the new joint filing system was taken, another seven states were actively considering it (Note 1950: 338–40). Representatives of common law states lashed out at community ownership as being 'alien and foreign' (Bright 1948: 82) while the Treasury's continued insistence on adopting UK-style marital aggregation (without splitting) led to the realization that aggregation would mean that all married couples—in both common law and community property states—would pay higher taxes.

In the aftermath of the Second World War, popular demand for tax breaks for married men converged with a growing backlash against women's paid work. In this climate, single-income married couples in community property states became cast as villains who were taking unfair advantage of 'individual filing', while husbands in common law states, who could only take advantage of transferable and special marital exemptions, were cast as victims of individual taxation. When representatives of community property states attempted to defend the unique tax benefits of their property laws by describing themselves as the true champions of women's equality because their state laws gave women immediate 50 per cent shares of all family assets and incomes (Lahey 2009b) 'individual taxation' became associated not just with proponents of community property law, but with the 'women's liberation movement' as well (Bittker 1975: 1411–12).

The resulting pressure to replace individual taxation with some form of marital aggregation—with or without the income-splitting feature—placed women's groups in a no-win situation. On the one hand, women could not openly criticize the claims that women in community property states were 'more equal' in family property law than women in common law states, even though women lawyers knew that these claims were deeply flawed (DeCrow 1974: 153; Smith 1998: 138–44) because it was clear that representatives of community property states were their strongest (and nearly only) allies in staving off any form of marital aggregation. On the other hand, women's groups could not acquiesce in the claim that income splitting recognizes women's inherent equality, because they understood full well that attributing any part of husbands' incomes to wives would result in over-taxing wives, would give husbands valuable tax benefits for having no-income or low-income wives and would create tax disincentives to women's paid work. This limited women's groups to simply opposing 'any law tending to establish the family as a tax unit' (Wiley 1947: 913–14)—a carefully-worded position that was never considered on its merits because of simplistic identifications between 'individual' taxation, the women's movement and the community property movement. In the end, even Douglas J of the US Supreme Court agreed that women's improving legal status did not prevent the government from shaping tax policy around the concept of fiscal coverture: 'I see no reason why that which is in fact an economic unit may not be treated as one in law' (*Fernandez v Wiener* 1945: 365).

The Gender Politics of US Income Splitting

The near invisibility of women in the litigation and legislation leading to enactment of joint filing/income splitting and the silence surrounding its negative impact on women did not mean that this policy process was largely devoid of gender politics. On the contrary, it is clear that many appreciated that it would operate as a new form of 'capture' of women in tax law.

As early as 1941, the focus of tax unit policy in the United States was to 'equalize the tax burdens of husbands and wives in non-community property States with those living in community States'—it was *not* to secure equity as between husbands and wives in single and dual-income couples (United States—Repr Dingell 1941: 5488). When Treasury officers lobbied in support of their joint filing proposal in the post-war years, appeals to 'equality' and 'equity' between married couples living in common law and community property states were tightly intertwined with criticisms of women in paid work and information on the tax benefits the new system would give high-income married men. Stanley Surrey, chief spokesperson for the US Treasury in this campaign, played a key role in its success, and his own publications reveal that he used sexist slurs, depersonalization of women and promises of greater wealth to men to win support for it. Like Douglas J in *Fernandez*, Surrey could not see women as economic actors in their own right (1946: 980–86). For those who worried that joint filing would unfairly discriminate against single taxpayers (which it necessarily does) Surrey foreshadowed the rapid increase in the marriage rate that followed its enactment by retorting '[L]et them get married'.

These views were widely shared by supporters of joint filing. Common law advocates pointed out that joint filing would put wives 'back in their home' to care for children, get them out of offices and businesses and let veterans and working men have the jobs (United States—Lowrimore 1947: 929, 931; Surrey 1948: 1111). Legislatures of states that were still considering community property legislation in 1948 quickly dropped those proposals as soon as joint filing was approved by Congress (Bright 1948: 68) and many of the states that had already adopted community property regimes began repealing them in order to free male-owned property from community claims of women (Note 1950: 338–40, 350).

These gender politics were not just played out in the rarified atmosphere of legislative debates. The popular press continually published stories on how women should get out of paid work, or at least get out of 'men's jobs', conform to new images of domesticity and orient their energies towards family and home. Women with careers were ridiculed (Skinner 1956), told why joint filing would make it almost impossible for them to take home much more than 25 per cent of their gross pay and were shown why, with joint filing, they could actually contribute more to the family budget by working in the home and serving as tax shelters for their husbands (Griswold 1949: 127). At the same time, single people were bombarded with financial information showing why 'it pays to get married' and why it does not pay for the wife to work (US News 1951: 17; 1957).

In the longer term, researchers have now concluded that US income splitting has actually had all of these effects, and more: joint filing has promoted heterosexual marriage at earlier ages for women, helped reinstate the principle of male ownership of property under common law doctrine, created large permanent tax incentives for women to specialize in unpaid work when paid work does not 'pay' and contributed to persistent gender gaps in the US in incomes, wealth, women's paid workforce participation rates, quality of work and equality. Detailed examination of these gaps is beyond the scope of this chapter, but two examples of these effects are given here to underscore the gender impact of joint filing.

First, while Surrey was campaigning for income splitting in 1946, he predicted that joint filing/income splitting would accelerate the accumulation of male wealth by leaving more after-tax income in the hands of single-income high-income couples (1946: 983). At the same time, the principle of gender-neutrality was used to take the focus away from husbands and wives/men and women, as postwar tax policy research programmes were established, and lack of gender specificity in statistical data made it difficult to assess the accuracy of these predictions. Thus, in 1951, the National Bureau of Economic Research studied changes in incomes in the postwar years for identical 'spending units'. The data were analyzed around every single variable—except sex—producing results showing 'no change' in levels of after-tax incomes even when the numbers of spending unit members engaged in paid work (wives, dependent children, etc) had changed (Katona and Fisher 1951: 94). Because gender breakdowns were not reported in the data, economists have only more recently been able to identify how joint filing had affected women (LaLumia 2006).

Secondly, a growing body of research has subsequently established that US joint taxation has a significant negative effect on women's labour force participation rates and thus on women's work lives and lifetime incomes. In the early 1980s, researchers found that eliminating income splitting would remove barriers to married women's labour force participation rates (Apps 1981; Leuthold 1984), that the non-taxation of women's unpaid work in the domestic realm creates biases against women's paid work (Leuthold 1983) and that reducing the over-taxation of married women's earnings would counter these effects (Apps 1981; Leuthold 1985). Subsequent research has confirmed these findings (for example, Boskin and Sheshinski 1983; Heen 1995; Gugl 2010); comparative research demonstrates that other forms of joint tax and benefit measures have the same negative effects on women (Apps 1999: 448–49; Briggs 1985; Smith et al 2003: 422; Crossley and Jeon 2007; O'Donoghue and Sutherland 1999: 589–91); and intersectional research has concluded that all these effects are exacerbated by other marginalizing characteristics, such as race and immigration status (Amott and Matthaei 1996: 412; Lipman 2006: 14–20).

If Surrey's projections as to the enhanced savings married men could expect in the first ten years of joint filing/income splitting are at all accurate, then this form of marital aggregation has been artificially reducing women's involvement in paid work for decades wherever it has been adopted. During the same period of time, the annual financial benefits of the system have been accruing largely to men.

BECOMING 'SUBJECTS' IN FISCAL POLICY: THE ONTOLOGICAL CHALLENGE

Debates over income splitting and other joint fiscal measures are no longer conducted in the blatantly sexist terms of the last two centuries. Providing tax incentives to taxpayers whose partners/spouses minimize paid work is now framed as a matter of 'choice', while using family income cutoffs to regulate access to social support payments is justified as 'target efficiency'. But while the language of this form of 'capture' of women has changed, the underlying realities of women's lives have not: women's involvement in good paid work remains vulnerable, women's access to livable incomes is still fragile and women have much heavier unpaid work loads and support obligations than men—yet the numbers and types of joint fiscal measures that continually reinforce these realities continue to proliferate.

It is urgent to continue mapping joint versus individual fiscal models across governance units and structures (Fagan and Hebson 2007: 68; Gustafsson 2005; Millar 2003; OECD 2007). However, the ontologies that have perpetuated the 'capture' of women in law and taxation, fiscal coverture under conditions of constitutional equality and the concentration of good work, sustainable incomes and bearable workloads in male hands must be addressed before fundamental change can be achieved. Given the reluctance in many countries to engage in meaningful gender-based analysis of fiscal law, gender mainstreaming and gender budgeting, the core problem remains: in too many nations, women are still not seen and experienced as full 'subjects' of the state. Between the early 1990s and 2005, for instance, Canada doubled the number of joint provisions in its income tax law, and in 2006, it actually enacted its first income splitting measure in exactly the same form as the upside down tax benefits for single-income couples provided by the original US joint filing system nearly 60 years earlier. The new pension income splitting system provides no tax benefits to couples with incomes of C$30,000 or less, but it provides tax benefits ranging from C$500 to C$11,216 for couples with incomes up to C$140,000 per year. While the rate at which countries are adopting the US joint tax unit is slowing, many countries classified as using individual tax systems have continued or even expanded their use of joint couple-based tax and benefit measures like those that still exist in the UK and Sweden (Brender 2005: 18; Brender and Strawczynski 2006: 55; Ketscher 2001: 165–66; Lahey 2001a; 2001b; Wennberg 2008: 312–20). For example, the 2009 Canadian income tax system provided for some C$20.8 billion in joint tax credits, tax deductions and direct benefits with significant gender effects, as compared with only C$12 billion in tax items that could be seen as supporting women's economic autonomy (Lahey 2009b: Tables 8, 9).

Gender mainstreaming is designed to bring transparency to governance, to make governments accountable to women as well as to men and to fashion programmes and policies that meet the evidence-based needs of women and of men. Yet Canada, a world leader in implementing gender mainstreaming, certainly does not appear to consider women to be 'subjects', and in recent years Canadian governments have taken major steps to intensify the concentration of wealth, income and power in male hands.

In part, the ontological challenge is posed by the very nature of fiscal analysis. Whenever political analysis of distributional and fiscal issues is allowed to operate at a high level of abstraction and stereotype, it is more difficult for women and other marginalized groups to be heard. Women were never really participants in the US tax unit debate: the original policy issues were designed by male tax planners; government reactions were shaped by male tax policy analysts; legal submissions were developed by male lawyers; new laws were written and shaped by male legislators; popular interpretations of the new laws were written by male authors to promote the interests of men generally; and women had limited access to key political, media and professional spaces. The submissions that women did manage to make were constrained by the non-feminist positions of power holders. Because the focus of the policy struggle was never really about individual husbands and wives, but was framed as an abstract debate about 'equality between couples' under different legal regimes, women were never able to participate as their full selves in this critical process. Failure to talk explicitly about the profound material and political differences between single-income and dual-income couples, for example, made the over-taxation of women in joint taxation models completely invisible, placing the burden on future women to find ways to deconstruct these false symmetries and abstractions (Lahey 2001a). Women especially 'need a ballast against tendencies that confuse theory with unconstrained play' (Hekman 2007: 6). For women, that means finding ways to present detailed and dynamic information on the material realities of women's lives, to demand that society and governments recognize 'economic woman' at the same time they use critical economic analysis when thinking through what *all* subjects need (Nelson 2003; Ketscher 2001: 236).

The ontological challenge, then, is not just to bring women fully into policy debates, but to change the forms and contexts in which women are seen and see themselves. Politicians are obviously more comfortable thinking about women in fiscal policy only to the extent that they are contained within the structures of masculine capture—the couple, the family, the household, the retired couple. But as Howell concluded in her study of women in the late medieval period, 'in practice, women [are] not contained' (1998: 119).

Women do not fit the models imposed on them by abstract categorical thought, but their variability and their capabilities cannot be 'seen' among the images used in the dominant discourse. The problems caused for women by tax laws of all kinds have common elements: they do not take seriously women's persistently low incomes, high levels of responsibilities and constrained mobility. Nor do they give sufficient weight to society's responsibility for sharing those burdens fairly, or the unacceptability of constructing male wealth out of those unequal burdens. The unrelenting focus on gender-neutral categories like 'the poor' or 'single parents' or 'children living in poverty' has made it seem as if women, whether contained in the couple, in the social assistance system or in parenting, do not matter unless they and their containers are 'poor' and serve worthy purposes. Thus, the greatest challenge may be to find ways to reveal the artificiality of the containers and to see women as being too variable, too self-defining, to be contained—to imagine women as fully human subjects with equal entitlements to all the opportunities life can offer (Garofalo and Marra 2007).

It is possible that if the US had not adopted the joint tax unit, most countries would have ended up following the example of Sweden and the United Kingdom in gradually moving to individual taxation. US joint filing, however, aggressively interjected another option into the process, offered a way to perpetuate fiscal and economic coverture long after it had been repealed in other areas of law and inspired other countries that sought similar results. But part of women's reality is that joint taxation perpetuates many of the fiscal barriers to greater gender equality. Individualized taxation, on the other hand, removes these barriers and makes possible more equalized sharing of work and wealth, income, and tax benefits between women and men (OECD 2008: indicator PF4).

Continuing to press for fully individualized tax and benefit measures cannot, by itself, eliminate women's disadvantaged status. But in fiscal systems that continue to measure women's tax liability and benefits on the basis of relational hierarchies, challenging masculine capture by revealing the material realities obscured by ancient and outmoded ideologies remains a critical strategic objective.

REFERENCES

Amott, T and Matthaei, J (1996) *Race, Gender, and Work: A Multi-cultural Economic History of Women in the United States* (Boston, South End Press).

Apps, P (1981) *A Theory of Inequality and Taxation* (Cambridge, Cambridge University Press).

—— (1999) 'Tax Reform, Ideology and Gender' 21 *Sydney Law Review* 437.

Baker, JH (1971) 'Baron et Femme: Unity of Person' and 'Succession' in *An Introduction to English Legal History* (London, Butterworths).

Barner, S (1959) *World Tax Series: Taxation in Sweden* (Boston, Little, Brown).

Barr (1980) 'The Taxation of Married Women's Incomes—Part II' 6 *British Tax Revue* 478.

Bittker, BI (1975) 'Federal Income Taxation and the Family' 27 *Stanford Law Review* 1389.

Bittker, BI and Stone, LM (1972) *Federal Income Estate and Gift Taxation* (Boston, Little Brown).

Björne, G (1972) 'Sweden's Report on the Income, Fortune and Estate Tax Treatment of Household Units' 2 *Cahier de droit fiscal international* 275.

Black, J et al (1997–2006) 'A Praise Poem of Ur-Namma (Ur-Namma C)' in *The Electronic Text Corpus of Sumerian Literature* (Oxford). Available online at ETCSL: www-etcsl.orient.ox.ac.uk/.

Blackstone, W (1765–69) *Commentaries on the Laws of England* vol 1 (Oxford, Clarendon Press).
Boskin, MJ and Sheshinski, E (1983) 'Optimal Tax Treatment of the Family: Married Couples' 20 *Journal of Public Economics* 281.
Bräutigam, DA (2002) 'Building Leviathan: Revenue, State Capacity and Governance' 3 *Institute for Development Studies Bulletin* 10–20.
Brender, A (2005) *Tax Benefits for Women in Israel: International Perspective and Benefit Take-up* (Tel Aviv, Research Department, Bank of Israel) (unpublished; copy on file with author).
Brender, A and Strawczynski, M (2006) 'Earned Income Tax Credit in Israel: Designing the System to Reflect the Characteristics of Labor Supply and Poverty' 3 *Israel Economic Review* 27.
Briggs, N (1985) 'Individual Income Taxation and Social Benefits in Sweden, the United Kingdom, and the USA—A Study of their Inter-Relationships and their Effects on Lower-Income Couples and Single Heads of Household' 39 (June) *Bulletin of the International Bureau of Fiscal Documentation* 243.
Bright, MH (1948) 'Community Property' 24 *North Dakota Bar Briefs* 66.
Byrd, RC and Wolff, W (2003) *Historical Statistics of the United States: Colonial Times to 1970* Parts 1–2 (House Document Series, no 93–78) (Washington, Census Bureau).
CBO (Congressional Budget Office), US Congress (1997) *For Better or for Worse: Marriage and the Federal Income Tax* (Washington, CBO).
CPS (Current Population Survey) (2005) *Annual Demographic Survey* (Washington, United States Census Department).
Chan, W (1999) 'Women, Childcare, and Taxation' 10 *King's College Law Journal* 71.
Coffield, J (1970) *A Popular History of Taxation: From Ancient to Modern Times* (London, Longman).
Cooper, JS (1986) *Clay Cones La 9.1 Presargonic Inscriptions* (New Haven, American Oriental Society).
Crossley, TF and Jeon, Sung-Hee (2007) 'Joint Taxation and the Labour Supply of Married Women: Evidence from the Canadian Tax Reform of 1988' 28 *Fiscal Studies* 343.
DeCrow, K (1974) *Sexist Justice* (New York, Random House).
De Funiak, W and Vaughn, M (1971) *Principles of Community Property* 2nd edn (Tucson, University of Arizona Press).
Delphy, C (1984) *Close to Home: A Materialist Analysis of Women's Oppression* (Amherst, University of Massachusetts Press).
'Does It Really Pay for the Wife to Work?' *US News and World Report* (March 1957) 154, 156.
Durant, W (1944) *Caesar and Christ* (New York, Simon and Schuster).
Eisenstein, Z (1979) *Capitalist Patriarchy and the Case for Socialist Feminism* (New York, Monthly Review Press).
—— (1986) *The Radical Future of Liberal Feminism* (Boston, Northeastern University Press).
Fagan, C and Hebson, G (2007) '"Making Work Pay" Debates from a Gender Perspective: Co-ordinators' Synthesis Report' in *Babies and Bosses—Reconciling Work and Family Life* (Paris, OECD).

Garofalo, MR and Marra, M (2007) *Work–Life Reconciliation Policies from Well-Being to Development: Rethinking EU Gender Mainstreaming* (Munich Personal Repec Archive). Available online at: www.mpra.ub.uni-muenchen.de/9598/1/MPRA_paper_9598.pdf.

Goetz, A-M (2006) *Gender and Accountability: Challenges for Reform in Developing States* (Boston, Tufts University Fletcher School). Available online at: www.genderandsecurity.umb.edu/Anne-Marie%20Goetz%204-10-06.pdf.

Griswold, EN (January 1949) 'Something for the Middle Class' *Fortune* 125.

Gugl, E (2010) 'The Behavioural Effects of "Joint" Tax and Benefit Laws on Women's Economic Lives' 22 *Canadian Journal of Women and Law* 109.

Gustafsson, S (2005) *Gender Impact of Income Taxes: On the Disincentives for Married Women to Work Created by Joint Income Taxation* Working Paper (Department of Economics, University of Amsterdam).

Gustafsson, SS and Bruyn-Hundt, M (1991) *Incentives for Women to Work: A Comparison between the Netherlands, Sweden and West Germany* Working Paper no 59 (The Hague, Netherlands Scientific Council for Government Policy).

Heen, M (1995) 'Welfare Reform, Child Care Costs, and Taxes: Delivery Increased Work-Related Child Care Benefits to Low-Income Families' 13 *Yale Law and Policy Review* 173.

Hekman, S (2007) 'Constructing the Ballast: An Ontology for Feminism' (Chicago, American Political Science Association, Report of the Annual Meeting of the American Political Science Association).

Howell, M (1988) *Women, Production, and Patriarchy in Late Medieval Cities* (Chicago, University of Chicago Press).

—— (1998) *The Marriage Exchange: Property, Social Place, and Gender in Cities of the Low Countries, 1300–1500* (Chicago, University of Chicago Press).

'It Pays to Get Married' *US News and World Report* (February 1951) 17.

Katona, G and Fisher, JA (1951) 'Part II Postwar Changes in the Income of Identical Consumer Units' in *Studies in Income and Wealth* (Washington, National Bureau of Economic Research) 62.

Kay, FM, Masuch, C and Curry, P (2004) *Turning Points and Transitions: Women's Careers in the Legal Profession: A Longitudinal Survey of Ontario Lawyers 1990–2002* (Toronto, Law Society of Upper Canada). Available online at: www.lsuc.on.ca/media/oct2604_turning_points.pdf.

Ketscher, K (2001) 'From Marriage Contract to Labour Contract: Effects on Care Duties and Care Rights' in K Nouvsiainen (ed), *Responsible Selves* (Aldershot, Dartmouth).

Knowles, L (1920) 'Reservation' in Royal Commission on Taxation, *Report of the Royal Commission on Taxation* (London, Queen's Stationer).

Lahey, KA (2000) *The Benefit/Penalty Unit in Income Tax Policy: Diversity and Reform*. Study prepared for the Law Commission of Canada. Available at: dalspace1.library.dal.ca/dspace/handle/10222/10400?show=full.

—— (2001a) *The Benefit/Penalty Unit in Income Tax Policy: Diversity and Reform* (Ottawa, Law Commission of Canada).

—— (2001b) 'The Impact of Relationship Recognition on Lesbian Women in Canada: Still Separate and Only Somewhat "Equivalent"' (Ottawa, Status of Women Canada). Available at: dsp-psd.pwgsc.gc.ca/Collection/SW21-82-2001E.pdf.

—— (2009a) *The 'Male Breadwinner' Model of Unemployment Insurance: Gender Analysis of Regular Benefits*. Report of the Standing Committee on the Status of Women (Ottawa, House of Commons). Available at: www2.parl.gc.ca/HousePublications/Publication.aspx?DocId=3690435&Language=E&Mode=1&Parl=40&Ses=2].

—— (2009b) 'Sexism in the Treasury—: Gender-Based Analysis, Tax Expenditures Analysis, and the Joint Tax/Benefit Unit' (forthcoming).

LaLumia, S (2006) *The Effects of Joint Taxation of Married Couples on Labor Supply and Non-wage Income* Working Paper no 28 (Williamsburg, Department of Economics, College of William and Mary).

Lefkowitz, MR and Fant, MB (1982) *Women's Life in Greece and Rome* (Baltimore, Johns Hopkins University Press).

Leuthold, JH (1983) 'Home Production and the Tax System' 3 *Journal of Economic Psychology* 145.

—— (1984) 'Income Splitting and Women's Labor-Force Participation' 38 *Industrial and Labor Relations Review* 98.

—— (1985) 'Work Incentives and the Two-earner Deduction' 13 *Public Finance Quarterly* 63.

Levi, M (1989) *Of Rule and Revenue* (Berkeley, University of California Press).

Lindencrona, G (1979) *Trends in Scandinavian Taxation* (Deventer, The Netherlands and Boston, Kluwer).

Lipman, FJ (2006) *Taxing Undocumented Immigrants: Separate, Unequal and Without Representation* Working Paper no 06-20, Legal Studies Research Paper Series (Orange, CA, Chapman University).

Locke, J (1824) *Two Treatises of Government* (London, Rivington) (originally published anonymously, 1690).

Lyon, CS and Eustice, JS (1962) 'Assignment of Income: Fruit and Tree as Irrigated by the P.G. Lake Case' 17 *Tax Law Review* 295.

Magnusson, L (2000) *An Economic History of Sweden* (London, Routledge).

Malmström, Å (1955) 'Matrimonial Property Law in Sweden' in W Friedmann (ed), *Matrimonial Property Law* (Toronto, Carswell).

Marshall and Walsh (1970) 'Marital Status and Variations in Income Tax Burdens' 4 *British Tax Review* 236.

Miles, JC and Driver, GR (1960) (trans) 'Laws of Hammu-Rabi' in *The Babylonian Laws* (Oxford, Clarendon Press).

Millar, J (2003) 'Squaring the Circle? Means Testing and Individualisation in the UK and Australia' 3 *Social Policy and Society* 67.

Nelson, J (2003) '"Free Market" Economics and Feminist Alternatives' (unpublished). Available online at: www.policyinnovations.org/ideas/policy_library/data/01016/_res/id=sa_File1/.

Note (1950) 'Epilogue to the Community Property Scramble: Problems of Repeal' 50(3) *Columbia Law Review* 332.

OECD (Organisation for Economic Co-operation and Development) (2007) *Babies and Bosses: Reconciling Work and Family Life* (Paris, OECD).

—— (2008) 'Neutrality of Tax/Benefit Systems' *Family Database* (Geneva, Social Policy Division) (indicator PF4).

O'Donoghue, C and Sutherland, H (1999) 'Accounting for the Family in European Income Tax Systems' 23 *Cambridge Journal of Economics* 565.

Royal Commission on Taxation (1920) *Report of the Royal Commission on Taxation* (London, Queen's Stationer).
Rice, RS (1955) 'Judicial Trends in Gratuitous Assignments to Avoid Federal Income Taxes' 64 *Yale Law Journal* 991.
Scott, SP (1932) *Corpus Juris Civilis: The Civil Law* (Cincinnati, Central Trust Co).
Severy, B (2003) *Augustus and the Family at the Birth of the Roman Empire* (London, Routledge).
Skinner, CO (December 1956) 'Women Are Misguided' *Life* 73.
Smith, BA (1998) 'Why the Community Property System Fails Divorced Women and Children' 17 *Texas Journal of Women and the Law* 135.
Smith, N et al (2003) 'The Effects of Taxation on Married Women's Labour Supply across Four Countries' 55 *Oxford Economic Papers* 417–39.
Steele, F (1948) *The Code of Lipit-Ishtar* (Philadelphia, University of Pennsylvania Press).
Sundberg, JWF (1975) 'Recent Changes in Swedish Family Law: Experiment Repeated' 23 *American Journal of Comparative Law* 39.
Surrey, SS (October 1946) 'Family Income and Federal Taxation' *Taxes* 980.
—— (1948) 'Federal Taxation of the Family: The Revenue Act of 1948' 61(1) *Harvard Law Review* 1097.
UNDP (United Nations Development Programme) (Current) *Human Development Reports*. Available online at: hdr.undp.org/en/reports/.
—— (2008) 'Canada' *Country Fact Sheets: 2008*. Available online at: hdrstats.undp.org/2008/countries/country_fact_sheets/cty_fs_CAN.html.
United Nations (UNDP, 1990–93) *Human Development Report*. Available online at: hdr.undp.org/en/reports/.
Watson, A (1970) 'Family Law' in *The Law of the Ancient Romans* (Dallas, Southern Methodist University Press).
Wennberg, L (2008) *Social Security for Solo Mothers in Swedish and EU Law: On the Constructions of Normality and the Boundaries of Social Citizenship* (Upsalla, Iustus Forlag).
Wiley, AK (1947) 'Letter' read into record by Mr Gearhart, Revenue Revisions, 1947–48, House of Representatives, Ways and Means Committee 913.
Williams, J (1910) 'Roman-Dutch Law' 19(3) *Yale Law Journal* 156.
World Economic Forum (2008) 'Canada' *Gender Gap Index 2008*. Available online at: www.weforum.org/pdf/gendergap/ggg08_canada.pdf.

Case Law

Fernandez v Wiener [1945] 60 F Supp 169, rev'd 326 US 340, 66 SCt 178 (Louisiana).
Poe v Seaborn 282 US 101 (1930).

Decisions, Reports and Opinions

United States—Opinions of the Attorney General, vol 38, 298 (10 September 1920); vol 37, 435, 458, 463 (26 February 1921).

United States—Repr Dingell, Michigan, HR 5488, 77th Con, 1st Sess (4 August 1941).
United States—Statement of Charles S Lowrimore, Murchison Building, Wilmington, NC, 927–33 at 929, 931 (1947).
United States—S, Treasury Decision No 2090 (14 December 1914).
—— Treasury Decision No 2137 (30 January 1915).
—— Treasury Decision No 3138 (26 February 1921); *Cumm Bull* No 4, 238.
United States—Victory Tax, 77th Cong, Sess II (1942), Ch 619, s 452.

2

Tax, Markets, Gender and the New Institutionalism

ANN MUMFORD*

TAX LAW AND policy in the United Kingdom experienced a tremendous amount of change under the New Labour regime of government, which began when Tony Blair was elected Prime Minister in 1997. Blair, and his historically long serving Chancellor of the Exchequer, Gordon Brown, issued new and dramatic modifications to the tax system, directly impacting on the relationship between gender and the fiscal state. This chapter will argue that the new institutionalist development in sociological theory provides a framework within which the impact on gender economic inequality of a pattern of governance in UK tax law under Gordon Brown's stewardship (both as Chancellor, and then as Prime Minister) might be considered.

The objective of this project is not to consider the sum total of the alterations in tax law, and to assess whether or not they benefit women economically—through requiring women to pay less in taxes; or, through requiring some taxpayers to pay more, so as to fund government programmes which target women. Rather, the chapter will argue that there is a layered relationship between tax and gender equity, the nature of which is more easily addressed through analysis of the points of interest suggested by a neo-institutionalist framework. Indeed, the chapter will propose that the theoretical bases of new institutionalism afford insight into the way that tax institutions are being given a key role in a new governance era, with specific and direct impact on gender equality. An inspiration for this approach is provided by the fact that New Labour was distinguished by having what appeared to be, with Anthony Giddens, a court philosopher

* A draft of this chapter was presented at a Queen Mary School of Law staff seminar series and has benefited enormously from assistance received on the day and, afterwards, from Kenneth A Armstrong and Kate Malleson. I am particularly indebted to Roger Cotterrell for drawing to my attention the importance of Philip Selznick's writings.

This chapter was completed before David Cameron was appointed Prime Minister on 11 May 2010.

(McRobbie 2000: 99; Bevir and O'Brien 2001: 536). Enormously prolific, Giddens appeared to publish a new book at the same pace that Tony Blair and his historically long-serving Chancellor issued new, and dramatic, changes to the tax system. Thus, modifications to tax law and policy in many instances were considered and thoughtful, even if reactive. The developments in tax law during this period were part of a New Labour 'philosophy', the terms of which this chapter aims to consider. The thesis is that some of these developments in tax law could be characterized as occurring within a pattern of change, along the lines described by new institutionalist theory.

There have been important administrative and bureaucratic changes to the Revenue during this period, some of which directly impact on the relationship between families and the state—and thus concern questions of gender equity, as women as a whole invest disproportionate hours of unpaid labour in the private sphere of the family. The managerial and bureaucratic adjustments that accompany such structural changes present an opportunity to engage with theories of organizational sociology, many of which have developed under the broadly conceived, neo-institutionalist school. The development of tax credits during this period is an obvious focus of attention, but this project will also address adjustments with important implications for women, that do not at first glance appear to be focused on questions of gender.

WHAT IS THE 'NEW INSTITUTIONALISM'?

The Old ...

Introduction to the 'new institutionalism' begins with a discussion of the 'old', institutionalist branch of sociological theory. After the Second World War, behaviouralism and rational choice theory dominated political science (Peters 2005: 1). Institutions were not thought to be very important according to these theories because the focus was on individuals, who presumed to make rational choices and to 'act autonomously' (Peters 2005: 1). Institutionalism, in part, involved a reaction against this, and developed a social and scientific analytical approach to institutions as an object of study, which allowed for the identification of patterns of behaviour and change across periods of space and time. Talcott Parsons was identified with some aspects of institutionalist thought. By the 1980s, institutionalism appeared to have fallen out of favour, and concern shifted to the 'public sector' and the influence it and other institutions wield over politics and individual choice (Peters 2005: 1).

What has been described as the 'new institutionalism' does not completely reject rational choice theory, but it does lessen its importance, thus building on and complementing the work of the earlier institutionalists.

Peters provides a useful example of this aspect of the difference between old and new institutionalism:

> [T]he old institutionalism argued that presidential systems are significantly different from parliamentary systems, based upon the formal structure and rules. The 'new institutionalism' goes further and undertakes trying to determine if these assumed differences do indeed exist, and if so in what ways do those two alternative ways of organizing political life differ, and what difference this makes for the performance of the systems (2005: 2).

The main difference is that institutionalists start from a point of assuming that the differences between parliamentary and presidential systems, for example, do matter, and 'new institutionalists' are not so sure (Peters 2005). Institutionalists start their study at a later point: having assumed that differences between the organization of public life matter, they then attempt to identify the differences and their impact. Essentially, however, for institutionalists and 'new institutionalists' the fundamental project is the same.

'Old institutionalism' continues to have an effect on new institutionalist theory but in a positivist way (McAnulla 2007: 314). The search for explanations behind the choices of actors—either through 'facts' (for example, poverty) or through laws—is an example of this (McAnulla 2007: 314). Perhaps because it lacked a common text, the 'old institutionalism' was concerned with excluding aspects of social life from its field of study. Thus, for example, the process of competition between actors was excluded from traditional, institutionalist studies (Lee and Pennings 2002: 144ff). By contrast, the new institutionalism is content to include competition within its focus (Lee and Pennings 2002: 144ff).

Parsons' impact on 'old institutionalist' thought was felt primarily in the United States (Beckert 2002: 137). Parsonian institutionalism involves the explicit rejection of the rational-actor model at the heart of economic theory (Beckert 2002: 137). The difference between Parsons' work (Parsons 1991: 87, 171, 198, 201, 210 and 215) and the 'new institutionalism' is that the latter 'seeks to explain institutions rather than simply to assume their existence' (Nee and Brinton 2001: 1). Parsons looked for institutions in many different places—even, for example, in the writings of Durkheim, whose methodological individualism is famed for its focus on *individuals* (not institutions). Yet Parsons' interpretation of Durkheim is widely held to be very valuable, and it contributed to the idea that Durkheim found institutions in untraditional places: '[I]nstead of being mere habits they are normative rules ultimately dependent upon common ethical values' (Parsons 1935: 649). Parsons suggested that 'Durkheim's "institutionalism" leads to the "romantic", not the "positivistic", side of the "economic" factor' (Parsons 1935: 650). Despite sometimes misleading interpretations, however, Parsons was not necessarily a strong supporter of the institutionalist school, and he criticized its members for tending to 'fall back into "psychologism" and "survivalism"' (Parsons 1932: 339 fn 6; Parsons 1990: 319). His primary complaint was related to the lack of a standard institutionalist text, which he argued stunted the potential development of institutionalism in social scientific theory.

As noted, Parsons' institutionalist approach ultimately became unpopular in the late twentieth century (Schmitter 2004; Swedberg 1996). Indeed, Schmitter has argued that '[n]o theory of regional integration has been as misunderstood, caricatured, pilloried, proven wrong and rejected as often as neo-functionalism' (2004: 1). There have been efforts, however, to revive the theory—most notably, Alexander's widely cited text *Neofunctionalism and After* (1998). In that analysis and elsewhere, Alexander conceded that Parsons' work was 'ambiguous' on certain points but insisted that in this, Parsons was no different from any other theorist (Alexander and Colomy 1985: 11). Alexander also identified, broadly, two modern strands of institutionalism.

First, Parsons studied culture, society and other social forms (for example, personality) as distinct institutions (Alexander 1998). Secondly, Parsons redefined 'institutionalisation' through his analyses of, primarily, Durkheim and Freud. In the first strand, what could largely be described as the interactions between culture, society and other forms are studied. In the second (what Alexander describes as the 'reductionist' strand), 'institutionalization becomes the internalization by personalities of common value patterns'. The second strand receives insufficient attention in anti-neofunctionalist literature and is complementary to arguments within new institutionalist theory.

The deviation from traditional (if it may be described as such—it is a very broad church) new institutionalism that this project will recommend will involve reconsideration of Parsons' role in institutionalist theory. Simply, it appears that some aspects of Parsons' neo-functionalism are more harmonious with new institutionalist concerns, and less positivistic, than is sometimes indicated in new institutionalist writings. It is worth noting that the new institutionalism has been described as 'the jurisprudence of values' (Smith 1988: 90), which perhaps presents further evidence of the suitability of this vein of thought for tax law. Thus, this chapter will argue that the patterns of change in the relationships between women, tax, markets and the state during the new Labour period of governance is best understood within a reconsidered new institutionalist framework. Tax law itself will be revealed as a semi-autonomous actor within a political, social and, above all, gendered historical process. Additionally, tax law is linked with reactive, but nevertheless institutional, change.

... And the New

So what constitutes the new institutionalism? One school suggests that Meyer and Rowan's classic 1977 article, 'Institutionalized Organizations: Formal Structure as Myth and Organization', marked the beginning of institutionalism as it is currently understood (Tolbert and Zucker 1999: 169). This article established the concept of institutional *rules*, which the modern state promulgates in increasing number, not only as the source of institutional structures, but as a form of myth (Meyer and Rowan 1977). It is only through their incorporation by the institutions that rules attain a form of legitimacy. Meyer and Rowan argue that this is a symbiotic process and that '[o]rganizations which incorporate institutionalized myths are more legitimate, successful, and likely to survive' (1977: 361).

This 1977 article more or less revived the Parsonian school of sociological thought, which was then out of favour. Indeed, by 1984, there was support for a pronouncement that institutionalism was firmly 'back on the agenda' (Cohn 1994: 433). Just over ten years later, in 1996, Hall and Taylor (1996: 936) observed that '[t]he "new institutionalism" is a term that now appears with growing frequency in political science' and then proceeded to consider the different ways in which what could be described as a philosophy of governance has been developed. A fresh look at (old) institutionalism had started a resurgence of sorts and initiated the development of what would become understood as the 'new institutionalism'. Three of the most important writers in this field, who will be addressed briefly here include Steinmo, Hall and North.

First, Steinmo has developed a historical institutionalism, which largely seeks to place the choices of individuals over a spectrum of time and within a wider social context (see, for example, Steinmo 2002, 2003 and Steinmo, Thelen and Longstreth 1992.) Hall adopts a similar approach, but she does not always do so within an historical context. Thus, she approaches judges' dissenting opinions (Brace and Hall 1990) and the process of reaching judicial consensus (Brace and Hall 1993) from the perspective of individual choices interacting within a wider, institutional process. Finally, the Nobel Prize winner Douglass North has been described as the 'most important proponent and theoretician of new institutionalism' (Hira and Hira 2000: 269). Among his contributions is the observation that increasing national income from tax is but one of a number of competing factors that rulers of states will consider when addressing the question of, for example, laws governing property (Vandenberg 2002: 228). Thus, other factors may include political popularity and the desire to be re-elected (North 1990, cited in Vandenberg 2002).

North has revolutionized understanding of the connection between taxes and the political process. For example, he has explained that the drive for lower taxes can itself be institutionalized, which has had enormous influence on sociological studies of the organization of local government in the United States (Miller and Banaszak-Holl 2005: 195). In addition, North's theory reveals that, when lower taxes are implemented, a resulting competition for resources between government agencies can forge new institutionalist forms. He has emphasized that this is particularly true in urban, local government (Boschken 1998: 606).

North, like Steinmo and Hall, works within a 'new institutionalist' movement that has been described as a 'convergence' of organizational sociology and the sociology of law (Suchman and Edelman 1996: 903). New institutionalism is attractive to analysts of tax and welfare in the modern state generally because it includes a strong focus on political behaviour (Searing 1991: 1239). For example, it supports the analysis of budget speeches and legislation within the context of press releases announcing their advent, as part of an effort to identify the emergence of a new institutionalism which actively involves the fiscal state.

This is evocative of Schumpeter's emphasis on the fiscal state as the blueprint of a state's ambitions (Schumpeter 1950; 1994). The idea of the fiscal state, Schumpeter's important contribution, dominates modern socio-political approaches to the interaction between taxation and politics. This chapter proposes that new institutionalist thought may deepen the understanding of the impact of this interaction on gender equality.

The reason for this is that new institutionalist analysis need not stop at the point of identifying a state's blueprint under the labyrinth of fiscal legislation—a place where fiscal sociology might stop. New institutionalism can be more ambitious than that; indeed, it can be teleological. Teubner predicted in 1983 that '[w]ith the coming of the welfare and regulatory state, greater stress has been placed on substantively rational law, ie, law used as an instrument for purposive, goal-oriented intervention' (1983: 240). Teleological deployment of a state's ambitions through tax was an inevitable part of this development, and tax law from the New Labour years presents a perfect example of Teubner's prediction/explanation that '[a] formal rational legal system creates and applies a body of universal rules, and formal rational law relies on a body of legal professionals who employ peculiarly legal reasoning to resolve specific conflicts' (1983: 240). It is especially when addressing women, markets and money, that New Labour tax law is intensely instrumentalist.

A 'REMATERIALIZED' NEW INSTITUTIONALIST APPROACH (AND HOW IT MIGHT BE APPLIED TO TAX LAW)

What Teubner referred to as a 'new' trend (in 1983) has been described as 'rematerialization' by some European legal scholars and not always without controversy. According to this trend, law does not protect the private sphere (and delineate activities that may occur within it); rather, it openly targets social behaviour. Yet the targeting process is diffuse, so it is difficult for analysts to capture a sense of what is happening. The legislative changes themselves are not subtle (there is little subtlety in a 'Working Families' Tax Credit' as the first New Labour re-launch of the Child Tax Credit was named). Rather, there is simply a great deal of change happening at once, and not all of it is legislative. Some of it is structural, some of it is managerial and some of it is organizational—classic subjects of the new institutionalism.

A template for this approach was provided by Moorhead (1998) who employed the dual perspectives of new institutionalism and 'new public management theory' to analyze New Labour changes to the legal aid system. He, too, endeavoured to capture a sense of what was happening, but in his case, New Labour changes were being made to the legal aid system. Moorhead's analysis was constructed from the starting point that legal aid was entering 'a new phase' and he 'sought to capture the complex forces shaping its future' (1998: 387). He selected a new institutionalist methodology (if it may be described as such) because it 'provide[d] a framework for understanding such processes of change and resistance' (1998: 386).

Other authors within the new institutionalist tradition include Seron and Munger, who have suggested that the importance of the new institutionalist approach lies in the fact that it identifies and acknowledges the significance of complex, changing 'patterns' in 'social life' (Seron and Munger 1996: 188). Seron and Munger—and Moorhead—have applied North's famed approach to institutionalism, discussed above, explicitly to sociological theory. Where North used quantitative economic analyses to explain institutional change, Seron and Munger have employed sociological theory to similar ends. Moorhead's approach is slightly different again, as he relies on the heterogeneous, sociolegal, approach to explain 'what is happening'.

Tax law, like the area of legal aid, which is the subject of Moorhead's work, has undergone an extraordinary period of change during the past ten years. Yet tax can be differentiated from legal aid because of the extraordinary role that Gordon Brown has played in its development since 1997. As a Chancellor with a strong presence, Brown's tax initiatives were widely identified with him and less so with Tony Blair. One possible legacy of this situation is that it was inevitable that the presence of Alistair Darling (Chancellor of the Exchequer, 2007–2010) would echo that of Tony Blair. Changes to tax law were driven in many ways by a single person. Of course Gordon Brown was still required to work within the strictures of politics and thus to accede to and accommodate the preferences of others. Brown, nonetheless, had the power to lead changes to the system, in order to bring about more easily the changes he wanted to see. Every prime minister is powerful, but not every prime minister has ascended to his position after acting as the longest consecutively serving Chancellor of the Exchequer in UK history. Beginning in 1997, the mechanisms of taxation and spending were central to Brown's attempts to effect political change. A new institutionalist approach would attempt to discern a pattern within this period of change.

A New Period of Gamespersonship: Rules and Structures

Many of Gordon Brown's most significant changes to tax law were structural. An example of this is provided by the introduction of the Pre-Budget Report. Before Brown assumed the chancellorship, a Chancellor of the Exchequer could be sacked (or worse) if he revealed the contents of the Budget. The Pre-Budget Report was introduced by Brown in 1998, with the objective of allowing public consultation on aspects of the forthcoming budget. It was used for two other purposes as well, both in the area of avoidance. First, if significant anti-avoidance measures were anticipated for the Spring, then in at least one instance (Mumford 2007: 573–76), the Pre-Budget Report has distracted the professions from this by not mentioning major upcoming legislative changes. Secondly, the Pre-Budget Report was used for the purpose of enabling partially retrospective legislation.

Partially retrospective legislation targets completed deals with pending (advantageous) tax consequences and is not uncommon. The Pre-Budget Report can assist partially retrospective legislation, as the impact of legislation can be predated to them, however broadly worded the report may be. The perceived need for partially retrospective legislation arises from the tax legislative process itself—as a response to tax loopholes. Tax loopholes may be the product of several factors, including broadly worded legislation. Consider that the definition of 'asset' in the Taxation of Chargeable Gains Act 1992 is, more or less, an asset (Taxation of Chargeable Gains Act 1992, section 1(1)). The modern trend for avoiding definitions was perhaps started by GSA Wheatcroft in 1955, when he declined to recommend a definition of income to the Royal Commission, out of fear that any such definition would lead to tax avoidance. The reaction to this report in many ways led directly to the enactment of capital gains tax ten years later (Williams 1966) and to overly targeted legislation, which may be so precisely drafted that it misses its target (Fraser 2004: 285). The relationship between the tax adviser and the Revenue would appear to be perfectly suited for game theory and systems analysis (Fraser 2004). This chapter, however, aims to consider a distinct period of change as part of a pattern of governance. Tax advisors and the Revenue are actors within that pattern.

A study of tax law is a study of ongoing change, for which institutionalist analyses would appear to be well matched, despite the difficulties inherent in engagement with a moving target. As Jane Jenson said '[a]nalysis of change is fraught with difficulty ... in large part because it is always occurring' (2004: 171). New institutionalist analysis may be approached from the perspective that some eras in history involve more change than others (Jenson 2004: 172). For UK tax law, the period including Brown's chancellorship and his time as Prime Minister would constitute one of the more important eras of change. The significance of the Pre-Budget Report and the increase in partially retrospective legislation was that tax law under New

Labour entered a new period of intense gamespersonship. The significance for gender is that even as the government relied on tax law more heavily than ever before (as part of its effort to influence people's choices outside the paid marketplace, within the private sphere), amendments were put in place which indicated distrust of the relationship between law and the market.

Games and Gender

In addition to these changes in the process of producing tax law, the former Inland Revenue assumed at least two new tasks under Brown's chancellorship. First, the Inland Revenue merged with the former Customs and Excise, to form Her Majesty's Revenue and Customs (HMRC). This merger was recommended by the O'Donnell Review, which investigated the circumstances leading to the collapse of a series of fraud cases (O'Donnell Review 2004). When dismissing the charges against the defendants in these cases, the court was particularly critical of the managerial culture within Customs and Excise which, among other problems, led employees to believe that they did not have to follow basic provisions of criminal procedure (O'Donnell Review 2004). Although the O'Donnell Review paid tribute to the fact that Customs and Excise had been operating for 'hundreds of years', it concluded that a merger of Customs and Excise with the more successful (by comparison) Inland Revenue would prove to be the best path forward.

Secondly, and significantly to the discussion in this chapter, many forms of benefits were allocated to HMRC for administration, including the Child Trust Fund, Child Benefit and child (and other) tax credits. The reasoning behind charging a tax collection agency with responsibility for administering benefits was layered. The ostensible justification offered for this change was that the (now) HMRC has a long history of dealing with money, employment, and families—what could be described as the technical, financial side of the public/private divide. This successful history is a product of its long administration of the Pay As You Earn System, which has been operating in its current form since the Second World War. Thus, in a relatively short period of time, HMRC took on major new responsibilities without concomitant investment in staff, despite the fact that staff enhancement was recommended by the O'Donnell Review. Indeed, staff were reduced. The fact that there was a child benefit data scandal in 2007 is perhaps understandable in this context.

Thus, an overstretched, under-resourced organization assumed a number of responsibilities involving women and the marketplace. HMRC collects taxes from women in paid employment, administers benefits to women living in poverty and coordinates information received from mothers, to ensure that the delicate combination of collected tax, with administered tax expenditures, encourages mothers to work in the paid marketplace and to 'resist' a life on benefits. This is a cycle of governance in which tax law was used to coordinate women's relationship between the paid and unpaid marketplace. The objective of coordination is clear: women are encouraged through financial incentives, either administered through tax or perhaps disguised as tax, to spend more time in the paid marketplace. The obligations of unpaid work are present and unavoidable and not as directly considered (for other discussions of the relationship and tensions between women's paid and unpaid work in tax law, see in this volume Philipps (Canada), de Villota (Spain) and Wersig (Germany)).

The tax credit system was implemented on the assumption that the problem presented by unpaid labour could be addressed by turning one person's unpaid labour into another person's paid work. Thus, the child of a mother who works may be cared for by paying another. The potential of the tax agency to forge a link between the paid marketplace and the family is noteworthy, as are the consequences of this attempted link for economic gender equality. Pierson observed in a new institutionalist analysis of welfare state politics, '[p]atterns of governance matter' (Pierson, 1996: 152). More significantly to this project, Pierson also suggested that the growing popularity of new institutionalism in political science was due to a recognition that political behaviour is marked by relatively few patterns of change (1996: 152). Changes to tax law under Brown were founded on fixed ideas about what a tax collector should do and, perhaps more importantly, what a tax collection agency could achieve if properly guided. The preference of government was that women should spend less time doing unpaid work at home unless their time there was funded privately (by men). This preference has been articulated through a series of reactive changes to tax as an institutional actor. It is significant that many of the changes described in this chapter were made not proactively, but reactively. As Philip Selznick, one of the foremost contributors to organizational theory, would have described them, the changes were 'born of social crisis, set out piecemeal as circumstances have demanded; they have not come to us as part of a broad and conscious vision' (Selznick 1984b: 1). Selznick, whose work on organizational theory has clear links to the new institutionalist analysis advanced in this chapter, has been writing for over 60 years on a vast array of subjects (Krygier 2002: 1). His immense legacy extends to the new institutionalist concern with rules as a form of interactive response, perhaps best exemplified in the modern concern with responsive law (Kagan 2002). He conducted studies of organizations as diverse as the Tennessee Valley Authority (Selznick 1984b) and the National Association for the Advancement of Colored People (NAACP), describing the latter organization as having a relationship between its members and its organizational centre akin to that between taxpayers and a governmental agency (Selznick 1984a: 52). In other words, the relationship was extremely loose and did not involve the exertion of strong elements of control. 'The result,' Selznick explained was 'an organization which ... [could not] easily be called upon to engage in unaccustomed types of action or to support precipitous policies' (Selznick 1984a: 53).

Although the changes to the production of tax law and the administration of benefits are obvious examples of what Selznick would describe as 'reactive' change, it is perhaps less obvious, but the expansion of earned income tax credits was also reactive. His 'structuration theory', however, presents parallels with Selznick's work, as it emphasized the importance of bureaucracies and institutions as sources of social change (Giddens 1985: 171). Giddens also often emphasized that society could no longer afford certain things. He described the decreasing influence of the gendered, pre-determined path which was which predicated on the assumption that women would work at home and that men would work in the paid marketplace as a recognition by society that 'we no longer live our lives as fate' (1999: 3).

Giddens did not romanticize the end of tradition (1999: 5) but argued that recognizing that traditionalized patterns had ended was crucial to the survival of the post-1945 welfare state (1999: 7). He suggested that, for example, the National Health Service was predicated on the assumption that traditionalized patterns of family life would continue and that failing to recognize that these patterns had ended was dangerous:

> In a world of more active engagement with health, with the body, with marriage, with gender, with work—in an era of manufactured risk—the welfare state cannot continue on in the form in which it developed in the post-1945 settlement.

Giddens constructed what he identified as necessary responses to the problems arising from the end of traditionalism. These suggestions have been criticized for an alleged over-reliance on some form of agency theory (Giddens 1985: 167). His 'structuration theory', however, presents parallels with Selznick's work, as it emphasized the importance of bureaucracies and institutions as sources of social change (1985: 171). In this context it is interesting to consider Giddens' arguments within the context of Selznick's writings. Giddens provided philosophical inspiration for the new Labour project. Selznick provides a context for understanding changes in bureaucracies brought about by developments within a new era of government, and in politics—two forums with important relevance for tax.

Games, Gender and Institutions

This chapter has argued that, under Gordon Brown, New Labour began to deploy the tax system in a 'strategic' way, interacting with players, markets and prevailing expectations of the tax system. Economic investment in bureaucratic tax structures was reduced even as these same structures assumed primary responsibility for the welfare state and, thus, the economic wellbeing of women. This final section will endeavour to articulate a sense of 'what is happening' as a result of these developments by relying on the analytical tools and touchstones provided within new institutionalist literature. It also will attempt to predict the significance of these developments to the status of women within the paid labour market.

New institutionalist theory suggests that law does not only monitor and regulate organisations. Rather, organizations are far from submissive and actually play a significant role in the formation of law and cultures of enforcement (Still 2008: 1510). What the Revenue preserves, and what the Revenue elects to attempt to change, are part of this interactive process. The interactive approach to tax law as an institution, or as a body of rules, faces a serious challenge when imbalances in power are considered. Women work longer than men, at work and at home, but are paid less. Similarly, when tasks typically performed as unpaid labour are placed within the paid marketplace, such as housework (Staudt 1996) the (largely, women) workers who take these jobs find that their labour is not highly compensated. Tax law in this context appears less interactive, and more prescriptive, at worst; at best, tax fails sufficiently to challenge existing inequities within the economy.

A new institutionalist approach to the gendered question of unpaid labour might suggest that the problem is that housework, for example, has been excluded from this interactive process; indeed, the problem is that women are excluded. The case for valuing unpaid labour—for bringing it into the paid marketplace, for *taxing it*—can be made powerfully (Staudt 1996). The argument often stops, however, at the criticism that what it ultimately will achieve is raising the level of taxation for middle and lower earning families. If unpaid labour is a taxable benefit on a progressive structure, the tax obligations of families will increase.

Whether or not increases in tax burdens for some taxpayers will lead to economic improvements for others—in other words, whether the imposition of a tax as described above ultimately will be worth it—is a question for economic analysis. Economists are concerned not with devising equitable rules, but, perhaps, with designing systems that distribute resources more equitably. Thus, economists have been described as both opposed to most laws and in favour of lowering most taxes (Beckert, Hollstein, Lehman, Marsden and Etzioni 2008: 1710). Neo-institutionalists, by contrast, are concerned with analyzing the rules that lawyers and economists produce and considering them as indicators of change.

Tax law is particularly receptive to the new institutionalist approach because it is sometimes understood as a 'primary legal rule', which should be applied by a judge in a 'predictable' way but without reference to 'basic issues of justice or public policy' (Kagan 2002: 87). Both the substance and the administration of tax law, however, are intimately connected with issues of justice and policy, perhaps especially in a system based on a merging of tax with the welfare state in an environment which promotes elements of political strategy. Who wins in this strategic interplay between the government and the market? Clearly, not women, who already lose in the connection between work and money, as they offer too many hours in service of the former, and receive too little of the latter in return. It is for this reason that, in many ways, this chapter hopes to function as a call to action for the fashioning of a feminist, new institutionalism.

Although institutional analysis, especially historically based, has a strong potential for feminist research, it is the identification of the internationalization of common value patterns that contributes most strongly to a feminist, new institutionalism. Both comparative and historical contexts, important schools within new institutionalist theory, are useful to understanding women's lack of power within the market economy. A feminist, new institutionalism would be useful both as part of a development away from earlier trends in political theory, and as the start of a process which aims to appreciate the importance of tax to women's economic wellbeing.

Any project that considers gender and politics could benefit from analyses that focuses on patterns of change. The patterns of change in the relationships between women, tax, markets and the state during the new Labour period of governance is best understood within a reconsidered neo-institutionalist framework that would perhaps aim to identify common patterns of values. This identification process is significant, because the production of tax law itself is laden with values. In some instances, the manner in which the tax law is produced can be at least as significant as the context of the legislation itself. Thus, merging tax and benefits, when the majority of taxpayers who live below the poverty line are women, is as important, if not more important, than the content of legislation outlining the structure and allocation of benefits.

A feminist, new institutionalism would focus on the interaction of power, change and gender. It would identify tax, itself, as an institutionalist actor. As Steinmo has emphasized, '[i]n the broadest sense, institutions are simply rules' (2001: 1) and frequently these rules are considered with reference to other systems. Differences in rules used by systems are a distinct part of the new institutionalist analysis. Indeed, the value of new institutionalism lies in the fact that it is primarily concerned with divergent responses to difference.

In so doing, new institutionalism builds on the insights of earlier work, such as that of Parsons, and of Schumpeter, but also asks new questions. For example, can a period of relative political stability, actually mask political turbulence along gendered lines? The New Labour project began in 1997 with a certain vibrancy, predicated—even by its name—on the idea of a new start, or a new approach, to entrenched problems. Many changes to the tax system were reactive, but these reactions revealed much about the way the tax system, and taxpayers, interact, and the effect of that interaction on society. Much has changed, but much also has stayed the same in terms of women's place within the economy. The value of a feminist, new institutionalism is that, through historic and contextual analyses, it reveals the gendered difficulties of effecting change upon 'new' political platforms, especially when these changes are predicated on old ideas about the economic valuation of women's work.

CONCLUSION

This chapter has sought to articulate, or to capture, an idea of what had changed, for women and for tax, during the New Labour era. The project was approached through the perspectives provided by a new institutionalist analysis of tax, markets and gender. Modern tax law became an instrument of government both within and without the market, and is thus particularly receptive to such an approach.

For tax law as an institutional actor, many things did change. The manner in which HMRC collects taxes from women in paid employment, administers benefits to women living in poverty and coordinates information received from mothers to run the welfare state, all changed in a variety of ways. The interaction between market citizens and the tax state also changed, and entered a new period of gamespersonship. For women, however, although many of these changes impacted on them, and although many of these effects were positive, several things, nonetheless, stayed the same. The dissonance between the amount of work that women perform, and the amount of economic power they have, persists. A new institutionalist analysis can help to explain what has emerged, and the persisting impact of entrenched beliefs and valuation processes—all constructive to the cause of determining what should be done next.

REFERENCES

Alexander, JC (1998) *Neofunctionalism and After* (Oxford, Blackwell Publishers).

Alexander, JC and Colomy, P (1985) 'Toward Neo-Functionalism' 3 *Sociological Theory* 11–23.

Beckert, J (2002) *Beyond the Market: The Social Foundations of Economic Efficiency* (Princeton, Princeton University Press).

Beckert, J, Hollstein, B, Lehman, EW, Marsden, D and Etzioni, A (2008) 'Twenty Years of "The Moral Dimension: Toward a New Economics"' 6 *Socioeconomic Review* 135–73.

Bevir, M and O'Brien, D (2001) 'New Labour and the Public Sector in Britain' 61 *Public Administration Review* 535–47.

Boschken, HL (1998) 'Institutionalism: Intergovernmental Exchange, Administration-Centered Behavior, and Policy Outcomes in Urban Agencies' 8 *Journal of Public Administration Research Theory* 585–614.

Brace, P and Hall, MG (1990) 'Neo-Institutionalism and Dissent in State Supreme Courts' 52 *The Journal of Politics* 54–70.

—— (1993) 'Integrated Models of Judicial Dissent' 55 *The Journal of Politics* 914–35.
Cohn, D (1994) 'Review' (untitled) 37 *Acta Sociologica* 433–35.
Fraser, R (2004) 'Tax scheme disclosure provisions' *British Tax Review* 282–95.
Giddens, A (1985) 'Marx's Correct Views on Everything: (With Apologies to L Kolowkowski)' 14 *Theory and Society* 167–94.
—— (1999) 'Risk and Responsibility' 62 *Modern Law Review* 1–10.
Hall, PA and Taylor, RCR (1996) 'Political Science and the Three New Institutionalisms' 44 *Political Studies* 936–37.
Hira, A and Hira, R (2000) 'The New Institutionalism Contradictory Notions of Change' 59 *The American Journal of Economics and Sociology* 267–82.
Jenson, J (2004) 'Changing the Paradigm: Family Responsibility or Investing in Children' 29 *Canadian Journal of Sociology/Cahiers canadiens de sociologie* 169–92.
Kagan, R (2002) 'On "Responsive Law"' in P Selznick, R Kagan, M Krygier and K Winston (eds), *Legality and Community: On the Intellectual Legacy of Philip Selznick* (London, Rowman & Littlefield).
Krygier, M (2002) 'Introduction' in P Selznick, R Kagan, M Krygier and K Winston (eds), *Legality and Community: On the Intellectual Legacy of Philip Selznick* (London, Rowman & Littlefield Publishers).
Lee, K and Pennings, JM (2002) 'Mimicry and the Market: Adoption of a New Organizational Form' 45(1) *Academy of Management Journal* 144–62.
McAnulla, S (2007) 'New Labour, Old Epistemology? Reflections on Political Science, New Institutionalism and the Blair Government' 60 *Parliamentary Affairs* 313–31.
McRobbie, A (2000) 'Feminism and the Third Way' 64(1) *Feminist Review* 97–112.
Meyer, JW and Rowan, B (1977) 'Institutionalized Organizations: Formal Structure as Myth and Ceremony' 83 *American Journal of Sociology* 340–63.
Miller, EA and Banaszak-Holl, J (2005) 'Cognitive and Normative Determinants of State Policymaking Behavior: Lessons from the Sociological Institutionalism' 35 *Publius* 191–216.
Moorhead, R (1998) 'Legal Aid in the Eye of a Storm: Rationing, Contracting, and a New Institutionalism' 25 *Journal of Law and Society* 365–87.
Mumford, A (2007) 'Inheritance in Socio-Political Context: The Case for Reviving the Sociological Discourse of Inheritance Tax Law' 34 *Journal of Law and Society* 567–93.
Nee, V and Brinton, MC (2001) *Sources of the New Institutionalism. The New Institutionalism in Sociology* (Stanford, Stanford University Press).
North, DC (1990) *Institutions, Institutional Change and Economic Performance* (Cambridge, Cambridge University Press).
O'Donnell, G (2004) *Review of the Revenue Departments*. Available at: www.hm-treasury.gov.uk/bud_bud04_odonnell_index.htm.
Parsons, T (1932) 'Economics and Sociology: Marshall in Relation to the Thought of His Time' 46 *The Quarterly Journal of Economics* 316–47.
—— (1935) 'Sociological Elements in Economic Thought: II. The Analytical Factor View' 1 *The Quarterly Journal of Economics* 646–67.
—— (1990) 'Prolegomena to a Theory of Social Institutions' 55 *American Sociological Review* 319–33.
—— (1991) *The Early Essays* (Chicago, University of Chicago Press).

Peters, BG (2005) *Institutional Theory in Political Science: The 'New Institutionalism'* (London, Continuum International Publishing Group).
Pierson, P (1996) 'The New Politics of the Welfare State' 48 *World Politics* 143–79.
Schmitter, PC (2004) 'Neo-Neofunctionalism' in A Wiener and T Diez (eds), *European Integration Theory* (Oxford, Oxford University Press).
Schumpeter, JA (1950) 'The March into Socialism' 40 *The American Economic Review* 446–56.
—— (1994) *Capitalism, Socialism and Democracy* (London, Routledge).
Searing, DD (1991) 'Roles, Rules, and Rationality in the New Institutionalism' 85 *The American Political Science Review* 1239–60.
Selznick, P (1984a) *Leadership in Administration: A Sociological Interpretation* (Berkeley University of California Press).
—— (1984b) *TVA and the Grass Roots* (Berkeley, University of California Press).
Seron, C and Munger, F (1996) 'Law and Inequality: Race, Gender ... and, of Course' 22 *Annual Reviews in Sociology* 187–12.
Smith, RM (1988) 'Political Jurisprudence, the "New Institutionalism", and the Future of Public Law' 82 *American Political Science Review* 89–108.
Staudt, NC (1996) 'Taxing Housework' 84 *Georgetown Law Journal* 1571–647.
Steinmo, S (2002) 'Globalization and Taxation: Challenges to the Swedish Welfare State' 35 *Comparative Political Studies* 839–62.
—— (2003) The Evolution of Policy Ideas: Tax Policy in the 20th century' 5 *The British Journal of Politics and International Relations* 206–36.
Steinmo, S, Thelen, KA and Longstreth, F (1992) *Structuring Politics: Historical Institutionalism in Comparative Analysis* (Cambridge, Cambridge University Press).
Still, MC (2008) 'Family Responsibilities, Discrimination and the New Institutionalism: The Interactive Process through which Legal and Social Factors Produce Institutional Change' 59 *Hastings Law Journal* 1491–515.
Suchman, MC and Edelman, LB (1996) 'Legal Rational Myths: The New Institutionalism and the Law and Society Tradition' 21 *Law and Social Inquiry* 903–41.
Swedberg, R (1996) 'Book Review of Nicos Mouzelis: Sociological Theory—What Went Wrong? Diagnosis and Remedies' 39 *Acta Sociologica* 116–18.
Teubner, G (1983) 'Substantive and Reflexive Elements in Modern Law' 17 *Law and Society Review* 239–85.
Tolbert, PS and Zucker, LG (1999) 'The Institutionalization of Institutional Theory' in SR Clegg and C Hardy (eds), *Studying Organization: Theory and Method* (London, Sage Publications).
Vandenberg, P (2002) 'North's Institutionalism and the Prospect of Combining Theoretical Approaches' 26 *Cambridge Journal of Economics* 217–35.
Williams, A (1966) Foreign Tax Policies and Economic Growth (NBER Conferences). Available at: www.nber.org/chapters/c1547.pdf.

Legislation

Taxation of Changeable Gains Act 1992

3

Gender Equity in Australia's Tax System: A Capabilities Approach

MIRANDA STEWART

ON 13 MAY 2008, following a '2020 summit' of ideas, the Australian Labour government announced a review of *Australia's Future Tax System*.[1] Known as the Henry Tax Review after its chair, Ken Henry (Secretary of the Treasury), the Review reported in December 2009. The Henry Tax Review was the most comprehensive review of the tax system since the Asprey Committee report (1975).[2]

Gender issues are at play at some crucial points in the Review's *Final Report* (Treasury 2009b), the *Architecture Paper* (Treasury 2008a) and the *Consultation Paper* (Treasury 2008b). This chapter analyses the 'gendered dynamics of tax policy' in the Henry Tax Review (Philipps 2002: 41). It focuses on the Review's analysis of the combined effect on individuals of the income tax system and the transfer (or welfare) system, referred to throughout this chapter as the 'tax-transfer system'.

The chapter's main focus is the 'capabilities' approach to equity in the tax-transfer system which was proposed by Ken Henry (2009), drawing on the work of Sen (1999). The chapter argues that the capabilities approach holds promise for enhancing gender equity in the tax-transfer system and defines some guiding principles for analysis of women's capabilities in tax policy. The chapter then examines whether the Review's analysis and outcomes live up to this promise. It discusses two issues with important implications for gender equity: first, the well-known debate about the

[1] Reports, commissioned research and submissions are available at http://taxreview.treasury.gov.au.

[2] The Review examined the income tax, transfer system, state and local taxes, resource taxes, excises and road pricing and the retirement savings system. The government insisted that retirement fund payouts should remain tax-exempt and excluded (for political reasons) the rate and base of the Goods and Services Tax (GST), a broad-based 10 per cent value-added tax.

tax-transfer unit, and secondly, the less visible issue of the impact of tax on women's saving and wealth.

TAXES AND GOVERNMENT

Australia has tax and spending levels of about 31 per cent of GDP, below the OECD average though higher than most neighbours in the Asia Pacific (OECD 2009: 40). Approximately one-quarter of federal taxes are redistributed in Australia's substantial but tightly means-tested transfer system (Treasury 2008a: 223). The Henry Tax Review affirms that the tax-transfer system is 'a fundamental part of Australia's social and economic infrastructure' and implicitly supports maintaining or even increasing the current size of government (Treasury 2008a: 3). In particular, it emphasises revenue 'sustainability' in the long term, taking into account Australia's ageing population.

The Review's support for a sustainable, redistributive tax-transfer system is positive for gender equity. Feminists have long emphasised the need for public provision to improve economic outcomes for women while also pointing to the complex interaction between the public and private domains in (re)producing gender inequity (for example, Boyd 1997; Cossman and Fudge 2002; Dahl 1984; WEL 2009).

However, while acknowledging the importance of government, the Review argues that Australia needs strong economic growth to drive increased well-being and tax revenues. It states that a pro-growth policy must be adopted in a context in which Australia is 'a small, open economy operating in an increasingly globalised world' (Treasury 2008b: 19–21). The overall approach of the Review is to recommend reform so as to reduce taxes on mobile capital investment and to encourage both market work and saving by Australians.[3]

EFFICIENCY AND EQUITY

The Henry Tax Review accepts the standard tax efficiency argument that 'all taxes and transfers affect the choices people and businesses make by altering their incentives to work, save, invest or consume'. It argues, therefore, that 'the tax and transfer system should raise and redistribute revenue at the least possible cost to economic efficiency' by minimizing the effect on these choices (Treasury 2009b: Part 1 Box 2.1, 17).

[3] The Review acknowledges that global capital mobility is imperfect and that in Australia's resource-based economy, the corporate tax may collect substantial economic rents (Treasury 2008b: 128).

In respect of equity, the Review conventionally, but still significantly, supports taxation on the basis of ability to pay (Treasury 2009b: Part 1 Box 2.1, 17):

> The tax and transfer system should treat individuals with similar economic capacity in the same way, while those with greater capacity should bear a greater net burden, or benefit less in the case of net transfers. This burden should change more than in proportion to the change in capacity. That is, the overall system should be progressive.

The Review takes both efficiency and equity into account in its analysis of the impact of the tax system on the choice to work. In this analysis, it explicitly acknowledges the issue of women's workforce participation (Treasury 2009b: Part 1, 18):

> International and Australian research has highlighted the different ways in which tax and transfer rules impact on the workforce participation of men, single and partnered women and women with children. In particular, partnered mothers and single parents are quite sensitive to the impact of taxes, transfer withdrawal rates and the level of transfer payments in deciding whether to undertake paid work.

In contrast, the Review does not directly refer to gender in its discussion of the impact of income tax on saving and investment.

The Review's *Architecture Paper* identifies a number of different perspectives on equity. These are 'inter-temporal equity'; 'intergenerational equity'; 'spatial equity'; equity in 'opportunity', 'freedom' and 'capabilities'; and 'rights-based frameworks' (Treasury 2008a: 178). The Review refers to gender only in this last category, in relation to which it affirms the need to 'rule out altogether' discrimination on grounds of 'gender', 'race' and 'sexual preference'. However, the Review interprets a 'rights-based' analysis narrowly as encompassing procedural fairness and the elimination of formal discrimination. It thereby ignores the important work identifying *substantive* gender and race inequality arising from formally neutral tax law and policy (see Gunnarsson, chapter four, this volume; Young 1997; Moran and Whitford 1996).

EQUITY IN CAPABILITIES

In a speech entitled 'How Much Inequity Should We Allow?' (2009), Ken Henry proposes a 'capabilities' approach to equity in the tax-transfer system. Henry draws explicitly on Sen's argument that 'the true measure of human development is that a person has the "capabilities" necessary to leading the kind of life they value and have reason to value'; thus, 'capabilities allow an individual to fully function in society; they are not "income" and, while they include basic civil rights and political freedoms, they are not limited to "rights"; they are "substantive freedoms"' (Sen 1999: 17).

Henry's speech identifies three important consequences for the tax-transfer system arising from the 'capabilities' approach. First, he states that it supports adequate basic incomes for all, and he thereby highlights the tax-transfer system as Australian society's main gesture toward equity. Secondly, he discusses the 'proper role of society' in 'fostering capabilities' of individuals. He states that public expenditures 'that directly address capability deficits' (for example, in education or health) 'may be more effective at raising long-term well being'. These remarks can be interpreted as an affirmation of a key role for public provision.[4] However, a capabilities approach does not mean equality of outcomes for Henry (or, probably, for Sen) and he accepts the 'relatively orthodox' economic view that a degree of income inequity is necessary to maintain incentives to earn income so as to generate economic growth (Kaplow 2008, in Henry 2009; see also, Sen 2009: 235).

Thirdly, 'and perhaps most importantly', Henry argues that the capabilities approach requires the tax-transfer system to support the development of individuals' capabilities that would improve their wellbeing in the longer term (2009: 2). The Review's final report states (Treasury 2009b: Part 1, 19):[5]

> In framing policies to alleviate disadvantage, a simple focus on the adequacy of income ... has been replaced by broader goals that focus on lifetime income and the capacity of people to engage in work and other social activities. In particular, there is greater awareness that assistance should not encourage short-term choices which compromise the development of capabilities that offer potential medium to long-term improvements in a person's wellbeing.

WOMEN'S CAPABILITIES

The implications of Sen's capabilities approach for women have been developed by a number of theorists. In particular Martha Nussbaum has sought to build a 'partial theory of social justice for women' based on the 'capabilities' approach (2000; 2002; 2003).[6]

[4] This may not have been what Henry intended, however, as he refers later in the speech to the possible withdrawal of the state from public housing (Henry 2009: 4).

[5] The Review also refers to 'social inclusion', a concept that has been adopted by the Labour government (see: www.socialinclusion.gov.au) in much the same terms as 'capabilities', eg, in discussing family and child payments (Treasury 2009b: Part 2, 556).

[6] See also 9 *Feminist Economics* (special issue of July 2003); Berik et al (2009); and Sen's own recent discussion of capabilities which refers frequently to gender issues (2009).

Nussbaum establishes a foundational list of 'women's capabilities', each of which is independent and necessary, in the sense that one cannot be substituted for another. Nussbaum's capabilities are, in brief summary: life; health, including food and shelter; bodily integrity and freedom from violence; sense, imagination and thought; emotions, including family attachments; practical reason, including being able to make moral choices; affiliation, including social interaction with others, self-respect, freedom of assembly and freedom from discrimination; living in relation to nature; play and recreation; and control, including control over material assets in the sense of equal rights to own property, the right to work and political participation (Nussbaum 2003: 41–42). Nussbaum's list is a reminder that income is just one component of wellbeing. Nonetheless, the list contains significant elements that relate to material wellbeing and that can enhance our analysis of the tax-transfer system.

Nussbaum's theory of women's capabilities places at the centre the issue of care. She observes that the 'capabilities' approach sees humans 'as animal beings whose lives are characterized by profound neediness as well as by dignity', so that (2002: 134; emphasis added):

> a good society must arrange to provide care for those in a condition of extreme dependency, *without exploiting women as they have traditionally been exploited, and thus depriving them of other important capabilities*. This huge problem will rightly shape the way states think about all the other capabilities.

Nussbaum also highlights the limits on individual agency generated for women in an inequitable society. Henry's speech does not explicitly acknowledge the limits on individual agency, although Sen is aware of 'adaptive preferences' restricted and shaped by societal norms (Nussbaum 2003: 34; Sen 1995). Berik et al express these three components nicely in proposing a feminist approach to development and economic growth (2009: 2):

> Human well-being requires at a minimum adequate provisioning (through interconnected paid labor and unpaid care activities and entitlements from the state or community); capabilities (the ability to do or be, based on provisioning); and agency (the ability to participate in decision making so as to shape the world we live in).

It is proposed that Nussbaum's approach to women's capabilities provides four principles for analysis of gender equity in Australia's tax-transfer system.

1. The capabilities approach supports a focus on the *individual* in the tax-transfer system. This does not mean, as Sen (2009: 244ff) is careful to point out, that individuals are not fundamentally influenced by each other or that individuals should not care about others. While family life and social connection are, of course, vital, it is fundamental to a

capabilities approach that each individual has dignity and is an 'end in themselves', so that his or her 'capabilities' relate to his or her own development and well-being. It is particularly important to emphasise women's *individual* capabilities in the present context, as women are so frequently embedded (and invisible) within families or households in tax policy discourse.

2. The capabilities approach requires an examination of the *lifecycle* of individuals. Capabilities are developed from infancy to old age and need to be fostered throughout one's life. This inter-temporal aspect of capabilities is clearly central to the Review's approach which looks at medium to long-term decisions and lifetime resources (Treasury 2008a: 178). For example, Henry's speech demonstrates an awareness of the long-term impact that a decision not to work may have on women's capabilities and the capabilities of children in the household (2009: 3).
3. Specific capabilities identified by Nussbaum include security of shelter and the capability of women to work and to own material assets. Here, it is important to take note of current gendered economic inequalities and not to lose sight of the goal of 'equality of outcomes' for women (Berik et al 2009: 5).
4. The capabilities approach requires the equitable distribution of the burden and cost of care. Valuing capabilities of each individual requires the distribution of the cost of care across all individuals; the tax-transfer system is a primary mechanism of the state to achieve this.

CAPABILITIES, CARE AND THE TAX-TRANSFER UNIT

The debate about the unit of assessment is a central trope in tax policy discourse. This apparently formal issue of tax law design hides a fundamental struggle about family, caring responsibilities and work. (See also Wersig, chapter eleven and Phillips, chapter twelve, this volume who address different facets of the tax unit debate.)

The Individual Tax Unit

The individual is the formal unit of assessment in Australian income tax. In 1975, the Asprey Committee stated that 'the right to be taxed as an individual has always been accorded in Australia'.[7] However, there have always been some aspects of the tax system that indirectly import a spousal unit, including the dependent spouse tax offset (credit); the spouse superannuation

[7] Asprey 1975: 134 [10–16]; for history, see Stewart 1999.

contribution tax offset; and joint income testing for the senior Australians tax offset, Medicare Levy and private health insurance tax offsets.

The Henry Tax Review affirms the individual tax unit (Treasury 2009b: Recommendation 3) for both efficiency and equity reasons. Its primary reason is the beneficial effect on work incentives (2009b: Part 2, 23–26):

> [I]n a couple where one partner is the primary earner and the other earns less, perhaps working part-time and caring for children, imposing the same marginal tax rate on both may cause the secondary earner to reduce their work effort. By contrast, a lower marginal rate for that person may encourage and support work. . . . A progressive individual tax system, with resulting lower tax rates for typically female secondary earners, is therefore more efficient than family taxation.

The Review also supports an individual unit based on horizontal equity between individuals. It therefore rejects the possibility, raised in an earlier paper, of adopting a family tax unit on the basis that this might 'better reflect the ability to pay of individuals in a family' (Treasury 2008a: 179). Finally, the Review describes the individual tax unit as more stable because 'families change over time, as people partner and separate, and society's conception of what constitutes a couple also changes' (Treasury 2009b: Part 2, 24). The Review does not, however, refer to the classic argument that *control* of income is the appropriate test for ability to pay (Simons 1938: [51]) so that the tax burden should be distributed according to each individual taxpayer's control over economic resources. In 1985, a previous Labor government adopted this argument as being 'consistent with Government policy of promoting equal employment opportunity and of furthering the independence of women' (Treasury 1985: 63).

Consistently with its position on the individual tax unit, the Review recommends removal of the various dependency tax offsets. It proposes a single 'dependant tax offset' payable if the dependant is unable to work due to disability, or carer responsibilities; or either the taxpayer or dependant has reached the age at which they would be eligible for the age pension (Treasury 2009b: Recommendation 6). Structurally, it appears that this dependant offset would directly benefit the taxpayer (the breadwinner) and not the dependant. If the dependant has no market income solely because of 'carer responsibilities', they are statistically much more likely to be female. In this case, it would seem more appropriate for the tax offset to be paid directly as an allowance directly to the carer, to alleviate her financial dependence on the breadwinner in the household. The Review's implicit assumption of income sharing in this recommendation is discussed further below.

The Review's recommendation for an individual tax unit must be placed in context of its proposal for reform of the tax rate structure by eliminating the targeted low income tax offset and replacing it with a high tax-free threshold (Treasury 2009b: Recommendation 2). The rate structure suggested by the Review is compared with the current rate structure in Table 1.

Table 1: 2010–11 Australian Personal Income Tax Rates compared with Henry Tax Review suggested Tax Rates (a)

Taxable income brackets 2010–11 ($) (a)	Marginal tax rate 2010–11 (a) %	Effective taxable income brackets 2010–11 with low income tax offset ($) (b)	Effective marginal tax rates 2010–011 with low income tax offset (b) %	Henry Tax Review suggested taxable income brackets (a)	Henry Tax Review suggested rates (a) %
0–6000	0	0–16,000	0	0–25,000	0
6001–37,000	15	16,001–30,000	15		
		30,001–37,000	19	25,001–180,000	35
37,001–80,000	30	37,001–67,500	34		
		67,501–80,000	30		
80,001–180,000	37	80,001–180,000	37		
180,000+	45	180,000+	45	180,000+	45

Notes:
(a) For current tax rates see www.ato.gov.au. For proposals, see Treasury 2009b: Part 1 29–30 and Recommendations 2 and 4.
(b) For 2010–11, the maximum low income tax offset will be $1500 and the phase-out limit will be $67,500. The offset raises the zero threshold to $16,000 and phases out at 4c in the dollar above $30,000 taxable income.

The Review's position on tax and work incentives for secondary earners might lead one to expect a recommendation to reduce rates in the lower middle income range that will affect most women seeking to increase working hours or a higher paying job. However, Table 1 reveals that the Review's proposal leaves current effective marginal rates more or less unchanged, and in fact would *increase* the marginal rates applying between $30,000 and $80,000 of income relative to 2010–11 rates.

Finally, the Review notes (as have many others) the risk of income splitting between family members to generate a de facto family tax unit and take advantage of an individual tax unit and progressive rates. As Grbich explains, income splitting is most effective in a traditional breadwinner-homemaker family, in which the taxpayer and his spouse are inevitably constituted in a hierarchical and gendered fashion (1987: 315). Income splitting has long been widespread in Australia, in particular by the 'professional and commercial classes' (Murphy J in *FCT v Everett* (1980) 143 CLR 440 at 457) but also by individuals providing personal services. Arrangements to ensure income splitting for tax purposes while still enabling the breadwinner to retain control of the disposition of income have often been upheld (see, for example, *DFCT v Purcell* (1921) 29 CLR 464). Today, discretionary trusts are widely used for this purpose.

The Review's proposal for an individual tax unit with a high tax-free threshold is likely to make the tax benefits of income splitting even more attractive. This will have to be addressed by tightening the income tax rules against income splitting.[8] One possibility is to apply automatic income attribution rules, like those applicable in Canada. However, such rules may themselves operate to undermine women's autonomy. Philipps (chapter twelve, this volume) suggests that income splitting could be tolerated to the extent that it provides women as 'recipients' of the split income with full control of the income. Such a proposal could be consistent with a capabilities approach as it would enhance women's economic independence within the family.

The Joint Transfer Unit

In Australia's contemporary tax-transfer system, the income tax unit is only half the story. In contrast to its support for an individual tax unit, the Review recommends joint (couple) income and asset testing for transfer payments such as unemployment benefits and the age pension, and testing on joint taxable income for family payments and childcare assistance. Its

[8] Reforms in the 1980s outlawed most income splitting with minor children and through short-term income assignments: Div 6AA and Div 7 of the Income Tax Assessment Act 1936. More recently attribution rules were enacted to prevent some personal services income splitting: Divs 84–87 of the Income Tax Assessment Act 1997.

main recommendation is to replace the current system of multiple family payments (with different tests) with a single payment, increased per child and phased out at an unspecified but 'low' rate tested on joint income (Treasury 2009b: Recommendations 89–96).

It has been exhaustively shown by Patricia Apps that in the current tax-transfer system, a joint unit prevails for most families raising children, as a result of the joint income-tested family payments introduced by the Howard Liberal-National (conservative) government during the 1990s.[9] In their recent analysis of the Review's proposals on this topic, Apps and Rees (2010) demonstrate that the Review's recommendations for family payments continue this joint family unit. Combined with the tax rate proposals outlined above, the Review proposals continue the trend to shift the tax burden towards middle income dual-earner families. This generates a significantly unequal tax burden and work disincentives for women through high effective marginal and average tax rates on secondary earners in a couple.

In respect of childcare payments, the Review proposes consolidation of the current system of two payments with a single payment based on a percentage of childcare costs, withdrawn on joint income but with a relatively high base level of assistance provided across the income distribution (Treasury 2009b: Recommendation 99; Part 2, 586). Here, the Review's stated purpose is 'to facilitate participation' and alleviate 'a number of biases against paid work'. Nonetheless, when childcare payment phase outs are layered on phase out of family payments, the significant effective marginal and average tax rates for secondary earners remain.

Why has the Review made recommendations for a joint unit for testing of family payments that contradict its stated policy in respect of the individual tax unit, in respect of the very people (mothers) who it identifies as most responsive to tax rates on work? The answer is that the Review considers itself bound by what it terms the 'iron triangle' of targeted means tested transfers in which (1) the level of payment must be balanced with (2) the cost to revenue and (3) impact on incentives to work (Treasury 2009b: Part 2, 498). The Review briefly refers to a system 'like those of Scandinavian countries', in which 'both parents, even of quite young children, are expected to work, just as any other capable adult is, but very extensive support is provided in the form of high-quality child care and early education' as well as 'family-friendly' workplaces (Treasury 2009b: Part 2, 527). However, the Review appears to conclude that Australia is not ready for this approach and, shackled by the 'iron triangle', it rejects universal family payments as 'extremely costly'.

The Review also relies on a 'horizontal equity' argument in support of a joint unit for family payments. In contrast to its discussion about equity

[9] In particular, Family Tax Benefit B is structured as a payment to a household with a breadwinner and dependent homemaker: Apps 2006; 2009; Apps and Rees (2010); see also Stewart (1999).

between *individuals* in the tax system, the final report frames the issue of family payments as being about equity between dual-earner and breadwinner-homemaker *couples* (Treasury 2009b: Part 2, 557):

> Horizontal equity can also refer to providing similar tax treatment to couples that receive their income primarily through one earner, relative to couples where both members undertake significant work. Because of the progressivity in the tax and transfer system, the couple where both members work pays lower net tax.

The suggestion that the breadwinner-homemaker family is worse off ignores the benefit to them of the non-taxation of home production, being the provision of childcare and other services in the home, relative to the dual-earner family who not only pay tax on both incomes but must pay out significant non-deductible costs of working and for care giving. The focus on the couple also renders invisible the negative effect of a joint unit on the woman within the couple. As the Review acknowledged in its *Architecture Paper*, the joint unit changes 'the distribution of tax *within* couples—with higher tax being paid by the lower income earner, though lower tax would be paid by the couple' (Treasury 2008a: 179).

An additional reason why the Review supports a joint unit is based on the argument that 'couples or families form a single economic unit' (Treasury 2008a: 179). The Review does not interrogate the assumption of income sharing that underlies this view. More than 30 years ago, it was observed that while 'much is jointly consumed' by married couples, 'in some marriages, and not by any means only unhappy ones, almost completely separate patterns of spending and enjoyment may be the rule. Between the extremes a whole range of intermediate arrangements will be found' (Asprey 1975: [10.18]). The Asprey Committee's scepticism about income sharing is supported by empirical studies demonstrating the wide variety of financial arrangements within couples (Gray and Evans 2008; Singh and Lindsay 1996; Kornhauser 1993).

Australia's tax-transfer system now defines a couple to include married opposite-sex couples and same-sex or opposite-sex couples who are 'living together as a couple on a genuine domestic basis'. Ironically, the 'rights-based' equity recently achieved for lesbian and gay couples serves also to embed the breadwinner-homemaker model of caring and work within same-sex couples, privatising care and reducing costs to government.[10] (See also Warman and Woolley, chapter nine, this volume.)

Overall, the policy direction of the Henry Tax Review is directed at the limited goal of encouraging mothers (back) into *part-time* work. The

[10] Same-sex couples were included effective 1 July 2009. The government estimated a saving of $60 million a year through a reduction of transfer payments because of testing on joint same-sex couple income: *Explanatory Memorandum* to the Same-Sex Relationships (Equal Treatment in Commonwealth Laws— General Law Reform) Bill 2008.

Review states this explicitly in its discussion of transfer payments: it aims to continue 'current policy' which is aimed 'at keeping primary carers in touch with the labour market. This usually means some form of part-time work' (Treasury 2009b: Part 2, 527). From a capabilities perspective, part-time work has the potential to enhance a mother's current income though it is unlikely to make much difference to her retirement savings. It also could contribute to other capabilities, including skills and social connection. In the event of divorce or other crisis, having employment may strengthen self-esteem and increase capacity to support herself and her family.

However, the goal of increasing women's capability to engage in part-time work is a minimal expression of the capabilities approach for women, for several reasons. First, while there is scope to increase Australia's participation rates for women with children that are among the lowest among rich countries (OECD 2010), the Review's proposals ultimately make very little change to the disincentives and unfair distribution of the tax burden on women that arise under the current system. Secondly, many mothers are *already* entering the workforce part time, even in the current system (these women simply bear an unfair share of the tax burden).[11] Thirdly, many part-time jobs are not good jobs: they are neither secure nor well paid and they may not provide a pathway to more sustaining work. Fourthly, even a good part-time job cannot generate sufficient reward to eliminate gender inequity in women's income or savings, or to prevent many women who are single parents from living in poverty.

Most importantly, the Review's proposals do not relieve women of primary responsibility for care. The focus on part-time work of a secondary earner who retains responsibility for parenting sidesteps the 'huge problem' in Nussbaum's words of ensuring that care is provided to all *and* that all are responsible for it *without exploiting women*.

CAPABILITIES AND SAVING

It seems at first blush more difficult to apply Sen's 'capabilities' approach to inequity of saving (the distribution of income and wealth) above a basic minimum. However, it is argued here that a capabilities approach to gender equity requires us to examine women's capability to enjoy economic security and independence over the lifecycle. In Australia, economic security requires both public and private provision and so women need to be able to accumulate savings. Furthermore, as Berik et al (2009) argue it is important not to lose sight of the goal of gender equality of outcomes.

[11] Seventy-three per cent of women (compared with 92 per cent of men) between the ages of 25 and 59 are employed and women's participation continues to trend upwards: Household Income and Labour Dynamics in Australia (HILDA) survey of 2005. The majority of women with young children work part-time and balance work and care responsibilities: ABS 2009.

The comprehensive or 'Shanz-Haig-Simons' income tax (Simons 1938) has long been the ideal benchmark against which Australia's income tax is evaluated. The Henry Tax Review departs significantly from previous Australian tax policy discourse in stating that 'comprehensive income taxation, under which all savings income is taxed the same as labour income, is not an appropriate policy goal or benchmark' (Treasury 2009b: Part 1, 32). Instead, it proposes to tax savings income 'at a lower rate than labour income' (Treasury 2009b: Part 1, 17). In support of this, the Review accepts the position, long argued by some economists, that imposing tax on capital income 'creates a bias against savings, particularly long-term savings' (Treasury 2009b: Part 1, 32; see, for example, Kaldor 1955; Bradford 1980). The Review considered a direct expenditure tax but ultimately does not make such a radical recommendation.[12]

Unlike its analysis of tax on work, the Review does not explicitly consider the gender implications of its shift towards a consumption tax benchmark. In general, there are reasons for feminists to be concerned about such a shift. As discussed below, women are generally poorer than men, save less, have fewer assets and have fewer opportunities to invest. Consequently, as a class, women would benefit much less than men from a shift to a tax system that entirely exempts savings. Women would also likely suffer more from any loss of tax revenues for public provision and welfare that would result from such a change. (Young (1997) makes a strong gender equity argument for removing tax concessions for saving and assets.)

However, Australia's income tax already exempts significant forms of saving from tax. The following forms of saving in Australia benefit from significant tax concessions that bring their taxation closer to a consumption tax benchmark:

1. Home ownership is completely exempt from income tax.
2. Private retirement saving is taxed at 15 per cent (in superannuation funds) and benefits are usually exempt on payout. This system may be even more generous than a consumption tax benchmark, which would fully exempt contributions and earnings but would tax payouts at individual marginal rates. Individuals or employers can contribute large sums on a deductible basis into superannuation (up to $25,000 annually).

[12] A consumption or expenditure tax is theoretically equivalent to a comprehensive income tax, except that it exempts the return to saving. The Asprey Committee was attracted by the 'philosophy' of an expenditure tax but it recommended retaining a progressive income tax and reforming it to be more in line with a comprehensive income tax benchmark (1975: [3.17]). The Henry Tax Review cites an OECD study (Johannson et al 2008) in support of an expenditure tax but relies on research carried out for the UK Mirrlees Review that suggests that it is more efficient to impose some tax on capital income (Diamond and Banks 2008; see Treasury 2008a: 216; 2008b: 64).

3. Only half of capital gains of individuals and trusts on other forms of investment such as shares or rental properties are taxed, applying the capital gains tax 50 per cent discount.

The only categories of capital income not eligible for a tax concession are interest on bank accounts and dividends on shares (which benefit from full dividend imputation providing a credit for company tax paid). It can be seen that, as in most countries, Australia's income tax is in reality a rather incoherent 'hybrid income-consumption tax' (Aaron et al 1988). We must make a realistic appraisal of the extent to which the income tax currently fails to tax capital income and the historical and current impediments (political, economic and administrative) that stand in the way of implementing a comprehensive progressive income tax.

From a capabilities perspective, I propose that we refocus the analysis to identify who benefits from tax subsidies for saving. A brief examination of components and distribution of wealth in Australia assists in this analysis. Average household wealth comprises 44 per cent home ownership (69 per cent of Australians live in their own home); 13 per cent private superannuation saving; and the balance being other real estate, financial investments and bank accounts (ABS 2007; Treasury 2008a: 181). However, the top 20 per cent of households have more than 20 times the wealth of the bottom 20 per cent and derive 65 per cent of capital income. Older households have higher wealth (and lower incomes), while younger households have higher incomes and lower wealth (Treasury 2008a: 182–84).

Overall, women have less income and assets than men (Jefferson and Ong 2010). Women's wealth is increasing over time as their participation in market work increases, but it remains limited because female working life is interrupted by care responsibilities (Kelly, Percival and Harding 2001; Tually, Beer and Faulkner 2007). Women's limited asset portfolios imply that women derive fewer and smaller capital gains than men and hence benefit less from the capital gains tax 50 per cent discount; there is evidence of this in similar countries (Young 1997; Philipps 1996 and Kornhauser, chapter fourteen, this volume). At the other end of the spectrum, women occupy many of the poorest households (Lloyd, Harding and Payne 2004: 5; ABS 2007b). Female-headed households make up more than 60 per cent of households in public housing or receiving rent assistance (Baker and Tually 2008: 129).

The remaining parts discuss the implications for women's capabilities of the two largest tax subsidies for saving: the exemption of home ownership from income tax and the massive tax subsidies for retirement saving. I then consider the Henry Tax Review's approach to these key elements of saving.[13]

[13] There is not scope to examine the Review's proposal for other savings, in which it essentially adopts a 'dual income tax' schedular approach similar to that adopted in some of the Nordic countries (Treasury 2009b: Recommendation 14).

Retirement Saving

While we do not know enough about women's overall wealth, it is well known that Australia's retirement savings system is highly gendered in both its structure and outcomes (Jefferson 2005, 2009; Sharp and Austen 2007). Tax subsidies for superannuation comprise the second largest measured tax expenditures in the income tax, estimated at $24.4 billion in 2009–10 (Treasury 2010: 4, Items C5 and C6). The bulk of this arises from tax deductibility of contributions and the 15 per cent tax rate on contributions and earnings in the fund. Like many tax expenditures, this is an 'upside-down' subsidy from which high income earners who work full time through their working lives benefit most. Middle-aged, full-time employed women have about 66 per cent of the superannuation balances of men, but women close to retirement have only 46 per cent (Tually, Beer and Faulkner 2007: 29). While women do benefit from a government co-contribution of up to $1500 a year and from the ability of a taxpayer to contribute up to $3000 to a superannuation fund for their spouse if the spouse has a low income, these are tiny subsidies by comparison.[14] Women represent 55 per cent of people over the age of 65 and two-thirds of people over 80; not surprisingly, more than half of age pensioners are women.

The Review acknowledges that women are differently situated because of their interrupted working lives (Treasury 2009a: 26, 45). However, the Review accepts the status quo of the 'three pillar' retirement system, comprising means tested age pension; compulsory employer superannuation contributions; and increased voluntary contributions to superannuation savings. It concludes that retirement security for 'people who have experienced broken work patterns'—that is, most women—'should be achieved through the Age Pension' (Treasury 2009c: 13). In this limited context, the Review proposes some minor superannuation reforms that would improve the equity of the superannuation tax system and go some way to ensuring an individual tax unit for retirement saving (Treasury 2009b: Recommendations 18–19). In spite of these minor improvements, the structural gender inequities in the retirement system are so stark that I suggest, as do others, that the best policy to ensure women's economic security over their lifetime would be to reduce tax subsidies for private superannuation saving significantly and use the tax funds to support the age pension.

Home Ownership

The largest component of Australian household wealth is the home itself, and 69 per cent of Australian households own or are purchasing a home

[14] Eg, the spouse co-contribution was estimated as a tax expenditure of only $9 million in 2009–10 (Treasury 2010: Item C10).

(ABS 2007). Home owners benefit from very large tax expenditures because imputed rent and capital gains are exempt from income tax. Applying a tenure-neutral benchmark that compares home owners with landlords, the Treasury estimates $19.5 billion in revenue foregone from home ownership tax expenditures in 2009–10 (2010: Table C1; Yates 2010). These subsidies mean that Australia's current income tax system essentially applies a consumption tax treatment to home ownership.[15]

The Review proposes to maintain the exemption of the home from income tax because it 'provides security, shelter and a savings vehicle' to millions of Australians (Treasury 2009b: 410). Shelter is a fundamental capability, and in a society such as Australia's, there is an argument that home ownership as a widely valued and secure form of shelter should be fostered. Australian renters are significantly worse off than home owners in terms of both income and wealth (Treasury 2008b: 203).

Women *do* benefit from home ownership tax concessions, in contrast to superannuation. For the majority of women, their home is the only asset of significant value that they accumulate during their lifetime (Jefferson and Ong 2010; Baker and Tually 2008). There is a particularly strong lifecycle element in home ownership and most people over the age of 65 own their home outright. The main residence is exempt from the age pension assets test and this is crucial for older women. Most women obtain housing wealth through home purchase while in a couple.[16] Single women have less housing wealth than couples or single men; however, when they do own a home, it comprises more than half of their total assets. On relationship breakdown, women frequently retain home ownership although divorce does generate housing insecurity for many women (Sheehan and Hughes 2001; De Vaus et al 2007).

Based on this brief analysis, it is argued that a capabilities approach to women would support the existing subsidies for home ownership. However, there is a good case for taxing high value capital gains on the home, either through a capital gains tax (and a bequests tax) or a land tax. The Review deals with this by recommending that land tax be extended to the home (Treasury 2009b: Recommendation 52). The Rudd Labor government rejected enacting a federal land tax; the result is that we are left with a very difficult political reform process for State governments.

The second limb of a capabilities approach to home ownership requires measures to extend access to home ownership to a wider class of low-income women and men. One approach would be to provide a subsidy to enable people to save for home purchase. In 2008, the Australian government established

[15] See further Stewart (2010).

[16] Almost 80 per cent of couples own or are purchasing a home and in 84 per cent of these couples, title to the home is held jointly: Jefferson and Ong (2010).

a First Home Saver Account (FHSA) scheme.[17] This scheme provides a low-tax house deposit savings strategy including a government co-contribution and 15 per cent rate which could be of great assistance to younger people, including women on relatively low incomes, seeking to purchase their first home. The revenue cost of FHSAs was estimated to grow from $156 million in its first year to $400 million in its fourth year of operation.[18] However, two years later, the direct expense of government contributions to FHSAs was estimated at only $23.6 million.[19] This dramatically lowered estimate reveals the main flaw of this programme, like many low income savings programmes, which is the very limited uptake by eligible individuals.

CAPABILITIES AND GENDER EQUITY

This chapter examined some aspects of Australia's recent Henry Tax Review from the perspective of gender equity and in particular the 'capabilities' approach to equity in the tax-transfer system.

If we are to take women's capabilities seriously as 'substantive freedoms', reforms to the tax-transfer system should expand the universe of choices for women. The Review's support for an individual tax unit is positive for gender equity. However, the Review's contradictory recommendations for maintaining a joint transfer unit in relation to family and childcare payments work against women's capabilities. They do not significantly change the institutional structures and pathways that limit women's capabilities in respect of work and care, constraining many women's ability to do significant paid work and to accrue significant saving for long term economic independence and security. The Review's emphasis on 'cost' of family payments suggests it continues to undervalue women's capabilities and does not come to grips with the principle of *sharing* the cost of care. It does not engage with a more fundamental approach to restructuring the tax-transfer system to enable a reconfiguration of care and work.

A 'capabilities' approach to women's saving demands that we examine the components of saving for individuals to determine where women would benefit from tax subsidies for saving and where, on the other hand, such subsidies reinforce gender inequity and public provision remains crucial. Those with retirement savings and those who own homes benefit from the largest tax expenditures in Australia's income tax, both of which shift the base toward a consumption tax benchmark. While all such subsidies benefit

[17] Division 345 of the Income Tax Assessment Act 1997; see: homesaver.treasury.gov.au/content/default.asp.

[18] Explanatory Memorandum to First Home Saver Accounts Bill 2008: 7.

[19] Treasury Portfolio Budget Statement 2010–2011 Table 2.1: 916. Available from: www.treasury.gov.au.

higher-income individuals more than low-income individuals, a capabilities approach to gender equity supports maintaining the tax subsidy for home ownership. However, there are compelling arguments to wind back tax concessions for superannuation saving as they exacerbate gender inequity in income over the lifecycle.

The 'capabilities' approach to tax equity proposed by Henry has significant potential to reinvigorate a gender equity analysis of tax-transfer policy. The analysis in this chapter shows that gender equity becomes visible in the Henry Tax Review's analysis where it would be consistent with the goals of efficiency and revenue raising, in particular the impact of tax on choices to do part-time work. Yet gender disappears, even at the expense of work incentives, where achieving it may be more 'costly' for the public sphere in the short term. Stark gender inequities in saving are not acknowledged in the debate. The most important function of the tax system for women's capabilities remains the fundamental goal of raising adequate tax revenues for public provision of retirement income and housing. We must be careful that 'capability' of individuals is not restricted to what is necessary for the market, leaving untouched gendered norms of work, care and wealth.

REFERENCES

Aaron HJ, Galper, H and Pechman, J (eds) (1988) *Uneasy Compromise: Problems of a Hybrid Income-Consumption Tax* (Washington, DC, Brookings Institution).

Apps, P (2006) 'Family Taxation: An Unfair and Inefficient System' 7 *Australian Review of Public Affairs* 77–101.

—— (2010) 'Labour Supply, Saving and Family Tax Reform' paper prepared for the conference on 'Australia's Future Tax System: A Post-Henry Review' (Sydney, 21–23 June 2010).

Apps, P and Rees, R (2010) 'Australian Family Tax Reform and the Targeting Fallacy' 43(2) *Australian Economic Review* 153–175.

ABS (Australian Bureau of Statistics) (2007a) *Household Wealth and Wealth Distribution 2005–06* (6554.0). Available at: www.abs.gov.au.

—— (2007b) *Low Income Low Wealth Households* (4102.0, Australian Social Trends). Available at: www.abs.gov.au.

—— (2009) *Work, Life and Family Balance* (4102.0, Australian Social Trends 2009). Available at: www.abs.gov.au.

Asprey Committee (Taxation Review Committee) *Full Report* (31 January 1975).

ATO (Australian Taxation Office) (2008) *Taxation Statistics 2006–07*.

Baker, E and Tually, S (2008) 'Women, Health and Housing Assistance: Implications in an Emerging Era of Housing Provision' 43(1) *Australian Journal of Social Issues* 123–38.

Boyd, SB (ed) (1997) *Challenging the Public/Private Divide: Feminism, Law and Public Policy* (Toronto, University of Toronto Press).

Berik, G, van der Meulen Rogers, Y and Seguino, S (2009) 'Feminist Economics of Inequality, Development, and Growth' 15(3) *Feminist Economics* 1–33.

Bradford, D (1980) 'The Case for a Personal Consumption Tax' in J Pechman (ed), *What Should Be Taxed: Income or Expenditure?* (Washington, DC, Brookings Institution) 75–112.
Cossman, B and Fudge, J (eds) (2002) *Privatization, Law and the Challenge to Feminism* (Toronto, University of Toronto Press).
Dahl, TS (1984) 'Women's Rights to Money' 12 *International Journal of the Sociology of Law* 137.
De Vaus, D, Gray, M, Qu, L and Standon, D (2007) *The Consequences of Divorce for Financial Living Standards in Later Life*, Australian Institute of Family Studies Research Paper no 38 (Melbourne, AIFS, February 2007).
Diamond, P and Banks, J (2008) 'The Base for Direct Taxation' in S Adam, T Besley, R Blundell, S Bond, R Chote, M Gammie, P Johnson, G Myles and J Poterba (eds), *Reforming the Tax System for the 21st Century: The Mirrlees Review* (London, Institute for Fiscal Studies). Available at: www.ifs.org.uk/mirrleesreview.
Gray, E and Evans, A (2008) 'Do Couples Share Income? Variations in the Organisation of Income in Dual-Earner Households' 43 *Australian Journal of Social Issues* 441–57.
Grbich, JE (1987) 'The Position of Women in Family Dealing: The Australian Case' 15 *International Journal of the Sociology of Law* 309.
Henry, K (2009) 'How Much Inequity Should We Allow?' Speech given at ACOSS national conference (3 April). Available at: taxreview.treasury.gov.au.
Jefferson, T (2005) 'Women and Retirement Incomes: A Review' 8 *Economic Record* 273–91.
—— (2009) 'Women and Retirement Pensions: A Research Review' 15(4) *Feminist Economics* 115–45.
Jefferson, T and Ong, R (2010) *Profiling Gender Differentials in Asset and Debt Portfolios in Australia*, Centre for Research in Applied Economics Working Paper Series no 2010/04 (Perth, Curtin University of Technology School of Economics and Finance).
Johansson, A, Heady, C, Arnold, J, Brys, B and Vartia, L (2008) *Tax and Economic Growth*, Economics Department Working Paper no 620 (OECD, Paris).
Kaldor, N (1955) *An Expenditure Tax* (London, George Allen & Unwin Ltd).
Kaplow, L (2008) *The Theory of Taxation and Public Economics* (Princeton, NJ, Princeton University Press).
Kelly, S, Percival, R and Harding, A (2001) 'Women and Superannuation in the 21st Century: Poverty or Plenty?' paper for the SPRC National Social Policy Conference University of New South Wales. Available online at: www.sprc.unsw.edu.au/nspc2001/NSPC%202001Papers/Kelly_Percival_Harding%20.pdf.
Kornhauser, M (1993) 'Love, Money, and the IRS: Family, Income-Sharing, and the Joint Income Tax Return' 45 *Hastings Law Journal* 63.
Lloyd, R, Harding, A and Payne, A (2004) Australians in Poverty in the 21st century (National Centre for Social and Economic Modelling (NATSEM), University of Canberra). Available from www.canberra.edu.au/centres/natsem/publications.
Moran, BI and Whitford, WC (1996) 'A Black Critique of the Internal Revenue Code' 4 *Wisconsin Law Review* 751.
Nussbaum, M (2000) 'Women's Capabilities and Social Justice' 1 *Journal of Human Development* 219–47.
—— (2002) 'Capabilities and Social Justice' 4 *International Studies Review* 123–35.

—— (2003) 'Capabilities as Fundamental Entitlements' 9 *Feminist Economics* 33–59.
OECD (2009) *Revenue Statistics 1965 to 2008* (Paris, OECD). Available at: www.oecd.org/ctp/revenuestats.
—— (2010) *Gender Brief*. Available at: www.oecd.org.
Philipps, L (1996) 'Tax Policy and the Gendered Distribution of Wealth' in I Bakker (ed), *Rethinking Restructuring: Gender and Change in Canada* (Toronto, University of Toronto Press) 141–64.
—— (2002) 'Tax Law and Social Reproduction: The Gender of Fiscal Policy in an Age of Privatization' in B Cossman and J Fudge (eds), *Privatization, Law and the Challenge to Feminism* (Toronto, University of Toronto Press) 41.
Sen, A (1983) 'Poor, Relatively Speaking' 35 *Oxford Economic Papers* 153–69.
—— (1995) 'Gender Inequality and Theories of Justice' in M Nussbaum and J Glover (eds), *Women, Culture and Development: A Study of Human Capabilities* (Oxford, Clarendon Press) 259–73.
—— (1999) *Development as Freedom* (Oxford, Oxford University Press).
—— (2009) *The Idea of Justice* (Cambridge, The Belknap Press of Harvard University Press).
Sharp, R and Austen, S (2007) 'The 2006 Federal Budget: A Gender Analysis of the Superannuation Taxation Concessions' (June) *Australian Journal of Labour Economics* 61–77.
Sheehan, G and Hughes, J (2001) *Division of Matrimonial Property in Australia* (Melbourne, Australian Institute of Family Studies).
Simons, H (1938) *Personal Income Taxation: The Definition of Income as a Problem of Fiscal Policy* (Chicago, University of Chicago Press).
Singh, S and Lindsay, J (1996) 'Money in Heterosexual Relationships' 32 *Journal of Sociology* 57–69.
Sorenson, P and Johnson, S (2010) *Taxing Capital Income: Options for Reform in Australia in Melbourne Institute: Proceedings of Australia's Future Tax System Conference* (Çommonwealth of Australia, 18–29 June 2009). Available at: taxreview.treasury.gov.au/content/html/conference/downloads/conference_report/09_AFTS_Tax_and_Transfer_Policy_Conference_Chap_9.pdf.
Stewart, M (1999) 'Domesticating Tax Reform: The Family in Australian Tax and Transfer Law' 21 *Sydney Law Review* 453–86.
—— (2010) 'Housing and Tax Policy: New Directions' in M Stewart (ed), *Housing and Tax Policy Conference Series No 26* (Australian Tax Research Foundation) 1–35.
Treasury (Australian) (1985) *Reform of the Australian Tax System: Draft White Paper* (Canberra, Australian Government Publishing Service).
—— (2008a, August) *Architecture of Australia's Tax and Transfer System*. Available at: taxreview.treasury.gov.au/content/Content.aspx?doc=html/pubs_reports.htm.
—— (2008b, December) *Australia's Future Tax System—Consultation Paper*. Available at: taxreview.treasury.gov.au/content/Content.aspx?doc=html/pubs_reports.htm.
—— (2009a, May) *Australia's Future Tax System. The Retirement Income System: Report on Strategic Issues*. Available at: taxreview.treasury.gov.au/content/Content.aspx?doc=html/pubs_reports.htm.

—— (2009b, December) *Australia's Future Tax System. Final Report to the Treasurer.* Available at: taxreview.treasury.gov.au/content/Content.aspx?doc=html/pubs_reports.htm.
—— (2010, January) *Tax Expenditures Statement 2009*. Available at: http://www.treasury.gov.au/contentitem.asp?NavId=022&ContentID=1465.
Tually, S, Beer, A and Faulkner, D (September 2007) *Too Big to Ignore: Future Issues for Australian Women's Housing 2006–2025* (Adelaide, AHURI Southern Research Centre). Available at: www.socsci.flinders.edu.au/ahuri.src/publications/2007/toobigtoignore.php.
WEL (Women's Electoral Lobby Australia Inc) (2009) *Submission to the Review of Australia's Future Tax System*. Available at: taxreview.treasury.gov.au/content/submission.aspx?round=2&pageid=004c.
Yates, J (2010) 'Tax Expenditures and Housing' in M Stewart (ed), *Housing and Tax Policy Conference Series No 26* (Australian Tax Research Foundation) 39–91.
Young, C (1997) 'Taxing Times for Women: Feminism Confronts Tax Policy' in R Krever (ed), *Tax Conversations: A Guide to the Key Issues in the Tax Reform Debate—Essays in Honour of John G Head* (London, Kluwer Law International) 261–92.

Legislation

Australian Commonwealth legislation, Bills and explanatory memoranda are available at: www.comlaw.gov.au/.
Income Tax Assessment Act 1997 (Cth).
Income Tax Assessment Act 1936 (Cth).
Explanatory Memorandum to the Same-Sex Relationships (Equal Treatment in Commonwealth Laws—General Law Reform) Bill 2008 (Cth).
Explanatory Memorandum to the First Home Saver Accounts Bill 2008 (Cth).

Cases

DFCT v Purcell (1921) 29 CLR 464.
FCT v Everett (1980) 143 CLR 440.

4

Challenging the Benchmarks in Tax Law Theories and Policies from a Gender Perspective—The Swedish Case

ÅSA GUNNARSSON

GENDER EQUALITY IS a constitutional principle in the European Union. Solely on this basis, legislative bodies within the EU should consider gender equality when making tax reforms. However, gender-responsive tax reforms are not guaranteed by a constitutional framework for gender equality, but rather by qualitative analyses concerning the substance of the welfare state, the labour market and family structures—a common approach in most gender-sensitive policy analyses (see O'Connor, Orloff and Shaver 1999). Considering contemporary and future social risks that the European welfare states are facing in connection with income protection for wage earners,[1] it is no exaggeration to claim that gender equality is probably one of the most important prerequisites for future welfare reforms. Overlooking gendered patterns of social power in designing the financing of welfare regimes may very well turn out to have devastating consequences for the future sustainability of tax regimes in many welfare states. Put frankly, gender blindness in tax policy making is, in the light of welfare futures, an irresponsible political standpoint.

In this chapter, I will try to identify some of the underlying normative foundations of tax theories and policies that mirror and reproduce gender inequalities and to provide some examples of how these normative benchmarks are applied in Swedish national tax law. The chapter picks up on several major policy debates about tax system design that are particularly

[1] See, eg, the identification of new social risks made by Giuliano Bonoli (2005). Bonoli points out that transformations of the labour market and of family structures have created new social risks, such as difficulties in reconciling work and family life, single parenthood, having responsibility for an ageing or disabled relative and possessing low or obsolete skills.

relevant to the gendered dimensions of how welfare is produced and distributed in the triangular relation between the market, the state and the household (which in the following I will label the 'social welfare triangle'). To capture the whole gendered context of social welfare, one also has to consider the exchange of time, care and economic resources within the households. Nordic feminist scholars have successively developed a model for analysing both the public and the private side of welfare production and distribution. By adding the private relations of exchange of time, care and economic resources to the public relations of the exchange of money and work between the state, the market and the household, it is possible to see structural patterns through which tax law reproduces the division between the public and private spheres, which, in turn, mirrors the division between male and female lives (see Ketscher 1998: 60–68; Stang Dahl 1988; Gunnarsson 2003). From this perspective, I will explore the gendered impact that the choices of tax units, tax mixes, quotas and tax equity principles can have, and I will also show that the concept of the public/private division of labour fails to capture gender-equality concerns in the tax system.

THE NEED FOR A CRITICAL EPISTEMOLOGY BASED ON A GENDER PERSPECTIVE

A report from the Swedish Inland Revenue (*Skatteverket*), published at the beginning of 2007, can serve as an example of lack of gender competence in tax policy making. The report is not of great significance for tax policy processes in Sweden, but it is the first of its kind. The subject of the report was whether simplifications of tax regulations would increase gender equality (2007: 2). The basic conclusion was that Swedish tax legislation is gender neutral but that in some areas of taxation, the system's impact on women causes them to suffer significant substantive inequalities. This inequality emanates, according to the report, from gender-related differences in work performance, entrepreneurship and investments. On the basis of this conclusion, the report stated that it would be more interesting, from a gender-equality perspective, to investigate and measure whether complex tax regulations result in differential treatment of men and women.

The statement in the report is representative of a formalist legal perspective. Traditional legal frameworks such as this do not provide a set of general implications for theorizing about gendered dimensions in the tax system. The only frame of reference for formalist legal analysis is the normative model, according to which all citizens are equal under a neutral law. Using such a uniform approach, it is impossible to identify those legal structures or legal discourses in which the patterns of social power reside and which reproduce gender inequalities between men and women, together with stereotyped gender constructions. Using this approach, it is also impossible to detect the possibility that the substantive preconceptions of legal forms, rules and principles can function to the social disadvantage of women (Young 2000).

By contrast, a more substantial and comprehensive gender approach may be taken to the questions of gender equality and taxation, based on international feminist revenue law research (see, for example, Apps 1984; Grbich 1990–91; McCaffery 1997; Staudt 1996; Young 1997 and 2000; Kornhauser 2005). According to this approach, a diversity of possible legal strategies for achieving gender equality (drawn from social, economic and political contexts) may be highlighted. The report touches upon three fundamental issues—work, entrepreneurship and investments—but it considers these issues as beyond the scope of law. In contradistinction to this perspective, a comprehensive gender approach recognizes that legal orders are not closed, normative systems; that legal research is about all aspects of legal norms; and that legal norms are not detached from the social and economic values that shape the conditions of life (see Gustafsson 2002, 84–87 and Hydén 2002).

A Matter for the Private Sphere

Mainstream revenue law scholarship that replicates the social meanings of productivity and wealth is based on economic rationalism, which represents the self-interested and socially isolated character of 'economic man' (Grbich 1993). Feminist legal studies about revenue law challenge the prerequisites for human agency imbedded in this approach. They also challenge a 'blind spot' in the mainstream perspective, which fails to take into account the fact that the gender relations shaped by the stratification of revenue and welfare arrangements prevents women from having equal access to the resources available to men (Liebert 2001: 268; Orloff 1996; Tronto 2001: 66–70).

One key factor in the elimination of this blind spot consists of analysing the context of the social location of the household (ie, the family). Women's living conditions are largely bound up with family life—and the normative and structural patterns that shape these living conditions emerge from traditional gendered functions within the family, as well as from the way the family as an institution is organized in society. The general picture of unequal distribution of power and resources between men and women shows that women's economic dependency resides in, and is reinforced by, the exchange of time, care and economic resources in the household, which in turn is replicated in the production of social welfare between the state, the market and the family. In other words, family life results in economic and social subordination for women, although in mainstream social and legal science and according to political notions of social justice, it is assumed that family institutions are just. However, the unequal distribution of responsibilities, financial resources, powers and time within the family is closely related to inequalities that exist in society outside the family. According to gender analysis (which challenges traditional normative foundations), welfare is produced in a cyclical process throughout the state, the market and the family and in structural terms, it reinforces the dominance of men over women—from the home to work to the welfare regime and hence back home again (Gunnarsson 2003: 22–23; Nyman 2002: Article 3; Okin 1989: 21–22, 92, 95, 113).

A Matter of Tax Equity and Social Justice

Viewing the taxation of work, entrepreneurship and investments from a gender perspective challenges the complexity of tax fairness. Tax equity can be many ways, but the core issues are always related to the mix of tax levels and tax structures. Tax equity is also part of the much broader context of social justice in the welfare state, which is a fundamental democratic issue. As John Head, an internationally recognized expert on tax principles and policies concerning tax fairness, puts it, 'The achievement of a fair tax system in a democracy is rightly regarded as a matter of high economic and social importance' (1993: 4).

A basic political issue for every welfare state is the identification of sustainable and legitimate tax structures that will allow citizens to equitably share the burdens of paying for benefits—by means of social contributions and by means of collective and individual and direct and indirect taxes. In theory, the recognition of citizens' social rights ought to correlate with an obligatory common responsibility to generate the public funding needed to pay for them. In that way, citizens' obligations are based on the legitimate demand that they support certain basic needs. From this perspective, tax equity, on an aggregated, collective level, is related to a fair and just connection between burdens and benefits (Lacey 1998: 50–52; Sjöberg 2001: 17–18; Young 2000: 7–8).

The relationship between revenue law and social welfare/social security law has to be viewed as a broad concept that includes the aspect of social power within legal structures. It ought to include both the right to receive welfare and the obligation to participate in generating public welfare. The structuring of taxation and social security has therefore become closely intertwined in welfare state policies. For instance, in countries like the United States and Canada, many social security programmes are now delivered legislatively and administratively through the tax system. From the point of view of women's economic equality and social security, it is therefore important to investigate both sides of the public budget by using theoretical and methodological concepts such as tax expenditures analysis (Young 2000) or gender budgeting analysis (Philipps 2006).

From the perspective of the social welfare triangle (the market, the state and the household) it is also important to investigate how revenue and social benefit regulations can promote gender equality by creating incentives and disincentives regarding central gender-equality issues, such as work decisions and family formations. The structures of entitlement to social provisions should be tested in terms of the way that social benefits and services contribute to women's autonomy or reinforce their dependency. Such a test ought to include the range of benefits and services, as well as underpinning criteria, such as coverage (including eligibility requirements), duration and benefit levels. In addition, the structures of revenue obligations should be tested in relation to the socio-economic realities of women's lives. The test could include both how social programmes are subsidized as tax expenditures through the tax system and how the mix of tax structures are constructed in relation to gendered patterns governing the exchange of time, care and economic resources in relation to the production and distribution of social welfare (see Orloff 2001: 135–36; Sainsbury 1996: 44–45; Young 2000).

THE IMPACT OF THE PUBLIC/PRIVATE DIVIDE ON TAX LAW

Our understanding of ourselves and the world around us is greatly influenced by the division of society into a public world and a private-domestic world. This division can also be found in various areas of research. It has a strong influence on philosophical thinking and on liberal ideas of justice (Okin 1989: 111–16; Svensson 1997: 312). One should not forget that the public/private dichotomy is of fundamental importance in the feminist movement and that it may even be, as Carole Pateman once expressed it, 'ultimate' (1983).

The theoretical framework of the public/private divide is based on gendered patterns governing the exchange of time, care and economic resources within the social welfare triangle, where the state and the market represent the public sphere and the household represents the private sphere. Feminist revenue law scholarship has pointed out the need for a wider explanation of gendered social relations in order to circumvent the mainstream gender analysis of the tax system, which feeds the public/private divide. This perspective is also relevant for interface issues concerning the interaction between the tax and benefit systems. By focusing on deconstructing the public/private divide from the perspective of the social welfare triangle (the state, the market and the family), it is possible to apply a method that can include women's care work and other domestic activities, part-time work and low wages as part of the analysis of tax equity and social justice (Apps 1984; Grbich 1987; McCaffery 1997; Staudt 1996 and Young 1997). Obviously, as shown by many of the authors in this book, this type of analysis can contribute to a deeper epistemological understanding of the normative patterns in revenue law that reproduces gender inequalities.

The outcome of the public/private divide is evident in tax expenditures and tax structures that are openly or unconsciously designed to reproduce relational dependency in the family or traditional notions of the productivity of women's labour and their contribution to the economy (Grbich 1990–91 and Young 1997). Tax expenditures are normally defined as tax rules that are designed technically to raise revenue and tax rules that deviate from this benchmark are defined as tax expenditures (Young 2000: 9). The distinction between fiscal and non-fiscal purposes has often been made on the basis of a specific interpretation of the theory of optimal taxation. In the Nordic countries, the benchmark view among leading tax law scholars is that non-distorting taxation should be seen as neutral taxation because neutral tax minimizes welfare losses and promotes an efficient allocation of resources.[2]

Tax expenditures can serve political redistributive purposes, either in redistributing wealth or in reducing income inequalities. Expenditures that depart from the 'normal' tax structure can also serve regulatory and stabilizing functions in relation to the economy, such as fighting inflation, unemployment, budget deficits and the growth of the shadow economy. Environmental and social programmes and programmes that mitigate demographic problems are other examples of tax expenditures. Some of these tax measures are the result of a political process, while others are imposed as a result of exogenous factors (Messere, de Kam and Heady 2003).

A common view among feminist tax law scholars is that tax structures that are clearly related to a gender-biased notion of dependency and productivity are chiefly present in the construction of the tax unit and the tax base. Much of feminist revenue research has focused on the relative merits of the individual versus the spousal couple as the appropriate tax unit from an ability-to-pay perspective, as well as on the impact of the choice of tax unit as an incentive or disincentive regarding women's participation in the labour market. The marital tax unit has been seen both as a defective indicator of ability to pay (Apps 1984: 472–74; Chan 1993: 64–65) and as a disincentive to women's autonomy and women's participation in the labour market. Sweden abandoned the joint taxation of spouses long ago, but the structure still exists in many OECD countries and also affects the

[2] Two annual reports produced by researchers connected with the Nordic Tax Research Council are representative of this view. One was published in 1983, and the other was forthcoming in 2009 (*Rapporter vid Nordiska skattevetenskapliga forskningsrådets* (seminarium i Saltsjöbaden i oktober 1983). *Nordiska skattevetenskapligaforskningsrådets skriftserie*, NSFS 13 and Bolander (2009).

outcome of case law in the European Court of Justice (Gunnarsson 2003: 48–53, 61–63).

On the basis of normative, foundational tax policy principles and tax theories on income, consumption and capital, a plurality of ideals has developed concerning the construction of a tax base and the mix of tax bases. Even though pure ideals transform into hybrids in the political landscape, both principles and theories have great impact on the way in which tax systems are constructed. The problem, of course, is that any framework for tax law reform very seldom includes a gender-equality perspective. For instance, the traditional view of fairness in taxation does not consider remedies for the gender-structured division of labour, which is characterized by women doing the majority of household and care work, working part-time, working for lower salaries and having greater responsibility for maintenance support for children and other dependants in the household. Household production is regarded as non-taxable imputed income[3] within the income tax base.

The Tax/Benefit Unit and Family Taxation

Family taxation can be defined in many ways, but among these different definitions, two normative positions are rather obvious. One is the taxable capacity approach and the other is the social welfare approach. The taxable capacity approach aims to preserve horizontal equity. It is based on principles such as equal treatment, non-discrimination, protection of the family and the ability to pay. Under the liberal, rule-of-law tradition, these are all recognized as outcomes of the state's obligation to protect citizens' freedoms and rights. In some states, these principles are established in the constitutions; in other states, they are considered to be fundamental general principles. One objective of the social welfare approach is to achieve vertical equity concerning socioeconomic issues of redistribution. According to this approach, taxation should be part of welfare programmes—in combination with social benefits or as a replacement for cash or in-kind benefits (Soler Roch 1999).

Compared with other European countries, Germany and France have extensive family taxation. In Germany, for instance, marriage and family are protected by the constitution (article 6(1) GG). One might think that this regulation would govern family taxation in the form of allowances for maintenance support and joint taxation in tax law. However, according to Joachim Lang, this type of family taxation is linked mainly to the

[3] Imputed income should be understood as the value of work and services taxpayers provide for themselves.

constitutional rule that all people have the right to be equal before the law and not the protection and support of marriage and family. He argues that equality of taxation is expressed in the ability-to-pay principle, which in Germany is interpreted as a base for neutrality in the taxation of different forms of cohabitation. In order to avoid tax discrimination against marriage, an income-splitting tariff was introduced through a Federal Constitutional Court decision in 1958. Spouses are generally assessed jointly, and a progressive income tax schedule is applied on the aggregated total income of both spouses, divided into two (Lang 1999; Olsson 2006: 154–57). Lang's opinion is confirmed by both Scheiwe and Wersig in this volume. In contrast to Lang, however, they both emphasize that the 1958 Federal Court decision indirectly draws on the constitutional protection of marriage and family by underlining the fact that husband and wife are free to make decisions concerning the division of household labour. As described by Wersig and Scheiwe, in its decision, the Court even included a rather radical twist in its argumentation in relation to the principle of gender equality.

Public policy governing family taxation in France is renowned for its history of supporting large, male-breadwinner families through an extensive form of joint taxation, which can be defined as a family-splitting system (Hantrais and Letablier 1996, and see also Wersig in this volume). After the Second World War, the tax unit, called the *foyer fiscal*, was introduced. The original idea was to include everyone sitting around the 'fireplace', which symbolized economic dependency on the breadwinner. This view constituted an extreme version of joint taxation, whereby the breadwinner was permitted to split his or her (usually his) income with all members of the *foyer fiscal*. Today, the tax unit includes spouses, cohabitant partners recognized under the *PACS*[4] and children and other family members claimed as dependants. Income splitting in relation to family size is called the *quotient conjugal* for income splitting between spouses and *PACS* partners, and it is called the *quotient familial* for income splitting between children and other dependent members of the household. Since French family taxation is based on a combined taxable capacity approach and social welfare approach, the *quotient conjugal* is based mainly on the same reasoning as the German joint taxation of spouses. That is, the primary objective is to ensure neutrality between single persons on the one hand and cohabiting partners on the other. The *quotient familial* (which is a form of extended joint taxation) has been linked to two objectives: one fiscal and one non-fiscal. The objective considered to be fiscal is to achieve neutrality between tax units with and

[4] Since 2004, a family also includes partners who are considered to be in a French civil union (*le pact civil de solidarité* [*PACS*]). This means that civil law has extended the family concept to other forms of cohabitation than the so-called nuclear family. However, a contract regulating mutual rights and responsibilities in the partnership is required, and partners must cohabitate for three years before they are considered to have the same legal status as a married couple.

without children, based on the ability-to-pay principle. The objective considered to be non-fiscal (David 1999; Gunnarsson 2003: 72–82; Thévenon 2008) is related to the social protection of families with many children, as the *quotient familial* has also been used as an instrument in the traditional concern about fertility rates in French family policy.

In Sweden, many arguments against joint taxation and family taxation were put forward over the years, but when joint taxation was replaced with individual taxation, it was the ability-to-pay principle, together with gender-equality objectives, that served as the rationale. Specifically, the abolition of joint taxation of spouses was based on knowledge of the correlation between the labour-market participation of women (married or living in partnerships) and the income of their husbands or partners. When individual taxation was first introduced, the incentives for wives and female partners to participate in the labour market increased. The effective marginal tax was generally higher for married men in relation to the marginal tax rates for women, so an increase in working hours for women was more beneficial for households. Since the 1970s, family taxation in Sweden has therefore been regarded as tax expenditure, but it has been replaced in part over the years with social benefits in cash or in kind (Gunnarsson 2003: 57–62). One explanation for the pragmatic use of the ability-to-pay principle in Swedish tax law reforms—used to argue both for joint and individual taxation in the name of fiscal neutrality—might perhaps be found in differences between Sweden on the one hand and Germany and France on the other, in relation to the legal status of family and marriage. In contrast to Germany and France, the only principles established in the Swedish Constitution that are relevant for this tax policy issue, are non-discrimination and equality of treatment.

The construction of tax units can be linked to how childcare costs are funded in the various countries, as joint taxation can also be part of how subsidies for childcare are delivered. Overall, one can say that there exist two normative models of welfare arrangements for how to subsidize childcare costs, which are mutually exclusive as they promote either gender equality or traditional life patterns for men and women.

Tax Bases and Quotas

In public finance, the concept of generating wealth is centred on the taxpayer's obligation to pay taxes and social contributions, constitute the main sources of revenue. In the OECD countries from 1965 onwards, the greatest share of revenues comes from personal income tax, which until the 1990s was far larger than any other revenue source. During the early 1970s and 1980s, social security contributions increased rapidly, and by the mid-1990s, they reached almost the same level as personal income tax as a revenue source. The share of total tax revenue raised from general consumption taxes has also increased, while tax revenues from property tax and corporate income tax have remained fairly constant and at a low level (Messere, de Kam and Heady 2003: 36–37).

For many years, the total tax ratio[5] in Sweden has, with few exceptions, been the highest among the OECD countries. Tax ratios among countries are difficult to compare for several reasons, of which various differences in the existence, levels and structures of social security contributions and taxes are the most pronounced (see, for example, Messere 1993: ch 3; Messere, de Kam and Heady 2003: 33; *Riksskatteverket* 2003). Even so, it is apparent that the tax ratio of the Swedish welfare state has been consistently high when the tax obligations of its citizens are measured.

Theoretically, the assumption is that the correlation between obligations and legitimate needs ought also to be strong in a country that wants to realize social justice through a hegemonic welfare state, expressed in the distributive principles of equality of opportunity and solidarity. However, such normative coherence does not exist between tax and social security law. In fact, the justification for tax fairness in relation to social security law is based on somewhat different distributive principles—ones that are duty oriented—and the source of taxation has an impact on how the need for distributive principles is articulated in theories and policies.

Taxation has many sources, including real estate, wealth, capital, beneficial transfers, consumption, goods, services, production, labour and income. The Swedish tax system draws, directly or indirectly, on all these sources, apart from beneficial transfers, which was recently abolished as a tax base. In effect, most economic activities are taxed. As a result, there is one basic problem: the tax system operates with a very diverse set of distributive principles, and the ways in which 'tax citizens' come to share a common tax burden is therefore not particularly transparent.

When a government structures taxation in relation to the economic activity within its jurisdiction, its income flow emanates from three main sources. Production is the original source from which income springs; the next step is transfer of income from production to households; and the third step is the use of incomes for consumption. The circle is then closed as income from consumption returns to production. On the level of production, the sum of gross incomes earned by a firm (the payroll of a company) constitutes the basis for assessing an employer's social security contributions. These contributions are structured as payroll taxes for employers and could easily be classified as a tax on investment in the productive factor, labour. Incomes from employment also constitute the tax base for income tax, for which employees are the tax subjects. This is an individual, direct tax on the

[5] The tax ratio expresses the total tax burden in a country calculated as total tax receipts to GDP at market prices.

basis of net income from earnings. The personal income tax base includes, in principle, all incomes and fringe benefits from the performance of work of all kinds. It also includes a large part of public social transfers. In general, benefits based on residence in a state and social assistance in the form of maintenance support are exempt from income taxation. Savings from earned income become capital, and income from that capital also constitutes a separate tax base. Certain capital possessions also constitute a tax base for a wealth tax. When using earned or saved income for private consumption, an indirect consumption tax is added to the consumer price for services or goods (SOU 2002:47, 53–56).

The multiplicity of taxation sources, the comprehensive use of broad tax bases and the combination of both direct and indirect taxation of individuals makes the concept of obligation to pay tax broader than qualifications for social entitlements in Sweden. In short, to become a taxpayer (tax citizen) is much easier than to become a social beneficiary (social citizen). There is no need for the subjects of obligations to meet demands for eligibility such as residence or work, which serve as qualification criteria for social entitlements under social security law (Gunnarsson 2007).

Economic Growth before Social Justice: A Disadvantage for Gender Equality

Commonly, the ability-to-pay principle has been used to express tax fairness in general, in terms of both tax equity and social justice. Tax equity is a formal aspect of tax fairness promoting impartiality in the treatment of taxpayers. Social justice has redistributive objectives, and when this principle is being applied, an individual's ability to pay should be assessed according to a progressive income tax rate schedule. In the 1991 Swedish tax reform, however, legislators changed the content of the ability-to-pay principle. Instead of applying a neutrality principle inspired by optimal tax theory or neoliberal economic ideas, it seems that the tax policy strategy was to keep the label but change the content. Ability to pay was transformed into a neutrality principle in order to legitimize the structuring of a uniform tax base for fiscal purposes. Social justice was also not served by the neoliberal tax ideology behind the restructuring of income tax during, inspired by the 1986 US tax reform. In that case, a line was also drawn between fiscal purposes and social justice.

The benchmark introduced during the 1991 Swedish tax reform stated that tax regulations with a social purpose were to be seen as political interventions in the market economy. According to the neoliberal economic philosophy of Friedrich A Hayek in particular, economic intervention creates excess burdens or welfare losses, which hinder economic growth (Hayek 1956; Korpi and Palme 1993). As redistribution of wealth and income is based on political ambitions concerning economic equality, they are seen as interventions that create inefficiency in the economy. This standpoint has resulted in a normative standard that distributional neutrality is a part of the concept of fiscal taxation. The distribution-neutrality objective aims to preserve the status quo, whereby no income group should benefit or lose more in relation to any other income groups as an effect of income taxation (Prop 1989/90:110, 620–32).

This benchmark of tax neutrality justified broader income and consumption tax bases, less progressive income tax and a shift from the equality of treatment of income tax subjects to equal treatment of income tax objects. That is, the equality of treatment of tax subjects with equal economic capacity has been transformed into a principle of equal treatment of equal incomes. The shift from subject to object is manifested in the change from a global to a dual income tax. Global income taxation, also defined as the conventional personal income tax, is regarded as the ideal for the ability-to-pay version of tax equity, as all incomes from different sources are assessed for each tax subject and taxed at the same rate. In a dual income tax system, however, each source of income is treated under a separate tax regime (Gunnarsson 1995; 1999; 2001). One can, of course, ask what difference for tax equity and social justice these tax structures make at the end of the day, since in reality, all income tax systems become imperfect through deviations from the original theoretical idea. This is true, but if one abandons the possibility of assessing the individual tax subject's ability to pay, many options for creating a tax system that is fair from a socio-economic point of view are also abandoned.

The 1991 reform had multiple objectives, but the focus was on cutting effective marginal tax rates on earned income. Those income earners with the highest incomes had the highest effective marginal tax rates, as the income-tax-rate scale had a redistributive, progressive profile. Unfortunately, during this process, the significant crossover effect between the marginal costs for women's paid work and the income of their husbands or partners (a gender-equality problem) were not taken into consideration. Not surprisingly, the cuts in the effective marginal tax rates had a moderating impact on women's paid work, as the marginal net of taxed salaries increased for men (Aronsson and Palme 1994). The shift from income tax to consumption tax also had a side effect that contributed to moderating women's labour supply. For the first time, a 25 per cent value added tax (VAT) was introduced on several services that could be regarded as substitutes for the type of household maintenance that is traditionally carried out by women. It therefore became more expensive for households to buy these services than for women in the households to perform those services themselves (Wennemo 1997: 18–19).

The 1991 tax reform clearly stated that family taxation and social justice objectives were to be regarded as non-fiscal. Welfare state schemes were delegated to the transfer system of the public budget and were not to be carried out as tax expenditures. In this context, social justice included every possible welfare state reform that could be based on a diversity of objectives in areas such as the labour market, the family, housing and infrastructure policies. To regard these objectives as non-fiscal is, again, political and normative. However, the inherent normativity of drawing the line between fiscal and non-fiscal was not recognized, and this may well be the reason why the Swedish strategy of avoiding unwanted welfare losses by cutting effective marginal tax rates (EMTR)[6] and abolishing the non-fiscal, social dimensions of income tax law, has not succeeded. A high EMTR in a progressive income tax system is regarded as an excessive burden for the economy when it becomes a disincentive for high-income earners to work. Unfortunately, the 1991 tax reform also exacerbated an existing EMTR problem. This was the result of a poorly coordinated combination of income-tested social benefits and fees for social services, such as municipal fees for childcare, an income-related basic deduction for low-income groups and tax reductions for certain categories of taxpayers with little ability to pay. The combined effects of these tax and social laws gave the welfare system as a whole a progressive profile for low-income households. This EMTR problem created disincentives in the form of poverty traps, which influence work and study decisions related to income (Gunnarsson 2003).

The dimension of social power is obvious in the discourse concerning income tax cuts. According to the hegemonic understanding of the connection between economic growth and cuts in high marginal tax rates, it should also be recalled that optimal tax theory recommends that married women should be taxed less and married men more. This analysis is based on the observation that men are inelastic in their work patterns and married women have high income elasticity relative to their husbands' incomes. Efficiency and wealth maximization would improve if married men paid more income tax than their wives. In terms of gender equality, such a reform would increase women's participation in the labour market and would thus improve economic growth (McCaffery 1997: 164–87).

THE DICHOTOMY BETWEEN PAID AND UNPAID WORK

The tax system's non-recognition of household production is based on positivist methodologies that preclude analysis of the gendered character of home-based activities. Such methodologies generally understand household production as leisure, valued according to the price the individual would accept in order to substitute it with market-based labour (Grbich 1990–91). This view of productivity is very problematical from a gender perspective. It

[6] Effective marginal tax rates (EMTR) can be defined as including both the tax paid on the last income earned and the loss of any social provision that occurs directly or indirectly because of an increase in gross income (St John 1993).

is based on a general assumption about non-market labour, shared by many around the world, that women are the ones who do the household work and that this work does not entitle them to wages or other economic benefits tied to traditional market employment (Staudt 1996: 1573). Consequently, women's unpaid labour in the home is ignored for tax purposes as being earned income in kind or a form of imputed income. As Claire Young has put it: 'The combination of the non-recognition by the tax system of household production and the low wages paid to women reinforces the sexual division of labour' (1997: 268). The tax equity issues raised in connection with this problem are contradictory. On the one hand, there are the market-oriented concepts of gender equality that argue for labour-market participation as the means for women to achieve economic autonomy and emancipation; on the other, there is the argument that by recognizing work in the home as valuable and productive (by, for example, taxing the value of imputed income), women's economic security would be improved (Staudt 1996).

In Sweden, there is a conflict between the normative model of gender equality and the real world for families with small children. The idea of gender equality in tax and social security law rests on two strategies: the combination strategy and the employment strategy. The combination strategy is Swedish family policy, and its purpose is to achieve welfare regimes that allow parents to combine work and family life when their children are small. (It is similar to what are called reconciliation strategies within family policy elsewhere in Europe.) The ideal nuclear family—mother, father and a couple of children—consists of two breadwinners, where work and family life have been reconciled for both parents, and where the parents are self-supporting individuals. In reality, the general structure of the exchange of time, care and economic resources within the triangular relation of state, market and family reveals that the life patterns of families with small children do not correspond to the normative ideal. The standard for a Swedish nuclear family consists of no more than one-and-a-half breadwinners, where normally the woman is not self-supporting in terms of money or time because of the unequal division of paid work and unpaid care work (Gunnarsson 2003). One of the basic obstacles to truly implementing a combination strategy is that the value of all productive work is not treated equally.

No tax system directly taxes the value of household labour. However, several tax reforms in various countries directly or indirectly address the issue. One such example is the Swedish tax credit for the employment costs of using household/domestic services (Lag (2007: 346) *om skattereduktion för utgifter för hushållsarbete*) which has its counterparts in many other countries. However, the tax credit in Swedish tax law has no connection with a theoretical framework for the valuation of women's household labour. The main policy objective is part of an employment strategy, with the task of stimulating certain branches of business.

From a gender perspective, the question of valuing and taxing household labour is extremely ambiguous. The dilemma resides in determining whether or not upgrading household labour so that it becomes an integrated part of a comprehensive income-tax base will actually help countries meet gender-equality objectives. Nancy Staudt has convincingly argued for the advantages of taxing household labour as a means of resourcing women. By pointing out the logic of tax neutrality for all productive work, she erases the distinction between the public and the private spheres and also recognizes all welfare produced in the social welfare triangle. In this way, care work, representing women's special contribution and relationship to the welfare state, is given economic value and also provides eligibility for social entitlements (1996: 1577). Obviously, many objections can be raised against Staudt's proposal. For instance, in a Swedish context, the strategy can be rather unpromising, in that married women are treated as autonomous individuals with economic rights to a much greater extent in Sweden than they are in the United States. In this volume, Philipps presents a different approach to the question of how tax reforms could contribute to providing economic support for the lower-earning spouse or cohabiting partner of the household who does most of the unpaid (non-market) work. This approach is much closer to the one followed in Sweden.

GENDER INEQUALITIES PERSIST

The normative structures reinforcing gender inequalities in tax law, expressed here in the context of the social welfare triangle, are not at all new findings. However, in this chapter, the aim has been to add to the common knowledge of feminist tax scholarship the realization that even a gender-egalitarian welfare state like Sweden, with advanced individualization of social rights and fiscal obligations, is trapped in the notion of a public/private division of labour. Thus, the benchmark of tax neutrality in the Swedish national tax system does nothing to promote gender equality. Conclusions that can be drawn are the need for gender sensitive analysis in how the taxation of capital, work, entrepreneurship and consumption constructs and reproduces gender relations in law and economy.

REFERENCES

Government Committees and Other Official Documents

Lag (2007) om skattereduktion för utgifter för hushållsarbete. (Law on Tax Credit for domestic work).

Prop 1989/90:110 Om reformerad inkomst- och företagsbeskattning. (Governments proposal on a reformed income and company taxation).

Skatteverket Report (2007) Enklare skatter för ökad jämställdhet. (Report from the Swedish Inland Revenue).
SOU (2002) Våra skatter? (Report from Government's Commission on the Tax Base).

Literature

Apps, P (1984) 'Tax Reform and the Tax Unit' 1 *Australian Tax Forum* 467–81.
Aronsson, T and Palme, M (1994) 'A Decade of Tax and Benefit Reforms in Sweden—Effects on Labour Supply, Welfare and Inequality' *3 Tax Reform Evaluation Report* (Stockholm, Ekonomiska rådet).
Bolander, J (ed) (2009) Yearbook for Nordic Tax Research 2009. The non-fiscal purposes of taxation (Copenhagen, Djöf Publishing).
Bonoli, G (2005) 'The Politics of New Social Risks: Providing Coverage against New Social Risks in Mature Welfare States' 33 *Policy and Politics* 431–39.
Chan, W (1993) 'Taxing the Female—as Woman or Wife' in C Scott (ed), *Women and Taxation* (Wellington, Institute of Policy Studies, Victoria).
David, C (1999) 'France' in MT Soler Roch (ed), *Family Taxation in Europe* (Dordrecht, Kluwer Law International).
Grbich, JE (1990–91) 'The Tax Unit Debate Revisited: Notes on the Critical Resources of a Feminism Revenue Law Scholarship' 4 *Canadian Journal of Women and Law* 512–38.
—— (1993) 'Writing Histories of Revenue Law: The New Productivity Research' 11 *Law in Context* 57–77.
Gunnarsson, Å (1995) *Skatterättvisa* (Uppsala, Iustus Förlag).
—— (1999) 'Equity Trends in Taxation—with Examples from Swedish and New Zealand Tax Reforms' in *Liber Amicorum Leif Mutén* (Amsterdam, Kluwer).
—— (2001) 'Familjen—genusforskningens utmaning' in M Burman and Å Gunnarsson (eds), *Familjeföreställningar. Om familjens betydelse inom juridik, ekonomi och forskning* (Uppsala, Iustus AB).
—— (2003) *Fördelningen av familjens skatter och sociala förmåner* (Uppsala, Iustus Förlag).
—— (2007) 'Gender Equality and the Diversity of Rights and Obligations in Swedish Social Citizenship' in Å Gunnarsson, E-M Svednsson and M Davies (eds), *Exploiting the Limits of Law. Swedish Feminism and the Challenge to Pessimism* (Aldershot, Ashgate Publishing).
Gustafsson, H (2002) *Rättens polyvalens: En rättsvetenskaplig studie av sociala rättigheter och rättssäkerhet* (Lund, Lund Studies in Sociology of Law).
Hantrais, L and Letablier, M-T (1996) *Families and Family Policies* (London, Longman).
Hayek, FA (1956) 'Progressive Taxation Reconsidered' in M Sennholz (ed), *On Freedom and Free Enterprise: Essays in Honour of Ludwig von Mises* (Princeton, Nostrands).
Head, J (1993) 'Tax Fairness and Principles' in A Maslove (ed), *Fairness in Taxation: Exploring the Principles* (Toronto, University of Toronto Press).
Hirschman, NJ and Liebert, U (eds) (2001) *Women and Welfare: Theory and Practice in the United States and Europe* (Brunswick, NJ, Rutgers University Press).
Hydén, H (2002) *Normvetenskap* (Lund, Lund Studies in Sociology of Law).

Ketscher, K (1998) *Socialret: Almindelige principper—Retssikerhed og administration* (Köpenhamn, GadJura).
Kornhauser, ME (2005) 'Choosing a Tax Rate Structure in the Face of Disagreement' 52 *University of California at Los Angeles Law Review* 1697.
Korpi, W and Palme, J (1993) *Socialpolitik, kris och reformer: Sverige i internationell belysning* (Stockholm, Institutet för social forskning).
Lacey, N (1998) *Unspeakable Subjects: Feminist Essays in Legal and Social Theory* (Oxford, Hart Publishing).
Lang, J (1999) 'Germany' in MT Soler Roch (1999) *Family Taxation in Europe* (Dordrecht, Kluwer Law International).
Liebert, U (2001) 'Degendering Care and Engendering Freedom: Social Welfare in the European Union' in NJ Hirschman and U Liebert (eds), *Women and Welfare: Theory and Practice in the United States and Europe* (Brunswick, NJ, Rutgers University Press).
McCaffery, EJ (1997) *Taxing Women* (Chicago, University of Chicago Press).
Messere, K (1993) *Tax Policy in OECD Countries. Choices and Conflict* (Amsterdam, IBFD Publications BV).
Messere, K, de Kam, F and Heady, C (2003) *Tax Policy: Theory and Practice in OECD Countries* (Oxford, Oxford University Press).
Nordiska skattevetenskapliga forskningsrådets skriftserie, NSFS 13 (1983), *Konflikten mellan beskattningens fiskala och icke-fiskala ändamål. Rapporter vid Nordiska skattevetenskapliga forskningsrådets* (seminarium i Saltsjöbaden i oktober 1983).
—— (2008) *Nordiska Skattevetenskapliga Forskningsrådets* (seminarium om Beskattningens icke-fiskala syfte).
Nyman, C (2002) 'Mine, Yours or Ours? Sharing in Swedish Couples' (Doctoral dissertation, Umeå University).
O'Connor, JS, Orloff, AS and Shaver, S (1999) *States, Markets, Families: Gender, Liberalism and Social Policy in Australia, Canada, Great Britain and the United States* (Cambridge, Cambridge University Press).
Okin, SM (1989) *Justice, Gender, and Family* (New York, Basic Books Inc Publishers).
Olsson, S (2006) *Författningsprövning i skatterätten—en studie kring svensk och tysk konstitutionell praxis påverkan på skatterätten* (Uppsala, Iustus förlag).
Orloff, AS (1996) 'Gender in the Welfare State' 22 *Annual Review of Sociology.*
—— (2001)'Ending the Entitlements of Poor Single Mothers: Changing Social Policies, Women's Employment, and Caregiving in the Contemporary United States' in N Hirschman and U Liebert (eds), *Women and Welfare. Theory and Practice in the United States and Europe* (Brunswick, New Jersey and London, Rutgers University Press).
Pateman, C (1983) 'Feminist Critiques of the Public/Private Dichotomy' in S Benn and G Gaus (eds), *Private and Public in Social Life* (London, Croom Helm).
Philipps, L (2006) 'Gender Budgets and Tax Policy-Making: Contrasting Canadian and Australian Experiences' 24 *Law in Context* 143–68.
St John, S (1993) 'The Tax/Benefit Interface' in C Scott (ed), *Women and Taxation* (Wellington, The Printing Press).
Sainsbury, D (1996) *Gender Equality and Welfare States* (Cambridge, Cambridge University Press).

—— (ed) (1999) *Gender and Welfare State Regimes* (Oxford, Oxford University Press).

Sjöberg, O (2001) 'Välfärdsstatens finansiering under 1990-talet: Välfärdens finansiering och fördelning' in *Antologi från Kommittén Välfärdsbokslut* (Stockholm, Graphium/Norstedts AB).

Soler Roch, MT (ed) (1999) *Family Taxation in Europe* (Dordrecht, Kluwer Law International) 27–54.

Stang Dahl, T (1988) *Women's Law* (Oslo, Norwegian University Press).

Staudt, NC (1996) 'Taxing Housework' 84 *Georgetown Law Journal* 1571–647.

Svensson, E-M (1997) *Genus och rätt: En problematisering av föreställningen om rätten* (Uppsala, Iustus förlag AB).

Thévenon, O (2008) *Does Fertility Respond to Work and Family-life Reconciliation Policies in France?* CESifo Conference on Fertility and Public Policy: How to Reverse the Trend of Declining Birth Rates (1–2 February 2008).

Tronto, JC (2001) 'Who Cares? Public and Private Caring and the Rethinking of Citizenship' in NJ Hirschman and U Liebert (eds), *Women and Welfare: Theory and Practice in the United States and Europe* (Brunswick, NJ, Rutgers University Press).

Wennemo, I (1997) 'Hushållsarbetets organisation och tjänstesektorns utveckling' in SOU 1997:17, *Skatter tjänster och sysselsättning. Betänkande av Tjänstemannautredningen.* (Report from Government's Commission).

Young, C (1997) 'Taxing Times for Women: Feminism Confronts Tax Policy' in R Krever (ed), *Tax Conversations: A Guide to the Key Issues in the Tax Reform Debate—Essays in Honour of John G Head* (London, Kluwer Law International).

—— (2000) *Women, Tax and Social Programs: The Gendered Impact of Funding Social Programs through the Tax System* (Ottawa, Status of Women Canada).

Part II

Bases and Rates: Structural Choices in Tax Policy Design

5

Taxing Surrogacy

BRIDGET J CRAWFORD*

SOME PREGNANCIES ARE and should be taxable. Admittedly, this claim is not typical conversational fare for tax policy makers and scholars, as participants in tax discussions do not always consider the impact that fiscal laws have on the human body. True, most countries have tax laws to address the treatment of employer-provided health insurance or damages received for personal injuries, but the specific statutes generally do not address the tax implications of corporeal functions.

In the United States, tax law collides with the human body at an unexpected juncture: surrogate motherhood. Surrogacy is legal in some parts of the United States and illegal in other places. Regardless, payments received by a surrogate mother for carrying and bearing a child for another party or other parties are universally taxable for federal income tax purposes, and in this chapter, it is argued that the taxation of surrogacy income is sound, both as fiscal policy and as social policy. Anecdotal evidence suggests, however, that not all surrogates' income tax reporting practices conform to the law. Some surrogates report their income, but others do not.

The next part of this chapter briefly describes two distinct areas of law in the United States: the law of income taxation and the law of surrogacy. The next part examines the limited available evidence concerning the reporting and non-reporting of surrogacy income and presents speculation about why some surrogates may report and others may not. This discussion is followed by a consideration of the economic, behavioural, social and cultural implications of taxing (and not taxing) surrogacy. Suggestions are then provided as to how a government agency like the United States Department of Treasury could encourage surrogates' greater compliance with applicable income tax laws. The chapter concludes with notes for further study of the

* For helpful comments and discussions, the author thanks Ann Bartow, Caitlin Borgmann, Kimberley Brooks, Dorothy Brown, Naomi Cahn, Danielle Citron, Kathryn Dean, Anthony C Infanti, Lily Kahng, Kimberly Krawiec, Sarah Lawsky, Darren Rosenblum and the other contributors to this volume.

ways in which tax law can contribute to gender equality, not only through enforcing the taxation of surrogacy income, but in other contexts.

OVERVIEW OF APPLICABLE AMERICAN INCOME TAX LAW

United States' income tax law is anchored by a broad definition of income, which states that income can be derived from services, property or any other source. The only distinction made between sources of income is in a rate preference for capital gains (gains from property held for investment) as opposed to ordinary income (like wages). Federal tax rates on ordinary income range from approximately 10 to 35 per cent. Moreover, US tax law makes no distinction between income derived from legal versus non-legal sources. Thus, a bank robber who fails to pay taxes on the value of a heist violates both the law against theft and the income tax law.

Diverse state laws create a heterogeneous legal landscape in the United States, particularly where matters of morality or social policy are involved. For example, the medicinal use of marijuana is legal in California but not in Ohio. Prostitution is legal in Nevada but not in Oklahoma. Similarly, the enforceability and legality of surrogacy contracts vary from state to state. Only a few states expressly permit or prohibit surrogacy. In New Hampshire, Florida and Ohio—to name just three—paid surrogacy agreements are enforceable, but they are subject to stringent regulations. In contrast, in New York and at least five other states, paid surrogacy agreements are void, unenforceable and potentially subject to criminal penalties. Most states, however, occupy a 'middle ground', with limited or no statutory or case law authority that speaks to the validity or enforceability of surrogacy contracts and with no civil or criminal prohibition either. In the United States, as elsewhere, there is deep ambivalence about the legality and morality of an arrangement in which a woman is paid to gestate a baby for another party or other parties. Nevertheless, gestational surrogacy is now the most common form of surrogacy in the United States.[1]

Perhaps reflective of this ambivalence is the fact that even states that treat paid surrogacy agreements as enforceable will not enforce agreements for payment of anything other than clearly defined and limited items, such as the surrogate's living expenses and medical expenses. (For a discussion of the deductibility of medical expenses paid to surrogates and implications

[1] Because of the decision in the *Baby M* case (109 NJ 396), as well as advances in medicine, most surrogates in the United States are gestational surrogates—that is, they bear no genetic relationship to the child that they carry (Brody 2009). For that reason, the discussion in this chapter is limited to taxation of payments received by gestational surrogates. (Gestational surrogates are implanted with an embryo created from the genetic material of one or both of the intended parents. The use of donated sperm or a donated egg is common [Ali and Kelly 2007].)

for heterosexual and gay or lesbian couples, see Infanti in this volume.) This prohibition resembles some states' restrictions in the analogous context of 'private placement' adoptions (ie, those arranged between the birth mother and the adoptive parents, without the involvement of an adoption agency, although usually with the involvement of a private attorney). In the state of Michigan, for instance, private placement adoption laws permit the adoptive parents to pay for expenses such as court-ordered psychological assessments, the birth mother's medical fees, the birth mother's legal fees and the child's medical fees. But the adoptive parents are not permitted to pay a 'fee' for the mother's relinquishment of the baby or for her 'services' of gestation (Michigan Compiled Laws Annotated 2009).

In the surrogacy context, to avoid a policy prohibition against, a contract may recite that the intended parents will pay the gestational surrogate a certain sum of money per month for rent or groceries, even if the contract does not require the surrogate to provide receipts for these expenses. At least one surrogacy agency has explained that clauses like this are included so that the surrogate will not have to declare payments as income. This particular agency informed an intended parent that by structuring payments to the surrogate as 'reimbursements' instead of as a fee, the surrogate would not recognize income (Joseph X interview 2009). This advice is almost certainly incorrect because any money that changes hands in connection with a surrogacy contract constitutes income under the broad US definition.

Given that any surrogacy receipts are income, what type of income is it? In two related contexts, courts have found that taxpayers were in the 'business' of selling their bodily fluids. In *Green v Commissioner* (1980), the United States Tax Court ruled that a taxpayer with a rare blood type who regularly sold her plasma was in the 'business' of doing so (at least for tax purposes) (Brown 2010). In connection with her 'business', the taxpayer was entitled to take deductions for the cost of specialty foods and for transportation to and from the laboratory where she made her deposits. Similarly, in a General Counsel Memorandum, the Department of the Treasury stated its intention to treat the sale of human breast milk as a commodity (Brown 2010; Internal Revenue Service General Counsel Memorandum 1975). Therefore, a taxpayer who sells human breast milk sells 'inventory' and experiences ordinary gain. The Treasury has not addressed the specific income tax consequences of gestational surrogacy, but by analogy with the blood and breast milk scenarios, it is likely that the surrogate would be permitted to take some deductions for costs associated with her pregnancy (such as the cost of vitamins or extra food) and that her income would be treated as ordinary.

Treating receipts from surrogacy as business-related income precludes its characterization as a damage award for personal physical injury (Internal Revenue Code 1986: § 104). US income tax law excludes from gross income any amounts received by a taxpayer on account of personal physical injuries that are not compensated for by insurance or otherwise. However, a different rule applies to damages received in a business context. If surrogacy, like the sale of blood or human breast milk, is a business, then it is not a 'personal physical injury' for income tax purposes. In any case, it would be difficult to characterize pregnancy, and even associated injections of fertility drugs as 'personal physical injuries' when the surrogate has contracted for the same.

In order to escape taxation, a surrogate might argue that the transfers to her by the intended parents are a gift and thus not taxable under US income tax rules (Internal Revenue Code 1986: § 102). This argument, however, is unlikely to succeed, since the transfer of funds from the intended parents to the surrogate is not the product of donative impulses. If it were not for the surrogate's promise to carry a child for the intended parents, the intended parents would not make payments to or on behalf of the surrogate. The absence of donative intent on the part of the transferors means that the transaction lacks the 'detached and disinterested generosity' required for the payment to be treated as a non-taxable gift (*Commissioner v Duberstein* 1960). No doubt, some intended parents may develop a true affection for a surrogate, but they pay (at least certain amounts) to her not because of donative intent, but because they are contractually obligated to do so.

Would the tax consequences be different if the surrogate were a relative of one of the intended parents, rather than a stranger? Assume that sister 'A' acts as a surrogate for sister 'B'. Sister B's egg is fertilized *in vitro* with the sperm of the intended father or a sperm donor. At the appropriate time, the embryo is transferred to the womb of sister A. Might financial transfers by B to A now qualify as tax-free gifts (Internal Revenue Code 1986: § 102)? Probably not, unless B could show, perhaps through a pattern of prior gifts, that donative intent, not A's promise to carry the fertilized embryo, motivated B's transfers. In the rare case that B could show from past practice that her transfers were part of a longer pattern of gifts, a different tax issue would arise. One would then have to ask whether the transfers by B would be subject to gift tax. United States' wealth transfer tax law imposes a tax on the value of lifetime transfers in excess of the amount of the gift tax annual exclusion (US$13,000, or approximately €9409, in 2009) (Internal Revenue Code 1986: § 2501). If B had a partner, then each of the intended parents could transfer US$13,000 to A tax-free (Internal Revenue Code 1986: § 2503(b)), and direct payments to medical providers would always be gift-tax-free (Internal Revenue Code 1986: § 2503(e)). However, a wholly donative scenario would likely be exceptional.

THE REPORTING AND NON-REPORTING OF SURROGACY INCOME

The American government keeps no records of surrogates, and although the Society for Assisted Reproductive Technology (SART) makes some effort to collect information on the number of surrogate births that occur in the United States each year, a significant percentage of fertility clinics do not report to SART. Therefore, SART's data are not precise. Furthermore, not all surrogates are patients of fertility clinics (Ali and Kelly 2007), some choosing to work with their own doctors, for example. One informed estimate placed the number of surrogate births in the United States in 2006 at approximately 1000, and the number of surrogate births trends upwards each year (Ali and Kelly 2007).

If it is difficult to determine the number of surrogates, it is nearly impossible to determine what income tax positions surrogates take. This is partly because the Internal Revenue Service does not ask taxpayers whether they have received or made payments under a surrogacy agreement. In addition, intended parents are not permitted to take any deduction in connection with payments to a surrogate (which might otherwise cause the tax authority to search for a corresponding inclusion on the payee's tax return) (see Lawsky and Cahn 2009 and Infanti in this volume). It might be possible to look for clues in the records of adoption proceedings, but many of these records are not publicly available. And even in the unlikely event that a researcher could assemble a representative sample of data, there would be no information about the tax treatment of payments to surrogates. The lack of tax data is not unique to the United States. As Villota and Spangenberg each point out in their respective chapters in this volume, the lack of tax data, especially gender-disaggregated data, is a problem for researchers in other countries, too.

In the absence of structured studies of the income tax positions taken by surrogates, the researcher must rely on the words of surrogates and intended parents themselves. In-person interviews and postings of surrogates to public internet discussion boards hint at a range of behaviours, including the fact that surrogates do not have a uniform approach to reporting income from surrogacy. A quick internet search reveals a popular online discussion forum where prospective surrogates can ask questions of experienced carriers. Prospective surrogates ask, for example, which surrogacy agencies issue a Form 1099-MISC, the official tax statement for amounts paid 'for services performed for a trade or business by people not treated as its employees' or 'rent or royalty payments'. Of the 18 agencies mentioned in one particular discussion, contributors reported that six agencies issue Form 1099 and 12 agencies do not (SMO 2008A).

Publicly available anecdotal information also suggests that not all surrogates understand their income tax reporting obligations. As one surrogate asked an online financial adviser, 'I served as a surrogate carrier in 2004 and gave birth earlier this year . . . . Do I have to report my compensation?' and she added the following statement: 'I do feel I shouldn't have to pay taxes for being compensated for helping a couple have a baby. What about all the needles, sticks, stretch marks and pain/suffering I went through?' (Saenz 2005). This woman's questions suggest that she sees surrogacy as simultaneously 'not work' and an activity deserving compensation. Her phrase 'helping a couple have a baby' suggests that she considers her activities to be altruistic, and the surrogate then posits that her generosity should not be subject to tax, presumably because gifts are not income taxable in the United States. (Conveniently and crucially, however, this surrogate ignores the fact that she received payment in return for her act of 'generosity'—and that takes the payment for the gestation and childbirth out of the realm of gratuitous transfers.) The surrogate also refers to the 'needles, sticks, stretch marks and pain/suffering' associated with pregnancy and childbirth. Framed in these terms, her activities are presented as a form of work—or perhaps even a type of injury ('pain/suffering')—for which she deserves to be compensated.

Another surrogate's posting to an online message board echoes the view that surrogacy is something other than work of the income-taxable variety. She explains her belief that it is utterly inappropriate for a surrogate to receive a Form 1099-MISC: 'I believe that most of the places that do 1099 think of us as "independent contractors" of which we are NOT!' (SMO 2008). She adds that 'MOST of the large agencies have been in business for some time and know the industry DO NOT 1099. They are in business and what their clients/surrogates do is not their business' (SMO 2008). This woman objects to agencies (and presumably a tax system) that treat surrogates as 'independent contractors' performing (taxable) services. In this surrogate's view, agencies that do send tax forms are misinformed, inexperienced or both. She distinguishes between the 'business' of the agency and the activities of the surrogate—implying both that the gestational mother is not in a 'business' (in a commercial sense) and that the surrogate's activities are her own 'business' (in a privacy sense). This surrogate would place her payments beyond the reach of the tax system because they derive from what she considers to be a non-commercial and non-public transaction.

In fact, an agency that was in the business of matching, supporting and facilitating payments to surrogates would ordinarily be expected to issue a Form 1099-MISC to its surrogates, but there is no indication that the Internal Revenue Service has ever sought to enforce this practice. Nevertheless, the failure of a surrogacy agency to issue a Form 1099 does not mean that payments to a surrogate are non-taxable because the United States has a self-reporting income tax system. Whether or not a payor issues a particular form has no bearing on the tax treatment of monies received by the payee.

IMPLICATIONS OF TAXING SURROGACY (OR NOT)

Economic and Behavioural Implications

The reporting or non-reporting of income by surrogates may have minor fiscal tax consequences in any one particular year, but it has longer-term economic and behavioural implications. In terms of lost tax revenue, it is difficult to estimate the fiscal consequences of the non-reporting of income by surrogates. A highly speculative and informal estimate might proceed from the roughest baseline assumptions—that surrogates receive somewhere between US$20,000 (approximately €14.269) and US$25,000 (approximately €17.836) upon birthing a child (Ali and Kelly 2007) and that there are, for this example's sake, 2000 surrogate births each year. Assuming, for purposes of simplicity, that no surrogate reports her receipt of US$25,000, then an aggregate of US$50,000,000 (approximately €35.905.00) goes untaxed. In light of the lost opportunity to impose a tax at the assumed highest marginal rate of 39.6 per cent, the forgone tax revenue is about US$19,800,000 (approximately €14.227.257). But this is not even two one-thousandths of a per cent of the total income tax collected in the United States in 2007 (Internal Revenue Service 2007).

Given the government's comparatively small revenue loss from surrogates' non-reporting of income, why should taxing surrogacy concern policy makers and scholars? The loss of revenue in any one particular year is admittedly minor, but over a period of years, the cumulative losses will have a greater effect. Of course, non-reporting of income puts each individual surrogate in a better immediate financial position than if she declared and paid tax on her receipts. At first glance, the non-taxation of payments will appeal to the surrogate who seeks to maximize the assets available to her. To attain this net increase, a surrogate who understands her income tax reporting obligations may be willing to risk audit, especially if she does not receive a Form 1099-MISC. For women as a group, however, surrogates' failure to report (and be taxed on) income from surrogacy contracts has longer-range implications for their economic wellbeing. As is the case with household labour and other caretaking activities, women who do not receive income (or who do not report it) do not contribute to social security and other benefits programmes whose future payments depend on the number of years the recipient has engaged in paid (and taxed) marketplace labour (Staudt 1996).

As Staudt has argued in the case of housework, failing to impose tax on women's work causes that work to become tax-preferred. (See Philipps in this volume for further discussion of tax incentives for women to engage in unpaid homemaking and caregiving activities, and see Warman and Woolley in this volume for a discussion of the benefits of one spouse or common-law partner being financially dependent on the other spouse or partner.) In other words, a worker may have a choice between job 'A' and job 'B', where both jobs are similar in kind and degree and both yield identical pre-tax compensation. If saving for social security is not a goal, and the worker will pay income tax on the wages from job A but not on the wages from job B, she always will be motivated to choose job B. In the case of US surrogacy arrangements, these motivational factors come into play, but it is important to note that surrogacy income is taxable, so the motivation to earn surrogacy income does not originate from the fact that such earnings are non-taxable, but from the fact that payment of taxes on surrogacy income is not well enforced. And because of the absence of meaningful enforcement, surrogacy is tax-preferred work. When faced with the choice of doing market labour or serving as a gestational surrogate, if the compensation is the same, a woman may be more motivated to act as a surrogate.

Comparing traditional market labour and surrogacy work has an acknowledged flaw: it fails to account for the ways in which surrogacy work is different from traditional market-based work. First, a surrogate may work mostly at home, apart from going to regular medical appointments and delivering the child (if the child is born away from home). Secondly, a surrogate may work as such while also engaging in other paid, market-based work. Thirdly, surrogates' duties may vary from week to week, or month to month, insofar as a woman may experience pregnancy as easier or more difficult at different times during the baby's gestation. The work of being three months' pregnant is different from the work of being nine months' pregnant. There are, however, some unique restrictions on surrogacy work that do not apply to traditional market labour—because surrogacy is a viable option only for women within a certain narrow age range and with certain medical histories. So, while taxation is a factor in the hypothetical woman's work decisions, fiscal considerations alone will not explain why she might prefer surrogacy over other types of work.

Surrogacy is also likely to have repercussions on women's subsequent participation in traditional paid labour. If a surrogate does not engage in traditional market labour while carrying and delivering the child, that time away from traditional work may make it more difficult for her to achieve long-term financial parity with men of equivalent ability. Buchanan and others (2008) have shown that women who leave the traditional workforce to bear and care for children earn substantially less over the course of their careers than male counterparts who do not leave the traditional workforce. One might reasonably assume that this holds true regardless of whether a woman bears a child who is biologically related to her (as is true for the overwhelming majority birth mothers) or whether the child is not biologically related to her (as is true for most gestational surrogates). Also, consider that every surrogate will eventually become ineligible or unable to serve as a surrogate—whether for reasons of biology, psychology, personal preference or some other factor. If that woman then enters the traditional labour force for the first time, she will have less seniority and experience than a man who has been working in the traditional labour force during the time period that the woman was a paid surrogate. Surrogacy may be a tax-advantaged choice in the short term, but it has long-term economic disadvantages for individual surrogates and for women as a group.

Clear signals or guidance that the government will seek to tax surrogates might have one or more economic or behavioural effects. If the government makes it clear that it intends to enforce a tax on surrogacy, the researcher can hypothesize different results, based on different assumptions about price sensitivity as well as theories of efficiency and taxation. (The importance of such baseline assumptions with reference to tax policy is emphasized in Stewart's chapter in this volume).

First, assume that intended parents have little or no price sensitivity. If that is true, then the price that intended parents pay a surrogate in a taxable environment (*P2*) must equal, on an after-tax basis, what they would have paid in the non-taxable environment (*P1*) in order for the number of surrogates to remain constant. Otherwise, the number of women willing to act as surrogates will likely decrease if *P2* and *P1* are the same (ie, the work becomes tax-disfavoured). These hypotheses assume, however, that fees drive the decision to become a surrogate—an assumption that surrogates themselves say is incorrect (Saenz 2005).

Some women may be so motivated by a desire to help another that they will be willing to act as a surrogate even if *P2* is lower, on an after-tax basis, than *P1*. Conversely, some women might consider taxation so antithetical to their work of 'giving life' that they would be willing to act as a surrogate, but refuse, on principle, to pay taxes on income received for that work. A third group of women might refuse to act as a surrogate at all, if the women knew monies received would be treated as income.

Secondly, and in an alternative scenario, assume that the intended parents are highly price sensitive. If surrogates are willing to receive either *P1* (non-taxable income) or *P2* (taxable income), one would still expect the intended parents to be more likely to pay *P1* because it would more likely be a lower price than *P2*. This is because the surrogacy fee within *P2* (taxable) would likely increase to account for the expected tax. It would then be likely that there would be a decrease in the number of intended parents willing and able to pay a surrogate the *P2* fee. Those who would have become parents in a tax-free context would more likely be pushed out of the market by the enforcement of the tax on the fee for surrogacy work. However, it is not clear what constraining effect price has on people who are deciding whether or not to use a surrogate. Given that surrogacy is the only option for some people who want a biologically-related child (see Infanti in this volume), price sensitivity may exist only in extreme cases.

Social and Cultural Implications

In addition to its economic and behavioural consequences, taxing surrogacy has social and cultural implications. In some contexts, for instance, being subject to taxation confers privilege and status. Contracts also have this effect in some instances, as described by Columbia Law School Professor Patricia Williams. She describes the experiences she and a colleague each had in searching for an apartment in a new city. Peter, a white male colleague, found an apartment and concluded the transaction with a handshake and a cash deposit. In contrast, Williams, who is African-American, signed a detailed written agreement with her new landlord:

> In my rush to show good faith and trustworthiness, I signed a detailed, lengthily negotiated, finely printed lease firmly establishing me as the ideal arm's-length transactor . . . [Peter and I] could not reconcile our very different relations to the tonalities of law. Peter, for example, appeared to be extremely self-conscious of his power potential (either real or imagistic) as white or male or lawyer authority figure. He seemed to go some lengths to overcome the wall that image might impose . . . On the other hand, I was raised to be acutely conscious of the likelihood that no matter what degree of professional I am, people will greet and dismiss my black femaleness as unreliable, untrustworthy, hostile, angry, powerless, irrational and probably destitute . . . [T]o show that I can speak the language of lease is my way of enhancing trust of me in my business affairs.

As this experience demonstrates, the way in which one views the law is a function of experience: 'On a semantic level, Peter's language of . . . informality . . . sounded dangerously like the language of oppression to someone like me who was looking for freedom through establishment of identity' (Williams 1991: 146–48). Similarly, for those women whose reproductive work has been historically devalued, treating reproductive labour like other, traditional work (ie, taxing it) can mark it as worthy and important.

Nevertheless, taxing surrogacy has two salient negative socio-legal consequences. First, placing a monetary value on women's ability to reproduce has a complex and painful history in the United States. Enslaved African and African-American women were valued for their fertility—the ability to bear children who, as slaves, would accrete to the wealth of the slave owner. Moreover, government intervention in reproductive matters has not protected women of colour—in fact, the results in this regard have been disastrous. The United States has a documented history of unconstitutional sterilization of Native-American women (Comptroller General 1975) Puerto Rican women, Mexican-American women (Sidel and Sidel 1984), disabled women and poor women of all colours (Rodriguez-Triaz, H 1998). Historically, the state's invasive regulation of women's bodies has damaged women's individual and collective wellbeing.

Critics have warned that surrogacy would lead to exploitation of poor women and women of colour (Macklin 1990). In fact, however, most surrogates are white, married, self-identified Christians and from working-class backgrounds. Most surrogates are between 20 and 40 years old and have children of their own (Ciccarelli and Beckman 2005). Disparities between surrogates and intended parents exist, but they are not the racial or extreme class differences that critics anticipated (Ciccarelli and Beckman 2005; Macklin 1990). Even so, proposals for increased state involvement in women's reproductive choices should be evaluated critically. After all, the decision to become a parent—or to assist another in becoming a parent—is a private decision about the use to which one will put one's own body and, ultimately, a significant portion of one's life. Yet this proposal to tax surrogacy is not a proposal to increase governmental involvement in women's decision making; it is a bid to increase the rate at which women report to the taxing authorities those payments that are clearly taxable. This improved reporting would increase the likelihood of women's reproductive labour being treated as making economic contributions equal to those of other, 'traditional' market-based work.

Those who disapprove of surrogacy on moral or religious grounds may or may not object to taxing surrogacy. They may argue that taxation represents recognition of the existence of the arrangement. In another context, in 2009 New York State governor David A Paterson proposed a tax on the download of internet pornography. Conservative political leaders criticized that proposal as 'legitimizing' the product and practice of pornography, saying that only Nevada 'legitimizes' the sale of sex by taxing it. Yet the conservative objection overlooks two nuances. First, taxing an activity can, but does not always imply approval—as is clear from the case of the robber who is taxed on the fruits of a heist. Secondly, taxes can discourage the behaviour that results in taxes being due. For example, the history of US tax law includes taxes on bowling alleys (Internal Revenue Code 1954: § 4471), adulterated butter (§ 4811) and filled cheeses (§ 4841). These taxes likely had social goals (limiting certain activities) more than economic goals (increasing government revenue). Similarly, taxing surrogacy could appeal to some opponents, on the grounds that taxation would discourage the practice.

COMPLYING WITH A SURROGACY TAX

A proposal to more rigorously enforce existing laws requiring income tax to be paid on surrogacy fees is grounded in the reality that surrogacy involves the exchange of money and a child. In the case of women who act as surrogates without compensation, the desire to help another may be the only motivation. And altruism may often play a role in the decision to become a surrogate, but it is not necessarily the principal motivation (or a motivation at all). Recall the surrogate who believed she 'shouldn't have to pay taxes for being compensated for helping a couple have a baby'. She characterizes the payment to her as recompenses for 'all the needles, sticks, stretch marks and pain/suffering (Saenz 2005). Nothing in the surrogate's statement suggests that she was altruistic or that she denies receiving income. Yet she uses a framework of injury compensation, not commerce. This suggests that calling the surrogacy payment anything else would conjure up morally repugnant phrases like 'baby selling' and 'womb renting'. Yet surrogates are indeed compensated, and that compensation is considered to be income under existing US tax laws.

Because the 'problem' with taxing surrogacy is not the law but rather compliance with the law, the solution should focus on compliance efforts. The government could increase compliance by issuing a revenue ruling or other administrative guidance that clearly states surrogacy agencies must issue a Form 1099-MISC and that surrogates must report payments as income. The ruling or other administrative guidance should provide, further, that if a surrogate receives payments from a private party (ie, from the intended parents as opposed to an agency), she must report these payments as income. The government has already issued guidance about the income tax consequences of selling or donating blood (Brown 2010; Private Letter Ruling 8814010, 1987) and administrative guidance on surrogacy should be consistent with the government's past positions on taxable income.

It could be argued that the problem of tax compliance could be solved through some mechanism other than the tax system. However, this raises significant privacy concerns. For example, a requirement for doctors to disclose names of patients who undergo *in vitro* fertilization would be an inappropriate intrusion into the doctor-patient relationship. Such a requirement also would be over-inclusive, insofar as it would include women who are implanted with their own eggs, women who do not in fact become pregnant and women who do not carry a pregnancy to full term. Even if patients were informed that their identities would be made available to the government only for purposes of income tax compliance, they might fear that the information could be given to insurance companies who might then deny insurance or charge higher premiums—or that it could be made available to neighbours or family members who might disapprove of a woman's decision to be a surrogate. Pregnancy is not usually secret, but actual gestational practices can be carried out in private, and some may object to government record-keeping as an invasion of this privacy.

BRINGING SURROGACY OUT OF THE SHADOWS

Liberal supporters of surrogacy rely on concepts like bodily integrity and a woman's right to be free from government interference in decisions about her body. But a right to be left alone need not be the only strain of discourse. If one inverts the paradigm, inviting the government into women's decisions might create new institutional pathways for securing women's equality. Governments can and should enhance the wellbeing of women, and taxation can be one way of accomplishing that. To tax an activity is to make it part of the public conversation about rights and responsibilities. Bringing surrogacy out of the shadows and into the sunshine of the law is a step toward recognizing the value of reproductive work. It is also a step toward normalizing a wide variety of family configurations.

A proposal to tax surrogacy is a proposal for formal equality, since it asserts that reproductive work should be valued as much as traditional work by taxing the income from both. Taxing surrogacy will benefit women's long-term economic strength because their otherwise unvalued or undervalued work will count as market labour for purposes of social security and other benefits.

It is important to recognize that, despite the importance of formal equality in tax law or fiscal policy relating to surrogacy and other women's endeavours, this type of legal and economic framework will not achieve substantive gender equality on its own. Meaningful social, political, economic and personal equality requires women to have employment opportunities and conditions equal to those of men. And such equality will not exist without a full range of legal, social, political and cultural shifts. Whether women are raising their own children, acting as surrogates, living in common law, married or lesbian partnerships or in their own individual households, they need to live in a context characterized by fair living wages, legal protections against sexual harassment and domestic violence, access to safe and legal contraception, affordable, quality childcare and non-gendered distribution of family and household responsibilities. Tax law and the enforcement of tax laws relating to surrogacy is a part of the progress towards justice for women, but it remains only one part.

REFERENCES

Ali, L and Kelly, R (2007) 'The Curious Lives of Surrogates' *Newsweek* (7 April).

Brody, JE (2009) 'Since Baby M, Much Movement in Surrogacy' *New York Times* (21 July).

Brown, DA (2010) 'Taxing the Body' in M Goodwin (ed), *Contested Commodities* (New York University Press, 21st Century Law Series) (forthcoming).

Buchanan, NH et al (2 October 2008) 'Why Do Women Lawyers Earn Less Than Men? Parenthood and Gender in a Survey of Law School Graduates' GWU Law School Public Law Research Paper no 449; GWU Legal Studies Research Paper no 449. Available at: ssrn.com/abstract=1280464.

Ciccarelli, JC and Beckman, L (2005) 'Navigating Rough Waters: An Overview of Psychological Aspects of Surrogacy' 61 *Journal of Social Issues* 21–43.

Internal Revenue Service, United States Department of the Treasury (2007) *Tax Stats at a Glance*. Available at: www.irs.gov/taxstats/article/0,,id=102886,00.html.

Joseph, X (adult male, who wishes to remain anonymous, who is an intended parent under a surrogacy agreement brokered by a large agency in the United States) (discussion with the author, October 2009).

Krawiec, KD (2009) 'Why We Should Ignore the "Octomom"' 104 *Northwestern University* Law Review 120-131 (2009), http://www.law.northwestern.edu/lawreview/colloquy/2009/34/LRColl2009n34Krawiec.pdf.

Lawsky, SB and Cahn, NR (2009) 'Embryo Exchanges and Adoption Tax Credits' 123 *Tax Notes* 1365.
Macklin, R (1990) 'Is There Anything Wrong with Surrogate Parenthood: An Ethical Analysis' in L Gostin (ed), *Surrogate Motherhood: Politics and Privacy* (Indianapolis, Indiana University Press) 60–63.
Rodriguez-Triaz, H (1998) 'Sterilization and Sterilization Abuse' in W Mankiller, G Mink, M Navarro, B Smith and G Steinem (eds), *Reader's Companion to US Women's History* (New York, Houghton Mifflin).
SMO (Surrogate Moms Online) (2008) Message Boards (29 December, 03:38 pm, posting from SusanFrmLA). Available at: www.surromomsonline.com/support/showthread.php?p=1604396.
Saenz, G (24 May 2005). Question from 'Alicia' sent to George Saenz: 'Do Surrogate Moms Have to Pay Income Tax?' Available at: www.bankrate.com/brm/itax/tax_adviser/20050524a1.asp.
Sidel, VW and Sidel, R (1984) *Reforming Medicine: Lessons of the Last Quarter Century* (New York, Pantheon Books) 116.
Staudt, NC (1996) 'Taxing Housework' 84 *Georgetown Law Journal* 1571–647.
Williams, PJ (1991) *The Alchemy of Race and Rights* (Cambridge, MA, Harvard University Press) 146–48.

Cases

Commissioner v Duberstein, 363 US 278 (1960).
Green v Commissioner, 74 TC 1229, 1234 (1980).
In the Matter of Baby M, 109 NJ 396 (1988).

Legislation and Administrative Materials

Comptroller General of United States (4 November 1975) *General Accounting Office Report*.
Internal Revenue Code of 1986, as amended, 26 USC §§ 1 *et seq* (2009).
Internal Revenue Code of 1954, as amended, 26 USC §§ 1 *et seq* (1954).
Internal Revenue Service (1975, Sept 15) General Counsel Memorandum 36,418.
Michigan Compiled Laws Annotated 710.44(5) and 710.54(2)(a)–(d) (2009).
New Hampshire RSA §§ 168-B:1 to 168-B:32 (2007).
NY CLS Dom Rel §§ 121–24 (2007).
Private Letter Ruling 8814010, 1987 PLR Lexis 4174.

6

A Gender Perspective Approach Regarding the Impact of Income Tax on Wage-earning Women in Spain[1]

PALOMA DE VILLOTA

IN SEVERAL COUNTRIES, special attention has been paid to comparing the impact of fiscal reforms on men and women. One example is the women's budget process initiated at an official level in Australia in 1985.[2] Another is the proposal presented by the Canadian Centre for Policy Alternatives and Choices: A Coalition for Social Justice within their 1998 Alternative Federal Budget (AFB).[3] This chapter will provide a detailed analysis of the way in which the latest changes in the Personal Income Tax (PIT) in Spain have affected men and women with regard to their specific position in that country's labour market.

A GENDER PERSPECTIVE ON BUDGETS

Budgetary policy has two well-defined aspects—income and spending—and in some ways, this shapes the behaviour of the social groups that are affected (Elson 2005). The purpose of income tax policy is to obtain sufficient

[1] This chapter is part of a research project financed by the Instituto de la Mujer. Data processing was completed in collaboration with Ignacio Ferrari.

[2] Eg, the Australian *Women's Budget Statement* of 1989 asserted that: 'The tax cuts announced in the Statement particularly benefited women workers. The reduction in the lowest tax rates were of most advantage to those on low pay, most of whom are women' *Women's Budget Statement* (The Parliament of the Commonwealth of Australia, 1989) 8.

[3] See I Bakker and D Elson, 'Towards Engendering Budgets' in *Alternative Federal Budget Papers* (Ottawa, Canadian Centre for Policy Aternatives and Choices: A Coalition for Social Justice,1998) 297–324, where the authors discuss the fiscal policy trend favouring tax cuts in Canada: 'Given fiscal pressures such as deficit reduction, it also undermines the state's ability to provide minimum levels of social security for those faring badly in the market or those who work in the care economy. It remains at best unclear, given remaining gender-based economic disadvantages, to what extent women will benefit from the increased consumption power supposedly generated by tax cuts' (at 317).

economic resources to meet public sector needs, while spending policy is the vehicle through which social policy, among other government policies, is implemented. The two policies work in tandem, and they are inseparable inasmuch as without economic resources, it is impossible to implement spending and without spending it is not possible to achieve redistribution of income. This perception must be completed by the inclusion of fiscal expenditure which—the Spanish constitution states—must also feature in the budget.

It would seem obvious that gender issues are related to social policy, as social policy may either foster or diminish equal opportunities. It is more difficult, however, to ascertain how gender issues are related to tax policy, and at first glance it may appear that taxes are unrelated to the gender of taxpayers. This is because, in theory, legislation does not distinguish between men and women, although empirical verification differs significantly from theoretical approaches and there are political and technical challenges to be studied from a gender perspective.

With regard to indirect taxation, such as VAT and sales taxes, it is also difficult to trace connections with gender issues, but these links undoubtedly exist and should be studied rigorously (see chapter seven by Wanjala and Were, this volume). There is no doubt, however, that direct taxation and, specifically, Personal Income Tax (PIT) in Spain can be seen as a paradigmatic case of indirect discrimination in the form of fiscal discrimination. In theory, direct taxation is irreproachably neutral, and taxpayers' sex or gender characteristics have no bearing on this form of taxation. However, this is not the case when the fiscal regime is not individual because some taxpayers benefit and some lose, depending on their marital status and/or the type of family to which they belong (Barnet and Grown 2004). In fact, in the European Union, non-individualized compulsory tax regimes may penalize the following groups: people living together as partners, one-parent families (where mothers are more often the sole parent than are fathers) and non-heterosexual relationships. At the same time, these regimes favour the traditional two-parent family with one income earner, as Wersig points out in this volume with reference to Germany. One flagrant example of indirect discrimination under these regimes can be seen in the case of income being accumulated and reported by the family unit. This results in the income of the secondary earner being taxed at the marginal rate of the primary earner, and this rate is always higher than the one that would be applied to the secondary earner's income if that secondary earner made an independent tax return. This method of reporting taxes was compulsory in Spain until 1989 and, regrettably, is still optional in spite of the fact that the European Commission (EC) (1982), in its first community action programme for equal opportunities between men and women, stated that one of its major goals would be to 'individualize social and fiscal rights'. This, the EC said, would enable 'men and women to act as independent individuals when seeking employment and combining working life and family life', thus preventing 'gender-based discriminatory treatment'.

In order to prevent all possible fiscal harassment, it is therefore essential to seek answers to the many questions regarding this matter—such as the following: are compulsory taxes based on a gender-biased, masculine model? Do tax benefits exclusively favour individuals who are legally married or may they be extended to all types of families, including one-parent families and heterosexual life partners? Which type of family receives greater tax benefits? Does fiscal neutrality exist from the perspective of marital status and gender?

The purpose of this chapter, however, is much more restricted, as it focuses on the gender disparities observed in wages in the labour market. It attempts to foster discussion, in the case of Spain, concerning the way that income tax is designed and concerning other possible options that would make employment more attractive, in order to increase female participation in the labour market and reduce other gender disparities.

These discussions will all reflect the persistence of patriarchy in the labour market, as Sylvia Walby (1986) has pointed out in her analysis. In the first section of this chapter, an uneven and traditional patriarchal division of work will be evident in the asymmetrical division of remunerated and unremunerated work and in the vast amount of domestic work that women still have to perform throughout Europe. Statistics from the Harmonized European Time Use Survey (HETUS) (European Commission, 2008) show that differences all over Europe are not always of the same kind, a circumstance that is also considered in the first section of this chapter.

The second section explains the principal characteristics of Spanish income tax and its evolution in recent years. During this period it has to be pointed out that, on one hand, there has been an important increase in the number of taxpayers from 1980 to 2004 and, on the other hand, there has always been a high proportion of income (79.6 per cent in 2004) related to waged work in the total amount of taxable income.

The third section analyzes gender asymmetric distribution in the Spanish labour market first by presenting a diagram showing a breakdown of labour income by gender and secondly by examining this asymmetry more deeply, through a density function diagram (see Figure 6 and Table 5) that reflects the real percentage of people at each income level (even though differences in labour income refer not only to wages, but to other incomes, such as contributory pensions and unemployment benefits).

In the fourth section, the marginal rates that make up the PIT taxation scale are superimposed onto the diagram corresponding to the density function, in an attempt to reveal the effect of taxation rates on different levels of income. This new diagram also sheds light on the proportion of men and women affected by the differing marginal rates applied in Spain, revealing where differing rates are concentrated and consequently showing how men and women are affected by lower or higher marginal rates.

The fifth section briefly presents the results obtained in the various parts of the study on which this chapter is based.

ASYMMETRICAL PARTICIPATION IN THE LABOUR MARKET IN EUROPE

Asymmetrical participation in the labour market can be seen clearly in the evolution of the activity rates (participation) of women and men during their lifecycles. Once they have finished their studies, men generally enter the labour market and remain in it without interruption throughout their working lives (unless they are forced to take early retirement after they reach the age of 50). Women, on the other hand, often leave the labour market when they marry and primarily, as is the case in a number of countries in the European Union, when they decide to have children and bring them up. Women do not always return to work once this stage of their life is over, and in many cases, the presence of young children causes an empirically demonstrable decline in women's participation in the labour market and even their total absence—owing, among other reasons, to a lack of adequate childcare services and to the fact that, socially, children continue to be considered the responsibility of the mother and not of both parents (see Figure 1).

Consequently, the graph representing women's working lives throughout their lifecycles differs from that of men. The patterns of activity for women also differ according to their country of residence. In some countries, there is a well-defined maximum of paid activity between the ages of 21 and 29 that drops sharply after that point, as a result of marriage and child rearing. This remains the situation in Ireland and Spain today, with few women returning to work at a later date. The result of this behaviour is that women, overall, have a very low rate of participation in the labour market. In other countries (for example, Germany and the United Kingdom), a second pattern appears, in which the lowest activity rate coincides with the years when women have small children. This indicates that reconciliation of employment and raising a family continues to be difficult in some European countries and that subsequent re-entry into the labour market is viable only when children are old enough to attend school. In the third group of countries (including Denmark), the pattern forms a curve in the shape of an inverted U, or plateau, which is very similar to the curve in Figure 2 (showing the labour-market activity rate of men).

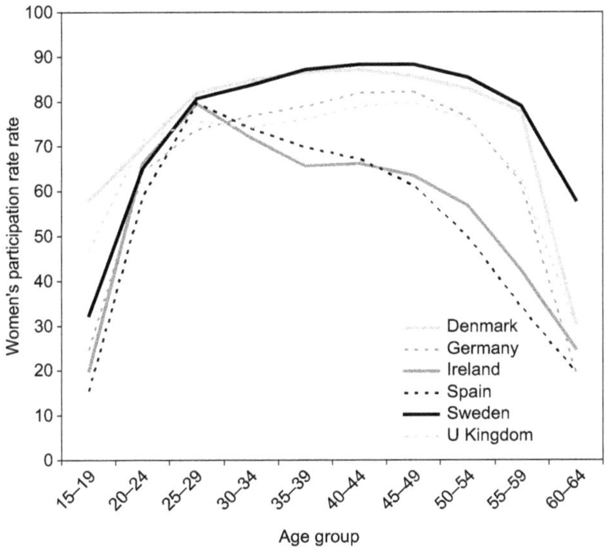

Figure 1: Women's Activity Rate and Lifecycle, 2004
Source: Eurostat Activity Rates by Sex, Age Groups and Nationality. Available at: epp.eurostat.ec.europa.eu/portal/page/portal/employment_unemployment_lfs/data/database. Date of extraction: 25 October 2009

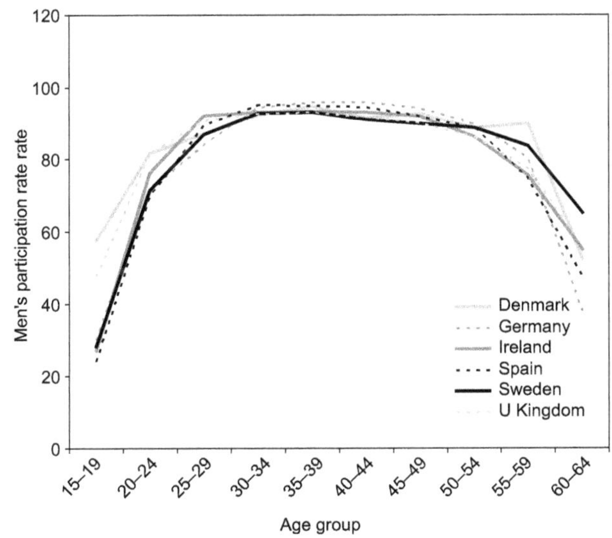

Figure 2: Men's Activity Rate and Lifecycle, 2004
Source: Eurostat Activity Rates by Sex, Age Groups and Nationality. Available at: epp.eurostat.ec.europa.eu/portal/page/portal/employment_unemployment_lfs/data/database. Date of extraction: 25 October 2009

The configuration of each of these profiles is closely interrelated with the existence or absence of fiscal and social policies that make it possible for men and women to reconcile their private and working lives by ensuring that adequate facilities and institutional and legal factors are in place to allow for the care of children and elderly and disabled family members. Institutional and legal factors include those relating to parental leave, flexible working hours and school hours. The combination of these factors is of fundamental importance in explaining the profile of women's participation in the paid workforce, in that they result either in women withdrawing temporarily or definitively from the labour market, or in women managing to integrate their professional lives and their family lives successfully throughout the different phases of their lifecycles.

From a gender perspective, the female workforce profile offered by Spain is very different from that of the male workforce. The latter is represented by an inverted U-shaped curve, with a participation rate of over 80 per cent between the ages of 20 and 55 (at which point the number of workers diminishes as a consequence of early retirement), whereas women show a far lower level of labour-market participation.

To explain the pan-European differences, the effect of taxation should be linked to that of public expenditure on family transfers, childcare and social services for the elderly. In this way, the combined effect of taxation and these public expenditures can be assessed when putting forward hypothetical explanations for the changes in female behaviour observed in the various countries.

The statistics from the Harmonized European Time Use Survey (EUROSTAT, June 2004) (reproduced in European Commission, 2008) also display these gender differences in time spent by women and men in unpaid work (especially in domestic work). This situation is understandable only if the persisting effects of the historical gendered division of labour in European societies are taken into account.

From the data shown in Table 1 it is possible to see that domestic work still constitutes the main activity of many women in all European countries, taking up a daily average of about four and a half to five and a half hours of domestic work. But in Sweden, Norway and Finland, women allocate less time to domestic tasks (fewer than four hours). The contrast in work patterns between the Nordic welfare states and other European countries may be closely related to differences in national social policy. For example, according to the interpretation presented by Lina Gálvez, Paula Rodríguez and Mónica Domínguez (2009), the situation in Italy and Spain could be explained in light of their fascist heritage, which built social policies whereby women became the main providers of domestic support for the family. Nevertheless, it has to be underlined that in most European countries, women spend more time than men on housekeeping and childcare when they also participate in the paid workforce.

Table 1: Time Use Structure for Women and Men aged 20–74 years (hours and minutes per day)

	Free time	Meals, personal care	Sleep	Travel	Domestic work	Gainful work, study	Unspecified time use	Total
Women								
Belgium	05:06	02:37	08:34	01:22	04:10	02:09	00:02	24
Denmark	:	:	:	:	:	:	:	:
Germany	05:15	02:43	08:15	01:19	04:14	02:09	00:05	24
Greece	04:18	02:04	08:26	01:02	04:53	03:12	00:05	24
Spain	04:26	02:33	08:32	01:05	04:55	02:26	00:02	24
France	04:05	02:58	08:55	00:54	04:34	02:31	00:03	24
Italy	04:06	02:53	08:19	01:14	05:20	02:06	00:03	24
Finland	05:17	02:06	08:32	01:07	03:56	02:49	00:12	24
Sweden	04:57	02:27	08:11	01:23	03:42	03:13	00:06	24
U Kingdom	04:55	02:16	08:27	01:25	04:15	02:33	00:10	24
Norway	05:40	02:17	08:10	01:11	03:47	02:53	00:03	24
Men								
Belgium	05:58	02:30	08:15	01:30	02:28	03:18	00:01	24
Denmark	:	:	:	:	:	:	:	:
Germany	05:42	02:32	08:08	01:29	02:22	03:42	00:05	24
Greece	05:02	02:11	08:24	01:12	02:33	04:33	00:04	24
Spain	05:16	02:35	08:36	01:16	01:37	04:39	00:02	24
France	04:44	02:59	08:45	01:03	02:24	04:03	00:02	24
Italy	05:05	02:59	08:17	01:35	01:35	04:26	00:03	:
Finland	05:56	02:01	08:22	01:12	02:16	04:01	00:12	24
Sweden	05:18	02:11	08:01	01:30	02:29	04:25	00:06	24
U Kingdom	05:22	02:04	08:18	01:30	02:18	04:18	00:08	24
Norway	05:52	02:10	07:56	01:21	02:21	04:16	00:03	24

Source: Eurostat (2008): *Living Conditions in Europe. Data 2003–05* (Luxembourg)

Considering data shown in Table 1, it can be observed that only in Sweden do men and women spend almost the same time in total work (domestic work and gainful work or study).[4] And it can be asserted, as Galvez et al have pointed out, that those countries in which there are more gender differences are the Mediterranean countries (in Italy women's total workload was seven hours and twenty-six minutes compared with six hours and one minute for men; and in Spain women worked a total of seven hours and twenty-one minutes compared with six hours and sixteen minutes for men).

Although there is no space here to comment on differences in the amount of leisure time[5] available in Europe for women and men, this should be considered as another kind of gender discrimination. Achieving more equality in this matter would lead to a better quality of life according to the capabilities approach developed by Amartya Sen (1993) and Martha Nussbaum (2003). The data from Table 1 show an important gender gap for Europe with regard to the amount of free time women in Spain and Italy have at their disposal as compared with the amount of free time available to women in Norway or Sweden.

For instance, historian Richard Wall (2009) outlines the discriminatory situation in which married women found themselves in Russia, using the data calculated by Tyazhelnikova (2006) for the city of Pskov in the 1960s, where '[M]arried men in full-time employment had 78 per cent more leisure time than married women who were employed full-time although the latter devoted almost as much time to paid employment as married men'.

GENERAL CHARACTERISTICS OF THE SPANISH TAX SYSTEM

Personal Income Tax (PIT), in its present form, was created when Spain changed to a democratic system of government and had its specific origin in the tax reform initiated on 14 November 1977 as part of the Tax Reform Emergency Measures Law 50/1977. This was the result of the Moncloa Pacts established by the government and almost all political parties and was signed by Adolfo Suárez (President of the Government), Leopoldo Calvo-Sotelo (UCD), Felipe González (Partido Socialista Obrero Español), Santiago Carrillo (Partido Comunista de España), Enrique Tierno Galván (Partido Socialista Popular), Josep María Triginer (Partido Socialista de Cataluña), Joan Reventós (Convergencia Socialista de Cataluña), Juan Ajuriaguerra (Partido Nacionalista Vasco) y Miquel Roca (Convergència i

[4] Table 1 shows just one minute of difference.

[5] According to the data of European Comission, EUROSTAT (2008) *Living Conditions in Europe. Data 2003–2006* (Luxembourg), there are great differences among European countries. Norway appears as the more egalitarian, with a difference of twelve minutes between men and women). Conversely, Italy can be considered the worst with almost one hour (59 minutes).

Unió). Manuel Fraga (Alianza Popular) only signed the economical part of the agreement and not the political.

The reform had three phases, related to tax administration, direct taxation and indirect taxation, respectively. In addition, the reformers aimed to implement a modern tax regime that would harmonize with already existing systems in the European Economic Community by including a value-added tax (VAT)—a key tax element with regard to Spain's entry into the EEC on 1 January 1986.

Personal Income Tax (PIT) which became law in Spain on 8 September 1978, was initially conceived as a uniform tax, which treated all incomes identically, regardless of their nature and origin. It was considered to be personal, since it allowed deductions for those who paid not only in proportion to their financial situation, but in relation to their personal and family circumstances.[6] The tax unit was considered to be the family unit, with all the latter's components being jointly and severally subject to the tax.[7] Moreover, capital gains and yields of all members of the family unit, whatever the financial regime of the husband and wife may be were to accumulate.[8]

Those who passed this legislation did not foresee the problems that accumulated taxation would cause from the perspective of gender, since they defined the family unit as being made up of a married couple and 'legitimate, legitimized, natural, recognized or adopted' children who were still underage.[9] Furthermore, one-parent family units were defined as those that resulted from 'marriages being annulled or dissolved or from legal separations' (cases of divorce were not recognized, as this was not yet legal) and those where single fathers or mothers had underage children in their care.

Throughout the 30 years since it was implemented, the PIT has undergone changes, especially as a result of the Constitutional Court's verdict of 20 February 1989, whereby compulsory joint taxation was deemed unconstitutional. This verdict meant that the PIT had to be modified and converted into an optional tax, so that individuals within a family would have the choice of filing either a joint tax return with the other members of the family unit, or an individual return (for further discussion of the differing effects of joint and individual tax filing, see the chapters by Lahey, Philipps, Wanjala and Were and Wersig, in this volume). As a result, family tax returns are still valid and affect a large number of taxpayers because the

[6] Art 1 of Law 44/1978.
[7] Art 4.2.
[8] Art 7.1.3.
[9] Art 51.1 Law 44/1978.

Table 2: Evolution of Number of Tax Returns (by type)

	2000	2001	2002	2003	2004
Individual	9,128,393	9,856,308	10,481,421	10,987,527	11,500,355
Joint	5,114,994	5,047,635	4,999,961	4,998,254	4,973,795
Total	14,243,387	14,903,943	15,481,382	15,985,781	16,474,150

Source: *Memoria de la Administración Tributaria 2005* (Ministerio de Hacienda, Madrid, 2007)

proportion of joint tax returns remains high, at over 30.19 per cent (that is, one in three tax returns filed are joint returns), as Table 2 shows.[10]

It can be seen that the number of tax returns from 1980, when the democratic fiscal reform was applied for the first time, reached the number of 5,776,620, which significantly outnumbered the expectations of the Ministry of Finance. But surprisingly ten years later, this cipher had almost doubled, reaching 10,975,073. The explanation for this fact can be found in the effectiveness of the official fight against fiscal fraud as well as the establishment of the individual tax return option for married couples, in 1992, the precise moment when the evolution of the joint tax return started to decrease.

On one hand, regarding those making PIT returns, it is also worth noting that the great majority obtain their earnings from labour income, as may be seen in Figure 3, taxed in 2004 according to a progressive tax rate structure at up to 45 per cent. Income from capital gains, on the other hand, was taxed at a flat rate of 15 per cent for the same year. This structural change in taxation occurred during the 1990s and has been retained by both conservative and social democratic governments.

From the 16,474,150 returns filed in 2004 it has to be underlined that 14,742,315 contained labour income and 14,369,105 contained dividends and interest, where average yields differed greatly (€18,214 for labour income and €805 for dividends and interest) and 1,538,883 returns contain capital gains with a mean of €10,169. So the great majority of taxpayers who declare capital gains report a lesser amount of money than those reporting labour income. Income from professionals and small business were declared by more than three million taxpayers, with a mean of €9380.

[10] Table 2 is based on tax returns filed in the Common Fiscal Territory (CFT), ie, the entire Spanish state, or all the Spanish Autonomous Communities apart from the Basque Country and the Navarra Autonomous Communities, as both have special autonomy agreements on taxation.

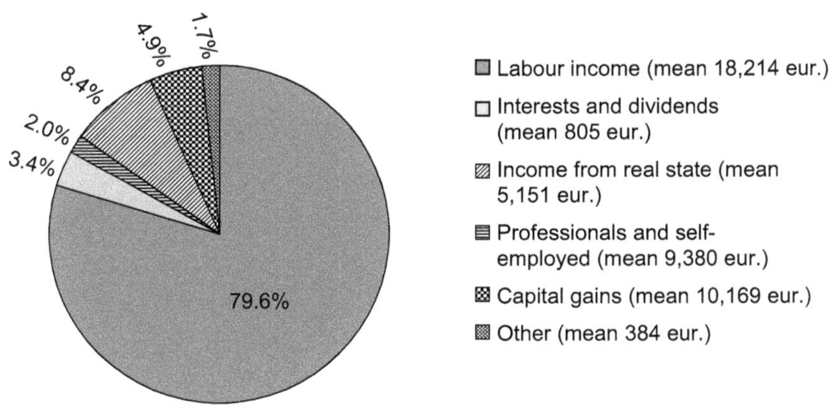

Figure 3: Structure of Taxable Incomes in Spain and Mean earned by Source
Source: Author's analysis based on *Memoria de la Administración Tributaria 2005* (Ministerio de Hacienda, Madrid 2007)

The dominance of labour income over other sources of income is reflected in the diagram below (Figure 3), which shows a breakdown of total income declared.

Labour income accounts for 79.6 per cent of the incomes declared, followed by self-employed and professional income (including agricultural businesses, professionals and small businesses) at 8.4 per cent and capital gains at 4.9 per cent. Interest and dividend income accounts for 3.4 per cent, with real estate income at 2.0 per cent. The relative insignificance of other income (at 1.7 per cent) is worthy of note. This category includes transparencia fiscal[11] and earnings from patrimonial and professional companies, etc.

The high proportion of income derived from labour is not unique to the Spanish income tax system: it is common to all tax regimes in developed countries. However, the quantitative importance of this category is not uniform for all those who declare taxable income because it varies according to amount of income, as shown in Figure 4.

At both extremes—that is, in the sections corresponding to the lowest and highest incomes—it can be seen that labour incomes make up a smaller proportion of total income than in the other sections. For those who earn between €12,000 and €51,000 in taxable income, labour income represents more than 80 per cent of all income declared, but beyond this threshold, the relative weight of labour income decreases until it reaches

[11] In order to prevent fraud, the Spanish Income Tax Law considers that under some circumstances some corporations are regarded as non existent, and their profits are directly attributed to shareholders.

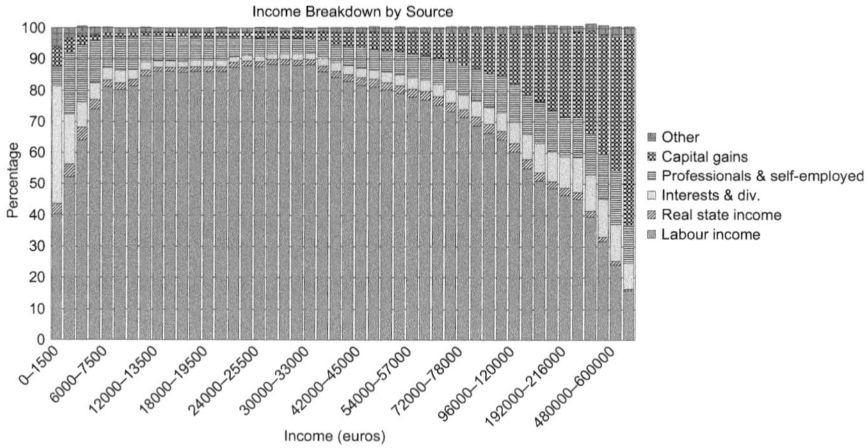

Figure 4: Income Breakdown by Source
Source: Author's analysis based on *Memoria de la Administración Tributaria 2005* (Ministerio de Hacienda, Madrid 2007)

its lowest point, just 17.9 per cent, in the 'over €600,000' section. In the highest bands, the significance of income from investments, capital gains and professional activities may be detected. In contrast, in the lower income bands, yields from self-employed activities have greater relevance (including income from shops and from personal services).

From a gender perspective, it would be interesting to ascertain income breakdown by source in the case of women. Until very recently, however, not much attention has been paid to this, so the lack of data is almost absolute, and mere estimates would not capture the reality.[12]

GENDER ASYMMETRIC INCOME DISTRIBUTION AND DIFFERING IMPACTS OF PERSONAL INCOME TAX ON MEN AND WOMEN IN SPAIN

Analyzing the differing impact personal income tax has on men and women is not an easy task, owing to the lack of taxation statistics broken down by gender, which would reveal this discrimination. Some advances have been made, however, by the Agencia Estatal de Administración Tributaria and the Instituto de Estudios Fiscales, which have been working together to elaborate on a sample with multiple data about payers of income tax from 2006 (*Muestra*

[12] In the 2002 PIT tax return, filed in June 2003, the declarer had to indicate gender. It is to be hoped that some relevant data may soon be obtained shortly as a result of this requirement.

IRPF 2002 IEF-AEAT, contribuyentes). The sample consists of almost a million items selected through a random statistics system, which includes three different categories of information: territorial (provinces), level of income and the type of tax return selected by taxpayers (individual or joint return). This sample opens a great range of possibilities for gender studies on taxation.

Unfortunately, the data are not yet completely broken down by gender. Individual taxpayers and one-parent families can be identified easily, but taxpayers who choose joint tax returns are not readily identifiable. In these cases, the situation is quite complex, especially as it is impossible for researchers to discover the amount of income that individual family members have contributed to total family income, as this information is lacking. Furthermore, until recently, only those legally married were allowed to choose between a joint or individual tax return. But it can be observed that in many cases, there is only one earner (breadwinner family model) or the level of income contributed by the secondary earner is irrelevant. To consider the economic rationality in choosing individual or joint tax returns for different kinds of families, see the study published by Villota et al (2008).

This sample constitutes a fundamental source of statistics for analyzing personal labour income distribution, as it allows for an analysis broken down by Autonomous Community and by province. Statistical use of this source is vital for the completion of the picture of income distribution that is currently available to us. The only drawback this data may have is that it is restricted exclusively to taxpayers who are affected by common tax regulations. The geographical area is the 'Common Fiscal Territory' that as noted above comprises the totality of the Spanish state, but excludes the Basque Country and the Navarre Autonomous Community, which are subject to autonomous tax regulations. Nevertheless, these statistics are a useful complement to the information supplied by the National Institute of Statistics. Similar data in other countries constitute the main source of information on wages. In France, for instance, since 1950, data has been available concerning the starting and finishing dates of work carried out by taxpayers, along with their working conditions.

The sample of income tax for 2004 (the latest available data) has been used as the basis of the graph in Figure 5, which shows the distribution of labour income for 15 Autonomous Communities in Spain (note that Spanish income tax considers as 'labour income' not only wages and salaries, but contributory pensions and unemployment benefits).

First, the great disproportion between the number of females and males in the labour market must be highlighted, since the former make up only 38.1 per cent of the total as compared with men, who make up 61.9 per cent of that total—that is, there are almost twice as many men as women participating in the labour market (see Table 3). Figure 5 clearly shows an asymmetric distribution biased towards men, with some exceptions for the group of labour-income earners who earn between €1800 and €9900

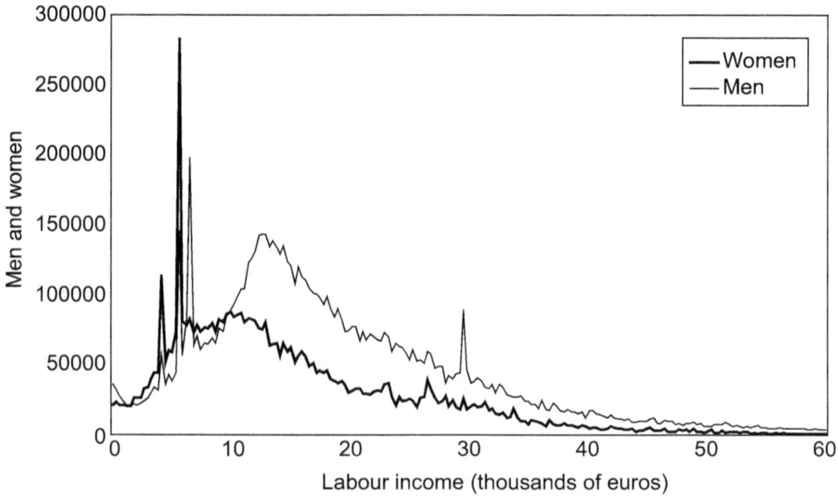

Figure 5: Distribution of Labour Income earned by Men and Women, 2004
Source: Author's representation of data from *Muestra IRPF 2004 IEF-AEAT, declarantes*

a year (but inside the group conversely there are more men than women for income between €6300 and €6900, as Table 4 shows).

All or some of the members of this group may have held jobs with an atypical legal workday (ie, part-time work) as the legal wage limit would not have permitted paying such low wage for a full day's work. These lower figures might also be attributable to payment received for a full-time job that was performed over a period of time shorter than a year—either sporadically and intermittently over this period or seasonally, owing to the kind of activity (agricultural or tourism, etc) performed.[13] Nevertheless, it must be stressed that the number of men and women is quite similar at the lower income levels, while it is possible to detect a greater male concentration in the income band between €12,000 and €24,000 (a distribution which shows a maximum in this bracket) (see Figure 6). In addition, according to statistics shown in Table 3, high incomes are earned mostly by males (260,947 men, as opposed to 43,785 women, had incomes higher than €60,000) and at incomes of €108,000 and higher, there are 88,051 returns from men as opposed to 9872 from women which means that nine out of ten income earners in this band are men (not shown in Table 3).

[13] These statistics refer to yearly amounts, but they do not reflect the kind of work carried out (part-time or full-time), nor do they reveal the type of employment contract (temporary or permanent).

Table 3: Distribution of Labour Income earned by Men and Women, 2004

Labour income (€)			Women	Men	Total	% Women	% Men
0	to	6,000	1,041,134	735,478	1,776,613	58.6	41.4
6,000	to	12,000	1,609,327	1,767,361	3,376,689	47.7	52.3
12,000	to	24,000	1,867,634	3,921,209	5,788,843	32.3	67.7
24,000	to	36,000	815,499	1,726,169	2,541,668	32.1	67.9
36,000	to	48,000	195,183	530,460	725,643	26.9	73.1
48,000	to	60,000	65,630	229,899	295,529	22.2	77.8
More	than	60,000	43,785	260,947	304,732	14.4	85.6
Total			5,638,193	9,171,524	14,809,717	38.1	61.9

Source: Author's representation of data from *Muestra IRPF 2004 IEF-AEAT, declarantes*

Table 4: Distribution of Labour Income earned by Men and Woman (detail up to €12,000) in 2004

Labour income (€)			No of women	No of men
0	to	300	20,994	35,632
300	to	600	22,949	32,433
600	to	900	20,786	27,518
900	to	1200	20,728	23,504
1200	to	1500	20,328	21,005
1500	to	1800	20,223	21,249
1800	to	2100	25,929	21,922
2100	to	2400	25,946	20,847
2400	to	2700	26,597	22,628
2700	to	3000	33,186	24,147
3000	to	3300	33,408	26,251
3300	to	3600	39,527	29,659
3600	to	3900	43,984	33,944
3,900	to	4200	44,505	31,213
4200	to	4500	113,906	57,266
4500	to	4800	52,049	35,922
4800	to	5100	60,239	42,835
5100	to	5400	58,816	38,153
5400	to	5700	73,428	43,982
5700	to	6000	283,605	145,368
6000	to	6300	80,797	56,478
6300	to	6600	77,735	82,246
6600	to	6900	82,357	197,643
6900	to	7200	72,613	64,087
7200	to	7500	78,188	70,290

(Continued)

Labour income (€)			No of women	No of men
7500	to	7800	73,810	60,698
7800	to	8100	76,183	65,427
8100	to	8400	75,892	64,327
8400	to	8700	79,724	69,166
8700	to	9000	73,868	65,418
9000	to	9300	82,130	75,553
9300	to	9600	80,264	73,723
9600	to	9900	85,895	84,485
9900	to	10,200	87,633	89,468
10,200	to	10,500	83,682	93,013
10,500	to	10,800	85,781	98,316
10,800	to	11,100	86,984	104,142
11,100	to	11,400	80,157	104,130
11,400	to	11,700	82,982	122,702
11,700	to	12,000	82,650	126,049

Source: Author's representation of data from *Muestra IRPF 2004 IEF-AEAT, declarantes*

This asymmetric distribution, from a gender perspective, may be seen more clearly in the density function diagram shown in Figure 6, which represents percentages of men and women earning the different levels of labour income.

The curve representing women's labour income (the thick line) is above the one for men (the thin line) for incomes up to €12,500, but beyond this level, the line representing women's income does not go above the line representing men's income again, except for some isolated peaks, specifically at €26,550 and €27,900. This is due to the large number of women who have found jobs as professionals in the public sector in recent years, and whose salaries match their status.[14] At the upper income levels, the line representing men's labour income is always higher than the line for women.

[14] For more information on this matter, see de Villota (2000).

The Impact of Income Tax Changes on Women's Labour Income

Figure 6 highlights the fact that women receive much lower incomes than men, in absolute terms and proportionally, and it reveals that the overall number of women participating in the labour market is lower than the number of men. This therefore demonstrates that the first marginal rates of the Personal Income Tax (PIT) will affect a higher proportion of women than men. Consequently, it may be stated unequivocally that any change in taxation that alters the lower bands of the tax scale will affect women to a greater degree, and if tax is reduced in the lower bands, a lower proportion of women will experience less tax pressure than men.

By superimposing the PIT taxation scale on the density function diagram shown in Figure 6, it is possible to obtain a complete picture of the impact of these rates of taxation on men and women (Figure 7). The diagrams in Figure 7 and Table 6 show the proportion of men and women affected by the different marginal rates—applied to the current rates in Spain—where it can be seen that women are concentrated at the lower marginal rates of 0 per cent and 15 per cent, respectively, while men outstrip women proportionally in the remaining taxation sections.

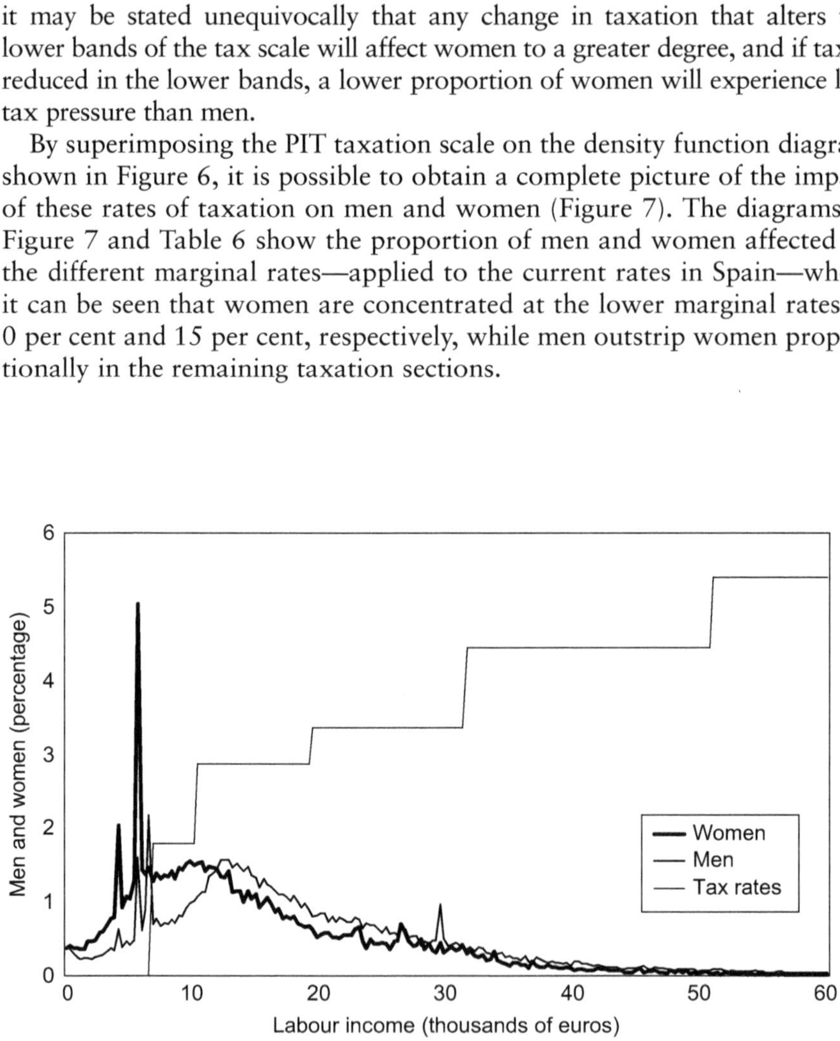

Figure 6: Percentage of Men and Women earning Different Levels of Labour Income, 2004

Source: Author's representation of data from *Muestra IRPF 2004 IEF-AEAT, declarantes*

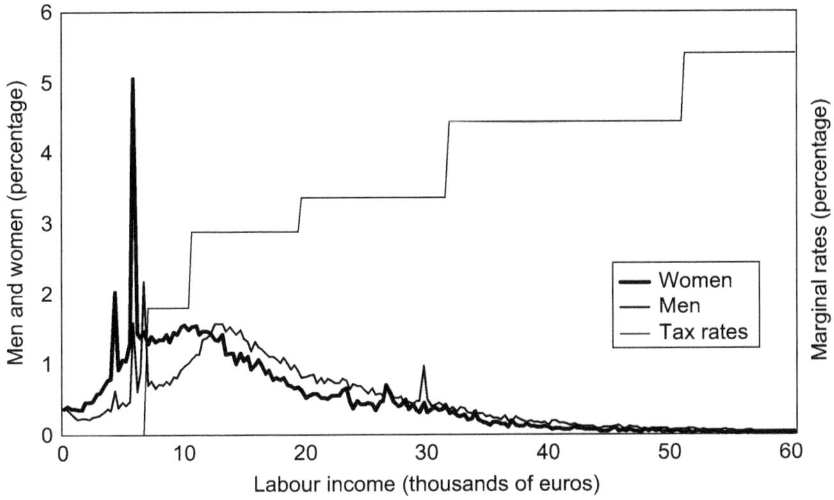

Figure 7: Marginal Tax Rates and Percentages of Men and Women earning Different Levels of Labour Income, 2004
Source: Author's representation of data from *Muestra IRPF 2004 IEF-AEAT, declarantes*

Table 5: Percentage of Men and Women earning Different Levels of Labour Income, 2004

Sections in thousands of €			% Women	% Men
0	to	6000	18.54	8.08
6000	to	12,000	28.65	19.41
12,000	to	24,000	33.25	43.06
24,000	to	36,000	14.14	18.24
36,000	to	48,000	3.47	5.83
48,000	to	60,000	1.17	2.52
More	than	60,000	0.78	2.87
Total			100.00	100.00

Source: Author's representation of data from *Muestra IRPF 2004 IEF-AEAT, declarantes*

The above analysis allows us to observe the impact of the latest PIT reforms on male and female workers, and these observations will be described in the following section.

Table 6: Distribution of Labour-income-earning Men and Women affected by PIT Marginal Rates, 2004

Tax marginal rate %	Women	Men	% Women	% Men
0.00	1,282,025	1,071,847	22.8	11.8
15.00	949,883	875,653	16.9	9.6
24.00	1,822,511	3,425,604	32.4	37.6
28.00	1,065,360	2,294,467	19.0	25.2
37.00	411,403	1,014,749	7.3	11.1
45.00	84,254	428,004	1.5	4.7
Total*	5,615,437	9,110,324	100.0	100.0

Source: Author's representation of data from *Muestra IRPF 2004 IEF-AEAT, declarantes*
*Returns with negative taxable income not included

The Gender Impact of the Latest PIT Reforms

To date, all changes made to PIT rates in Spain, from their original design in 1979 to the present day, have been implemented without consideration of their gender impact. The effects of these changes on the amount of tax collected have been analyzed in detail, as has the distribution of the tax burden among taxpayers, but the tax burden distribution has been seen as neutral because taxation is not viewed from a gender perspective.

Nevertheless, marginal rates have undergone continual changes throughout the lifecycle of the PIT, as shown in the following table (Table 7) which indicates the minimum and maximum marginal rates for the years 1979 to 2004.

Another vital aspect regarding the tax unit, or persons liable for payment of PIT, must not be overlooked. The fact is that until 1988 it was compulsory to file tax returns jointly in Spain. It is therefore extremely difficult, if not impossible, to measure the impact of lower rates of taxation on married women, as the latter were bound by the marginal rate of the principal breadwinner who was almost always the husband. The impact of the variation in the lower marginal rate affects all taxpayers, but it has the greatest effect on women because the reduction of the tax burden affects those with lower incomes proportionately more, and this is where women are more concentrated than men. For instance, 39.7 (22.8 + 16.9) per cent of women and 21.8 (11.8 + 9.6) per cent of men are taxed at the two lowest PIT marginal rates (see Table 6).

Table 7: Minimum and Maximum Marginal Tax Rates for the Years 1979–2004

Year	Minimum rate	Maximum rate
1979	15.00	43
1984	16.14	46
1985	8.00	46
1988	25.00	56
1992	20.00	56
1999	18.00	48
2004	15.00	45

In Table 7, a sharp drop may be observed in the minimum marginal rate in 1985 which undoubtedly led to a reduction in tax liability for taxpayers with lower incomes and this would apply particularly to single, divorced or widowed women workers. In contrast, in 1988—the first year that saw an application of the Constitutional Court's ruling that compulsory joint tax returns were unconstitutional,[15] the minimum rate rose to 25 per cent (representing an increase of 17 percentage points over the previous year), while the maximum marginal rate rose by 10 points, to 56 per cent. This extreme increase in rates resulted from the fear that the introduction of optional taxation might result in less tax being collected. The minimum rate of 25 per cent was maintained until 1992, when it was reduced to 20 per cent, and it remained unchanged until 1999, when the 1998[16] PIT reform was applied. This reform is still in force, although it has undergone some slight modifications, one of which was the reduction of the minimum marginal rate to 15 per cent, beginning in 2003.[17] Before the 1998 reform, the PIT instituted by Law 18/1991, which adapted the tax to the ruling of the Constitutional Court, continued to be applied, with a first marginal rate of 20 per cent. This translated into a reduction of five percentage points.

Law 40/1998 (which was passed on 1 January 1999, and remained in force until 2003 without any significant change) profoundly reformed the PIT and dismantled the basic tax scheme that had been valid for 20 years by converting tax credits for personal and family reasons to allowances and replacing the 'zero rate band' of the tax schedule with an allowance

[15] Ruling of 20 February 1989.
[16] Law 40/1998.
[17] Law 46/2002.

in taxable income called a 'personal minimum'. There is no doubt that those changes are regressive from the point of view of social equity, as they generate a tax reduction that increases with income level. This personal minimum proved to be arbitrary and discriminatory from a gender perspective, as it discriminated against one-parent families (the majority of which have women as their heads) as compared with two-parent families, and also because it eliminated the tax credit that favoured mothers with children under the age of three doing paid work outside the home. This measure was rectified by the reform brought about by Law 46/2002. (The impact of taxation on labour-market participation by female caregivers is also discussed in chapters by Scheiwe and Wersig, this volume.)

It must be pointed out, however, that Law 40/1998 improved women's tax situation in that the first marginal rate was decreased by two percentage points, leaving it at 18 per cent, and the next level was increased by one point (from 23 to 24 per cent). The taxpayers who benefited most, however, were those with the highest incomes, since the maximum marginal rate was drastically reduced, from 56 to 48 per cent. The following table (Table 8) shows the PIT marginal rates in 2002, the last year of the implementation of Law 40/1998.

The figures in Table 8 reveal that 21.0 per cent of female labour-income earners are not sufficiently remunerated to be liable for personal income tax (assuming earnings such as these are a woman's only income and that she files an individual tax return, rather than a joint one with her spouse).

Table 8: Distribution of Labour-income-earning Men and Women affected by PIT Marginal Rates, 2002

Marginal rate %	Women	Men	% Women	% Men
0.00	955,082	958,554	21.0	11.3
18.00	731,824	898,569	16.1	10.6
24.00	1,586,333	3,160,834	34.9	37.3
28.30	949,099	2,225,545	20.9	26.3
37.20	253,784	793,067	5.6	9.4
45.00	58,792	326,896	1.3	3.9
48.00	12,232	114,102	0.3	1.3
Total	4,547,147	8,477,567	100	100

Source: Author's representation of data from *Muestra IRPF 2002 IEF-AEAT, declarantes*

Should a woman opt for family taxation, her income would be liable to be taxed at the marginal rate of her spouse—that is, at a rate of at least 18 per cent. Those within this group who are entering the labour market for the first time, or who are re-entering it, would see their incomes taxed at a rate of at least 18 per cent, even though their incomes might possibly be so low as to be exempt from taxation if they filed separately. This would amount to the highest possible jump within the tax scale and would therefore represent an injustice for the affected taxpayers. In addition, a higher proportion of women are visible in the next bracket, corresponding to low wages liable to be taxed at the minimum rate of 18 per cent. In contrast, in the higher income brackets, men prevail in both absolute and relative terms. Table 8 also reveals that more than a third of women (21.0 + 16.1 per cent) are, or will be should their income increase, liable for inclusion in the 18 per cent rate, the first PIT bracket, as opposed to just 21.9 per cent of men (11.3 + 10.6 per cent).

Consequently, given the shape of the Spanish labour market,[18] variations in the minimum marginal income tax rate affect women predominantly, while any change in the highest marginal rates affect men to a greater degree, as they have higher incomes. It cannot be denied that any tax reform, like that of Law 40/1998, which reduces the highest marginal rates in the tax scale, has a definite gender impact and clearly benefits men—and vice versa. For instance, the tax modification introduced in Law 46/2002, which came into force from 2003 to 2006, lowered the minimum tax rate from 18 to 15 per cent, and this positively affected a greater proportion of women than men by reducing their tax burden. This, in turn, had the potential to motivate women to remain in the labour market. The reduction in tax rates of the first two brackets, after the fiscal reform of year 2003, along with a number of complementary measures, such as the increase in the personal minimum, have meant that 22.8 per cent of working women in 2004 are exempt from tax and 16.9 are liable at a marginal rate of 15 per cent (Table 6), which is an improvement with respect to the previous situation in 2002. On the other hand, the reduction of the upper marginal rate benefits 12,232 women, as opposed to 114,102 men (Table 8).

THE CONTINUANCE OF TRADITIONAL GENDERED DIVISIONS OF LABOUR

Given the persistence of patriarchal relations in Spain, the traditional gendered division of labour shapes the Spanish labour market at the present time,[19] thus maintaining and even exacerbating the asymmetrical distribution

[18] According to the data obtained for the Common Fiscal Territory.
[19] This conclusion is based on data obtained for the Common Fiscal Territory.

of domestic work. As a result, variations in the minimum marginal income tax rate predominantly affect women, while any change in the highest marginal rates affect men to a greater degree, as they have higher incomes. Consequently, it can be said that any tax reform that reduces the highest marginal rates in the tax scale has a definite gender impact and clearly benefits men. This was the effect of the reform brought about by Law 40/1998. Conversely, the tax modification introduced in Law 46/2002, which lowered the minimum tax rate from 18 to 15 per cent, positively affected a higher proportion of women than men by reducing their tax burden. This also had the potential of making women's contribution to paid work more attractive and therefore motivating them to participate, or to continue to participate, in the labour market. Although the latter reform improved the situation of many women, a number of issues still need to be addressed if Spain and Europe are to move towards complete gender equality. For example, measures need to be taken to deal with the issue of women's predominance in the lower tax brackets and with the fact that women in many European countries still do more daily domestic work than men. For instance, macroeconomic policies, including fiscal policy, should also be designed to prevent the persistent asymmetrical division of remunerated and non-remunerated work between genders that still exists in many European countries.

REFERENCES

Bakker, I and Elson, D (1998) 'Towards Engendering Budgets' in *Alternative Federal Budget Papers* (Ottawa, Canadian Centre for Policy Aternatives and Choices: A Coalition for Social Justice) 297.

Barnett, K and Grown, C (2004) *Gender Impacts of Government Revenue Collection: The Case of Taxation* (London, Commonwealth Secretariat).

Elson, D (2005) *Seguimiento de los Presupuestos Gubernamentales para el Cumplimiento de la CEDAW* (Washington, UNIFEM).

European Commission (1982) *First Community Action Programme for Equal Opportunities between Men and Women* (Brussels).

European Comission, EUROSTAT (2008) *Living Conditions in Europe. Data 2003–2006* (Luxembourg).

Gálvez Muñoz, L, Rodríguez Madroño, P and Domínguez Serrano, M (2009) 'A Comparative Analysis of "Total Work" by Gender in EU Countries and by Group of Welfare State Systems', paper presented at the 4th Symposium. Gender and Well-being: the Role of Institutions from Past to Present, Cost Action A-34 (Madrid, 25–28 June 2008). Available at: www.ub.es/tig/GWBNet/MadridPapers/Galvez%20et%20al.pdf.

Instituto de Estudios Fiscales (2006) *Muestra IRPF 2002 IEF-AEAT, declarantes* (Madrid).

—— (2008) *Muestra IRPF 2004 IEF-AEAT, declarantes* (Madrid).

Nussbaum, M (2003) 'Capabilities as Fundamental Entitlements: Sen and Social Justice' 9 *Feminist Economics* 33–59.

Parliament of the Commonwealth of Australia (1989) *Women's Budget Statement.*
Secretaría de Estado de Hacienda (2008) *Memoria de la Administración Tributaria, 2006* (Madrid, Ministerio de Economía y Hacienda).
Sen, A (1993) 'Capability and Well-being' in M Nussbaum and A Sen (eds), *The Quality of Life* (Oxford, Clarendon Press).
Spain (1998) *Empleo, salarios y pensiones en las fuentes tributarias, 1996* (Madrid, Instituto de Estudios Fiscales, Ministerio de Hacienda).
Tyazhelnikova, V (2006) 'The Value of Domestic Labour in Russia, 1965–1986' 21 *Continuity and Change* 159–93.
Villota, P (2000) *Análisis comparativo desde una perspectiva de género de la situación socioeconómica de las mujeres de la Comunidad de Madrid con el Estado español* (Madrid, Editorial de la Comunidad de Madrid).
—— (2004) *La imposición personal española desde una perspectiva de género Economía* (Mexico DF, Facultad de Economía de la Universidad Nacional Autónoma de México).
—— (2005a) 'Approach to Fiscal Policy from a Gender Viewpoint: The Cases of Germany and Spain' in E de Sotelo (ed), *New Women of Spain* (Münster, Lit Verlag).
—— (2005b) 'Fiscal Policies and Women's Employment in the EU' in M Jerneck, M Mörner, G Tortella and S Akerman (eds), *Different Paths to Modernity: A Nordic and Spanish Perspective* (Lund, Nordic Academic Press).
Villota, P and Ferrari, I (2004) *Aproximación al análisis de las figuras impositivas del sistema fiscal español desde una perspectiva de género* (Madrid, Instituto de la Mujer, serie Estudios, núm 80 Ministerio de Trabajo y Asuntos Sociales).
—— (2005) *Reflexiones sobre el IRPF desde la perspectiva de género: la discriminación fiscal del/de la segundo/a perceptor/a* (Madrid, Instituto de Estudios Fiscales, Ministerio de Economía y Hacienda). Available at: www.ief.es/Publicaciones/Investigaciones/Inves2004_09.pdf.
Villota, P et al (2008) *El Impuesto sobre la Renta de las Personas Físicas en Castilla y León desde la perspectiva de género. Una propuesta a favor de las mujeres asalariadas* (Valladolid, Consejo Económico y Social de Castilla y León). Available at: www.cescyl.es/pdf/coleccionestudios/Colecc08.pdf.
Walby, S (1986) *Patriarchy at Work: Patriarchal and Capitalist Relations in Employment, 1800–1984* (Oxford, Polity Press).
Wall, R (2009) 'Gender-Based Economic Inequalities and Women's Perceptions of Well-Being in Historical Populations' in B Harris, L Gálvez and H Machado (eds), *Gender and Well-Being in Europe: Historical and Contemporary Perspectives* (Burlington, Ashgate).

7

Gender and Taxation in Kenya: The Case of Personal Income and Value-added Taxes

BERNADETTE M WANJALA AND MAUREEN WERE

TAXATION IS ONE of the ways by which modern governments raise finances. In practice, there are three common objectives of tax systems: (1) to raise revenue to fund government operations; (2) to assist in the redistribution of wealth or income; and (3) to encourage or discourage certain activities through the use of tax provisions (Karingi and Wanjala 2005). The extent to which these objectives are met differs between countries. Countries worldwide have made considerable attempts to reform their tax systems, the impetus coming from the increasing complexity of the tax codes, narrow tax bases and concerns about horizontal equity.[1] One of the most important outcomes of Kenya's tax reform efforts is the fact that this country, unlike many other sub-Saharan African nations, is a high-tax-yield state with a tax-to-GDP ratio of over 20 per cent. The country is able to finance a large share of its budget so that external donor finances cover a much lower proportion of expenditures than is the case in other countries in the region. However, there are still major concerns regarding the impact and distribution of this tax burden among Kenyan citizens.

From a public finance perspective, tax systems are evaluated in terms of three main criteria: equity, efficiency and administrative ease. In this chapter, our fundamental concern is to analyze the Kenyan taxation system from a gender perspective and to identify any gender biases in the system by discovering who actually bears the burden of personal income taxes and value-added taxes. This involves asking what constitutes a fair distribution of the burden of a given tax between men and women. Emerging literature indicates that taxation policies are likely to affect men and women

[1] A system is horizontally equitable if persons or businesses in similar circumstances (in terms of welfare) have similar tax burdens.

differently, since they play different roles in society and also demonstrate different consumer behaviours (Barnett and Grown 2004). There have also been concerns worldwide that tax policy is biased against women because it tends to increase the incidence of taxation of the poorest women while failing to generate enough revenue to fund the programmes needed to improve these women's lives (Barnett and Grown 2004).

The government of Kenya acknowledges that the pace of development can best be accelerated and sustained if the creative and productive potential of both men and women is fully mobilized (Government of Kenya 2002). Attempts have also been made to engender the budgeting process, but as is the case in most economies, the focus has been on the expenditure side. Institutions such as the Department of Gender in the Ministry of Gender, Culture, Sports and Social Services and the National Commission on Gender and Development have been created, but there is no explicit policy on engendering the fiscal policy framework, especially with regard to taxation.

The scope of this chapter's analysis is limited to personal income tax and the value-added tax (VAT) for three reasons. First, these two taxes are important sources of government revenue, given their contribution to total revenue. For instance, income taxes accounted for about 38.5 per cent of total revenue in 2005, while the VAT accounted for 26 per cent over the same period. Secondly, the two taxes directly affect the majority of taxpayers, whereas the excise tax, for instance, is levied on only a few selected commodities. Lastly, our analysis is limited by the availability of gender-disaggregated data, which is insufficient to carry out comprehensive incidence analysis for all tax handles.

The next section provides a profile of men and women in Kenya, with the emphasis on employment, income and expenditure patterns. The chapter then reviews the structure and history of reform of both the personal income tax and the VAT, and discusses sources of possible gender bias in each. The final section analyzes gender disaggregated data on the incidence of the VAT on different households.

AN OVERVIEW OF SOCIO-DEMOGRAPHIC AND EXPENDITURE PROFILES OF MEN AND WOMEN IN KENYA

A description of the socio-demographic and expenditure patterns of men and women in Kenya will provide a basis for analyzing the relationship between gender and taxation. It will also help identify the gender impacts and biases resulting from the structure of the economy.

According to the 1999 census of Kenya's population, the proportions of men and women in the country are almost equal: 49.5 per cent and 50.5 per cent, respectively (Government of Kenya 2003). Males 0–14 years of age accounted for 22.1 per cent of the population, while females in this age bracket accounted for 21.6 per cent, although there are more females than males in the 35–64 years age bracket. Despite a slightly higher proportion of females in the active labour force age group (15–64 years), employment trends show that, on average, females constitute only 29 per cent of the total formal wage sector employment and earn 33 per cent less than their male counterparts (Government of Kenya 2006; Were and Kiringai 2004).

Statistics on wage employment by industry show that females were employed mainly in the education sector (27 per cent of total female employment), agriculture (15 per cent) and other services (12 per cent), while men dominated education, agriculture, manufacturing, trade, transport and communication (Government of Kenya 2006). In 2005, sectors with the highest levels of average wages were finance, insurance, real estate and business services; transport and communications; electricity and water; and trade, restaurants and hotels, respectively. These sectors are mainly male dominated, and this partly explains the discrepancies in incomes between males and females. There were 1,180,458 males earning more than 6000 Kenya shillings (Kshs) per month in 2004, as compared with only 502,758 females (Government of Kenya 2005b).

In terms of employment status, statistics indicate that about 80 per cent of poor females in 1998[2] were own account and unpaid family workers, whereas only 62 per cent of the males were in these categories (Government of Kenya 2000). For the non-poor households, males were predominantly skilled regular employees (28.3 per cent) and own account workers (36.4 per cent), while females were predominantly own account workers (43.5 per cent) and unpaid family workers (32.4 per cent).

A survey of the socio-demographic profile of Kenyan households with regard to gender reveals that a majority of households are male headed. According to the 1999 population census, only 37 per cent of the households were found to be female headed (Government of Kenya 2005b). This was the case mainly as a result of divorce, separation or widowhood.[3]

Wide disparities also exist in mean monthly expenditure patterns between poor and non-poor male-headed and female-headed households in both rural and urban areas (Government of Kenya 2000). While rural poor male-headed households were found to spend on average about 3188.5 Kshs on food, their female-headed counterparts spent 2405.2 Kshs (Government of Kenya 2000). Non-food expenditures were also higher for male-headed households than for female-headed households, for both the poor and the non-poor.

[2] These statistics were synthesised from the *Integrated Household Labour Force Survey Database* (Government of Kenya 1998).

[3] However, the existence of polygamy and the migration of husbands to urban centres to look for jobs complicates this definition.

This brief gender profile provides an indication of the likely incidence of taxes and also suggests that gender biases exist in the tax system. For instance, given that males dominate formal wage employment, it is expected that they would bear a larger income tax burden than females. In addition, the incidence of VAT payments will depend on existing expenditure patterns.

TAX STRUCTURE, TAX REFORMS AND IMPLICATIONS FOR GENDER EQUITY

Structure of the Personal Income Tax

This is a direct tax that is imposed on income derived from business, employment, rent, dividends, interest and pensions, among other sources (Government of Kenya 2004b, *The Kenya Income Tax Act, Cap 470*). Income from employment is taxed according to the pay-as-you-earn principle (PAYE), whereby the employer deducts tax directly from the employee's wages and remits that amount to the revenue authority at the end of each month.

The income tax structure is schedular, meaning that different types of income attract different rates. Each individual taxpayer is also required to file a tax return at the end of every calendar year, indicating a summary of all incomes, tax liability and the amount of tax that is collected at source (PAYE and withholding tax).

Personal Income Tax Reforms and Implications for Gender Equity

Major tax reforms in Kenya occurred under the Tax Modernisation Programme (TMP), which was initiated in the 1980s (Government of Kenya 1986). The impetus behind these reforms was mainly the need to restore buoyancy to revenues, reduce complexity in the tax system and address equity[4] in the distribution of tax burden, as well as in the composition of the tax structure. The TMP also aimed at strengthening tax administration, expanding the tax base and improving service delivery to taxpayers.

Reforms in the income tax system have taken place mainly in the areas of expanding the tax base, widening tax brackets and lowering top tax rates. Regular adjustments were made to tax brackets, largely to counter inflation creep, while marginal rates were lowered mostly to encourage savings for both households and enterprises. Income taxes in the pre-reform period (the 1960s and 1970s) were characterized largely by multiple tax brackets (eight during that period), with very high marginal tax rates (reaching 65 per cent). The multiple rates were used to achieve nominal progressivity,

[4] This did not necessarily include addressing gender equity.

guided by the principle that taxpayers should pay more income tax as a percentage of their income as they earn more. The number of brackets was gradually lowered to five and the top marginal rate reduced to 30 per cent in 2006/07. Empirical evidence indicates that the use of high and increasing marginal tax brackets and rates imposes a trade-off between growth and equity (Koester and Kormendi 1989; Mullen and Williams 1994; Becsi 1996; and Engen and Skinner 1996, quoted in Emes, Clemens, Basham and Samida 2001). High and increasing marginal tax rates have negative effects on economic growth mainly through their negative effects on savings and investments, which are key ingredients for long-term growth.

The way in which income tax returns are filed could result in gender bias. With individual filing, this bias might originate from several sources: allocation of non-labour and business income; allocation of tax preferences and allocation of tax rates (Stotsky 1996). Non-labour income may be allocated in several ways: attributing all of it to the higher earner, equal allocation between the spouses, allowing couples to decide on allocation or allocating the income to the spouse who has legal ownership of the enterprise. Business income may be allocated to either the husband or the wife, but in most cases, it is allocated to the husband. However, spouses may opt to declare income on the tax return of the spouse who pays a lower marginal tax rate, and this can be a form of tax avoidance. In the case of joint assessment, biases would exist if the couple moved into higher marginal tax rates, with the bias falling on whoever bears the additional tax burden resulting from movement into higher marginal tax brackets.

Kenya's experience reveals that, in the 1960s and 1970s, women's income was lumped together with the husband's for tax purposes. The practice was that the income of a married woman was deemed to be the income of the husband's for the purpose of determining his total annual taxable income. A wife who was engaged in gainful employment paid taxes on the basis of the PAYE system, which means that the taxes were directly deducted by her employer. However, at the end of each year, her income was lumped in with the husband's income, and since this moved her income into a high marginal tax bracket, it meant that she had underpaid her taxes through the PAYE system (Government of Kenya 1977/78 *Budget Statement*). The husband was then required to pay this liability. This shows that the filing system was biased against men, given that they had to bear the burden of the higher marginal rates resulting from lumping the husband's and wife's incomes together. However, starting on 1 January 1978, a system was devised whereby, with the written authorization of the wife, the tax could be deducted from her salary by her employer at a higher income tax rate to avoid the income tax arrears at income tax filing time. Therefore, the entire burden of joint filing was shifted to the wife (representing a gender bias against the wife).

In 1980, the wife's employment income was separated from the husband's for tax purposes. Further, the wife's professional income was separated from the husband's income in 1988/89 mainly to give impetus to women's professionalism and also to increase women's participation in formal employment. This meant that a woman's professional self-employment income was given the same treatment as a wife's employment income. The practice today is that the wife and husband are treated separately for tax purposes, even though there is still an option of joint filing.[5] In 2008–09, in order to grant women their own rights as taxpayers, women were allowed to declare income they had received from sources such as interest and rent (these had previously been declared by their husbands). The gender bias in joint filing has therefore been eliminated over time, except for the fact that the Kenyan tax system still assumes that a taxpayer is male as evidenced by the language used in the income tax return forms. Despite the assumption that most taxpayers are male, most women earning income file their tax returns separately.

Many reforms have also been made with regard to tax exemptions and other tax reliefs. In the 1960s and 1970s, the income tax system was characterized by exemptions and relief that varied according to the marital status[6] of an individual (married, single or special single—single with children) and also the individual's age. This differentiated structure of relief contained a discriminatory element, since married men had a higher level of relief than married women and single men and women. The probable reason behind such a policy was the assumption that high levels of relief for married men would benefit entire households. Over time, the levels of relief have gradually increased, the most significant reform being the unification of all types of relief into one in 1996–97, thereby removing the discriminatory element.

The main reason for increasing the level of relief (and, consequently, tax threshold) has been to exempt low-income earners. Statistics (Karingi and Wanjala, 2005) show that the income tax threshold is currently four times Kenya's national per capita income, which implies that a considerable number of taxpayers have fallen out of the tax net over time. Given that women constitute a smaller percentage of wage earners than do men[7] and that those who do engage in paid labour are mainly in the low-income cadre, it is expected that women are more likely to fall outside the direct income tax net and will therefore bear a smaller direct income tax burden than men. These gender differences are largely a result of the existing socio-economic structure.

[5] However, even with joint filing, the husband's and wife's incomes are not lumped together, and therefore they do not enter into higher marginal tax rates.

[6] Only married men were treated as married, while married women were in the category of singles (Government of Kenya 1994–95 *Budget Statement*).

[7] About 29% of total wage employment.

In addition to personal tax relief, special allowances have been made for individuals who were single but aged. For instance, in 1965–66, single men over 65 and single women over 60 were entitled to an allowance of about 8640 Kshs annually. No explicit justification was given for the difference in age threshold for men and women. However, these types of allowances were eliminated in the 1960s and have not featured in the tax system since then.

Allowances[8] and relief for households also varied, depending on the number of children. For instance, in 1964–65, the allowances for children were 1500 Kshs for a child under six years old and up to 5000 Kshs for a child over 17 years of age who was engaged in full-time post-secondary education. The maximum allowance per household was 9600 Kshs. Then, in 1965–66, to make the system less complex, allowances were unified at 2400 Kshs per child for up to four children per household (the maximum age being 19 years).[9] Children's allowances were given only to men. Even though women were not entitled to the allowance, any individual woman's income was lumped in with their husband's for tax purposes. Children's relief was incorporated into married relief in 1977–78, and this implied that all married couples were treated the same, regardless of the number of children they had.

The structure of income tax thresholds was similar to that of personal relief, varying according to marital status and number of children per household. For instance, in 1974–75, when the Income Tax Act was passed, the threshold exemption limit was 14,400 Kshs per annum for married individuals with four children, 7200 Kshs per annum for a married person with no children and 3600 Kshs for a single person or a single person with children. The exemption limit for married persons was four times higher than for singles, which implied that singles entered the tax net at much lower income levels than did married taxpayers. This could have had an effect on working incentives for singles. Meanwhile, these rates have been gradually increased, and the discriminatory element was removed when the rates were finally unified at 72,000 Kshs per annum in 1996–97.

The Structure of the Value-Added Tax (VAT)

When the VAT was introduced in Kenya in 1990, it replaced the sales tax and was charged on taxable goods or services made or provided in Kenya and on taxable goods or services imported into Kenya. At the time of the

[8] These are deductions from taxable income, not direct transfers. They have the effect of creating a reduction in taxable income.

[9] This implies that individuals with more than four children were disadvantaged.

VAT's introduction, the input credit system,[10] based on the destination principle,[11] was also adopted.

Under the VAT Act, there are three different classes of goods and services: designated, zero-rated and exempt[12] (Government of Kenya 2004b). Designated goods and services are those that are deemed taxable at other than the zero rate. The 2008–09 VAT structure has two main rates: the standard VAT rate, which is 16 per cent, and a lower rate of 12 per cent, which is applicable to supplied and imported electricity, energy and fuel oils. Several basic goods and services are exempt, which, as will be discussed in the next sections, has implications for reducing the regressivity of the VAT.

VAT Reforms

When it was introduced in 1990, the VAT had 15 rates, with a standard rate of 17 per cent. The highly complex system encouraged tax avoidance and evasion and also acted as a disincentive for both savings and investments especially for corporate taxpayers. The only advantage of having such a differentiated rate structure was that policy makers regarded the system as more progressive than the flat rate. The VAT Act can be said to be gender-blind, given that it applies only to goods and services, but it does have implicit gender biases, determined largely by consumption patterns.

The VAT's structure has changed over time, both in terms of the composition of the base and the rate structure. The number of rates was reduced from 15 at inception to only 3 by 2003–04. The standard rates have also been changed over time, ranging mainly between 18 per cent and 15 per cent. These reforms occurred for various reasons. The major objective was to improve administrative efficiency through rationalization of rates. Other objectives were to remove misclassification and ease administration, improve compliance, reduce smuggling and reduce requests for exemptions. The continued rationalization of rates has involved both lowering the top rate and reducing the number of tax rates.

As for the tax base, its composition has changed over time. Most of these changes did not have direct implications for gender equality. However, various policy reforms were carried out that would have an implicit impact on gender equality. For instance, reducing a tax on cooking energy (charcoal, kerosene, cooking gas and electricity) has implicit

[10] According to the input credit system, all VAT registrants are obliged to collect and remit the VAT on their taxable goods and services, with an allowance to recover tax paid on purchases made on items needed to carry out the business that is VAT registered.

[11] According to the VAT destination principle, goods are VATable when they reach their destination, and this implies that exports are not VATable in their country of origin.

[12] Goods and services that are zero-rated are deemed taxable but at the rate of zero per cent, while exempt goods and services are not taxable.

benefits for women more than for men, given that the women are the main consumers of cooking energy. These have been addressed in the Kenyan tax system through reduction of the VAT on kerosene in 1991–92, exemption of domestic electricity consumption of less than 200 kilowatts per month and eventual zero-rating of the same in 2001–02, lowering of VAT on sanitary towels in 1998–99 as well as eventual zero-rating in 2004–05 and exemption of liquefied petroleum gas in 2004–05. The objectives of these measures were varied, but they were carried out mainly in tandem with poverty alleviation and energy conservation strategies. The VAT on sanitary towels was lowered in 1998–99, a move that was widely applauded, but this change had a major limitation in that the majority of Kenya's poor cannot afford sanitary towels, therefore limiting the effectiveness of the measure in achieving gender equality. In 1996–97, there was a move to exempt basic commodities such as wheat, wheat flour, bread, maize and maize flour, rice and milk, but this was mainly to ease administration of the VAT, not to address the regressivity of the tax. Only in 2000–01 was it acknowledged that these exemptions could act as relief for low-income earners.

VAT INCIDENCE ANALYSIS

Consumption taxes are widely considered to be highly regressive (Bird and Miller 1989; Bourguignon and Da Silva 2003; Cnossen 2003; Entin 2004; Fullerton and Metcalf 2002; Martinez-Vazquez 2001; Metcalf 2006; Zodrow 1999). It is argued that the burden is higher for low-income individuals because they spend a higher percentage of their income on consumption than do high-income individuals. Countries that maintain progressive tax systems therefore take several measures to remove the regressivity of the VAT. These measures include (1) exempting food and social necessities and (2) taxing luxuries at higher rates and necessities at lower rates. Of the 105 countries that have a VAT, about 50 developing countries exempt foodstuffs from tax, while 26 (mainly industrialized economies) apply reduced rates (Cnossen 2003).

As discussed above, rationalization of VAT rates in Kenya (including zero rating and exempting of basic commodities) was carried out not only to simplify the tax system, but to reduce its regressivity. However, this approach of reducing the tax burden on the poor through exemptions and zero rating has been found to be unsound in some countries. For instance, findings from the Katz Commission[13] into Tax Reform in South Africa in 1994 indicated that 'providing relief to the poor through exemptions and

[13] *Commission of Inquiry into Certain Aspects of the Tax Structure of South Africa.*

VAT zero-rating was likely to be both unsound policy and ineffective social policy'. This is because poorer households spend much less than richer households in absolute terms, and richer households tend to buy more expensive varieties of food. These findings have also been confirmed in other countries, such as Ireland and New Zealand (Cnossen 2003).

From a gender perspective, the biases in the VAT are mainly implicit and could arise through preferential treatment on some products (zero rating or exemption of specific items) or through differential consumption patterns by men and women. There is a general belief that women spend more of their income on basic services than men do and that they would therefore bear a greater burden if basic commodities were not exempted or zero-rated (Barnett and Grown 2004).

How does the VAT tax burden vary with gender in Kenya? To answer this question, we conducted an incidence analysis to determine how the VAT tax burden is distributed across individuals. From a gender perspective, this involves calculation of how much tax males and females pay, based on their levels of expenditure. For this particular analysis, an expenditure measure of tax burden (in monetary terms) was used as opposed to an income measure. This was done for three main reasons (See Bird and Miller (1989) for further details). First, primary data on expenditures is more reliable than data on incomes. Secondly, expenditures are more objectively observed and more understandable than consumption levels and income measures. Thirdly, expenditures provide a better measure of wellbeing especially with respect to the poor, since they fluctuate less than their income, given that the poor mostly smoothen consumption.[14] To carry out incidence analysis, household data on consumption patterns from the *Kenya Integrated Household Budget Survey* Database was used (Government of Kenya 2005c). Several assumptions are required for an incidence analysis. Conventional incidence analysis assumes that the final burden of direct taxes is borne by factors of production (labour and capital), while indirect taxes are borne by consumers (Elson 2006; Martinez-Vazquez 2001; Stotsky 1996). It is therefore assumed that indirect taxes on goods are shifted entirely to consumers if markets are competitive and taxes apply to final sales, so that consumers bear the tax burden in proportion to their purchases of taxable goods (Bird and Miller 1989; Elson 2006; Martinez-Vazquez 2001). The statutory tax burden can be computed by multiplying the base (expenditure in this case) with the statutory tax rate. The rates that we applied are as specified under the VAT

[14] Most poor households maintain a more constant pattern of consumption even in cases of lower incomes by, for instance, borrowing or relying on remittances from other family members.

Act,[15] whereby goods and services are characterized as either designated, exempt or zero-rated. For *ad valorem* rates, the tax paid is given as:

$$T_{i,j} = t_j p_{i,j}\, x_{i,j} = \frac{t_j}{1+t_j}\, e_{i,j}$$

Where $T_{i,j}$ is household i's total loss in purchasing power for a tax on good j; $p_{i,j}x_{i,j}$ is household i's pre-tax amount of expenditure on good j; t_j is the tax rate; and $e_{i,j}$ is the post-tax amount of expenditure on good j. The tax burden is then computed as the ratio of the tax payable ($T_{i,j}$) to total expenditure. The incidence analysis is based on the ability to pay principle, which implies that those with higher incomes should pay a larger share of the tax burden than low-income individuals (see Entin 2004, Fullerton and Metcalf 2002, Metcalf 2006, Zodrow 1999). This concept implies that a tax system should be progressive. In the case of a tax on goods and services, a tax is said to be progressive if the tax burden (ratio of tax payable to total expenditure) rises with expenditure, regressive if it falls with expenditure and proportional if it remains constant, no matter what the level of expenditure (adopted from Bird and Miller, 1989).

Given that the incidence of a tax depends on consumption patterns, it is important to analyze the consumption patterns of the different categories of households before computing their level of tax burden. The data shows that the proportion of food expenditure to total expenditure increases by quintiles, which are based on per capita household expenditure (Table 1). Quintile 1 represents the lowest level of expenditure, while quintile 5 represents the highest level of expenditure. This could be attributed to the fact that most poor households, mainly rural, consume un-marketed production, which is not included in their expenditure basket. In addition, there is no significant difference between the male-headed and female-headed households, or between rural and urban areas.

The incidence analysis was carried out at two levels. First, it was assumed that all goods and services were designated and were therefore taxable at the same standard rate. Secondly, the rate structure of designated, exempt and zero-rated, which depicts the current VAT structure, was applied. This comparison reflects how the distribution of the tax burden is affected by zero rating, exemptions and use of a differentiated tax-rate structure. Different levels of household classification were adopted: (a) by gender and per capita expenditure quintiles; (b) by gender, whether the individual was

[15] Since the 2005 *Household Database* was used, we applied the 2005–06 tax rates. The 2005–06 VAT structure has two main rates: the standard VAT rate, which is 16%, and a lower rate of 14%, which is applicable to hotels and restaurant services. Also included under the 14% are accommodation and all other services provided by hotel owners or operators, including telecommunications, entertainment, laundry, dry cleaning, storage, safety deposits and conference and business services.

Table 1: Household Consumption Patterns

Household category	Food	Non-food	Total
Male-rural—1st quintile	63.93	36.07	100.00
Male-rural—2nd quintile	71.17	28.83	100.00
Male-rural—3rd quintile	95.60	4.40	100.00
Male-rural—4th quintile	98.27	1.73	100.00
Male-rural—5th quintile	99.06	0.94	100.00
Male-urban—1st quintile	61.62	38.38	100.00
Male-urban—2nd quintile	79.02	20.98	100.00
Male-urban—3rd quintile	84.58	15.42	100.00
Male-urban—4th quintile	97.93	2.07	100.00
Male-urban—5th quintile	99.18	0.82	100.00
Female-rural—1st quintile	59.70	40.30	100.00
Female-rural—2nd quintile	69.60	30.40	100.00
Female-rural—3rd quintile	95.56	4.44	100.00
Female-rural—4th quintile	98.56	1.44	100.00
Female-rural—5th quintile	98.58	1.42	100.00
Female-urban—1st quintile	76.23	23.77	100.00
Female-urban—2nd quintile	76.50	23.50	100.00
Female-urban—3rd quintile	83.45	16.55	100.00
Female-urban—4th quintile	97.45	2.55	100.00
Female-urban—5th quintile	99.42	0.58	100.00

Source: Authors' computation based on KIHBS 2005.

farming or not and without regard to size of agricultural land; and (c) by gender and marital status.

In the 2005 *Kenya Integrated Household Budget Survey*, the head of the household is defined as the individual who is the key decision maker in the household. In this case, an economic provider is not necessarily the household head. Age plays a major role, as the oldest adult male is often considered to be the head of the household. Following this definition, female-headed households are therefore those where adult males are not present (ie, the male could be working in urban areas; the woman could be separated or divorced; the home could be polygamous, with the man living away from the household; or the woman could be single).

Looking at the tax structure, the analysis reveals that, except for the fifth quintile, which represents the highest total expenditure, over 80 per cent of food consumption is exempted from the VAT, as compared with less than 10 per cent of non-food consumption (Table 2). Consequently, smaller proportions of food expenditures are taxable as compared with over 80 per cent of non-food expenditures. Generally, except for the second quintile, the percentage of exempt expenditures slightly decreases with the level of total food expenditure, while it increases for non-food expenditure. Thus, the tax system that applies to food items can be said to be neutral or slightly progressive, while taxation of non-food items is regressive.

Table 2: Share of Exempt, Zero-rated and Taxable Expenditures for Food and Non-food items

	Exempt	Zero-rated	Taxable	Total
Food expenditures				
1st quintile	88.67	12,000	28.65	100.00
2nd quintile	90.50	24,000	33.25	100.00
3rd quintile	89.74	36,000	14.14	100.00
4th quintile	89.78	48,000	3.47	100.00
5th quintile	78.72	60,000	1.17	100.00
Non-food expenditures				
1st quintile	3.49	5.29	91.22	100.00
2nd quintile	6.30	8.15	85.55	100.00
3rd quintile	7.31	10.30	82.39	100.00
4th quintile	9.93	10.67	79.40	100.00
5th quintile	20.73	11.80	67.47	100.00

Source: Author's computation based on KIHBS, 2005

Table 3 shows the VAT tax burden for food consumption by sex of the household head and region. When zero-rated or exempted, households in lower expenditure quintiles (ie, the first quintile) bear a slightly higher tax burden on food consumption as compared with the case for the higher quintiles. Without exemptions or zero-rating, proportionate tax burden

Table 3: VAT Burden for Food Consumption by Region and by Sex of Household Head

Household category	Tax burden with zero rating and exemptions	Tax burden without zero rating and exemptions
Male-rural—1st quintile	2.39	15.0
Male-rural—2nd quintile	1.49	14.8
Male-rural—3rd quintile	1.57	15.3
Male-rural—4th quintile	1.75	16.0
Male-rural—5th quintile	2.78	16.0
Male-urban—1st quintile	2.17	14.7
Male-urban—2nd quintile	1.99	14.2
Male-urban—3rd quintile	1.96	13.5
Male-urban—4th quintile	1.82	15.9
Male-urban—5th quintile	3.66	16.0
Female-rural—1st quintile	2.11	15.2
Female-rural—2nd quintile	1.21	15.5
Female-rural—3rd quintile	1.22	15.8
Female-rural—4th quintile	1.15	16.0
Female-rural—5th quintile	1.35	16.0
Female-urban—1st quintile	1.69	15.3
Female-urban—2nd quintile	1.55	15.1
Female-urban—3rd quintile	1.12	15.0
Female-urban—4th quintile	1.14	15.9
Female-urban—5th quintile	2.36	16.0

Source: Authors' computation based on KIHBS 2005.

for food consumption generally increases with expenditure quintiles. This implies that lack of exemptions and zero rating results in a more progressive tax structure than does exempting and zero rating. For male-headed households, the tax in the case of zero rating and exemptions is generally slightly higher in urban areas than in rural areas, but the trend is mixed for female-headed households.

Table 4 shows the VAT tax burden for food consumption by sex of household head, whether the household is farming or not, and in the case of farming, the size of the agricultural land. Without zero rating and exemption of food items, the tax burden is higher for female-headed households than for male-headed households. Female-headed households who do not own any land bear the greatest VAT burden. With zero rating and exemptions on most food items, male-headed households bear a greater tax burden than do female-headed households, with male-headed households who farm on more than five owned acres bearing the greatest VAT burden. For households with owned land in the category of zero rating and/or exemptions, the VAT burden is higher for male landowners than for females. Since land ownership is a sign of wealth, the higher tax burden carried by landowners (a majority of whom are male) would imply progressivity of the VAT system.

Table 4: VAT Burden for Food Consumption by Sex of Household Head, whether Farming or not and According to Size of Agricultural Land

Household category	Tax burden with zero rating and exemptions	Tax burden without zero rating and exemptions
Male-farming—no land	1.96	14.4
Male-farming—0.1 to 5 acres	2.20	15.2
Male-farming—5.1 acres to 10 acres	2.40	15.2
Male-farming—>10 acres	2.44	15.0
Male-not farming—no land	2.21	15.3
Female-farming—no land	0.73	16.0
Female-farming—0.1 to 5 acres	1.54	15.5
Female-farming—5.1 acres to 10 acres	1.78	15.4
Female-farming—>10 acres	1.09	15.8
Female-not farming—no land	1.50	15.7

Source: Authors' computation based on KIHBS 2005.

Table 5 shows that without tax exemptions or zero rating, the tax burden is highest for female-headed households where the women are divorced/separated, widowed or never married. The tax burden is much lower for males who are divorced/separated, widowed or never married. The reverse applies for cases where food consumption items are exempted or zero-rated, as male-headed households where the man is divorced/separated, widowed or never married bear the greatest burden, especially males who have never married bearing the highest burden of all. This can arguably be attributed to unmarried men's habit of eating out—which implies more expenditure on food.

Table 6 shows the VAT tax burden for non-food consumption by region and by sex of the household head. The tax burden with zero rating or exemptions decreases with quintiles, with those in the upper quintiles of total expenditure incurring lower tax burdens. This could imply that it is the non-poor who benefit from zero-rated or tax-exempted non-food products. In the literature, it has been argued that zero rating and exemption of non-food items will not have a major distributional impact because it is applied uniformly across all households, suggesting that both poor and rich households would benefit from the zero rating or exemption of commodities (Bird and Miller 1989; Bourguignon

Table 5: VAT Burden for Food Consumption by Sex of Household Head and Marital Status

Household category	Tax burden with zero rating and exemptions	Tax burden without zero rating and exemptions
Male—monogamous/living together	1.97	15.4
Male—polygamous	1.97	14.7
Male—separated/divorced	3.41	14.1
Male—widower	2.77	14.3
Male—never married	4.74	13.0
Female—monogamous/living together	1.38	15.1
Female—polygamous	1.61	14.4
Female—separated/divorced	1.45	15.5
Female—widow	1.49	15.6
Female—never married	2.02	15.5

Source: Authors' computation based on KIHBS 2005.

Table 6: VAT Burden for Non-food Consumption by Region and by Sex of Household Head

Household category	Tax burden with zero rating and exemptions	Tax burden without zero rating and exemptions
Male-rural—1st quintile	14.48	16.00
Male-rural—2nd quintile	13.48	16.00
Male-rural—3rd quintile	12.78	15.97
Male-rural—4th quintile	12.33	15.99
Male-rural—5th quintile	9.92	15.95
Male-urban—1st quintile	15.07	16.00
Male-urban—2nd quintile	14.25	15.96
Male-urban—3rd quintile	14.21	16.03
Male-urban—4th quintile	12.96	16.00
Male-urban—5th quintile	11.04	16.04
Female-rural—1st quintile	14.83	16.00
Female-rural—2nd quintile	13.87	16.00
Female-rural—3rd quintile	13.43	16.02
Female-rural—4th quintile	12.47	16.01
Female-rural—5th quintile	10.73	16.04
Female-urban—1st quintile	14.88	16.00
Female-urban—2nd quintile	14.65	16.00
Female-urban—3rd quintile	12.79	15.97
Female-urban—4th quintile	14.11	15.98
Female-urban—5th quintile	12.82	16.00

Source: Authors' computation based on KIHBS 2005.

and Da Silva 2003; Cnossen 2003; Entin 2004; Fullerton and Metcalf 2002; Martinez-Vazquez 2001; Metcalf 2006 and Zodrow 1999). However, it is also often argued by analysts that richer households would consume more expensive non-food items, implying that the overall tax burden would be less regressive as expected.

Table 6 also indicates that the tax burden is generally higher for those in urban areas (both male and female) than those in rural areas. This is mainly because rural households consume unmarketed or own-production commodities, which are not captured in the tax basket. This makes their total consumption of non-food items generally lower than that of their urban counterparts. However, compared with male-headed urban households, the tax burden for female-headed urban households with zero rating or exemptions is generally higher (especially for the fourth and fifth quintiles). On the other hand, the tax burden without zero rating is slightly higher for male-headed urban households at higher quintiles (the third to fifth quintiles). Hence, zero rating and exemptions seem to favour products mainly consumed by men at higher expenditure levels.

Table 7 shows the VAT tax burden for non-food consumption by sex of household head, whether farming or not and according to size of agricultural land. The tax burden with zero rating and exemptions is higher for female-headed households (regardless of whether farming or not or with land or not). For both female-headed and male-headed households, those farming but with no land bear the highest tax burden—and the burden is

Table 7: VAT Burden for Non-food Consumption by Sex of Household Head, whether Farming or not and According to Size of Agricultural Land

Household category	Tax burden with zero rating and exemptions	Tax burden without zero rating and exemptions
Male-farming—no land	13.67	16.00
Male-farming—0.1 to 5 acres	11.70	16.01
Male-farming—5.1 acres to 10 acres	12.11	16.01
Male-farming—>10 acres	9.39	16.01
Male-not farming—no land	11.19	15.99
Female-farming—no land	14.93	16.00
Female-farming—0.1 to 5 acres	12.31	16.00
Female-farming—5.1 acres to 10 acres	13.03	15.97
Female-farming—>10 acres	9.82	16.01
Female-not farming—no land	13.11	16.03

Source: Authors' computation based on KIHBS 2005.

slightly higher for females (14.93 per cent) than for males (13.67 per cent). However, the tax burden decreases, in general, as land size increases. In the case of tax burden without zero rating and exemptions, there are no significant differences between female- and male-headed households.

Table 8 shows, in terms of marital status, the tax burden for non-food consumption with zero rating and exemptions is highest for never-married females (13.63 per cent) and for the separated or divorced—both for males (13.21 per cent) and for females (13.81 per cent). The tax burden in this category for female-headed households where the women are in monogamous marriages is slightly higher (12.84 per cent) than for male-headed households where the men are in monogamous marriages (11.84 per cent). Similarly, with zero rating and exemptions, the tax burden on females who have never married is much higher (13.63 per cent) than on males who have never married. This clearly demonstrates the differences in the consumption patterns of men and women. For example, women would spend more on personal care effects than men. It is therefore not surprising that even with zero rating, their tax burdens are higher, since most of these products are not exempted or zero-rated.

Table 8: VAT Burden for Non-food Consumption by Sex of Household Head and Marital Status

Household category	Tax burden with zero rating and exemptions	Tax burden without zero rating and exemptions
Male—monogamous/living together	11.84	15.99
Male—polygamous	9.48	16.00
Male—separated/divorced	13.21	15.97
Male—widower	11.34	15.99
Male—never married	9.51	15.99
Female—monogamous/living together	12.84	16.01
Female—polygamous	11.64	16.02
Female—separated/divorced	13.81	15.97
Female—widow	11.85	16.01
Female—never married	13.63	16.00

Source: Authors' computation based on KIHBS 2005.

CONCLUSION

In this chapter, we have examined the gendered impact of taxation in Kenya, with a focus on personal income tax and the Value Added Tax (VAT). From the analysis, it has been shown that numerous efforts have been undertaken to reform the tax system, and in most cases, these changes have been found to promote gender equality. For personal income taxes, effective progressivity has been achieved through a flatter tax structure, accompanied by a more gender-equal structure of exemptions and reliefs (even though some implicit differences still exist). The personal income tax structure of the 1960s, 1970s and 1980s was gender biased, given that lumping the incomes of husband and wife together moved the couple into higher marginal tax brackets. The structure of exemptions and relief was based on marital status, number of children and age of the taxpayer, which were avenues for discrimination. But the evolution of the personal income tax structure has resulted in a more unified tax structure (including tax rate, tax exemptions and relief).

For food consumption, VAT incidence analysis indicates that households in lower expenditure quintiles bear slightly higher tax burdens, even with zero rating or exemptions, implying that the VAT is still regressive despite the exemptions and zero rating of basic commodities. The tax burden is also slightly higher for male-headed households, especially in urban areas. However, without zero rating or exempting certain food items from taxation, the tax burden would be higher for female-headed households than for male-headed households, especially for females who do not own any land. Hence, women would benefit more than men from zero rating and tax exemptions on food items, since they are likely to spend more on food than their male counterparts.

For non-food consumption, the tax burden is higher for urban households (both male and female) than for those in rural areas. However, compared with male-headed urban households, female-headed urban households bear a slightly higher tax burden with zero rating or exemptions at higher quintiles. Hence, male-headed urban households benefit more from the zero rating and exemptions applied to non-food items than do female-headed urban households. The regime seems to favour products consumed mainly by men over products consumed mainly by women at higher expenditure levels. Moreover, regarding non-food items, the tax burden borne by single, never-married females is much higher (13.63) than for single, never-married males, depicting gender differences in consumption patterns and the unique non-food consumption needs of women. In general, the tax burden on food items is slightly less regressive than the tax burden on non-food items.

Gender and taxation continue to form part of the public finance policy debate worldwide, as the gender blindness of taxation has become a growing concern. In this chapter, we have sought to contribute to the debate by showing that the Kenyan tax policies are not gender-neutral, as previously assumed. We hope that as a starting point, this study will serve as a platform for further research in the area of gender and taxation. The study was largely constrained by lack of adequate data for incidence analysis and lack of adequate information for more elaborate classification of households, given the debate about the definition of household headship. Other appropriate ways of classifying households could be pursued in future research activities, such as exploring further the heterogeneity of female household headship.

REFERENCES

Barnett K and Grown, C (2004) *Gender Impacts of Government Revenue Collection: The Case of Taxation* (London, Commonwealth Secretariat).

Besci, Z (1996) 'Do State and Local Taxes Affect Relative State Growth?' 81 *Federal Reserve Bank of Atlanta Economic Review* 2, 18–36.

Bird, RM and Miller, BD (1989) 'The Incidence of Indirect Taxes on Low-Income Households in Jamaica' in J Strauss (ed), *Economic Development and Cultural Change* (Chicago, University of Chicago Press) 393–409.

Bourguignon, F and Da Silva, LAP (2003) 'Evaluating Poverty and Distributional Impact of Economic Policies: A Compendium of Existing Techniques' in F Bourguignon and LAP Da Silva (eds), *The Impact of Economic Policies on Poverty and Income Distribution: Evaluation Techniques and Tools* (Washington, DC, World Bank).

Cnossen, S (2003) 'The Incidence of Consumption Taxes in Member Countries of the South African Development Community', paper prepared for the Southern African Conference on Excise Taxation (Gauteng, South Africa).

Elson, D (2006) *Budgeting for Women's Rights: Monitoring Government Budgets for Compliance with CEDAW* (New York, United Nations Development Fund for Women (UNIFEM)).

Emes, J, Clemens, J, Basham, P and Samida, D (2001) 'Critical Issues Bulletin on Flat Tax Principles and Issues' (The Fraser Institute, Canada). Available at: old-fraser.lexi.net/publications/critical_issues/2001/flat_tax/index.html.

Engen, E and Skinner, J (1996) 'Taxation and Economic Growth' Working Paper no 5826 (Cambridge, National Bureau of Economic Research).

Entin, SJ (2004) 'Tax Incidence, Tax Burden, and Tax Shifting: Who Really Pays the Tax?' A Report of the Heritage Centre for Data Analysis (Washington, DC, The Heritage Foundation) CDA04-12.

Fullerton, D and Metcalf, GE (2002) 'Tax Incidence' in AJ Auerbach and M Feldstein (eds), *Handbook of Public Economics* vol 4 (New York, Elsevier Science BV) ch 26, 1787–1872.

Karingi, S and Wanjala, B (2005) 'The Tax Reform Experience in Kenya' Research Paper no 2005/67 (World Institute for Development Economics Research of the United Nations University, (UNU-WIDER), Helsinki, Finland).

Kenya, Government of (1986) *Sessional Paper No 1 of 1986 on Economic Management for Renewed Growth* (Nairobi, Government Printers).

—— (1994–95) *Budget Statement*.

—— (1997–98) *Budget Statement.*
—— (1998) *Integrated Household Labour Force Survey Database.*
—— (2000) Ministry of Finance and Planning *Second Report on Poverty in Kenya: Poverty and Social Indicators* (Nairobi, Government Printers).
—— (2002) *National Development Plan 2002–2008* (Nairobi, Government Printers).
—— (2003) Central Bureau of Statistics *Report of the 1998/99 Labourforce Survey* (Nairobi, Government Printers).
—— (2004a (rev edn) *The Value Added Tax Act, Cap 476.*
—— (2004b) (rev edn) *The Kenya Income Tax Act, Cap 470.*
—— (2005a) *Statistical Abstract* (Nairobi, Government Printers).
—— (2005b) *Geographic Dimensions of Well-Being in Kenya: Who and Where are the Poor? A Constituency Level Profile* (Nairobi, The Regal Press Kenya Ltd).
—— (2005c) *Kenya Integrated Household Budget Survey* Database (KIHBS).
—— (2006) *Economic Survey.*
Koester, R and Kormendi, R (1989) 'Taxation, Aggregate Activity and Economic Growth: Cross-Country Evidence on Some Supply-Side Hypotheses' 27 *Economic Inquiry* 367–86.
Martinez-Vazquez, J (2001) 'The Impact of Budgets on the Poor: Tax and Benefit Incidence' Working Paper no 01-10 (Andrew Young School of Policy Studies, International Studies Program, Georgia State University).
Metcalf, GE (2006) 'Tax Incidence' Working Paper Series (Tufts University, Department of Economics). Available at: ase.tufts.edu/econ/papers/200607.pdf.
Mullen, J and Williams, M (1994) 'Marginal Tax Rates and State Economic Growth' 24 *Regional Science and Urban Economics* 687–705.
Stotsky, JG (1996) 'Gender Bias in Tax Systems', IMF Working Paper no 96/99. Available at: ssrn.com/abstract=882995.
Were, M and Kiringai, J (2004) 'Gender Mainstreaming in Macroeconomic Policies and Poverty Reduction Strategy in Kenya' in LM Wanyeki and A Patel (eds), *GTZ/African Women's Development and Communication Network (FEMNET)*: Available online at: www.femnet.or.ke/documents/gender_mainstreaming.pdf.
Zodrow, GR (1999) 'Incidence of Taxes' in JJ Cordes, RD Ebel and JG Gravelle (eds), *The Encyclopaedia of Taxation and Tax Policy* (Washington, DC, Urban Institute Press).

Part III

The Family in Tax Policy

8

Dismembering Families

ANTHONY C INFANTI*

> The concept of the body politic is not new. Elaborate organic images for human society were richly developed by the Greeks. They conceived the citizen, the city, and the cosmos to be built according to the same principles. To perceive the body politic as an organism, as fundamentally alive and as part of a large cosmic organism, was central for them. To see the structure of human groups as a mirror of natural forms has remained imaginatively and intellectually powerful.
>
> The union of the political and the physiological ... has been a major source of ancient and modern justifications of domination, especially of domination based on differences seen as natural, given, inescapable, and therefore moral.
>
> (Haraway 1991: 7–8) (citation omitted from original quotation)

IN THE ESSAY from which I took this excerpt, Donna Haraway, a professor of the history of consciousness and feminist studies at University of California–Santa Cruz, cautions us not to underestimate the extent to which 'the principle of domination is deeply embedded in our natural sciences', especially 'if we are to work effectively for societies free from domination' (1991: 8). This cautionary note set me to thinking about the primary place where science intersects with the individual US federal income tax—that is, in the deduction for medical expenses under section 213 of the Internal Revenue Code (26 USC section 213). By chance, as I was reading this essay and pondering its implications for the medical expense deduction, I also happened to be watching same-sex couples around me expand their families with the help of assisted reproductive technologies (for example, intrauterine insemination, *in vitro* fertilisation, intracytoplasmic sperm injection and surrogacy). Given the general heteronormativity of our tax

* Thanks for comments and helpful suggestions on earlier drafts of this chapter go to Kim Brooks; the participants at the May 2009 conference on *Challenging Gender Inequality in Tax Policy Making* at the International Institute for the Sociology of Law in Oñati, Spain; and the participants at the April 2009 *Critical Tax Conference* at Indiana University–Bloomington, including, especially, Kerry Ryan and Ted Seto.

laws, I naturally began to wonder whether section 213 treats the expenses that these same-sex couples incur to have children in the same way that it treats precisely the same expenses when different-sex married couples incur them to overcome fertility problems that prevent a more 'natural' form of procreation.

It did not take long to realise that section 213 treats the expenses for infertility treatments incurred by so-called traditional families differently from—and more favourably than—the same expenses when incurred by same-sex couples or others in non-traditional family arrangements. That much was, quite honestly, not a surprise to me—nor should it be a surprise to anyone who has ever heard of the Defense of Marriage Act (1 USC section 7), which, for purposes of federal law, refuses recognition to same-sex marriages. More interesting to me, though, was *how* section 213 privileged traditional over non-traditional family arrangements. As I came to see it, section 213 privileges traditional over non-traditional family arrangements through the construction, corporealisation and even dismemberment of families. In this chapter, I invite you to accompany me on a short journey as I explain how I see this process of constructing, corporealising and dismembering families play out in the text and context of section 213.

SECTION 213 OF THE INTERNAL REVENUE CODE

Section 213 of the Internal Revenue Code (Code) (26 USC sections 1ff) allows a deduction for expenses paid during the taxable year for 'medical care', which is defined to include 'amounts paid ... for the diagnosis, cure, mitigation, treatment, or prevention of disease, or for the purpose of affecting any structure or function of the body'.[1] To prevent a taxpayer from reaping a double benefit, the deduction is limited to medical expenses that have not been previously reimbursed by insurance or otherwise (for example, by a tortfeasor). And a built-in statutory 'floor' disallows any deduction for medical expenses not in excess of 7.5 per cent of the taxpayer's adjusted gross income. The purpose of the statutory floor is twofold. First, it ensures that the deduction is available only if the taxpayer has incurred 'extraordinary' medical expenses that affect her ability to pay federal income tax. Secondly, it mitigates the possibility that the deduction will contribute to rising medical costs, because an unlimited deduction would

[1] The United States lacks a comprehensive national health insurance programme. For decades, commentators have been arguing over whether s 213 has any place in a well-constructed income tax or whether it is no more than a poor substitute for a national health insurance program (see, eg, Andrews 1972: 334–35; Kahn 2002: 27–29; Surrey 1973: 20–23). My purpose here is not to add to (or detract from) that debate but to take s 213 as a given and to examine the ways in which heteropatriarchal domination might be embedded in that provision.

create an incentive to incur medical expenses and discourage the purchase of private insurance (see Joint Committee on Taxation 1983: 24).

From this brief description, section 213 does not seem a likely candidate for being tagged as furthering domination in American society. After all, from its inception, this provision has aimed to alleviate extraordinary financial burdens on taxpayers who already suffer from significant medical problems—and who, by definition, lack the help of insurance to relieve those burdens (US Congress 1942: 7800, 8469). But, as laudable as this goal might be, careful attention to the wording of section 213 reveals that it does not apply to all taxpayers equally. In fact, section 213 draws sharp distinctions between different types of families. It furthers the domination of the so-called traditional family and concomitantly contributes to the subordination of lesbian, gay and other non-traditional families.

Section 213 furthers this domination and contributes to this subordination in a curious way. There are certainly a number of Code sections that draw distinctions between different types of families. For example, educational provisions in the Code allow tax relief for education provided to the taxpayer, a spouse or dependants (for example, Internal Revenue Code 26 USC sections 25A, 221); the general fringe benefits provision in the Code allows certain fringe benefits to be provided on a tax-free basis to the spouse, dependants and even parents of employees (section 132(h), (j)(4)); the more specific exclusion for employer-provided meals and lodging applies not only to food and shelter given to the employee, but sometimes also to food and shelter given to a spouse and dependants (section 119); and the various attribution rules in the Code amalgamate ownership among family members, often adopting different (ie, broader or narrower) definitions of the 'family' depending on the particular purpose of the attribution rule (for example, sections 267, 318; see Crawford 2005). Yet, section 213 seems to go beyond merely identifying the relevant economic unit for tax purposes—it actually corporealises that unit. To paraphrase Haraway (1991), section 213 maps the physiological onto the political and creates the 'body family'.

CONSTRUCTING FAMILIES

As a first step towards understanding the creation of the body family, let's consider how section 213 constructs the 'family' and what type of 'family' it constructs. Section 213 allows a deduction not only for expenses paid during the taxable year by the taxpayer for his own medical care, but for expenses paid for medical care rendered to his spouse and dependants. Thus, an individual taxpayer is able to combine the medical expenses of others together with his own medical expenses both for purposes of determining whether he has exceeded the rather high statutory floor on deductibility and, if that floor has been exceeded, for purposes of obtaining the tax benefit from the deduction. Thus, by seeing the taxpayer not just as an individual but also as a head of household, section 213 creates a family unit and determines the deductibility of medical expenses on the basis of that unit.

Notably, this facet of section 213 dates back to its original introduction into the Internal Revenue Code in 1942 (Revenue Act 1942: section 127(a)). That historical fact is noteworthy because, in the early days of the federal income tax, it appears that Congress assumed 'that the taxpaying unit would be the individual' (Cain 1991: 100). Indeed, it was not until 1948 that Congress introduced the joint federal income tax return as we now know it (Revenue Act 1948: sections 301, 303); it was not until 1951 that Congress created a separate rate schedule for heads of household (Revenue Act 1951: section 301); it was not until 1984 that Congress fully embraced the idea of the different-sex married couple as a single economic unit for income tax purposes (Cain, 2000: 680; US Congress 1984: 1491); and it was not until 1986 that Congress enacted the 'kiddie tax' that makes the family a quasi-taxable unit (at least with respect to the unearned income of minor children) (Tax Reform Act of 1986: section 1411).

When departing from the early norm of focusing on the individual as the taxable unit, Congress had a specific family structure in mind—that of the traditional, 'nuclear' family. The relevant family unit for purposes of the medical expense deduction consisted of (and still consists of) the taxpayer, the taxpayer's spouse and the taxpayer's dependants. In 1942, the only 'spouses' were the husbands and wives of married different-sex couples. It was not until nearly 55 years later that Congress took the possibility of same-sex marriage seriously by enacting the Defense of Marriage Act in 1996. Even so, the focus on different-sex married couples was made abundantly clear in legislative history that described the proposed deduction in the following terms:

> The committee bill allows, within prescribed limits, the deduction of expenses for the medical care of the taxpayer, *his wife*, and *his* dependents.
>
> (US Senate Report 77-1631, quoted in Seidman 1954: vol 1, 1397) (emphasis added)

Therefore, in enacting the predecessor of section 213, Congress undoubtedly had in mind a taxpayer/husband. This taxpayer/husband could deduct the expenses paid for medical care rendered to his (presumably, stay-at-home) wife.[2] He could also deduct the expenses paid for medical care rendered

[2] This mental picture is consistent with the general mental picture of the framers of the Code, who consistently refer to taxpayers in the masculine gender (1 USC s 1) and who included many features in the Code that

> reflect the assumption that our society is composed of heterosexual married couples, with men occupying the 'public' sphere and women occupying the 'private' domestic sphere. (Staudt 1996: 1571)

Indeed, s 213 still speaks of a deduction 'for medical care of the taxpayer, *his* spouse, or a dependent'. (emphasis added)

to his 'dependants'. For this purpose, Congress borrowed the definition of 'dependant' from then section 25(b)(2)(A), which allowed a credit for dependants. In 1942, section 25(b)(2)(A) allowed the taxpayer a $350 credit 'for each person (other than husband or wife) dependent upon and receiving his chief support from the taxpayer if such dependent person is under eighteen years of age or is incapable of self-support because mentally or physically defective'. As originally enacted in 1917, the tax allowance for dependants was available only with respect to children who were under the age of 18 or who were incapable of supporting themselves because they were 'mentally or physically defective' (War Revenue Act 1917: section 1203). Thus, the children who round out the traditional, nuclear family form the core of the tax concept of 'dependant'.

Since 1917, Congress has supplemented this core by allowing other individuals to qualify as dependants. As mentioned above, even before it enacted the predecessor of section 213 in 1942, Congress marginally expanded the definition of 'dependant' by allowing any individual (and not just a child) who was 'incapable of self-support because mentally or physically defective' to qualify as a dependant (Revenue Act 1918: section 216(d)). Since then, Congress has further relaxed the definition of 'dependant' to embrace more than just the taxpayer's children and 'defective' individuals who are incapable of caring for themselves and whom the taxpayer supports; nonetheless, the focus is still squarely on relatives of the taxpayer and his spouse (ie, the 'extended' nuclear family).[3] Indeed, to be a dependant, an individual must either meet the requirements for being treated as a 'qualifying child' or a 'qualifying relative' of the taxpayer (Internal Revenue Code 26 USC section 152(a)). Thus, the basic picture of the household painted by the predecessor of section 213 was (and, arguably, still is today) that of the traditional, nuclear family with a breadwinner husband and a wife and children.

CREATING THE BODY FAMILY

However, in section 213, Congress does not merely construct a picture of the family that replicates the traditional, nuclear family norm. Neither does Congress merely sketch out what it considers to be the appropriate taxable unit. Instead, in section 213, Congress creates the body family as a separate person.

[3] There is a catch-all category for anyone else who has the same principal place of abode as the taxpayer and who is a member of the taxpayer's household (Internal Revenue Code 26 USC s 152(d)(2)(H)). Nevertheless, given the further requirement that the taxpayer must provide more than one-half of a dependant's support, this catch-all category covers same-sex couples or unmarried different-sex couples at best only tangentially (s 152(d)(1)(C)).

Since the enactment of the predecessor of section 213 in 1942, the traditional family has had the ability to aggregate its medical expenses regardless of whether the couple files a joint federal income tax return or two separate returns, and, since 1948, regardless of whether the couple avails itself of the income-splitting privilege afforded to married different-sex couples through the joint return. (For more on income splitting, in Canada, see chapter twelve by Philipps in this volume.) In other words, even today, a taxpayer can deduct expenses paid for medical care rendered to his spouse (and dependants), notwithstanding that the taxpayer and his wife file separate federal income tax returns.

This ability to aggregate expenses even if the spouses actually constitute two separate taxable units is atypical. The payment of one taxpayer's expenses by another does not normally give rise to a deduction in the hands of the payor (*Jenkins v Commissioner* 1983; *Welch v Helvering* 1933). Instead, the taxpayer whose expenses were defrayed has additional income—potentially includible in her gross income—and that taxpayer is normally the only one entitled to a deduction (*Estate of Slater v Commissioner* 1962; *Old Colony Trust Company v Commissioner* 1929; Treasury Regulations 26 CFR section 1.164-1(a); Revenue Ruling 75-301, 1975-2 CB 66; IRS Private Letter Ruling 87-33-002; see Dorocak 2001: 5–27). Thus, the norm of focusing on the individual as the appropriate unit for federal income tax purposes usually dictates that spouses must file a joint federal income tax return—and become a single taxable unit—before one spouse can deduct (or obtain a credit for) expenses paid with respect to the other spouse (see, for example, Internal Revenue Code 26 USC sections 21(e)(2), 25A(g)(6), 135(d)(3), 221(e)(2), 222(d)(4); but see also section 911(c)).

Section 213 takes exactly the opposite approach. It allows expenses to be aggregated across otherwise separate taxable units. A number of other Code provisions echo—and reinforce—this special treatment by allowing the traditional family to aggregate medical expenses even if the couple files separate federal income tax returns (see, for example, Internal Revenue Code 26 USC sections 35(b)(2), (g)(5), 105(b), (c), 162(l), 220, 223; Treasury Regulations 26 CFR section 1.106-1). Taken together, these provisions create a separate entity—the body family—that exists wholly apart from the individual taxable units of husband, wife and child (or children).

Though it is unusual to aggregate the expenses of separate taxable units across returns, Congress's creation of the body family as a separate person for purposes of section 213—while otherwise continuing to treat the individual components of that body as separate taxable units—is not so unusual. Tax is an area that is replete with instances of embodiment and disembodiment—that is, of merging two separate persons into one, of splitting one person into two and of recognizing a collective as a group at some points and as a separate entity at others.

For example, the joint federal income tax return and the combination of sections 1041, 2056 and 2523 merge two separate and distinct individuals—the husband and wife—into 'one economic unit' for tax purposes (US Congress 1981: 127). Yet, even though the marriage continues, the 'innocent spouse' rules can cleave this single economic unit into two when necessary to prevent the innocent spouse from being forced to pay for the tax misdeeds of the other spouse (Internal Revenue Code 26 USC section 6015(b)). Conversely, even after the marriage ceases and the couple formally becomes two separate taxpayers, the single economic unit will remain intact for tax purposes if either (1) the couple elects to continue income splitting under the alimony inclusion-deduction regime of sections 71 and 215 or (2) the couple makes property transfers to each other that are incident to their divorce and subject to section 1041.

In addition, an individual taxpayer can create a single-member limited liability company (LLC) in many states. By default, such an entity will be disregarded for federal income tax purposes, meaning that these two persons (ie, the LLC and its owner) will be treated as one for tax purposes (Treasury Regulations 26 CFR section 301.7701-3(b)(1)(ii)). At some later point, however, the single owner could simply file the appropriate form with the Internal Revenue Service (IRS) and elect to have the LLC treated as a separate entity, splitting the one taxpayer into two (Treasury Regulations 26 CFR section 301.7701-3(c)(1)(i)). Similarly, a corporation will be recognized as a separate entity 'even if it has only one shareholder who exercises total control over its affairs' (*Commissioner v Bollinger* 1988), effectively allowing an individual taxpayer to split herself into two (or more) at will.

Partnerships are perhaps most emblematic of how the Code can recognize a collective as a group at some points and as a separate entity at others. Partnerships are generally treated as an aggregate of individuals, as evidenced by section 701, which states:

> A partnership as such shall not be subject to the income tax imposed by this chapter. Persons carrying on business as partners shall be liable for income tax only in their separate or individual capacities.

At the same time, however, a partnership is treated as an entity for purposes of making most elections (for example, of accounting and depreciation methods) (Internal Revenue Code 26 USC section 703(b); Treasury Regulations 26 CFR section 1.703-1(b)(1)), for purposes of audit (Internal Revenue Code 26 USC sections 6221–31) and generally for purposes of determining the character of gain or loss on the disposition of an interest in the partnership (Internal Revenue Code 26 USC section 741; but see section 751). Similarly, S corporations are sometimes treated as an aggregate of individuals and sometimes as a separate entity (see Internal Revenue Code 26 USC sections 1363, 1366, 1371, 1374).

All these examples—from the coexistence of the joint return and the innocent spouse rules to the tension between the aggregate and entity treatment of partnerships and S corporations—underscore the mutability of personhood for tax purposes. If one taxpayer can so easily become two, if two or more can become one and if they can all move continually and seamlessly back and forth between these statuses, then it should not be at all surprising to find that same mutability surfacing—however partially—in the seemingly innocuous word 'body' in section 213.

CORPOREALISING THE BODY FAMILY

Yet, in creating the body family, Congress appears to go a step beyond its usual fluid notions of personhood. Through section 213, Congress appears to have actually mapped the physiological onto the political (and politicized) construct of the nuclear family for purposes of determining which expenses will be deductible as 'medical care'. In short, Congress appears to have corporealised the 'body family'.

For purposes of section 213, 'medical care' is defined in part as 'amounts paid for the diagnosis, cure, mitigation, treatment, or prevention of disease, or for the purpose of affecting any structure or function of the *body*' (emphasis added). What 'body' is Congress referring to in the latter part of this definition? At first glance, one would likely interpret the word 'body' to refer to the individual, physical bodies of the taxpayer, his spouse and his dependants. But, given the manner in which section 213 aggregates expenses and creates the body family as a separate person independent of the actual taxable unit, is that really the best or most appropriate interpretation of this word? Might this reference to the 'body' not more easily and logically be read as a reference to the collective, constructive 'body family'?

It is common for illness or disease that strikes one part of your body to affect other parts of your body, whether directly or indirectly. Healing from surgery is usually a whole-body experience, laying you up for days or weeks. Even something as minor as the common cold can leave you feeling 'tired and miserable' because your body has directed all of its energy at fighting a virus in your nose or throat (WebMD 2009). It is also common for an illness or disease that strikes one member of a family to affect other family members, whether directly or indirectly. You might catch that cold that your spouse or child brought home, or you might fight it off but still have to care for the person who is not feeling well. Some serious illnesses—for example, Alzheimer's disease—can actually have an arguably more serious impact on those surrounding the person with the disease than they have on the afflicted individual.

Section 213 maps these effects of illness onto a 'body'—namely, the body family. If illness or disease strikes one part of the body family, the entire body family is considered to be affected in just the same way as other parts of the body are affected when a person suffers a head cold. So, even if the taxpayer/husband is not ill, an illness or medical condition that strikes his spouse or dependants (ie, other parts of the body family) is treated as affecting (infecting?) him too, thereby permitting the taxpayer—as titular head of the body family—to take a deduction for medical expenses incurred to diagnose, treat or cure that illness.

This corporealisation of the body family is perhaps most easily understood when considered from the perspective of the reproductive functions of the body. Reproduction is not a solitary function, by which I mean that the taxpayer/husband cannot reproduce on his own.[4] Rather, it takes the taxpayer *and* his wife—each contributing genetic material through a sexual union of two bodies—to reproduce on *their* own. In the context of section 213, reproduction can be seen not as a function of the individual taxpayer's body but as a function that can only truly be fulfilled by and through the body family, of which the individual taxpayer's body forms no more than a part.

The different-sex married couple contemplated by section 213 may, however, experience fertility problems. In that situation, it will be necessary for the couple to seek outside medical assistance to fulfill their desire to reproduce. Different-sex couples 'are generally advised to seek medical help if they are unable to achieve pregnancy after a year of unprotected intercourse' (American Society for Reproductive Medicine 2009).

Most infertility problems are treated with medication or surgery (American Society for Reproductive Medicine 2009; Pratt 2004: 1133). Intrauterine insemination may also be used to overcome certain problems (Pratt 2004: 1133). If the couple still cannot achieve a pregnancy, then assisted reproductive technologies (ART) such as *in vitro* fertilisation, intracytoplasmic sperm injection, and/or surrogacy (possibly with the help of a sperm or egg donor) may be contemplated (Pratt 2004: 1133–34). These treatments can be rather costly and often are not covered by insurance, making them an excellent candidate for a deduction under section 213 if they qualify as 'medical care' (Pratt 2004: 1123, 1135).

Though there has been some debate about whether infertility treatment qualifies as 'medical care' for purposes of section 213, commentators have made a strong case for allowing a deduction for the costs of such treatment. These commentators have argued that infertility treatment qualifies as 'medical care' under both prongs of the definition of that term in section 213: Infertility treatments both mitigate or treat a recognized medical condition (ie, infertility) *and* affect a structure or function of the body (ie, reproduction) (Pratt 2004: 1126, 1144–61; Benjamin 2004: 1130–32; Maule 1982: 663). In addition,

[4] This may change if human cloning is permitted; however, even were cloning to be permitted, the individual to be cloned would still need to have a qualified individual perform the procedure. So, except in the rare instance of a scientist who clones herself, even cloning should not be a solitary experience.

the IRS has issued a private letter ruling indicating that the costs associated with securing an egg donor qualify as medical expenses under section 213 (IRS Private Letter Ruling 2003-18-017). Similarly, the costs associated with surrogacy should qualify as medical expenses under section 213 because they constitute 'payment for a substitute for the . . . diseased or impaired body part, . . . just as the costs of seeing eye dogs, human guides, and note takers are deductible' (Pratt 2004: 1158–59). Furthermore, in its most recent publication explaining the medical expense deduction to taxpayers, the IRS listed 'fertility enhancement' as a type of medical expense covered by section 213 (IRS 2008). Even Congress seems to expect that the cost of infertility treatments will normally qualify as a deductible medical expense (Pratt 2004: 1160).

The different-sex married couple's ability to deduct the costs of using ART to achieve a pregnancy as medical expenses not only squares with, but also squares, the corporealisation of the body family. Infertility treatments, including ART, can easily be described in the reinterpreted terms of section 213. A function of the body family is to procreate (ie, to grow or extend the body family). If the body family attempts to procreate for a year without success (ie, if the different-sex couple working *together* cannot achieve a pregnancy in that time), an infertility problem is considered to exist. The body family must then seek medical treatment so that the illness or disease can be diagnosed and treated or, at the very least, mitigated. Naturally, the purpose of this treatment is to affect the reproductive function of the body family, by hopefully restoring it to good working order.

Section 213 further reifies the corporealisation of the body family when the incidence—and perceptions about the incidence—of infertility are also taken into account. In about 67 per cent of all cases, the infertility giving rise to the need for medical treatment (and, hence, deductible medical expenses) is associated with one or the other spouse, with the incidence split about evenly between male and female infertility factors (American Society for Reproductive Medicine 2009). In 20 per cent of cases, the cause of an infertility problem is unexplained and it is only in about 10 per cent of cases that both spouses experience infertility (American Society for Reproductive Medicine 2009). Accordingly, in the vast majority of cases, it is the infertility of a single spouse (or an undetermined factor) that affects the couple's ability to reproduce as a whole.

Given the incidence of infertility, the taxpayer/husband will, in many cases, have no fertility problems himself. Nonetheless, he will be allowed a deduction for his wife's infertility treatments so that *they* can reproduce *together*. In fact, as mentioned earlier, section 213 should go so far as to allow a deduction for the taxpayer/husband's expenses in obtaining replacement genetic material from an egg donor or a replacement womb from a surrogate (or possibly both) in order to mitigate his wife's infertility problems so that the couple can reproduce together. Although the wife's infertility treatment is directed at curing or mitigating her infertility issues, it cannot escape notice that the medical treatment of, or a medical substitution for, the infertile wife directly benefits the fertile husband by allowing him to fulfill his reproductive function. In other words, the infertility treatments of one spouse benefit both spouses—that is, they benefit the body family as a whole—by allowing them each to carry out (or obtain a suitable substitute or replacement for) their separate reproductive functions that can result in procreation only when the two work in tandem as the body family.

The benefit of medical treatment to both spouses/the body family is even clearer when the taxpayer/husband himself experiences infertility. Notwithstanding its actual incidence, infertility tends to be gendered feminine (Ikemoto 1996: 1008). This is especially so when we think of ART, because no matter which spouse is infertile,

> the technology is used on the woman. And it is the woman who is not pregnant. Therefore, as a normative matter, it is the woman who is in/fertile.
>
> (Ikemoto 1996: 1037).

Thus, when the taxpayer/husband is infertile and it is necessary to resort to ART, the fertile wife must still undergo medical procedures to overcome the taxpayer/husband's infertility and become pregnant. For example, the fertile wife might have to undergo intrauterine insemination. Or she might have to have her eggs extracted, fertilised *in vitro* (possibly using intracytoplasmic sperm injection) and implanted into her uterus. Or she might have to undergo both of these procedures multiple times to achieve a pregnancy. When resort to a sperm donor is necessary because of the taxpayer/husband's infertility, the wife must still undergo the same procedure(s) to achieve a pregnancy. In this situation, the taxpayer/husband is allowed a deduction under section 213 for medical treatment of his wife—who has no fertility issues at all. The purpose of the wife's treatment is not to cure or mitigate an illness or disease that she has or to affect a structure or function of her healthy body but to overcome a disease (ie, infertility) that afflicts the taxpayer/husband. The corporealisation of the body family cannot be more clearly illustrated than when, as here, section 213 allows a deduction for the cost of medical treatment of a healthy person in order to mitigate the impact of a disease on the reproductive functioning of a different person's body so that the two can together—as the body family—fulfill their collective desire to procreate.

FURTHERING DOMINATION

Medicalising Procreation

By medicalising procreation as it does, section 213 of the Internal Revenue Code (Code) always already furthers heteropatriarchal domination. Hopefully, the discussion in the previous sections provided ample evidence of the patriarchal aspect of this domination. With its construction and corporealisation of the body family, section 213 certainly betrays an outsized focus on the traditional family model of the taxpayer/husband, wife and dependants.

At a more basic level, the patriarchal and heterosexual aspects of this domination stem from the unceasing reference to 'infertility' treatments. Referring to ART as 'infertility treatment' conjures up the image of a different-sex couple encountering difficulties in getting pregnant. But this paints only the most partial of pictures of the groups who use ART to procreate (Ikemoto 1996: 1053–57).

Increasingly, same-sex couples and single men and women (whether straight or gay) use ART to create nontraditional families:

> This is not a brave new world, but a fertile new world. Right up to the present we seem to exclusively link assisted reproductive technology with infertility. We have books like *Beyond Infertility: The New Paths to Parenthood* that itemize all of the assisted reproductive techniques to help a couple get a child of their own once they have confronted their inability to conceive. No mention is made of gay, lesbian, or single people who have no problems with their fertility. Yet increasing numbers of prospective single, gay, or lesbian mothers and fathers are availing themselves of these new paths to parenthood. For individuals in same-sex couples and for single people, the problem is not that their bodies do not work, but that they do not have another's body to work with.
>
> (Ehrensaft 2005: 5)

Same-sex couples and singles encounter few legal impediments to accessing ART because, as Crawford also notes in her discussion of taxing surrogacy in chapter five, US states have generally refrained from regulating the use of this technology (Kindregan and McBrien 2006: 24–25, 193–96). Nonetheless, in 2005 and 2006, Bills were introduced in the Indiana and Virginia legislatures to restrict access to ART to married different-sex couples, but these Bills were not enacted into law (Daar 2008: 45–46). The States of Texas and Florida do, however, limit the legal enforceability of surrogacy contracts to those entered into by married different-sex couples (Daar 2008: 46). Yet, same-sex couples and singles can easily circumvent such restrictions (as well as more generalized uncertainty about the legal enforceability of surrogacy contracts in some states) by simply working with a surrogate in a state with a receptive legal environment.

A more formidable obstacle to accessing ART is provider discrimination, which occurs when an individual doctor refuses to provide treatment to unmarried couples and single individuals (Daar 2008: 43). The extent to which such discrimination occurs is unclear (Daar 2008). It is worth noting, however, that a recent decision from the California Supreme Court held that an individual doctor could *not* refuse to provide ART treatment to a lesbian woman on the grounds that providing such treatment conflicted with his religious beliefs (*North Coast Women's Medical Care Group v Superior Court* 2008).

Given the general accessibility of ART to same-sex couples and singles in the United States, psychologist Diane Ehrensaft (2005) has suggested that we 'take the emphasis off the problem of infertility and put it on the solution—a solution that embraces not just problems with an individual's reproductive system but also the choice to have a child without the traditional male–female coupling'. Ehrensaft prefers the more accurate and inclusive term 'assisted conception' to refer to the use of these technologies in place of the more common—and overweeningly heteronormative—'infertility treatment' (or the IRS's slightly more euphemistic 'fertility enhancement').

Dismembering Families

Yet, picking up again on the discussion in previous sections, there is a deeper level to section 213's furtherance of heteropatriachal domination. As this chapter was being written, the US Tax Court issued a decision in *Magdalin v Commissioner* (96 TCM (CCH) 491 (2008)). In that case, William Magdalin, a medical doctor who already had twin sons 'born through natural processes' during a former marriage, had two children using an egg donor and a surrogate. One child was born in 2005 and the other was born in 2006. Dr Magdalin did not suffer from infertility problems; in fact, '[a]t all relevant times, his sperm count and motility were found to be within normal limits'.

This case was before the Tax Court because Dr Magdalin claimed a deduction under section 213 for the expenses incurred with respect to the egg donor and the surrogate in these two pregnancies. Those expenses totalled $52,310 in 2004 and $43,593 in 2005, the taxable years at issue in the case. After taking into account the 7.5 per cent statutory floor on the deduction, Dr Magdalin claimed a $34,050 medical expense deduction on his 2004 tax return and a $28,230 medical expense deduction on his 2005 tax return.

The Court ultimately decided that Dr Magdalin's expenses did not qualify as amounts paid for 'medical care', as that term is defined in section 213. The expenses did not satisfy the first prong of that definition because Dr Magdalin was not suffering from an illness or disease (for example, infertility) that required diagnosis or treatment. The expenses did not satisfy the second prong of the definition of medical care because the treatments did not affect a structure or function of Dr Magdalin's body. Failing to qualify as medical expenses under section 213, the expenses that Dr Magdalin incurred with respect to the egg donor and surrogate were held to be non-deductible personal expenses (Internal Revenue Code 26 USC section 262).

The Tax Court's treatment of Dr Magdalin in this case portends the tax treatment of other non-traditional families attempting to conceive through the use of ART. In Dr Magdalin's case, the Tax Court and the IRS focused their attention both on the need for a medical diagnosis of infertility and on the taxpayer's 'male body'. The focus on the taxpayer's own individual body in this case contrasts sharply with section 213's construction and corporealisation of the body family in the case of different-sex married couples. This dual focus on a diagnosis of infertility and the corporeal body of the individual taxpayer creates the possibility of a constellation of tax treatments that vary depending on the composition of the non-traditional family.

In the case of unmarried different-sex couples, resort to ART will be necessary only where infertility actually does exist. As a result, they should be able to deduct at least some of the costs of ART under section 213 because ART will be used to treat a recognized medical condition (ie, infertility) and that treatment will affect a structure or function of the taxpayer's body. However, unless one partner is the dependant of the other for purposes of section 213 (see note four above), the Tax Court's and the IRS's focus on the effect of medical treatments on the taxpayer's own individual body raises a question as to how far deductibility will go. For example, if the male partner in an unmarried different-sex couple is infertile, will treatments of the female partner be deductible because they mitigate the male partner's infertility or will the treatments be nondeductible because they do not affect the male partner's own individual body?

In the case of same-sex couples and single individuals, the Tax Court's and the IRS's dual focus may significantly limit the possibility of deducting expenses associated with ART. For lesbian couples and single women without fertility issues, it seems likely that the cost of obtaining donated sperm would not be deductible because of the lack of an infertility diagnosis and because the donated sperm does not, by itself, affect a structure or function of the woman's body.

The cost of intrauterine insemination using that donated sperm raises interesting questions. If the woman is fertile, would a deduction for the intrauterine insemination be disallowed on the ground that the procedure is not medically indicated but merely a result of her personal choice as to how to reproduce? Or would a deduction be allowed on the ground that intrauterine insemination affects a structure or function of her body? Or would that ground for deductibility also be jeopardised by arguments about personal choice, especially in view of congressionally imposed restrictions on the deductibility of cosmetic surgery, which are based on just such arguments? Compounding these questions, the IRS specifically argued in Dr Magdalin's case that it did 'not believe that procreation is a covered function of petitioner's male body within the meaning of section 213(d)(1)'. Though unexplained, this assertion certainly lends itself to the interpretation that section 213 does not cover procreation as a function of an individual taxpayer's body but only as a collective function of what I have termed the 'body family'. This assertion may therefore indicate incipient hostility on the part of the IRS toward arguments that an unmarried individual should be allowed to deduct the cost of ART under the second (ie, 'structure or function') prong of the definition of medical care in section 213.

If the woman is experiencing fertility problems (for example, there are several rounds of intrauterine insemination without producing a pregnancy), then it would seem that the cost of *in vitro* fertilisation (or possibly even a surrogate) would more likely be deductible as a medically indicated treatment for infertility (or as a substitute for the impaired body part). But is the cost of donated sperm a part of this medically indicated treatment or, in keeping with the IRS's views concerning section 213's limited coverage of the procreative function, just an action by an indispensable 'other'?

For gay couples and single men without fertility issues, Dr Magdalin's case is particularly instructive. For them, none of the expenses of ART will be deductible—both because they lack a diagnosis of infertility and because none of the ART procedures will be performed on their bodies. For a man with infertility issues, a question arises as to what exactly will be included under the rubric of infertility treatment for purposes of section 213. Will the costs associated with *in vitro* fertilisation and surrogacy be deductible because they mitigate the effects of male infertility? Or, as with unmarried different-sex couples, will these costs not be deductible because the treatments do not affect the man's own body?

Encouraging One Family Form and Discouraging All Others

In each of these situations, the questions about the deductibility under section 213 of expenses associated with ART stem directly from the sharp distinctions drawn in that provision between traditional and non-traditional families. On the one hand, section 213 both constructs and corporealises the traditional family. By treating the traditional family as a single 'body', section 213 elides questions about the necessary identity of the recipient of medical treatment. This is best illustrated by the ability of an infertile taxpayer/husband to deduct the cost of ART treatment administered to his fertile wife. On the other hand, in the case of non-traditional families, section 213 places questions about the identity of the recipient of medical treatments front and centre in any analysis of the deductibility of expenses associated with ART. These questions come to the foreground because section 213 generally works to dismember non-traditional families. In other words, section 213 refuses to see the non-traditional family as a unit capable of procreation. Instead of seeing a family, section 213 sees an individual who, by himself or herself, is incapable of procreation.[5]

[5] These sharp distinctions between traditional and non-traditional families are replicated and reinforced wherever s 213 and its standards are incorporated by reference in the Code.

This dismembering of non-traditional families contributes significantly to section 213's furthering of heteropatriarchal domination. For unmarried heterosexual couples experiencing infertility problems, section 213 creates a powerful economic incentive to marry so that the federal government will help to defray the costs of potentially expensive infertility treatments. For same-sex couples and singles, section 213 either denies them that subsidy outright or effectively denies it to them because their claim is sure to be met with a hostile reaction from the IRS and the Tax Court. The result is that ART is placed out of the reach of all but the most affluent of same-sex couples and singles (ie, those who can afford to pay for these procedures out of their own pocket). Thus, even beyond the normative privileging of traditional over non-traditional family arrangements, section 213 creates a financial incentive for affected different-sex couples to marry and erects a financial barrier to procreation by same-sex couples and single individuals.

REFERENCES

American Society for Reproductive Medicine (2009) 'Frequently Asked Questions about Infertility'. Available at: www.asrm.org/Patients/faqs.html#Q2.

Andrews, WD (1972) 'Personal Deductions in an Ideal Income Tax' 86 *Harvard Law Review* 309.

Benjamin, AL (2004) 'The Implications of Using the Medical Expense Deduction of IRC § 213 to Subsidize Assisted Reproductive Technology' 79 *Notre Dame Law Review* 1117.

Cain, PA (1991) 'Same-Sex Couples and the Federal Tax Laws' 1 *Tulane Journal of Law and Sexuality* 97.

—— (2000) 'Death Taxes: A Critique from the Margin' 48 *Cleveland State Law Review* 677.

Crawford, BJ (2005) 'The Profits and Penalties of Kinship: Conflicting Meanings of Family in Estate Tax Law' 3 *Pittsburgh Tax Review* 1.

Daar, JF (2008) 'Accessing Reproductive Technologies: Invisible Barriers, Indelible Harms' 23 *Berkeley Journal of Gender, Law and Justice* 18.

Dorocak, JR (2001) 'The Clintons' Legal Defense Fund: Income from Payment of Legal Expenses of Another and Deductibility of Such Expenses' 104 *West Virginia Law Review* 1.

Ehrensaft, D (2005) *Mommies, Daddies, Donors, Surrogates: Answering Tough Questions and Building Strong Families* (New York, Guilford Press).

For example, even if ART treatments are covered under an employer-provided health insurance plan, s 105(b) allows a plan's reimbursements for such treatments to be excluded from gross income only if those treatments qualify as 'medical care (as defined in section 213(d))'. In addition, a payment of another's medical expenses cannot escape gift tax unless it is made to a person who provides 'medical care as defined in section 213(d)' (Internal Revenue Code 26 USC s 2503(e)(2)(B)).

Haraway, DJ (1991) *Simians, Cyborgs and Women: The Reinvention of Nature* (New York, Routledge).
Ikemoto, LC (1996) 'The In/Fertile, the Too Fertile, and the Dysfertile' 47 *Hastings Law Journal* 1007.
Internal Revenue Service (IRS) (2008) 'Medical and Dental Expenses' publication no 502.
Joint Committee on Taxation (1983) *General Explanation of the Revenue Provisions of the Tax Equity and Fiscal Responsibility Act of 1982* (Washington, DC, US Government Printing Office).
Kahn, JH (2002) 'Personal Deductions—A Tax "Ideal" or Just Another "Deal"?' 2002 *Law Review of Michigan State University–Detroit College of Law* 1.
Kindregan, CP and McBrien, M (2006) *Assisted Reproductive Technology: A Lawyer's Guide to Emerging Law and Science* (Chicago, American Bar Association).
Maule, JE (1982) 'Federal Tax Consequences of Surrogate Motherhood' 60 *Taxes* 656.
Pratt, KT (2004) 'Inconceivable? Deducting the Costs of Fertility Treatment' 89 *Cornell Law Review* 1121.
Seidman, JS (1954) *Seidman's Legislative History of Federal Income and Excess Profits Tax Laws: 1953–1939* (New York, Prentice-Hall).
Staudt, NC (1996) 'Taxing Housework' 84 *Georgetown Law Journal* 1571.
Surrey, SS (1973) *Pathways to Tax Reform: The Concept of Tax Expenditures* (Cambridge, MA, Harvard University Press).
WebMD (2009) 'Understanding Common Cold—Basics'. Available at: www.webmd.com/cold-and-flu/cold-guide/understanding-common-cold-basics.

Cases

Commissioner v Bollinger, 485 US 340 (1988).
Estate of Slater v Commissioner, 21 TCM (CCH) 1355 (1962).
Jenkins v Commissioner, 47 TCM (CCH) 238 (1983).
Magdalin v Commissioner, 96 TCM (CCH) 491 (2008).
North Coast Women's Medical Care Group v Superior Court, 44 Cal. 4th 1145 (2008).
Old Colony Trust Company v Commissioner, 279 US 716 (1929).
Welch v Helvering, 290 US 111 (1933).

Legislation and Rulings

Defense of Marriage Act (1996) Public Law 104-199, 110; *Statutes at Large* 2419.
Treasury Regulations 26 Code of Federal Regulations.
Internal Revenue Code 26 US Code.
IRS Private Letter Ruling 87-33-002.
IRS Private Letter Ruling 2003-18-017.
Revenue Act 1918, ch 18, 40; *Statutes at Large* 1057.

Revenue Act 1942, Public Law 77-753, 56; *Statutes at Large* 798.
Revenue Act 1948, Public Law 80-471, 62; *Statutes at Large* 110.
Revenue Act 1951, Public Law 82-183, 65; *Statutes at Large* 452.
Revenue Ruling 75-301, 1975-2 CB 66.
Tax Reform Act 1986, Public Law 99-514, 100; *Statutes at Large* 2085.
US Congress (1942) *Congressional Record* vol 88.
—— (1981) 'Economic Recovery Act of 1981' *Senate Report* 97-144.
—— (1984) 'Deficit Reduction Act of 1984' *House of Representatives Report* 98-432.
War Revenue Act (1917) ch 63, 40; *Statutes at Large* 300.

9

*The Tax/Benefit Implications of Recognizing Same-sex Partnerships**

CASEY WARMAN AND FRANCES WOOLLEY

INTERNATIONALLY, CANADA HAS been at the forefront in recognizing same-sex relationships. Federal (nationwide) legislation in 2000 'extended the benefits and obligations of common-law status to same-sex couples' (Smith 2002). By 2005, same-sex couples were allowed to marry anywhere in Canada.[1] Legal recognition of same-sex relationships has benefited many couples by allowing access to a partner's health benefits, say, or greater pension rights. Yet it has been argued that this legal recognition is 'less than fully positive' (Young and Boyd 2006: 214).

From the perspective of taxation and benefits, legal recognition of same-sex partnerships has had decidedly mixed impacts. There are benefits to having a recognized partnership: for example, it provides an opportunity to claim a same-sex partner as a dependant, to transfer credits and to transfer capital assets on a tax-deferred basis. For people with certain types of retirement savings or pension income, partnership also provides

* While the research and analysis in this paper are based on data from Statistics Canada, the opinions expressed do not represent the views of Statistics Canada. The data was accessed at the Queen's RDC in Kingston, Ontario, Canada. We would like to thank participants at the *Challenging Gender Inequality in Tax Policy Making* workshop and Alan Macnaughton and Lisa Philipps for helpful comments and suggestions.

[1] For the areas of law discussed in this chapter, common law and formal marriages are equivalent. However this is not universally true. For example, in Quebec, common law partners have different rights in the event of a separation. A 'common-law' marriage is one where the partners are in a conjugal relationship and have lived together for a period of time. The relevant period of time varies—eg, for taxation purposes, a couple has a common-law marriage if they have lived together for a year or more, while for claiming social assistance in Ontario, a couple is treated as if they were married if they have been living together for three months.

opportunities for income splitting. There are also costs. Although the Canadian tax system is based primarily on the individual, eligibility for some benefits is based on a couple's total income. Consequently, legal recognition of a same-sex partnership can result in a loss of benefits, especially for low-income individuals.

In this chapter, the Canadian Community Health Survey (CCHS) will be used to create a demographic profile of self-identified gays and lesbians in Canada. Provisions in the Canadian tax and benefit system will also be identified—provisions that can lead to a change in a person's taxes or benefits on marriage or on formation of a common-law union. The potential impact of these provisions on the gay and lesbian community will then be considered, by identifying the portion of the gay and lesbian population who would, potentially, be affected by these changes.

Our research indicates that gays and lesbians have diverse economic experiences. On average, married and common-law same-sex couples have household incomes as high as, or higher than, their heterosexual counterparts, and they are less likely to be in a dependant/provider relationship. Because partners in lesbian and gay relationships typically have fairly similar income levels, legal recognition of these relationships has relatively few tax consequences in the context of the Canadian income tax system. These results are in stark contrast with those of Alm, Badgett and Wittington (2000), who found that tax recognition of same-sex marriage in the United States would generally decrease homosexuals' tax liabilities. However, they are similar to Australian estimates (Australia 2008: 6) that recognition of same-sex relationships would have a negligible effect on tax revenues.

There is, however, a significant low-income and middle-income homosexual population—including a substantial number of single parents—who are at risk of losing benefits as a result of formal recognition of same-sex relationships, a possibility that was recognized as early as 1994 by Young (1994). Lahey (2001) began to quantify the potential cost of recognition of same-sex relationships for low-income lesbians and gays. Unfortunately, she did not have access to data that allowed her to identify single gays and lesbians, hence could not estimate the effects of recognition of same-sex relationships on singles. Australian estimates of the impact of recognizing same-sex relationships identified these benefit-side impacts as much more substantial than the tax impacts, projecting that by 2010–11, recognition of same-sex relationships would generate savings of AUS$25.2 million for the Department of Families, Housing, Community Services and Indigenous Affairs and another AUS$32.1 million for the Department of Employment, Education and Workplace Relations through the reduction of benefits paid (Australia 2008: 6). In this chapter, potential negative impacts will also be highlighted.

A PROFILE OF THE GAY AND LESBIAN COMMUNITY IN CANADA

This study uses cross-sectional data from Statistics Canada's cycles 2.1, 3.1 and the first half of cycle 4.1 of the Canadian Community Health Survey (CCHS), for which information was collected in 2003, 2005 and 2007, respectively.[2] The survey asked each respondent the following question:[3]

Do you consider yourself to be:

1. Heterosexual? (sexual relations with people of the opposite sex).
2. Homosexual, that is lesbian or gay? (sexual relations with people of your own sex).
3. Bisexual? (sexual relations with people of both sexes).

(The terms in parentheses were used as prompts when people hesitated when responding.) Since the CCHS did not indicate whether people who responded 'bisexual' were in same-sex relationships or opposite-sex relationships, and since our focus in this chapter is on the implications of recognition of same-sex relationships only, we dropped bisexuals from our sample and focused only on self-identified homosexuals and heterosexuals. We also restricted the sample to people aged 18 to 59 and excluded those who described themselves as 'unattached' but living with others—for example, young adults living at home or students in shared housing.[4]

One concern with the CCHS, as with any survey that asks about sexual orientation, is of non-disclosure: in this case, respondents may have been reluctant to admit that they were gay or lesbian.[5] There is some evidence of non-disclosure in the CCHS in that those who self-identified as gay and lesbian in the survey differ demographically from the Canadian population as a whole. In particular, as shown in Table 1 below, they are less likely to be immigrants than are other Canadians. Although it is possible that the smaller fraction of gays and lesbians in immigrant communities reflects differences in the number of people choosing to be homosexual, we suspect that the difference is driven more by the relatively high level of acceptance of homosexuality in Canada. People growing up in countries such as India where, until 2009, homosexuality was illegal,[6] might be

[2] The cycle refers to the collection series number of the CCHS dataset. Starting with cycle 4.1, information was collected for two years but released annually, whereas for cycles 2.1 and 3.1, the data was collected biennially.

[3] See: www.statcan.gc.ca/imdb-bmdi/instrument/3226_Q1_V4-eng.pdf.

[4] In the 3.1 and 2007 CCHS, the sexual orientation question was restricted to people aged 18 to 59.

[5] Access to the sexual orientation question is restricted to the Statistics Canada Research Data Centres for which output is vetted and access is granted through a government-approval process.

[6] See: www.nytimes.com/2009/07/03/world/asia/03india.html?_r=1.

Table 1a: Males

	Married/ common-law heterosexual	Married/ common-law gay	Single heterosexual	Single gay
Personal income	$59,326	$50,467	$46,597	$49,018
Household income	$87,748	$92,834	$48,275	$50,329
Personal/household (× 100)	67.6	54.4	96.5	97.4
Percentage with Bachelor's degree or greater	26.8	43.1	22.6	42
Percentage immigrants	21.5	14.9	15	10.8
Percentage Vancouver/ Toronto/Montreal	32.5	60.3	33.6	58.4
Age	42.5	40.7	40.8	41.8
Observations	40,400	250	19,200	670

Notes: Income is adjusted for inflation using the Consumer Price Index, with 2005 as the base year
Source: Calculated by authors from the Canadian Community Health Survey

Table 1b: Females

	Married/ common-law heterosexual	Married/ common-law lesbian	Single heterosexual	Single lesbian
Personal income	$31,030	$44,158	$35,475	$36,874
Household income	$82,393	$88,400	$38,278	$40,289
Personal/household (× 100)	37.7	50	92.7	91.5
Percentage with Bachelor's degree or greater	26.1	43.5	24.7	31.7
Percentage immigrants	20.4	13.4	16.8	11.7
Percentage Vancouver/ Toronto/Montreal	32.4	46.3	35.9	49.2
Age	41.1	41	41.5	42
Observations	44,190	235	22,300	300

Notes: Income is adjusted for inflation using the Consumer Price Index, with 2005 as the base year
Source: Calculated by the authors from the Canadian Community Health Survey

more likely to be 'closeted' and not report their 'true' sexual orientation. However, non-disclosure is not a major problem, given that our focus in this chapter is on formal recognition of same-sex partnerships, and we hypothesize that people who do not disclose their relationships in a survey such as the CCHS would also be unlikely to reveal their sexual orientation by checking the 'married' or 'living common-law' box on their income tax return and providing the social insurance number of their same-sex partner. Consequently, they would tend to be less affected by formal recognition of same-sex relationships. Carpenter (2008: 1251) compares the CCHS data with information from the 2001 Canadian Census, arguing that his comparisons

> [p]rovide strong evidence that the CCHS and the Canadian Census are capturing basically the same groups of people . . . Overall, the CCHS patterns for demographic characteristics align very closely with the associated patterns from the 2001 Canadian census for gay and lesbian couples and married couples.

While there may be some problems with non-disclosure in the CCHS, they cannot be resolved by using another dataset. Moreover, no other Canadian dataset and very few internationally contain information about both single and partnered gays and lesbians. Hence, the CCHS is invaluable as a source of information about gays and lesbians. (As an aside: throughout this chapter we will use 'gay' to refer to gay men.)

The picture of the gay and lesbian community drawn from the CCHS is consistent with what is known about gay and lesbian communities in the United Kingdom, the United States and elsewhere (Arabsheibani and Wadsworth 2005; Badgett 2003). As shown in Table 1, gays and lesbians are highly educated. The gay and lesbian population is more urban than the heterosexual population, with gay men in particular being concentrated in Vancouver, Toronto and Montreal. Partnered gay men are on average slightly younger than partnered heterosexuals, while single gay men are on average slightly older. Given the extremely favourable labour-market characteristics of gays and lesbians—native born, urban and highly educated—one would expect them to have high earnings. But do they?

The Canadian Community Health Survey (CCHS) asked respondents: 'What is your best estimate of the total income, before taxes and deductions, of all household members from all sources in the past 12 months?' and also 'What is your best estimate of YOUR total personal income, before taxes and other deductions, from all sources in the past 12 months?' Table 1 summarizes responses to these questions (with the results from the 2003 and 2007 surveys converted into 2005 dollars). If we average all men, partnered and unattached, we find that gay men earn less, on average, than heterosexuals. The slightly higher earnings of unattached gays relative to single heterosexuals are overwhelmed by the substantially higher earnings of partnered heterosexual men relative to partnered gays. Lesbians, regardless of relationship status, earn more than heterosexual women.[7] As noted above, the self-identified lesbian and gay community differs in education and other labour market characteristics from the heterosexual community. But as argued in LaFrance, Warman and Woolley (2009) and as Carpenter (2008) also shows, even controlling for these differences, there is still an earnings penalty associated with being a gay male and an earnings premium associated with being lesbian.

Much of what is known about gay men and lesbians is gathered from information about people of the same sex who live together (not necessarily gays/lesbians) in large national surveys. Table 1 shows, however, the danger of generalizing from the situation of gay and lesbian couples to all gays and lesbians. For men, the earnings premium enjoyed by heterosexuals shrinks dramatically if only the unattached are considered. Partnered lesbians have the highest average earnings of any group of women, enjoying a substantial earnings premium over heterosexuals (attached and single) and unattached lesbians.

There is a variety of possible reasons why partnered people might earn more than singles. Higher-income people might be more desirable marriage partners and so might be more likely to get married. Some couples choose to divide their labour and specialize in the areas where they are relatively more productive. One person takes on the role of provider, devoting most of his (or her) time to the labour market, while the other takes on the bulk of domestic tasks, freeing the first from household responsibilities. This division of labour will tend to increase the earnings of the person specializing in paid, market work, and decrease the earnings of the homemaker. People with partners can also earn more if their partner provides them with work-related support, for example, social hosting, or performing routine work-related tasks, for example, wordprocessing (LaFrance, Warman, and Woolley [2009] and Badgett [2009] explore these issues in more detail.) In this paper we explore the possibility that partnered people have more earnings in part because partnership has more tax and benefit-related advantages for high-income people than for low-income people, prompting high-income people to live together and keeping low-income people single. In the next section, we will set out the tax-related benefits and costs of marriage and cohabitation in Canada and argue that, indeed, the benefits are experienced primarily by higher-income individuals.

[7] Given the large size of the earnings differentials, and given that several studies in other countries have found a gay earnings penalty and a lesbian earnings premium (see, eg, Arabsheibani and Wadsworth 2005; Badget 2003), we do not believe that the lesbian earnings premium is entirely generated by low-income lesbians being more reluctant to disclose their status. Having said this, LaFrance, Warman and Woolley (2009) find that self-reported bisexuals typically have very poor economic outcomes and, as noted earlier, the rate of self-reported homosexuality among immigrants is relatively low, suggesting that there is some amount of closeting in certain communities. Statistics based on self-identified gays and lesbians do not capture the entire queer experience.

THE BENEFITS OF DEPENDENCY

Since Canada's tax system is individually based, a person's tax liabilities are based primarily on his or her own income. For people whose incomes come entirely from employment, there are few tax advantages to being married or in a common-law relationship. Most of these advantages are what Young (2000) terms dependency provisions.

If a taxpayer's spouse or common-law partner earned less than $9600 (in 2007), the taxpayer can claim a non-refundable 'spouse or common-law partner amount' tax credit of 15 per cent of $9600 less the partner's actual earnings[8] (for brevity, we will refer to this credit as the 'spousal amount' below). This tax credit reduces the amount of federal tax owing by up to $1440. Similar credits are available in most provinces that reduce provincial tax owing, although the value of the credit varies from province to province. In Ontario in 2007, the maximum value of the credit was $439. Spouses/common-law partners can transfer credits to each other. For example, if one spouse has tuition expenses but his or her income is so low that he or she pays no taxes, then the credit (worth, federally, 15 per cent of expenses) can be transferred to the other spouse, resulting in tax savings.

For a more complete discussion of the tax advantages of marriage, see Young (2000). These tax advantages are of greatest relevance when the lower-income partner has very little earnings. Because Canada delivers personal reliefs mainly through tax credits, rather than through deductions, the value of, say, a tuition tax credit is largely independent of a person's income level.[9] Transferring credits provides few tax advantages if the couple's earnings are somewhat unequal but both pay income taxes. The two exceptions to this rule are charitable donations and medical expenses, where couples can reduce their taxes (for charitable donations, by $28 federally) by consolidating the credits on one return and having just one spouse claim the credit.

Table 2 compares the extent of dependency in the same-sex couples and heterosexual couples surveyed in the CCHS. The first row of the table shows the percentage of couples where the respondent's income was less than one-quarter of the total household income—ones where the respondent might be thought of as being dependent on his or her partner. The next two rows capture more egalitarian relationships, where the respondent's income is between 25 and 75 per cent of total household income. The fourth row captures couples where the respondent is a provider, earning over 75 per cent of

[8] Canada Revenue Agency, 'Income Tax Package' (2008). Available at: www.cra-arc.gc.ca/formspubs/t1gnrl/on-eng.html.

[9] There is a slight advantage in transferring credits to the higher-income partner in Ontario, Nova Scotia, Prince Edward Island and the Yukon, where provincial/territorial surtaxes, or taxes on tax owing, are in place.

Table 2: Married/Common-law Distribution of Personal Income as a Percentage of Household Income

Respondent income as percentage of total household income	Heterosexual men	Gay men	Heterosexual women	Lesbians
Less than 25%	2.9	7.4	30.6	10.1
25% to 50%	21	38.1	45.6	39.3
50% to 75%	40.2	38.3	17.4	38.1
Over 75%	35.9	16.2	6.4	12.5
Percentage able to claim the spousal amount credit	27	17.2	25	18.3

Notes: Income is adjusted for inflation using the Consumer Price Index, with 2005 as the base year
Source: Calculated by the authors from the Canadian Community Health Survey

the household income. Table 2 reveals that same-sex couples in Canada, like the same-sex couples identified in the US by Alm, Badgett and Wittington (2000), tend to have more egalitarian relationships than their heterosexual counterparts. In the case of same-sex relationships, 20 to 25 per cent fall into the dependant/provider categories as we have defined them here, compared with 35 to 40 per cent of heterosexual relationships. As a result, fewer people in same-sex relationships benefit from dependency provisions.

We estimated the proportion of gay and lesbian households that would be able to claim the spousal amount credit by calculating those where the respondent income or the household income minus the respondent income was less than the amount of the credit. As shown in the last row of Table 2, 17.2 per cent of gay households and 18.3 per cent of lesbian households could, by our estimates, potentially claim the spousal amount credit. Most heterosexuals do not benefit from dependency provisions either: the *Leave It to Beaver* model of the family captures few people's realities. But still, the one quarter or more of heterosexual households who are, potentially, eligible for the spousal amount is substantially more than the portion of same-sex couples who may be eligible.

MUTUALITY

Young (2000) uses the term 'mutuality provisions' to describe those aspects of the tax system that are based on the assumption that spouses share and pool their economic resources. These mutuality provisions can provide significant benefits to couples, especially older couples with substantial assets or pension income, but they can also be costly in that they limit couples' asset holdings in certain ways. The major mutuality provisions in Canada's income tax code relate to the treatment of pension income and transfers of assets.

On 31 October 2006, the Canadian government introduced pension income splitting, whereby couples are permitted to allocate any pension income received so as to minimize the total tax paid on that income (Woolley 2007). For heterosexuals, this is advantageous for a fairly small number of retired couples—those where one spouse has a high pension income and the other has very little by way of pension income (see Kesselman 2008: 30). However, same-sex couples would appear to be even less likely to benefit from pension income splitting. Although Table 2 shows results only for people aged 18 to 59, it is a useful indicator of what the future holds. Same-sex couples typically have fairly similar income levels, and as shown in Table 1, gays and lesbians are less likely than married heterosexual men to have high incomes.

Canadian couples have other opportunities to lower their total tax burden by transferring income-generating assets to the lower-income spouse (who, in a progressive tax system, will pay a lower rate of tax on income earned). The higher-income spouse can contribute to a spousal Registered Retirement Savings Plan, thus generating tax savings because, while the tax deduction for the savings plan contribution is claimed by the high-income earner, the income generated by the plan is taxed in the hands of the low-income spouse. Special provisions of the Income Tax Act also allow spouses, in certain circumstances, to transfer property to each other during their relationship—or on death or relationship breakdown—without triggering a capital gains tax liability. (See Philipps [2009] for exceptions to attribution rules, and Young [2000] for more details.) Kesselman (2008: 19) details several other ways in which spouses can decrease their taxes by splitting their incomes.

Unfortunately, the CCHS does not provide information on asset holdings or on sexual orientation for people over the age of 59, so we cannot use the survey to assess the importance of these mutuality provisions for gay and lesbian couples. However, from what we know from other sources, access to special spousal asset transfer rules is not necessarily an unmitigated blessing. Without legal recognition of their relationships, gays and lesbians would not be subject to 'attribution rules', which restrict couples' freedom to make tax-effective transfers of income-generating assets from the higher-income spouse to the lower-income spouse. Other mutuality provisions also place same-sex couples at a disadvantage. Without formal recognition of their relationship, members of a same-sex couple could potentially designate two homes as principal residences and would therefore benefit twice from the non-taxation of capital gains on a principal residence. With formal recognition, people in a married and common-law relationship can claim only one residence as principal residence, even if they work in different cities and maintain more than one home.[10] Unfortunately, we simply do not know whether the benefits of access to income-splitting provisions offset the cost of being subject to attribution rules and the restriction to one principal residence.

It is also not clear that economic mutuality, with the underlying assumption that assets and incomes are pooled, is an appropriate model for same-sex relationships (or, for that matter, many heterosexual relationships). In a qualitative study of same-sex couples in the UK, Burns, Burgoyne and Clarke (2008), found that 'A degree of financial autonomy was an important ideal highlighting a valuing of co-independence rather than financial "merging" for lesbian and gay couples.' Klawitter (2008), using the US Survey of Consumer Finances, found that 'married couples are much more likely to hold money jointly than are same-sex or unmarried different-sex couples'. A more inclusive definition of the couple in the Canadian Income Tax Act could call into question the assumption of economic mutuality, just as it calls into question assumptions about dependency.

DOES SAME-SEX MARRIAGE SHIFT THE COSTS OF CHILDREN TO FAMILIES?

Canada's tax system recognizes the dependency of children, as well as the dependency of spouses, but in somewhat atypical ways. Unlike many other developed nations, Canada had, until 2007, no universal recognition of the effect of children on ability to pay taxes. Instead, support for children was (and, to a large extent, still is) targeted toward single parents and low to moderate income households. Single parents can claim an 'amount for an eligible dependant' (for brevity, referred to the 'dependant amount' here). This is essentially the spousal amount described in the section 'The Benefits of Dependency' above, but it is for a child, rather than a dependent spouse. The major programmes providing support for children are refundable credits, the Canada Child Tax Benefit and the National Child Benefit Supplement. These credits are targeted towards low to moderate income families, with eligibility based on a measure called 'net family income', which is the combined income of a child's parents (when a child lives with both of his or her parents) or the child's custodial parent and any new partner, if the child's parents are separated.

[10] Although, for convenience, I have discussed this under 'Mutuality', the principal residence deduction limitations could also be thought of as recognizing the economies of scale enjoyed by two-person households.

Table 3: Benefits available, two adults with pre-tax incomes of $20,000 each, Ontario, 2008

	Taxed as two single parents (one child each)	Taxed as one single parent with two children and one unattached adult	Taxed as married couple with two children
Equivalent-to-married amount (Federal + Ontario, 2008)	$3,772	$1,886	$0
Canada Child Tax Benefit	$9,031.68	$8,792.88	$3,446.16
GST credit	$1,252.00	$1,134	$371.56
Total benefits	$14,056	$11,813	$3,818
Cost of marriage	$10,238	$7,995	n/a

Source: Calculated by the authors from the Canadian Community Health Survey. Details of Canada Child Tax Benefit calculations can be found in Woolley (2010)

The original rationale for Canada's current system of benefits was fairness. The system 'provides the same level of benefit per child to families in similar financial circumstances' (Canada, Department of Finance 1992: 138). Yet the fairness of providing benefits based on total family income assumes mutuality—that everyone shares equally in the family income. The fairness of providing the same benefits to two-adult and one-adult families at the same income level assumes strong economies of scale: only if two adults can really live as cheaply as one do two-parent families and one-parent families with the same income have 'similar financial circumstances'.

The assumptions of mutuality and economies of scale underlying Canada's child benefit programme create costs for low-income single parents who choose to form partnerships. For example, suppose Anita and Susan each earn $20,000 per year—just over what someone working full time, full-year at the Ontario minimum wage would earn. They have two children. Table 3 compares the amounts they can claim in dependant amount credits and refundable child tax benefits when they are taxed as (a) two single parents, each of whom has one child; (b) one single parent with two children and one unattached adult; (c) a couple with two children. Table 3 also includes a smaller refundable credit, the Goods and Services Tax (GST) credit, which is designed to offset consumption taxes for low-income households. The GST credit also assumes economies of scale and is more generous for single-parent households. As Table 3 shows, the loss of benefits associated with the formal recognition of their relationship can be quite substantial—over 25 per cent of Anita and Susan's combined pre-tax income. It could be argued that we have simply chosen this particular example because it illustrates a very large marriage penalty, and it is not realistic. What, then, is the situation of a typical gay or lesbian parent?

Table 4 provides information on the portion of gays and lesbians who live in a household with a child between 0 and 11, and on the portion receiving child tax benefit for single individuals (including those who are separated, divorced or widowed) and for partnered lesbian, gay and heterosexual individuals. This table is particularly important because it presents information about the prevalence of lesbian single parenthood that is not generally available. The information about children is gathered from the question 'What are the names of all persons who usually live here? ... What is [name]'s age?' The respondent may not be the biological or adoptive parent of the child in question if, for example, the child is the respondent's partner's child from a previous relationship. Alternatively, the respondent might have children from a previous relationship who live with another parent so are not included in the CCHS information. Therefore the percentage of gay or lesbian households containing a child is only an approximate estimate the number of gays and lesbians who are adoptive or biological parents. Table 4 shows that lesbians are much more likely than gay men to live in households with children. Two-adult households are more likely to contain children than one-adult households—which is not surprising, given that there is twice the number of potential parents. The percentage of gay (male) couples with children (6.2 per cent) in the CCHS is higher than the 2006 census estimate of 3.4 per cent of couples, perhaps because the CCHS sample is restricted to people under 60. On the other hand, the percentage of lesbian couples with children in the 2006 Census estimates—16.8 per cent—is higher than the CCHS sample (9.5 per cent), perhaps because the CCHS sample only considers children under 12 (Statistics Canada 2007)[11] or perhaps because the 2006 census was carried out after the first two CCHS cycles and there has been a 'gayby' boom with more children born in gay/lesbian households. All groups of gays and lesbians are less likely to have children than their heterosexual counterparts, although the difference is much more marked for men than for women. Most single lesbians are not single parents, but a significant minority are: about 7 per cent of single lesbians are the lone parent of at least one child under 12.

Information on receipt of benefits was gleaned from the question 'Thinking about the total income for all household members, from which

[11] In the 2.1 CCHS, it is not possible to identify the number of children 12 and over in the household, while in the 3.1 and 2007 CCHS data, it is possible to identify the number of persons 15 years old or less in the household and the number of dependants 16 or 17 years old in the household.

Table 4: Households with Children, receiving Canada Child Tax Benefit (CCTB)

Percentage reporting:	Females		Males	
	Child under 12	CCTB	Child under 12	CCTB
Heterosexual married/ common law	38.9	28.0	41.7	25.7
Heterosexual unattached	22.0	25.9	5.8	3.4
Lesbian/gay married/ common law	9.5	6.2	6.2	3.0
Lesbian/gay unattached	6.8	15.2	—[a]	—

Notes: [a]Gay (male) observations omitted due to low cell size
Source: Calculated by the authors from the Canadian Community Health Survey

of the following sources did your household receive any income in the past 12 months? ... Canada Child Tax Benefit'.[12] For unattached females, the percentage of households reporting the Canada Child Tax Benefit (CCTB) is a good estimate of the number of women who are lone parents, since most female lone parents have low enough incomes to be eligible for CCTB. Using receipt of CCTB as a measure of the presence of children, 15 per cent of unattached lesbians are lone parents. Although lesbian couples are more likely to report having a child under 12 in their household, singles are more likely to receive CCTB. For heterosexuals, if we consider only people with children, singles are again much more likely to receive CCTB. Recall that eligibility for CCTB is based on a measure of the combined income of a child's custodial parent and that of her/his partner, called net family income. It is fairly obvious that net family income will usually be higher for a parent with a partner than for a single parent.

Just over one in seven unattached lesbians is a single parent receiving CCTB. For these women, recognition of same-sex relationships is potentially disadvantageous. Previously, entering a new cohabiting relationship would have had no impact on CCTB. But now that same-sex relationships are recognized, entering a relationship can mean losing CCTB. One could argue that this is what equality is about: heterosexuals, lesbians and gays are all subject to the same penalties and privileges. However, lesbians face a different dynamic from heterosexual women. Because women earn less than men on average, a lesbian stands to gain less income from welcoming

[12] See: www.statcan.gc.ca/imdb-bmdi/instrument/3226_Q1_V4-eng.pdf.

a new woman into her life than a heterosexual woman typically gains from welcoming a new man.

SOCIAL ASSISTANCE

In Canada, much of the income support for low-income persons is delivered outside the tax system through a variety of provincial level social assistance plans. Although every province has its own social assistance programme, there are some commonalities across the country. Eligibility for benefits is subject to tight income and asset tests, so only very low-income persons are able to benefit. Both eligibility and the benefits to which a person is entitled are based on family status. The maximum income that a single parent on social assistance could receive from all sources of benefits—social assistance as well as refundable tax credits—varies from a low of $14,041 per year in Nova Scotia to a high of $17,850 in Newfoundland (National Council of Welfare 2008). A couple with children typically receives only marginally more by way of social assistance than a single person.

Table 5 shows the number of females and males in the Canadian Community Health Survey reporting receiving any social assistance income. The number of married or cohabiting gay men reporting social assistance was so low that we were unable to report these numbers due to confidentiality concerns. The numbers in Table 5 represent the percentage of households reporting receiving any income from social assistance over the course of the year, and they show that social assistance is an important source of income for single lesbians. One in seven single lesbians reported receiving some social assistance income. As Table 5 shows, it is rare for couples, heterosexual or same-sex, to receive social assistance: rates of social assistance for two-adult families are so low that if any employment is available, it is generally the preferable option. Or, given that benefits available through

Table 5: Households receiving any Social Assistance

Percentage reporting social assistance	Female/lesbian	Male/gay
Heterosexual married/common law	2.1	1.7
Heterosexual unattached	13.2	7.5
Lesbian/gay married/common law	2.3	—[a]
Lesbian/gay unattached	14.2	8.2

Notes: [a]Observations omitted due to low cell size
Source: Calculated by the authors from the Canadian Community Health Survey

social assistance are so similar for one and two-adult households, it makes sense to split up and claim as two households. The point of Table 5 is to illustrate another cost to gays and lesbians from formal recognition of relationships: potential loss of social assistance income.

CONCLUSION: WHY SAME-SEX MARRIAGE?

> MPs, like most Canadians, have come to understand that equal marriage doesn't harm anyone, it only makes life better for some.[13]

In this chapter, we have argued that formal recognition of same-sex marriage has few tax advantages for working aged gays and lesbians. For lesbians and for single parents, in particular, legal recognition of relationships can lead to a substantial loss of benefits. So why is there such a firmly held belief that, as quoted above, 'equal marriage doesn't harm anyone'?

One possible explanation is that the demographic harmed by the formal recognition of same-sex marriage—low-income single parents, especially lesbian single parents—is not very visible. The research we undertook for this chapter is the first, to our knowledge, to report even such basic information as the receipt of CCTB or social assistance for single gays and lesbians. Because few surveys ask about sexual orientation, most formal studies of the gay and lesbian population in Canada are based on same-sex couples. However, as we have demonstrated, this group is different from single gays and lesbians. Not only is statistical information about single gays and lesbians lacking, but the members of this group who are most at risk (lone parents) are also those with the least time for self-advocacy. Those engaged in advocacy—high-income, highly educated individuals with pensions, assets and health plans—have little to lose from recognition of their relationships, and often something to gain.

A second explanation is that the adverse consequences of living together can easily be avoided by not disclosing one's relationship. Because Canada has a system of individual filing, each member of a couple could simply file an individual return and tick 'single' in the marital status box. It should be noted, however, that the Canada Revenue Agency (CRA) does audit returns to identify couples posing as singles. For example, one parent must provide the other parent's social insurance number when claiming child tax benefits. So if the two parents used the same address for tax purposes but claimed to be singles, this could trigger a CRA investigation. It is questionable whether the Canada Revenue Agency would be able to enforce rules

[13] Source: www.equal-marriage.ca.

requiring disclosure of common-law status, but the issue has not yet been completely tested.[14]

Alternatively, the increasing visibility of gays and lesbians associated with the gay rights movement could inevitably have led to the retraction of benefits such as social assistance from partnered gays. Indeed, Young (1994: 551) reports an example of this happening in the early 1990s. A gay man was denied the coverage of medical expenses that would typically be available to singles with no other source of income because he had a 'spouse', but his partner was not able to claim those medical expenses on his income tax return, because he was not a spouse for income tax purposes. Given the inevitable loss of social assistance and other government transfers, it would only make sense to fight for the rights and entitlements associated with marriage and common-law partnerships.

Finally, it is only fair to note that a number of advocates for the rights of gays and lesbians, such as Claire Young (2000), have been sceptical about the value of broadening marriage to include gays and lesbians. Indeed, *Beyond Conjugality*, a report of the Law Commission of Canada (2001) argued for replacing conjugality in income taxation with other measures of economic dependence and interdependence.

What we have learnt in this chapter is that for most gay and lesbian couples, little is gained or lost through taxation as a result of formal recognition of their relationships. Gay and lesbian relationships are typically egalitarian, so people in such relationships have few opportunities to take advantage of dependency provisions. Although there are some potential gains from recognition of mutuality, there are other potential losses—for example, the loss of the provision for a second principal residence. One of the largest costs of relationship recognition is the potential loss of child benefits for single-parent families. Here, as in other aspects of the income tax system, recognition of the costs experienced by gay and lesbian families points to areas where policy reform may be needed, since Anita and Paul would experience costs as great as those incurred by Anita and Susan were each of these couples to marry. As Canadian families grow, change and evolve so must the Canadian income tax system.

REFERENCES

Alm, J, Badgett, MVL and Whittington, LA (2000) 'Wedding Bell Blues: The Income Tax Consequences of Legalizing Same-Sex Marriage' 53 *National Tax Journal.* Available at: ssrn.com/abstract=228874 or DOI: 10.2139/ssrn.228874.

[14] Alan Macnaughton, editor, *Canadian Tax Journal* (personal communication to the authors).

Arabsheibani, AGR and Wadsworth, J (2005) 'Gay Pay in the UK' 72 *Economica* 333–47.
Australia. House of Representatives (2008) Same Sex Relationships (Equal Treatment in Commonwealth Laws—General Law Reform) Bill 2008, Explanatory Memorandum. Circulated by the authority of the Attorney-General, the Hon Robert McClelland MP.
Badgett, MVL (2003) *Money, Myths and Change: The Economic Lives of Lesbians and Gay Men* (Chicago, University of Chicago Press).
—— (2009) *When Gay People Get Married: What Happens When Societies Legalize Same-Sex Marriage?* (New York, New York University Press).
Burns, M, Burgoyne, C and Clarke, V (2008) 'Financial Affairs? Money Management in Same-Sex Relationships' 37 *The Journal of Socio-Economics* 481–501.
Canada. Department of Finance (1992) *The Budget 1992: Budget Papers* (Ottawa, Department of Finance).
Carpenter, C (2008) 'Sexual Orientation, Work, and Income in Canada' 41 *Canadian Journal of Economics* 1239–61.
Kesselman, JR (2008) 'Income Splitting and Joint Taxation of Couples: What's Fair?' 14 *Institute for Research on Public Policy Choices.*
Klawitter, M (2008) 'The effects of sexual orientation and marital status on how couples hold their money' 6 *Review of Economics of the Household* 4, 423–46.
LaFrance, A, Warman, C and Woolley, F (2009) 'Sexual Identity and the Marriage Premium', working paper (Queen's University, Department of Economics).
Lahey, KA (2001) 'The Impact of Relationship Recognition on Lesbian Women in Canada: Still Separate and Only Somewhat "Equivalent"' (Ottawa, Status of Women Canada). Available at: dsp-psd.pwgsc.gc.ca/Collection/SW21-82-2001E.pdf.
Law Commission of Canada (2001) *Beyond Conjugality: Recognizing and Supporting Close Personal Adult Relationships* (Ottawa, Law Commission of Canada).
National Council of Welfare (2008) *Welfare Incomes 2006 and 2007.* Available at: www.ncwcnbes.net/documents/researchpublications/OtherPublications/2008 Report-WelfareIncomes2006-2007/Report-WelfareIncomes2006-2007E.pdf.
Philipps, L (2009) 'Income Splitting and Gender Equality: The Case for Incentivising Intra-Household Transfers' in K Brooks, A Gunnarson, L Philipps and M Wersig (eds), *Challenging Gender Inequality in Tax Policy Making* (Oxford, Hart Publishing, 2011).
Smith, M (2002) 'Recognizing Same-Sex Relationships: The Evolution of Recent Federal and Provincial Policies' 45 *Canadian Public Administration/Administration publique du Canada* 1–23.
Statistics Canada (2007) *Families and Households: 2006 Census* cat no 97-553-XWE2006024. Available at: www.statcan.gc.ca/bsolc/olc-cel/olc-cel?lang=eng&catno=97-553-X2006024.
Woolley, F (2007) 'Policy Forum: Liability without Control—The Curious Case of Pension Income Splitting' 55 *Canadian Tax Journal* 603–25.
—— (2010) 'Ending Poverty through Child Benefits: Hitting the Wall?' in CM Beach, B Dahlby and PAR Hobson (eds), *The 2009 Federal Budget: Challenge, Response and Retrospect* (Montreal, McGill-Queen's University Press).

Young, C (1994) 'Taxing Times for Lesbians and Gay Men: Equality at What Cost?' 17 *Dalhousie Law Journal* 534–59.
—— (2000) *What's Sex Got to Do with It? Tax and the 'Family'* (Ottawa, Law Commission of Canada). Available at: epe.lac-bac.gc.ca/100/206/301/law_commission_of_canada-ef/2006-1206/www.lcc.gc.ca/pdf/young.pdf.
Young, C and Boyd, S (2006) 'Losing the Feminist Voice? Debates on the Legal Recognition of Same Sex Partnerships in Canada' 14 *Feminist Legal Studies* 213–40.

10

Income Redistribution through Child Benefits and Child-related Tax Deductions: A Gender-neutral Approach?

KIRSTEN SCHEIWE

INCOME AND DIVISION of labour in a household are affected in various ways when there are children in the family who need to be cared for and whose expenses need to be paid. Since childcare is a highly gendered activity, gendered outcomes are also heavily influenced by situations where families need to care for children. Tax legislators and social policy makers can react in different ways to this situation: if having a child is considered to be a purely private decision, tax legislators may ignore the situation and impose equal taxes on taxpayers whether or not they have children and therefore childcare obligations. However, since the development of modern family policy in some European countries in the 1920s and 1930s, child benefits have been provided (first in Belgium and France), along with tax deductions and loans for married couples. Modern family policy differs from historical systems of poor relief in that it focuses not only on the poorest strata of society, but on working-class and middle-class families, who now receive child benefits and/or tax deductions for raising children.

This means that, nowadays, having a child matters under tax law in Germany. According to the case law of the German Federal Constitutional Court dating from the 1990s, tax legislators must take into account unavoidable expenses for the maintenance of members of the immediate family and cannot reject these as purely private, since they reduce the taxpayer's ability to pay and therefore have to be acknowledged according to the principle of tax fairness.[1] This principle has been applied in case law not only to maintenance costs for raising children, but to costs incurred in the

[1] BVerfGE 43, 108 (120); 82, 60 (87); 99, 216 (232ff).

support of a divorced spouse or the parents of a taxpayer (Schuler-Harms 2008: 37). The significance of supporting family members has been firmly established in tax law as a public and constitutional concern, but is gender equality woven as tightly into German concepts of tax fairness?

Two interacting systems need to be examined in order to answer this question: the system of tax deductions and that of child benefits, which have common goals but are regulated by different legal and organizational principles. In the case of tax deductions, those paying few or no taxes do not benefit from them much (if at all) compared with those with higher taxable income, especially if progressive tax rates are applied. Child benefits are designed in very different ways (as universal benefits or as means-tested schemes and as part of social insurance systems or as tax-financed benefits), but deductions and benefits both affect family taxation and have the common purpose of redistributing income for the benefit of families. From a gender perspective, it is important to analyse these two interacting systems together, since both take into account the direct and indirect effects of children on parents' income. In this chapter, I have opted to take a *broad view of taxation*, which encompasses taxes, social security contributions and certain child-related social benefits for families (regarded as negative taxes),[2] since they have a combined effect on the distribution of income towards different types of households and families. They are also based on underlying gender assumptions and have a gendered impact. (For more on the gendered impact of family-related tax provision, see Young [2000] and Gunnarsson, chapter four in this volume. For a discussion of patterns of male and female contributions to social security and benefits in Germany, see chapter thirteen of this volume by Spangenberg.)

However, undertaking this type of analysis is not an easy task, since the two interacting systems are only partially overlapping and their internal structures differ considerably in terms of policy goals, guiding legal principles, redistributive effects and the potential incentives they create. There are at least four dimensions of inequality to be distinguished: vertical inequality between households at different income levels; horizontal inequality between households with or without children; the tax treatment of one-earner versus two-earner households; and gender inequalities cross-cutting these three inequality levels.

GENDER INEQUALITIES HIDDEN BY COMPLEX SYSTEMS AND MULTIPLE POLICY GOALS

The goal of promoting gender equality is only one of many political goals in Germany. Although it is the guiding legal principle of non-discrimination

[2] This approach is also taken, eg, by O'Donoghue and Sutherland (1998); Parker and Sutherland (1991); Figari et al (2007); Maucher (2001); and Dingeldey (2000a; 2000b).

on the basis of gender, and although it is also the principle behind the state's constitutional objectives of promoting the implementation of equal rights for women and men and of moving toward the elimination of existing disadvantages (German Basic Law, article 3 section 2(2)), many other social objectives are on the state's agenda. If complexity is increasing and legislators are pursuing multiple normative goals at the same time (as is usually the case), the goal of combating gender disadvantages risks being neglected (possibly unintentionally) just because it is only one goal among others. Other goals, for instance, may be considered to be more important in the case of conflicts between goals. In addition, increasing interdependency and interaction between different sub-systems may cause more frequent occurrences of dysfunctional effects and non-intended outcomes that place women at a disadvantage because it is difficult to foresee the potential consequences of new legal measures.

Gender is often neglected, and especially in the case of family-related policies—whether in tax law or in social law—women are frequently disappearing 'within the family', based on the obviously erroneous but still extant assumption that 'what is good for the family is good for women'. This assumption fails to take into account the many differences among women (and men) according to income situation, family status and family form; employment status; and number and age of children. By contrast, any gender analysis must include an understanding of which family type is most favoured by tax deductions and social benefits (traditional family, single-parent family or others) and which person within the family is entitled to claim and to receive benefits or to make tax deductions. The gender dimension is different, for instance, under strictly individualized tax systems with tax rebates directed towards children (O'Donoghue and Sutherland 1998: 9) than in systems based on a hierarchical male-breadwinner model or on a dual-earner model. Furthermore, the gender dimension for parents living together or living apart has different connotations, since two parents can make different arrangements as to how to share time, employment and care than can a single parent.

This chapter will outline the complexities involved in discovering the gender dimension of policy goals and their potential redistributive effects in relation to child-related and childcare-related tax regulations and social benefits. It does not look at marriage-related tax deductions or benefits for a dependent partner, since this is the subject of other chapters in this volume (for example see chapters eleven and twelve by Wersig and Philipps, respectively). Another focus of my argument is the general trend to dissociate the regulation of marriage from the rights and obligations based on the child-parent relationship. This trend is favoured from a feminist perspective, since it reduces the dependency of caregivers on marriage and a traditional family form and places more importance on the societal dimension of organizing child support and care. Despite this trend, however, the advantages linked to marriage are still very strong in Germany under both tax and social security law.

OVERVIEW OF FAMILY POLICY IN GERMANY:
CHANGING PARADIGMS, CHANGING LEGAL INTERPRETATIONS

Historical Background

Modern family policy was institutionalized in some European countries in the 1930s through systems of child benefits and tax deductions for married couples. Belgium and France were the pioneers of child benefits as a wage supplement based on the idea that men were the earners of a 'family wage' (Montanari 2000), and the two countries institutionalized these benefits as part of their social security systems in 1930 (Belgium) and in 1932 (France). These benefits were financed through employers' contributions (Bahle 1995). In Germany, instruments of family policy were introduced in the 1930s during the Nazi regime. These included family benefits and income tax scales recognizing family burdens. These measures were introduced under the terrorist Nazi regime and served as a means of preserving mass loyalty; at the same time, they were elements of the modern welfare state.

Although neither family ideologies nor family policies were monolithic but, rather, diverse and contradictory expressions of a poly-centred system (Voegeli 2003), these new instruments constructed the husband as the head of the family and as entitled to social benefits and tax relief. They represented an extension of the traditional male-breadwinner model and of perceptions of the family that were inherent in social security schemes developed incrementally since the Bismarckian reforms of the 1880s. These social security measures included the introduction of survivor benefits, co-insurance of family members under the breadwinner's health insurance and maternity protection (Scheiwe 2005). Under the Nazi regime, marriage loans were granted (under racist eugenic conditions) to the husbands, beginning in 1933, on condition that the wife would not be (or would no longer be) employed in the paid workforce. These loans were granted independently of household income, and the repayable part of the loan was reduced by 25 per cent for each child born to the husband and wife. The marriage rate increased considerably after this measure was introduced, and only 8 to 9 per cent of children were born out of wedlock between 1935 and 1938 (Voegeli 2003: 134). Child benefits were introduced in 1935/36, and these were of particular advantage to workers with three or more children and to single parents.

Tax reductions for families were introduced between 1934 and 1938. A distinction was made between married couples with children and those without children, and single individuals were taxed at a higher rate—up to 180 per cent of the normal rate for married couples without children. In 1938, racist selection was established within the tax system: Jews and other so-called non-Aryans were always taxed at the highest tax rate for single individuals regardless of the size of their families (Voegeli 2003: 141). For the rest of the population, tax reductions were significant for families with three or more children, while direct transfer payments through the child benefit scheme were much more advantageous for low-income families.

These measures contained racist values and entitlement conditions (only so-called Aryan families were entitled) and served to secure mass loyalty. However, at the same time, they represented the beginning of a modern family policy that used tax law and social law as regulatory instruments in the manner of similar measures in France and fascist Italy (Saraceno 1990). The husband as head of the family was entitled, privileging marriage and men as husbands/married fathers, but unmarried single mothers were also entitled to some social benefits (though to a lesser degree than husbands/ married fathers). While single mothers were excluded from marriage loans, they could claim child benefits. Since 1937 when general conscription was reintroduced, children born out of wedlock could claim public support benefits if the father had been conscripted to the army, but only on the condition that the father had recognized paternity or had been sentenced to pay maintenance by a court and paid it efficiently (Buske 2004: 176). This policy measure was designed to bolster loyalty; already the First World War had led to the extension of claims to orphan pensions of children born out of wedlock of a father who died as a soldier (although under restricted conditions).

In other European countries, child benefits developed mainly after the Second World War as universal systems independent of parental income and employment status (in Ireland in 1944; the United Kingdom in 1946; Iceland in 1946; Norway in 1946; Sweden in 1947; Finland in 1948; and in Denmark in 1950). The basic idea was that of redistribution of income towards children through universal, tax-financed benefits. Germany introduced a very limited system of child benefits in an insurance-based system in 1954. During the subsequent decades, the system underwent various changes, starting as an insurance-based system and evolving into a universal system of child benefits especially in 1961 and 1975, but the comparatively low level of child benefits remained intact until 1996.

The Childcare Expense Reforms of 1996: Untaxed Minimums and Deductions

In 1996, a major reform was introduced under the influence of a 1990 judgment of the Federal Constitutional Court, in which it was decided that the legislator was obliged to refrain from taxing a minimum amount (called 'the existence minimum') to financially support a child. This interpretation was derived from the equality principle of German Basic Law (article 3 section 1) whereby tax fairness required that the portion of the family income necessary to cover a child's existence minimum cannot be taxed. In 1996, legislation introduced a dual system, a mix of tax and cash benefits for a child: a high tax deduction covering the existence minimum of a child, split between the two parents. For individuals with no or low taxable income who cannot fully benefit from the child tax deduction, a child benefit is granted. This dual system provides a refundable tax credit[3] in the form of a monthly tax refund, differentiated according to birth rank of the child to all taxpayers, and it builds on a complex interplay between child benefit and child tax deduction (Lang 1999; Maucher 2001). Thus, the so-called '*Kindergeld*' is a monthly tax refund for taxpayers who paid 'too much' (compared with those without children), based on the principles of tax fairness and equal treatment. Only for those who pay no or few taxes is it considered to be a social benefit. However, if the child receives means-tested public income support, the child benefit is fully deducted as income from the child's means-tested benefit.

Another family-related tax instrument comes in the form of *employed parents deducting childcare expenses* from taxable income. Although one policy goal of the German welfare state is to incentivize maternal employment through tax law,[4] in Germany tax law has not been used much to incentivize maternal employment (Daly and Scheiwe 2010). In fact, the possibility of deducting childcare expenses from taxable income is rather limited, and from 1984 to 2000, this option was open only to single parents.[5]

Tax Deductions for Single Parents and All Parents, Employed and Unemployed

Special tax rules for single parents were challenged before the Federal Constitutional Court in 1998 and declared to be in breach of the Constitution because married parents were disadvantaged compared with unmarried parents.[6] The regulation in question granted a 'household allowance' to a single parent that corresponded to a married couple's basic tax-deduction. This measure was intended to provide a single parent with partial compensation for being excluded from advantages that married couples had under joint taxation, thus alleviating single parents'

[3] Refundable or non-wastable tax credits are benefits that are paid in cash when the tax liability of a family is not large enough to make use of (or full use of) a particular fiscal advantage or tax credit.

[4] For an economic discussion and modelling of the impact of childcare costs and tax-benefit policies on parental employment, see Immervoll and Barber (2005).

[5] For details, see Ahmann (2002); Hey (2006) and Hölzer (2008).

[6] BVerfGE 99, 216 (238ff).

special burdens and the costs of educating a child alone. This particular tax deduction for single parents was gradually phased out, and instead, a considerably lower deduction was introduced from 2000 onwards[7] for a 'real' single parent living with a minor child but without any other adult person in the household. A parent cohabiting with another adult of the opposite sex or living in a registered same-sex partnership is not considered to be a 'real' single parent. In addition, the single-parent tax deduction cannot be split between separated parents if both care for the child and the child is considered to live alternately in each parent's residence. (See chapter nine by Warman and Woolley for a discussion of child benefits provided to single parents and heterosexual and lesbian/gay couples in Canada.)

Between 2000 and 2006, all parents caring for a child at home or spending money on childcare could deduct a lump sum for care and educational needs whether they were employed or not. Hence, home-based care for children by a non-employed parent was deductible on the same terms as childcare expenses of employed parents. Since 2006, however, the tax deductions for the latter have been more generous: if a single parent or both parents are employed (or self-employed), they are allowed to deduct two-thirds of their childcare expenses (for a kindergarten, after school care, child day care or professional caregiver at their home) up to a maximum of €4000 per year until the time when the child is 14 years old. If only one parent of the couple is employed, these costs are deductible only until the child is three years old and under more restricted conditions.

Low-income families benefit little from this tax advantage, as for them and for single mothers, a reduction of fees for public childcare is much more valuable than a deduction of childcare expenses from their income tax. And for single mothers on income support, the single-parent supplement under this scheme is more valuable. It should be noted that provision of childcare facilities (through kindergartens, crèches or day care centres) comes under the jurisdiction of the local municipalities and is tax-financed. Although parents have to pay fees, these can be reduced or waived for low-income households. Contrary to the situation in the United Kingdom and Canada, tax deductions for childcare expenses are not seen as an important instrument for incentivizing the supply of childcare or for encouraging people to enrol their children in day care, since direct subsidies are granted to the providers of childcare facilities by the local authorities responsible for youth and family support.

[7] Since 2004, a lone parent (defined as a parent with a minor child not cohabiting with another adult) can deduct €1308 per year or € 109 monthly from taxable income (para 24b Income Tax Act).

Gender Equality versus General Equality

The constitutional principle of gender equality (German Basic Law, article 3 section 2) played an important role in tax law decisions of the Federal Constitutional Court in the 1950s but later lost importance, while the general equality principle (German Basic Law, article 3 section 1) and the demand for tax fairness, combined with the protection of the family (German Basic Law, article 6 section. 1), have gained ground in the legal argumentation of the Court. The landmark 1957 decision[8] on the taxation of a married couple[9] argued that it was unconstitutional and an infringement of the gender-equality principle that the legislator tried to 'bring the wife back into the home' through legislative measures that disadvantaged a wife's employment and personal earnings. Such an intended 'educational effect' (to promote a particular role model) was rejected, and the Federal Constitutional Court stressed the personal right of a wife to be employed and 'to earn market income with the same legal chances and on the same terms as each male citizen'.[10]

This far-reaching critique of particular role models or intended 'educational effects' caused by tax legislation was weakened later on. In a later decision of 1978, concerning the non-deductibility of expenses for a household helper who cared for the children of an employed couple, the Federal Constitutional Court rejected the argument that this was an infringement of the gender-equality principle, stating that not only the mother but also the husband had to pay part of the expenses for this in-house child caregiver and therefore there had been no discrimination against the wife. There was no indication in the judgment that since women are usually the caregivers, non-deductibility of caregiver expenses (no matter which spouse pays for them) would tend to encourage one of the spouses (likely the wife) to stay at home. Therefore, the net effect would be a disincentive for women to enter or stay in the paid workforce. The Court judgment was given within the context of formal equality, and in that context, it is much more difficult to prove discrimination (and particularly indirect discrimination) against women. Furthermore, the gender-neutral normative role model of shared parenting and of a couple's democratic, joint decision making concerning division of labour is taken as a justification for not undertaking an empirical investigation of gender inequalities that may actually exist within that framework. Engaging in such empirical investigations is also hampered because gender-differentiated data on inequalities under tax law are largely missing in Germany (Mückenberger, Spangenberg and Warncke 2007).

[8] BVerfGE 6, 55.

[9] At the time, a married couple was the tax unit and was taxed jointly without splitting; due to progressive tax rates, a married couple paid higher taxes than two individuals being taxed separately.

[10] BVerfGE 6, 55 (82).

In the case law of the Federal Constitutional Court, it is not gender equality but the general equality principle and the unequal treatment of taxpayers with children compared with those without children that have gained the most attention. These concepts are connected with the principle of tax fairness, which has been based on a number of different legal principles and sources: the principle of equal treatment under tax law, the principle of fairness according to merit and the principle of equal tax burden.[11] Far-reaching legal reforms increasing gender inequality in the areas of family taxation and child benefits have also been instigated by the case law[12] of the Federal Constitutional Court, especially during the period from 1987 to 1999, when Paul Kirchhof, now professor of tax law at Heidelberg University, was a judge and a member of the Court's second senate.[13] In summary, the basic constitutional requirement for tax laws is that a realistic amount of the existence minimum of each individual, including the child has to remain untaxed; therefore income below this threshold is not taxed, and a parent can deduct the amount to cover the existence minimum of the child from her or his taxable income. The calculation of the existence minimum, based on the means-tested income support benefits designed to cover the existence minimum, has become a point of convergence between tax law and social law, since the calculation of the existence minimum is also the basis for calculating the level of income support benefits.

THE DOWNGRADING OF GENDER-EQUALIZING POLICIES: INSTRUMENTS USED AND THE EFFECTS OF CONFLICTING GOALS

To analyse ways in which gender-equalizing policies have been downgraded after the late 1950s, it is important to first examine the potential distributional effects of the treatment of children and the family under tax law and social law. Hypotheses regarding these effects have been offered by O'Donoghue and Sutherland (1998) and by Figari et al (2007), and they are as follows:

a. A universal child benefit is capable of delivering resources to all children, but on a proportional basis, the increase in income is greater for poorer children. Under a more progressive tax structure, tax deductions for children are of greater proportional benefit to those who pay higher income tax.

[11] Schuler-Harms (2008: 35).

[12] Especially the decisions concerning the 'Kindergeld' BVerfGE 82, 60 and the child tax deduction, BVerfGE 82, 198ff.

[13] He holds rather conservative views on the family and the woman's role within the family and ran as a candidate for the Christian Democratic Party (CDU) during the federal election campaign of 2005 as a proposed minister of finance. But his radical proposal to introduce a general, flat-rate tax of 25% for all, with hardly any exemptions or tax deductions met with resistance from all sides, so he was dropped as a candidate.

b. Child benefits should in the first instance be paid to the main caregiver (usually the mother). Tax deductions that are not refundable can be of use to the family only if the person to whom they are allocated has sufficient taxable income to set against them. Thus, under joint taxation, the family as a whole may benefit, but the cash is likely to be channelled through the father's income. Under independent taxation, the family will benefit to the greatest degree if the parent to whom the tax deduction is allocated has the higher income or if the tax deduction is transferable between spouses.
c. In the case of child benefits (or tax credits that are refundable to individuals who pay no taxes), payment to the mother does not compromize the positive impact on family income.
d. Non-means-tested benefits, including universal family benefits, as well as insurance-based, out-of-work benefits, can have a positive or negative effect on women's share of income, depending on who is most likely to receive these benefits.
e. Means-tested benefits are more valuable to people on lower incomes and contribute most to equalization in the bottom quintile.
f. Social security contributions tend to be progressive at lower earnings levels (due to contribution thresholds) and regressive for earnings close to the contribution ceiling. Accordingly, they can play a minor equalizing role at lower income levels but can exacerbate gender inequalities at high income levels.

Table 1 shows the instruments and policy goals and the redistributive effects and gender-equality effects of tax law, social law and social security benefits in Germany. These elements provide the basis for a discussion of the gender dimensions of redistributive effects and the connected (dis)incentives for taking up employment. A great deal of economic and social science literature is available on these issues,[14] usually built on model calculations for different types of household income before and after taxes. However, the elements shown Table 1 will provide a more general and abstract view for purposes of comparative discussion. (The footnotes give more information on specific instruments used under German law.)

CONCLUDING REMARKS

The interaction between social benefits and tax deductions or credits that are designed to support children or childcare is becoming more complex as time goes on. Different groups are affected unevenly (high income versus low income earner; single parent families versus two-parent families; one

[14] See Dingeldey (2000a), (2000b); OECD (2005); Figari et al (2007) and the work of Sutherland (1997), who explicitly includes distribution of income between men and women in her analysis.

Table 1: Instruments, multiple policy goals, and the Redistributive Effects and Gender Equality

Instrument	Policy goal	Redistributive effects and the gender dimension
	TAX LAW	
Tax deduction for a child[1]	Tax fairness; no taxation of the existence minimum	Income redistribution toward families; gender effect depends on the entitlement structure and who is the recipient; higher benefits for high-income families due to progressive tax structure
Tax deduction for childcare expenses[2]	Recognize childcare as employment-related expenses if both parents are employed; tax fairness for employed parent; equal treatment with other employment-related tax-deductible expenses	Compensate for employed mothers/parents opportunity costs, esp. single parents; higher benefits for higher-income groups
Childcare and educational tax deduction for a child[3]	Supplement family income (loss); recognition of family care	Redistribution toward one-earner family; the higher the taxable income, the greater the benefit
Tax deduction of maintenance payments[4]	Tax fairness; leave existence minimum untaxed	Depends on the entitlement conditions; can prolong the advantages of joint taxation after separation or divorce
Tax deduction for single parent[5]	Compensate for special income disadvantages; achieve equivalence with married couples benefiting from joint taxation	Women are the main beneficiaries; disincentive to cohabit with another adult
Care-related social benefits do not count as taxable income[6]	Supplement caregiver's income; recognize care; enhance supply of unpaid care	Main beneficiaries of the social benefits and the tax exemption are female
Tax deductions for the employment of caregivers or household helpers in private household[7]	Set incentives for regular employment in private households and shift such work out of the shadow economy	Higher tax gains for high-income households; expansion of a private market for low-paid feminized jobs

(*Continued*)

Table 1: Continued

Instrument	Policy goal	Redistributive effects and the gender dimension
	SOCIAL LAW	
Universal child benefit[8]	Support all families	Depends on the entitlement conditions (split between both parents or entitlement of the caregiver)
Means-tested income support for a child[9]	Reduce child/family poverty	Beneficiaries are mainly single-parent families and low-income families with many children; gender and class redistributional effects
Single-parent income support supplement[10]	Reduce poverty; recognize special costs of single-parent family, ensure care for children	Redistribution is mainly toward poor women as single parents
Unemployed caregiver's right to refuse a job offer under income support regulation[11]	Reduce family poverty and ensure personal care for the child up to a certain age; recognition of care	Redistribution is mainly toward women, esp. single parents/ income security of a caregiver at a low level/possibly negative employment incentive and poverty trap (depending on earning capacity)
Care-related social benefits do not count as income under means-tested schemes	Supplement caregiver's income; recognize care; enhance supply of unpaid care	Mainly female beneficiaries
	SOCIAL SECURITY BENEFITS	
Orphan's pensions	Secure maintenance of the child	Benefit amount is based on contributions paid by the deceased insured person
Child-related supplement to social security benefits	Status maintenance of the insured person's child	Flat-rate supplements redistribute more towards low-income recipients (women are over-represented in this group), while proportional benefits advantage higher-income insured persons

(*Continued*)

Table 1: Continued

Instrument	Policy goal	Redistributive effects and the gender dimension
Contribution reduction for parent	'Contribution fairness'; reduce financial burden for families	Higher-income insured person benefits more from the reduction (contribution rates are not progressive)
Free health insurance for child under statutory health insurance and statutory care insurance	Redistribution toward families; enhance child welfare and health	Lower and middle-income families profit (not those privately insured); also single parents/ mothers whose access conditions to statutory health insurance improved
	SOCIAL SERVICES	
Public supply of childcare and after-school care provision[12]	Promote maternal/parental employment; promote children's education	Distributive effects depend on fees and subsidies for low-income/single parents

[1] The refundable tax credit for a child is calculated on the basis of the existence minimum of a child. In 2010, it was €2184 per year for each parent and thus €4368 per year (monthly €364) for both (Income Tax Act [ITA], para. 32 s 6). The amounts indicated in the following notes relate to 2010.

[2] Since the 2006 reform, childcare expenses for a child up to the age of 14 years may be deducted up to €1500 per year. However, these expenses are not placed on an equal footing with other employment-related expenses; for the legal debate and controversies, see above.

[3] In addition to the tax credit for a child, there is a tax deduction of €1320 per year for each parent (of €2640 per child) which is intended to cover care and the educational needs of the child (in 2010). Adding up both tax credits for a child—for cash and for care—the total amount is €7008 per year.

[4] This is a subsidiary tax deduction for maintenance payments up to €7680 per year if these expenses are not yet covered by another tax relief. It may have importance for intergenerational support payments, especially to parents of a taxpayer.

[5] Since 2004, a single parent (defined as a parent with a minor child not cohabiting with another adult) can deduct €1308 per year or €109 monthly from taxable income (Income Tax Act, para 24b).

(*Continued*)

Table 1: Continued

[6] Two care-related benefits are not taxed as income: the parental leave benefit is non-taxable income up to the minimum flat rate of €300 per month (higher amounts are taxed) and the care benefit paid to the non-professional caregiver of a severely disabled person (a social insurance benefit) is not taxed either.
[7] Twenty per cent of the expenses for an employee in a private household of a maximum up to €20,000 per year can be deducted from taxable income; the task can be caregiving activities or any other household help or related services.
[8] The dual structure of *Kindergeld* as refundable tax credit has been explained above; the amount is €184 monthly for the first and the second child; €190 for the third child and €215 for the fourth and each subsequent child (2010).
[9] The benefits shall cover the existence minimum of a child (this includes a share of the housing costs plus monthly €215 for a child up to 5 years; €251 for a child aged 6–13 years; €287 from 14–24 years if the child which has reached the age of majority is still cohabiting with a parent. The child benefit is deducted as income of the child under means-tested schemes.
[10] A single parent who cares for one child below the age of 7 or for two or three children below the age of 16 receives a supplement of 36% of her income support benefit of €359 monthly. In 2010, this was a monthly supplement of €129. The supplement is 12% for one child over 7 years of age. For more than three children, the supplement is increased by 12% for each child up to a maximum of 60% of the single parent's income support.
[11] A parent receiving means-tested income support has the right to refuse an employment offer from a job centre if adequate care for the child is not guaranteed, in general until the child has reached the age of 3 and possibly longer (the burden of proof that no adequate childcare is available lies with the parent if the child is above the age of 3).
[12] In 1991, children aged 3and above were given the right to a place in a kindergarten. This was supplemented in 2008 by children aged 1and above being given the right to a place in a crèche or in day care. The latter provision is enforceable beginning in 2013.

earner versus dual earner households); and gender impact differs alongside these cross-cutting cleavages, as Table 1 shows. Because these measures have multiple policy goals (for example, to combat poverty or to facilitate parental/maternal employment or to favour families with more than one or two children), it is becoming increasingly difficult to analyse their impact on gender equality. The interaction between these various systems produces a number of unintended effects, and tax deductions and transfers also cause strategic behaviour on behalf of beneficiaries. This makes it difficult to identify clear tendencies in the development of child-related tax relief or social benefits and to describe their potential impact on gender inequality. It is also difficult to formulate recommendations as to how to design such measures in order to reduce gendered inequality. Although a gender-neutral model of shared parenting has been a normative goal, shaping family law regulation, particularly over the last two decades, the gendered practice of mothers being the main caregivers for children is still ongoing. The design of child-related benefits and tax relief is formally gender neutral, so benefits and tax relief tend to be split evenly between both parents (if the child is not the recipient in its own right). This corresponds to a gender-neutral normative model of shared and equal parenting, but in many cases there is not real division of time and labour between parents.

From a gender perspective, one might prefer the following design: a clear distinction should be made between tax deductions or transfers linked to the maintenance costs of the child (at least at the level of the existence minimum of the child) and those directed at covering the risks of a caregiver. The latter should be dissociated from marriage and granted as a direct entitlement of the caregiver. For children, dissociation from marital status has already happened, since the child tax credit is granted independent of the marital status of the child to both parents.

In fact, all regulations must take into account the different situations of parents living together or apart. Benefits or tax deductions to cover risks of the caregiver are a contested issue. Although feminists would agree that care should be acknowledged and that it should be a basis for social rights, there is controversy concerning how this should be done and how the public and the private burden should be divided. Furthermore, the situation of a one-parent household is different from parents living together in terms of dividing time between employment and care and sharing income and social security. How should tax law and social law take these differences into account when constructing tax deductions or benefits for those caring for children? An alternative choice is to implement public commitment to, and financial support for, day care services. This may be an appropriate substitute for, or even a complement to, tax deductions and benefits connected with childcare.

It has been shown that the re-distributional effects of different measures and packages are multifaceted and do not allow for a single solution from a gender perspective. Class and gender effects are intertwined, and this affects the gendered outcomes of the measures discussed. If policymakers in complex systems pursue different goals at the same time, gender issues risk being submerged by other goals. Great effort is therefore needed to make gender-equality impacts visible. At minimum, it might be possible to come to a consensus on the recommendation that the state should strengthen its commitment to providing public childcare and educational services to meet the demand. Feminists may also need to strive for a simplification of the system of tax deductions and social benefits as a means of reducing the complexity of interactions, thus diminishing unintended consequences and making the effects of tax legislation on gender equality more obvious.

REFERENCES

Ahmann, R (2002) 'Die berufstätige Mutter—das Stiefkind im Steuerrecht' 55 *Neue Juristische Wochenschrift* 633, 638.

Bahle, T (1995) *Familienpolitik in Westeuropa: Ursprünge und Wandel im internationalen Vergleich* (Frankfurt/M., Campus).

Buske, S (2004) *Fräulein Mutter und ihr Bastard: Eine Geschichte der Unehelichkeit in Deutschland 1900–1970* (Göttingen, Wallstein).

Daly, M and Scheiwe, K (2010) 'Individualisation and Personal Obligations—Social Policy, Family Policy and Law Reform in Germany and the UK' 24 *International Journal of Law Policy and the Family* 3, 177.

Dingeldey, I (2000a) 'International Comparison of Tax Systems and Their Impact on the Work-Family Balancing' manuscript (Gelsenkirchen, Institut für Arbeit und Technik).

—— (ed) (2000b) *Erwerbstätigkeit und Familie in Steuer- und Sozialversicherungssystemen: Begünstigungen und Belastungen verschiedener familialer Erwerbsmuster im Ländervergleich* (Opladen, Leske & Budrich).

Figari, F, Immervoll, H, Levy, H and Sutherland, H (2007) *Inequalities within Couples: Market Incomes and the Role of Taxes and Benefits in Europe*. IZA DP no 3201, Discussion Paper Series (Bonn, Forschungsinstitut zur Zukunft der Arbeit).

Hey, J (2006) 'Der neue Abzug für Kinderbetreuungskosten' 59 *Neue Juristische Wochenschrift* 2001, 2007.

Hölzer, C (2008) 'Abzugsfähigkeit von Kinderbetreuungskosten erwerbstätiger verheirateter Eltern—Licht am Ende eines dunklen Tunnels' 61 *Neue Juristische Wochenschrift* 2145, 2150.

Immervoll, H and Barber, D (2005) *Can Parents Afford to Work? Childcare Costs, Tax-Benefit Policies and Work Incentives*, Social, Employment and Migration Working Paper no 31 (Paris, OECD). Available at: www.oecd.org/els/workingpapers.

Lang, J (1999) 'Germany' in MT Soler Roch (ed), *Family Taxation in Europe* (Dordrecht, Kluwer Law International) 55, 69.

Maucher, M (2001) 'The Interplay of Cash and Tax Benefits for Children in Ten European Countries' *EURODATA Newsletter* (Mannheim, MZES) 1, 17.

Montanari, I (2000) From 'From Family Wage to Marriage Subsidy and Child Benefits: Controversy and Consensus in the Development of Family Support' 10 *Journal of European Social Policy*, 307, 333.
Mückenberger, U, Spangenberg, U and Warncke, K (2007) *Familienförderung und Gender Mainstreaming im Steuerrecht* (Baden-Baden, Nomos).
OECD (2005) *Taxing Working Families: A Distributional Analysis Text* (Paris, OECD).
O'Donoghue, C and Sutherland, H (1998) *Accounting for the Family: The Treatment of Marriage and Children in European Income Tax Systems*, Innocenti Occasional Papers, Economic and Social Policy Series no 65 (Florence, United Nations Children's Fund/International Child Development Centre).
Parker, H and Sutherland, H (1991) *Child Tax Allowances? A Comparison of Child Benefit, Child Tax Reliefs, and Basic Incomes as Instruments of Family Policy*, Suntory and Toyota International Centres for Economics and Related Disciplines, Occasional Papers 16 (London, London School of Economics and Political Science).
Pechman, JA and Engelhardt, GV (1990) 'The Income Tax Treatment of the Family: An International Perspective' 43 *National Tax Journal* 1, 22.
Saraceno, C (1990) 'Women, Family, and the Law, 1750–1942' 15 *Journal of Family History* 427, 142.
Scheiwe, K (2005) 'Soziale Sicherungsmodelle zwischen Individualisierung und Abhängigkeiten—verliert das traditionelle "Ernährermodell" im Sozialversicherungsrecht an Bedeutung?' 24 *Kritische Justiz* 127, 151.
Schuler-Harms, M (2008) 'Regelungsmodelle des Familienleistungsausgleichs zwischen staatlicher Nachwuchssicherung und familiärer Gestaltungsfreiheit—Deutschland, Frankreich und Großbritannien im Rechtsvergleich' in K Scheiwe and M Schuler-Harms, *Aktuelle Rechtsfragen der Familienpolitik aus vergleichender Sicht* (Baden-Baden, Nomos) 14, 77.
Soler Roch, MT (1999) (ed), *Family Taxation in Europe* (Dordrecht, Kluwer Law International).
Sutherland, H (1997) 'Women, Men and the Redistribution of Income' 18 *Fiscal Studies* 1, 22.
Voegeli, W (2003) 'Nazi Family Policy: Securing Mass Loyalty' 28 *Journal of Family History*, 123, 148.
Young, C (2000) *Women, Tax and Social Programs: The Gendered Impact of Funding Social Programs through the Tax System* (Ottawa, Status of Women Canada).

11

Overcoming the Gender Inequalities of Joint Taxation and Income Splitting: The Case of Germany

MARIA WERSIG*

IN GERMAN INCOME tax law, the male breadwinner is still considered to have an obligation to maintain the family, and this is demonstrated through joint taxation of married spouses according to a lower tax rate based on income splitting. That is, a married couple may choose to calculate their income taxes according to the assumption that each spouse earned half the household income. This form of taxation has existed since 1958. Because income tax in Germany is progressive, income splitting cuts the tax rate in half, and the largest savings are realized when only one partner has earned all the household income. This form of taxation is criticized as privileging marriages where there is only one breadwinner and as discriminating against married women because it includes disincentives for a second wage earner to work. Legally recognized same-sex couples are not permitted to choose the income-splitting option, even though their maintenance obligations are crafted after the model of marriage. This chapter analyses the debate about the gendered impact of joint taxation and income splitting in Germany and the model of family it implies, as well as effective strategies for change and resistance to these strategies.

Since their introduction in 1958, joint taxation and reduced tax rates created by income splitting have been controversial in Germany. It is argued that this form of taxation creates and perpetuates inequality between women

* My special thanks go to the editors and all participants in the workshop *Challenging Gender Inequality in Tax Policy Making*, held in Onati in May 2009 for their helpful comments on the various draft versions of this paper. Particular thanks to Gerhard Wagenhals for providing me with his graph illustrating the effects of income splitting in Germany. Many thanks to Tibor Fedke and to Kathryn Dean for their help with my English. All remaining errors are, of course, my own. At last I would like to thank the Hans-Böckler-Foundation for funding my work through their scholarship programme.

and men, married and unmarried couples and high and low incomes, as well as between taxpayers in the eastern and western parts of Germany[1] (Berghahn 2004; Färber, Spangenberg and Stiegler 2008; Sacksofsky 2000; Spangenberg 2005; Vollmer 1998). Notwithstanding such political and scholarly controversies, many scholars believe that the law is unlikely to be changed (Rüling and Kassner 2007: 83). Some attribute this to the fact that any new legislation would likely be overturned by the Federal Constitutional Court (the *Bundesverfassungsgericht*); others point out the important role of income splitting within the well-established male-breadwinner model of the German welfare state (Daly 2000: 94; Dingeldey 2001). From an international perspective, it seems that income splitting is more difficult to overcome in Germany than in other countries.

JOINT TAXATION AND INCOME SPLITTING: HISTORY, EFFECTS AND THE LEGAL DEBATE

According to German income tax law (*Einkommenssteuer*), married spouses[2] are permitted to choose to be taxed as one taxpayer (joint filing, § 32 a Abs. 5 EStG) at a rate determined by income splitting (§ 32 a Abs. 5 EStG). The income of both spouses is first added up and the sum is then divided by two. The standard rate of income tax is then applied to half the joint income. The amount of tax thus calculated is doubled to give the couple's accrued taxes for the year. When there are differences in the size of income between the partners, and particularly when one of them has little or no income, applying this method for calculating tax burdens means that the total household income is subject to a significantly lower tax rate than would be applied to the earnings of single people. This is called a 'splitting effect'. Because of the progressive tax scale, the 'splitting effect' results in the greatest savings if only one partner earned the total household income, and if both partners earned the same amount, the rate would be the same as that applied if each was taxed individually. The 'splitting effect' also varies according to the difference between the incomes earned by the spouses. Figure 1 illustrates[3] the potential 'splitting effect' per year where one partner earned the total household income (*Verhältnis* proportion 100:0) versus the tax effect for couples where both are breadwinners (with income proportions of 90:10, 80:20 and 60:40).

This form of taxation is criticized as privileging marriages where there is only one breadwinner or where there is a significant difference between the spouses' incomes. Couples in these categories achieve a tax reduction that

[1] Because of lower differences between the earnings of spouses in East Germany, couples there seldom profit from income splitting.

[2] Cohabiting unmarried couples or same-sex partners are not eligible for joint taxation.

[3] The horizontal axis shows taxable income in euros; the vertical axis shows the splitting effect in euros.

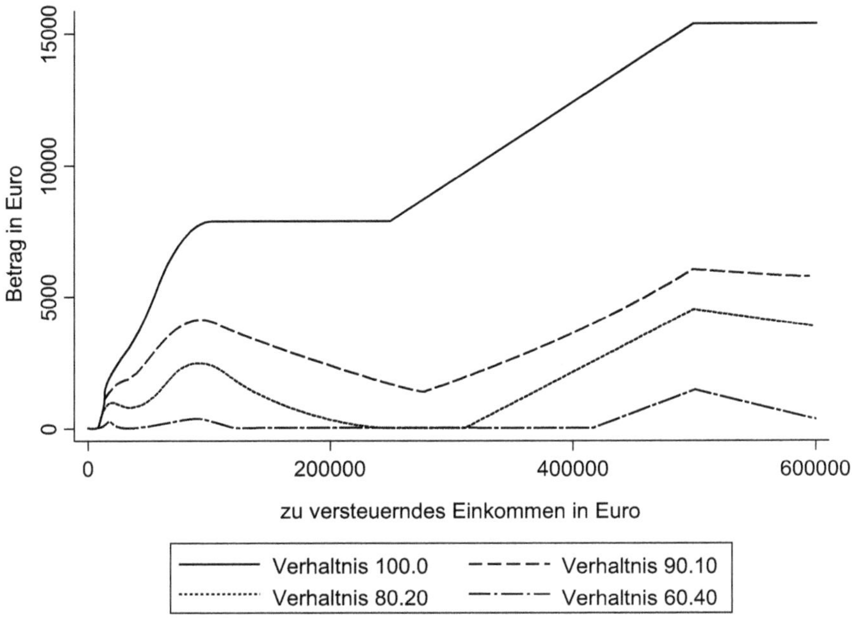

Figure 1: Annual 'Splitting Effect' if one Partner earned Total Household Income (base tax year 2007)
Source: Gerhard Wagenhals. Originally published in Wagenhals 2007: 247.

dual-earner couples are unable to achieve (Sacksofsky 2000: 1898; Vollmer 1998: 127). Supporters of income splitting argue that this method of taxation conforms to the ability to pay principle and that it is supported, if not called for, by the constitutional protection of marriage (Kirchhof 2000).

FAMILY POLICY IN THE 1950S, THE FEDERAL CONSTITUTIONAL COURT AND THE INTRODUCTION OF INCOME SPLITTING IN 1958

Income splitting was introduced in 1958, when West German family policy focused on protecting the nuclear family against perceived 'dangers', one of which was the gainful employment of married women and mothers. Family policy was shaped according to a strong male-breadwinner model, with the husband and father earning the family wage and the wife and mother taking care of the children at home. This gendered division of labour within the family was part of family law, and it was supported by a number of social security and tax regulations, as well as by public opinion. Politicians like Franz-Josef Wuermeling, the first minister of family affairs, argued that the family needed to be protected against 'the wrong kinds' of interpretations of gender equality, by which he meant interpretations that included working women and mothers. At the time, public policy in East Germany supported women and mothers who wanted to work (Joosten 1990: 29), but in West Germany, gender equality in the 1950s was defined by an 'equal but different' approach, whereby women and men were to play different roles in the family and in society. The aim was not only to re-establish a traditional family model and gender roles after the Second World War, but to demonstrate dissociation from the competing political system in the socialist Federal Republic of Germany.

Income splitting was introduced as a result of a decision of the Federal Constitutional Court, which rejected the former mandatory joint taxation method without an income-splitting option as unconstitutional.[4] This old taxation system was held to be unconstitutional, since the progressive tax system and the joint taxation of married couples could result in a marriage penalty (ie, the married couple could end up paying overall higher taxes than if they were taxed individually). The Court concluded that this would function as a disincentive for the secondary wage earner (married women) to enter or stay in gainful employment.[5] (For a discussion of Canadian incentives encouraging secondary earners to enter or stay in the labour market, see Philipps, chapter twelve in this volume.) The Court argued that the constitutional principle of gender equality and non-discrimination based on sex (German Basic Law, article 3 section 2) included women's right to work with the same opportunities and earning prospects as men.[6] Any tax law that had the indirect effect of encouraging women to withdraw from the labour market would therefore be unconstitutional. The Court also pointed out that income splitting was one constitutional option available to the legislator.[7] Even before the Court made this ruling, however, Parliament and the media had discussed the splitting method as an alternative, since that method was said to have been successful in the United States. The introduction of income splitting was a compromise (Niehuss 2001: 194) and aimed to enable married women to work without wage penalties (Seel 2007: 2) as well as supporting the male-breadwinner marriage.

ASSESSING THE CURRENT EFFECTS OF INCOME SPLITTING

International studies have shown the impact of joint taxation on women's participation in the labour market. Since the 1950s, women's participation

[4] BVerfGE 6, 55 (77).
[5] BVerfGE 6, 55 (77).
[6] BVerfGE 6, 55 (77).
[7] BVerfGE 6, 55 (77).

in the labour market has increased and marriage is no longer the single dominating socially accepted lifestyle or context for starting a family (Rosenfeld, Trappe and Gornick 2004). Nevertheless, large differences remain between women's and men's participation in the labour market. A majority of men still play the role of the main breadwinner in families, and most women, on the other hand, are still faced with part-time work, lower wages and financial dependence on maintenance payments or (in the absence of a breadwinner) social welfare payments. The labour-market participation rate of married women, at 68 per cent, is 10 percentage points lower than that of single women. The opposite is the case for men. Their labour-market participation rate, at 88 per cent, is 13 percentage points higher than that of single men (Dressel 2005). Higher proportions of women than men also tend to move into marginal part-time employment. In 2003, for instance, two-thirds of all employees in marginal part-time employment were women, three-quarters of them married (Spangenberg 2005: 27).

Even though only a minority of Germans today favour a traditional, strictly gendered distribution of labour, vast differences in attitudes regarding working women and mothers can still be observed in eastern and western Germany, 20 years after the reunification of the country. Acceptance of the male-breadwinner model was measured to be as high as 30 per cent in western Germany as opposed to 16.9 per cent in eastern Germany in 2005 (Dorbritz, Höhn and Naderi 2005: 49). Because policy in the Federal Republic of Germany included the promotion of women's labour-market participation, acceptance of working women/mothers is far greater in eastern Germany than it is in western Germany. Mothers in the eastern part work more often than mothers in the western part, and they more often work full hours (Dorbritz, Höhn and Naderi 2005a: 44). When asked which lifestyle they preferred, 43 per cent of women in eastern Germany answered that they preferred to work full time and care for children (while only 13 per cent of women in western Germany preferred this arrangement). In the western part of the country, women preferred part-time work and caring for children.

Childcare for very young children is also more readily available in the eastern states than in the western states. In the east, 41.2 per cent of children under the age of three have a place in public childcare facilities, while in the west, only 9.9 per cent of children under the age of three have access to public childcare. Women's labour-market participation, however, is still being judged in connection with the number of children living in the household (Dorbritz, Höhn and Naderi 2005: 50), though this is not the case for men. It is important to keep in mind these differences in attitudes, childcare policy and working hours within Germany, in order to understand the underlying conflicts that have governed gender-equality politics in Germany.

Women's working patterns are also affected by the tax and transfer unit (see chapter three by Stewart in this volume). Joint taxation has been shown to have a disproportional impact on women's workforce participation and to create a bias against women's entry into waged work in comparison with men's entry into the workforce (Apps 1981; Gustafsson 1992; Leuthold 1984; LaLumia 2008). On the other hand, there is no evidence that married men's participation in the labour market is affected by joint taxation (LaLumia 2008). For women, however, incentives and disincentives, taxation and other factors (such as, in Germany, the availability and costs of childcare) affect willingness to move from unpaid to paid work. As Gustafsson stated in a comparison of the Swedish and German models, 'The German wife . . . has to earn enough to offset the marriage gain, before she contributes to family income, and marginal earnings of the second wage earner are hit by a high tax rate' (1992: 61).

Many questions remain unanswered about the gendered impact of taxation in Germany, especially the question of who profits from tax benefits within the 'black box' family, which is usually seen as a unit, with the couple as 'one taxpayer'(Spangenberg 2005: 20). However, the redistributional effects of income splitting have been analysed (Bach and Buslei 2003) and these include differences between single-breadwinner and dual-breadwinner marriages, marriages in eastern and western Germany, married couples with and without children and finally, married couples with high and low or mid-range incomes.

In 2007, the overall volume of tax benefits resulting from the income-splitting method was €18.5 billion (Wagenhals 2007: 247). Of this amount, 76 per cent (or €14 billion) was received by single-breadwinner couples (Wagenhals 2007: 253). However, there are a number of structural differences between families in the eastern and western parts of Germany—regarding marriage rates, women's participation in the labour market and wages (the gender pay gap in the eastern states is not as high as it is in the western states). These caused married couples in western Germany to profit most from the income-splitting method. Specifically, in 2007, 90.8 per cent of the overall tax savings generated by the joint taxation method (€16.8 billion) accrued to couples in the western part of Germany (Wagenhals 2007: 253).

Supporters of income splitting often argue that it is part of family policy, since it takes into account income differences resulting from unpaid caregiving within the family (Lietmeyer 1998: 849). Studies to back up this argument have aimed to show that the majority of couples profiting from income splitting have children (Gottfried and Witczak 2006). However, there are wide variances in the effects of income splitting, depending on the tax brackets of different married couples with children. The tax relief varies between €17 and €5300 per year (Spangenberg 2005: 24). Further inequalities are created by the fact that many families are not eligible for joint taxation—for example, parents who are not married, who are divorced, who are living in a same-sex partnership or who are solo parents.

CURRENT CRITICISMS OF JOINT TAXATION AND INCOME SPLITTING

Gendered Impact of Income Splitting

The effects of taxation on individual decisions to enter or withdraw from the labour market cannot be viewed without reference to social security law, other welfare state regulations and, particularly, employment and family policy. Other important factors to consider include the cultural environment, couples' and individuals' preferences regarding the amount of time they spend working per year and general attitudes to balancing family responsibilities and paid work (Dingeldey 2001). While income splitting in Germany was introduced as part of a male-breadwinner welfare state model, this model has recently begun to change. Since 2005, the governments of the Social Democrats (SPD), the Christian Democratic Party (CDU) and the Christian Social Party (CSU) have focused on family policy and especially on the reconciliation of work and family obligations. A number of legal reforms in different areas of federal law have been introduced to support families and to enable parents to work, including a new parental benefit, better options for deducting childcare costs from taxes and increased public spending on childcare.

The introduction of a new parental benefit in 2007 aimed to increase women's labour-market participation and to bolster the financial security of the caring parent. (See also chapter twelve by Philipps in this volume for recommendations for increasing the financial security of primary caregivers in Canada through refundable tax credits or other state transfers.) For the first time, fathers have been addressed specifically as caregivers: parents now receive an extra two months' worth of benefits if both parents take time off work or work part time to care for a newborn or newly-adopted child. The government introduced options for recognizing childcare costs under tax law in 2006 and plans to improve the availability of childcare for young children The government aims to reach a 35 per cent rate of available childcare for children under three years of age, and starting in October 2013, every child in Germany will be legally entitled to a place in public childcare after his or her first birthday. Amid all these changes, the privileges of the breadwinner have also been considered, with a view to offering greater privileges to families where both parents are breadwinners. While the new developments could mark a turning point in the progress towards gender equality, other aspects of the male-breadwinner model are persistent. For instance, joint taxation and the accompanying income splitting can be identified as two elements of the traditional German welfare state whose proponents are still resisting change.

Income splitting therefore remains one of the most contested elements of the traditional German welfare state from a feminist point of view. Feminists argue that this form of taxation makes the usually lower income of the secondary wage earner (who is often the woman) seem more dispensable. Her work is then economically advantageous to the family only if she can earn more than the tax savings created by not working. Even if the secondary wage earner earns only a small amount, this will result in a significant diminishment of the tax savings because of the splitting effect (Spangenberg 2005: 19). Taking into account the inadequate childcare infrastructure in Germany and the fact that there are restrictions on setting off childcare expenses against tax liability, the incentive for married women, especially mothers, to reduce their labour-market participation is high. (For more on child tax benefits and deductions in Germany see Kirsten Scheiwe, chapter ten in this volume.) Supporters of income splitting do not see this disincentive as a problem, relative to the importance of the main breadwinner's ability to pay taxes. They stress the point that a family with one spouse who earns €50,000 per year and another who doesn't work is no wealthier than a couple where each earns €25,000 annually. Yet without income splitting, the former will be taxed at a higher rate due to progressive taxes.

Unmarried Couples and Same-sex Partnerships

From a family policy point of view, it can be argued that single-parent families and couples who are not married (including same-sex partners) do not have the option of splitting income under joint taxation, even though their ability to pay may be compromised by their family situation in the same manner that a married couple's ability to pay would be compromised. An increasing number of parents (20 per cent in the western part of Germany and 25 per cent in the eastern part) are not married and therefore do not have the option of choosing joint taxation. In the legal discourse, however, these arguments have not convinced the courts thus far to order any extension of the applicability of income splitting to unmarried partners. Since 2001, same-sex partners in Germany have been permitted to enter into a legally recognized partnership similar to marriage (the *eingetragene Lebenspartnerschaft*, or civil partnership). Although this type of partnership is designed after the model of marriage in terms of maintenance and other obligations, many legal privileges connected to marriage (including joint taxation) have not been extended so far to this arrangement. But is equal treatment in taxation not required for partners who decide to take on a legal commitment similar to marriage? Since the introduction of legally recognized partnerships for same-sex couples, the question of equal treatment of marriage and partnership has been raised, and same-sex spouses have claimed that they should be placed on the same footing as married couples.

However, many legal privileges connected to marriage (including joint taxation) have not yet been extended to partnerships. Even though maintenance obligations exist and may affect ability to pay, the income-splitting option has not been offered to unmarried partners, and they are still taxed individually (with limited options for deducting maintenance payments). Several finance courts, including the Federal Court of Finance (the *Bundesfinanzhof*), have rejected the applicability of income-splitting rules to same-sex partnerships. The Courts stressed the point that income splitting exists for married couples only and the legislator is permitted to extend taxation privileges exclusively to marriage, since only marriage is protected by article 6, paragraph 1 of German Basic Law.[8] However, because of the importance of the issue, the most recent court decision has been accepted for appeal to the Federal Constitutional Court.[9] At present, however, the second senate of the Federal Constitutional Court is more conservative than the first senate and will most likely not rule in favour of extending joint taxation to same-sex partners. In a long-awaited decision in 2009, the first senate of the Federal Constitutional Court has taken a close look at the state's obligation for equal treatment of marriage and civil partnerships in the case of widows/widowers pensions.[10] The Court ruled that the mere reference to the constitutional protection of marriage is not enough to justify privileges that are extended to married couples but denied to couples in similar actual and legal circumstances. The Court therefore asked for another reason to justify unequal treatment of marriage and civil partnership and ruled for the case of widows/widowers pensions in a corporate pensions scheme that there is no such reason, since the circumstances the law was dealing with (death of a spouse/partner who has a pensions claim) are similar and can occur in heterosexual marriages as well as same-sex civil partnerships. The Court decision also mentioned taxation as one example, where the legislator may take the economic responsibilities taken on by married couples into account and extend privileges on that basis, while denying them to others. But the Court pointed out that there is no difference between marriage and civil partnership concerning the life-long economic obligations and mutual responsibilities that these couples take on. Even though the decision was not concerned with joint taxation in the beginning, it pointed out one possible way to decide on this issue, because the reasoning of the Court points in this direction. Whether the second senate will follow this argument remains to be seen.

[8] BFH (19 October 2006), III R 29/06; BFH/NV 2007, 663–66.
[9] BFH (14 December 2007), III B 25/07; BVerfG 2 BvR 288/07.
[10] BVerfG (7 July 2009), 1 BvR 1164/07.

Interdependence of Taxation and other Areas of Law

The effects of income splitting need to be examined in connection with other areas of law, particularly with social security law. In Germany, the secondary breadwinner encounters further disadvantages because of the interaction between a number of legal fields and the consequences of those interactions. This situation is exemplified by the *Lohnsteuerklassen*: the interaction between monthly tax collecting and women's marginal part-time employment. Income tax is collected on a monthly, pay-as-you-earn basis (the *Lohnsteuer*), whereby the breadwinner's income is once more privileged. According to this pay-as-you-earn system, spouses have the option of calculating the monthly payment by taking into account the differences between their incomes. If the secondary earner pays tax at a higher tax rate, the monthly income of the main breadwinner can be increased because deductions that the secondary earner would otherwise have used are applied to the income of the main breadwinner. As a result, spouses with the lower income (usually wives) have an incentive to participate less in the labour market, in order to use this method to reduce taxes on the entire household income. The educational effect or incentive to adjust labour-market participation, which some people attribute to income splitting, is therefore part of the monthly income of many married women. If couples choose the option of taking into account the difference between spouses' incomes, almost all tax exempt amounts of both husband and wife are used to reduce the monthly tax burden of the spouse with the higher income (Spangenberg 2005). The person who earns less pays part of the main breadwinner's taxes and therefore has a reduced amount available at the end of the month; and 91 per cent of those who agree to pay more taxes in order to reduce the tax burden of their spouse are women. It appears more economically advantageous to calculate taxes in this way if the couple's income is viewed as one unit, since as one unit, there is more money left at the end of the month.

However, under social security law, many benefits (for example, unemployment benefits and parental benefits) are calculated based on an individual's monthly income after deductions. Married women's entitlements are therefore often lower than those of married men. And if one of the spouses (usually the woman) enters marginal part-time employment where no social security insurance is provided (such as health insurance or pensions), her income from this line of work will not be taken into account when the monthly pay-as-you-earn taxes are calculated. However, despite the lack of social security benefits and the inability to deduct those lost amounts from monthly income tax, it can seem more advantageous to take on a marginal part-time job than to work more and pay more taxes.

A reform of the *Lohnsteuerklassen* has been demanded for many years, but only in 2009 were preparations finally being made to do this. Unfortunately, however, legislators did not choose to dispose of the *Lohnsteuer* option for single-breadwinner couples. Instead, they decided to offer one more option. This new option results in a more equal distribution of the tax burden between spouses. And even though it is known that discriminating effects can be caused by one spouse giving up tax deductions in order to reduce the tax burden of the other spouse, couples are still legally permitted to choose that method of collecting the *Lohnsteuer* instead of the new, more egalitarian method.

The Constitutional Debate

As mentioned by Scheiwe (chapter ten, this volume) the demand for tax fairness and the principle of the protection of the family (German Basic Law, article 6, paragraph 1) have been stressed to a great extent in decisions regarding taxation made by the Federal Constitutional Court. Nevertheless, since the important decision regarding joint taxation in 1957, its implications for gender equality and non-discrimination based on gender have not been explored extensively. The question of how the law regarding joint taxation favours a gendered division of labour and could thus cause indirect discrimination against women has been raised by feminist scholars but has not, thus far, been picked up by the courts or by mainstream legal scholars.

Under German constitutional law, marriage is conceptualized as a place of security, a safe haven. Specifically, according to German Basic Law, article 6, paragraph 1 (regarding rights of the family), 'Marriage and family shall enjoy the special protection of the state'. This represents a strong, shared belief that the state should protect, yet not intrude into, the private family sphere.[11] Included in this understanding of protection and guaranteed freedom from intrusion are decisions about the division of labour between spouses, and it is argued that the traditional 'housewife marriage' has to remain an option. 'Protection' is also interpreted as providing access to the institution of marriage and not blocking such access through incentives that make marriage unattractive compared with other lifestyles (Gröschner 2004: 34).

Since the constitutional protection of marriage upholds the idea of freedom in making decisions about the division of labour between husband and wife, income tax law must take into account households where either one or both of the spouses acts as breadwinner. Spouses with two incomes are therefore not placed at a disadvantage because their ability to pay is to be judged differently from spouses with only one income (Kirchhof 2000; 2003). Income splitting, according to this point of view, is the only form of taxation that can take into account the ability to pay based on the division of labour between spouses and is therefore the only constitutional option

[11] The private sphere is, of course, not entirely inaccessible to the law: abuse and violence, including sexual violence, for example, are not accepted and may be combated with several legal strategies.

for the taxation of married couples. However, many others regard income splitting as only one of many options available to the legislator.

To date, the Federal Constitutional Court has not made a clear statement about income splitting. In 1982 it noted that the taxation of spouses is not variable at will and is not to be viewed as a taxation privilege but as one possible form of taking into account both ability to pay and the protection outlined in article 6, paragraph 1 of German Basic Law (regarding the protection of marriage).[12] Income splitting, the Court argued, would enable spouses to determine the division of labour within their households. In addition, however, the Court pointed out that different regulations could be left to the discretion of legislators. Critics of income splitting interpret this last point as meaning that married couples may also be taxed in other ways. Supporters of income splitting, on the other hand, use the ruling to argue that this form of taxation is necessary to comply with the Constitution.

Feminist legal scholars have argued that gender equality and the obligation of the state to ensure equality between women and men (German Basic Law, article 3, paragraph 2) calls for individual taxation (Spangenberg 2005; Vollmer 1998). German Basic Law, article 3, paragraph 2 states: 'Men and women shall have equal rights. The state shall promote the actual implementation of equal rights for women and men and take steps to eliminate disadvantages that now exist'. Furthermore, feminist scholars have challenged the assumption that couples freely decide on the division of labour within their households, without influence of gender roles or economic conditions. Vollmer has stressed the point that regulations favouring a division of labour tend to discriminate against women and not men, even if the black letter law is gender neutral and does not assign gendered responsibilities according to sex (1998: 125). In social reality, however, men are frequently assigned the role of breadwinners, enjoy a socially and economically secure position as part of the workforce that will not be threatened by laws aiming to support the male-breadwinner model. Women, on the other hand, will be expected to withdraw from the labour market if economically possible and to take on the gendered role of unpaid caregiver. Favouring the male-breadwinner model will therefore lead to discrimination against working women. On the other hand, unpaid caregiving puts the caregiver at a disadvantage because it does not result in the same level of financial and social security and independence. No measures have been taken to ensure that the unpaid caregiver actually receives part or all of the tax savings of the breadwinner. The educational effect of tax law is therefore that married women are encouraged to withdraw from the labour market, even though the Federal Constitutional Court ruled this to be unconstitutional in 1957, and this effect is still very much in existence today (Vollmer 1998: 131).

[12] BVerfGE 61, 319, 347.

Joint taxation is also based on the assumption that married couples pool their income and share it equally and therefore are treated as 'one taxpayer'. However, this assumption has been called into question (Spangenberg 2007). Arguments supporting this assumption are of an empirical and legal nature, drawing from family law. For instance, the maintenance obligations of married couples (as well as separated or divorced couples) are cited to support the assumption of pooled income, and it is also argued that the average happily married couple (the *intakte Durchschnittsehe*) in reality shares all income equally, even if they are not obliged to do so by law (Spangenberg 2007: 56). In fact, however, maintenance law does not support the assumption that household income is shared equally. No legal claim entitles the unpaid caregiver to half the breadwinner's income while the married couple cohabitates. Only after separation and divorce can maintenance claims be made to more than 'pocket money', but separated or divorced couples are not eligible for joint taxation. If joint taxation is in fact one way of recognizing maintenance obligations between adults, the maintenance obligations of legally recognized same-sex partners would also have to be recognized in the same way as those of married couples. In addition, empirical studies do not support the claim that in reality, income is pooled on an equal basis within the average marriage. On the contrary, inequality between women and men seems to exist in the realm of money management and expenditures within a marriage as well as in society at large (Ludwig-Mayerhofer 2007). Empirical studies have revealed many ways of managing funds in a partnership or marriage (see Vogler 2005 and Stewart, chapter three in this volume), and the reality is more complex than the fictional 'average marriage' implies (Spangenberg 2007: 68).

So far the constitutional arguments regarding gender discrimination and joint taxation have not resulted in change; in fact, they have not even made it to the courts. Nevertheless, a number of policy alternatives are being proposed in Germany, and these will be discussed in the next section.

POLICY ALTERNATIVES

Two policy alternatives are being discussed: (1) individual taxation combined with new forms of taking maintenance obligations into account and (2) a reduced tax rate based on 'family splitting'—a form of income splitting that takes into account the number of family members (including children).

Individual Taxation

Individual taxation of married couples is favoured by those who regard the current law as leading to discrimination against women. Because of the rulings of the Federal Constitutional Court regarding fairness in taxation and the need to leave the existence minimum of each family member untaxed, maintenance obligations must be taken into account. Therefore, one popular proposal has been the introduction of individual taxation, with the possibility of deducting one spouse's existence minimum from the other spouse's taxable income if he or she had no taxable income (Spangenberg 2005). However, a simulation of the introduction of legislation like this in Germany has found that it would have only minor effects on women's participation in the workforce (Steiner and Wrohlich 2006). The same study has demonstrated that there could be a significant increase in the willingness of wives from western Germany to enter the workforce if Germany were to switch to a system of individual taxation in which there was no possibility of deducting one spouse's existence minimum from the other spouse's taxable income.

Family Splitting

Some proponents of 'family splitting' see it as a way of allocating more money to families with children, while others hope to eliminate secondary earners' strong disincentive to work under the existing income-splitting policy for married partners. The Christian Democratic Party (CDU) favours the introduction of some form of family splitting in addition to income splitting for married couples, and this has been part of their election platforms since 2008. The Federal Minister of Family Affairs, Senior Citizens, Women and Youth, Ursula von der Leyen, also declared her preference for this concept, but during her time in office from 2005 until 2009 she was not able to introduce the concept during the administration of the coalition government consisting of the CDU and the Social Democrats (SPD).

It is not by accident that conservative politicians now favour family splitting because, as I pointed out at the beginning of this section, family policy has been widely supported in Germany over the last few years. Reforms introduced by the current government, such as a new parental benefit (the *Elterngeld*) and investments in childcare infrastructure have been met with much approval. There could also be great pressure from the general populace to decrease the tax burden of families with children, as well as opposition to the introduction of a 'family splitting' policy, even though it has been shown, empirically, that a 'family splitting' model like the one used in France would not affect the labour supply of married women (Althammer 2000; Beblo, Beninger and Laisney 2004). If the French system of family taxation were to be introduced in Germany it would lead to lower average tax rates than the German system (over a large range of income distribution) only for families with three or more children (Baclet, Dell and Wrohlich 2005). Because of these impacts of 'family splitting', this option is generally rejected by opponents of the current regulations. In 2007 a large group of NGOs concerned with family policy and gender equality, and in favour of individual taxation, made a public statement asking the government to work on establishing family policies that support all families, not only the ones with high incomes and/or a large number of children.[13] The federal government elected in 2009 and comprised of conservative Christian Democrats (CDU), their Bavarian sister party the Christian Social Union (CSU) and the liberal Free Democrats (FDP) has no plans to change the law or to pursue the family splitting option any further at the moment. Current debates about the necessary budget cuts on the federal level also include changes in the parental benefit[14] and several other planned changes in family benefits have been put on hold. It is of no surprise, therefore, that the government does not pursue the introduction of family splitting as this change in tax law would cost an estimated €4–5 billion at least and would only benefit families within the higher income brackets.

STRATEGIES FOR CHANGE

When the introduction of joint taxation and income splitting was discussed in Canada in 2005, there was much opposition to it. In particular, it was argued that such a policy would bring the greatest benefit to male-breadwinner marriages with a stay-at-home wife, thus investing billions of dollars in one lifestyle. This argument applies to Germany as well. Billions of euro are invested to support single-breadwinner marriages, especially ones in the high-income brackets in the western states of Germany. Nevertheless, there is still a great deal of reluctance to attempt to change the law, largely because of the perceived importance of the 'housewife marriage' in the western part of Germany. This lifestyle has been favoured and nurtured by various means and strategies and was the leading model for family and social policy for many years.

As is probably the case in most countries around the globe, arguments indicating that certain regulations have gendered impacts do not alone ensure legal reforms, especially if discrimination against women or other groups is being caused by the state and not a private entity. So how can effective strategies for change be developed and applied? Does the German case of joint taxation suggest that legal change can be brought about only after society at large has changed? It is often suggested in the debate about income splitting that it will continue to be difficult to eliminate this policy in Germany, since income differences between married spouses as well as the male-breadwinner marriage are still very dominant. By contrast, in countries like Sweden, where working patterns have changed and the dual-earner family is now the normal

13 Originally published in Frankfurter Rundschau, 13.1.2007. Available at: www.sozialpolitik-aktuell.de/tl_files/sozialpolitik-aktuell/_Politikfelder/Familienpolitik/Dokumente/Verbaende_FR_Doku.pdf.

14 Costs for the parental benefit will be cut from €4.5 billion a year to €3.9 billion.

family, individual taxation has been successfully introduced. By contrast, it is argued that if Germany introduced individual taxation, many married couples would face hardship. On the other hand, since rules and regulations, especially the redistributing effects of tax law, play a major role in shaping the conditions of couples' and individuals' decision making, these rules must be changed if they discriminate against women.

If the necessity for reform were widely accepted, the question of how to change the law would still remain. For instance, transitional regulations leading to individual taxation could be introduced, and today, even severe critics of income splitting have shown some openness to such regulations (Spangenberg 2008: 167). In the case of joint taxation, an attempt made in 1999 to introduce a law that at least puts a cap on the effect of income splitting was not followed through by the coalition governments of the Social Democrats (SPD) and the Greens (Bündnis 90/Die Grünen) due to the opposition the proposal faced. Nevertheless, both parties demanded adjustments of joint taxation once more in their 2009 federal election platforms (the Greens demanding individual taxation and the Social Democrats asking for a cap on the possible effects of income splitting). How can legal changes promoting gender equality be introduced? In the past, claims for legal change in the interests of gender equality were successful in Germany only if other interests also called for these reforms, if the socio-economic framework supported the changes and if interest groups within and/or outside the government were aware of the gendered dimensions of the problems (Lucke 1996). However, legal reforms are not often debated under such conditions, which means that the interests of gender equality are often sacrificed or at least compromised to some extent due to 'political necessity'. Sometimes, on the other hand, gender equality is promoted because legal reforms leading to greater equality are already on their way for other reasons or the reforms simply go through unnoticed or by accident, for example, in the case where a law concerning another issue has the unintended consequence of increasing gender equality.

New developments in international law can also provide leverage for changes at the national level. For example, the European Union is currently discussing a draft for a new directive that would oblige EU Member States to introduce laws ensuring that civil partnerships for same-sex couples are put on an equal footing with marriages (if some form of legal partnership option for same-sex couples already existed in that state).[15] On the topic of joint taxation with income splitting, the OECD[16] and the United Nations CEDAW Committee[17] have made statements asking Germany to review the effects of tax law on married women's participation in the labour market. Yet the current government has not even included a statement about taxation in the

[15] KOM 2008/420.
[16] See: www.oecd.org/dataoecd/27/35/40382005.pdf, 13.
[17] CEDAW/C/2000/I/CRP.3/Add.7

Sixth Periodic Report of the Federal German Government on the CEDAW Convention. Nonetheless, pressure at the international level can still be used by interest groups on the national level to argue for legal reform. The best chances for success seem to occur when strong national and international pressures for legal changes are combined.

In areas other than gender equality, pressure from the European Union has resulted in the introduction of better anti-discrimination laws. Unfortunately, however, in the area of taxation, there is no legal basis for interventions from the European level. Because of this and because increasing attention is being paid in Germany to supporting families, it is more likely that some form of family splitting will be introduced, rather than individual taxation. Arguments based on gender discrimination may prove to be less effective than the argument that the changed nature of family makes it necessary to allow families with unmarried parents to use the income-splitting strategy. This line of thought is also supported by the fact that changes in family policy are being made to support an increased birth rate in Germany.

CONCLUSION: CONTINUED RESISTANCE TO CHANGE

Fifty years after joint taxation and income splitting were introduced in Germany, chances of reform are still limited. There are many reasons to overcome joint taxation and to introduce a more individualized form of taxation. However, although feminists have succeeded in introducing alternatives to income splitting into the debate within political parties and NGOs, the resistance to change remains strong. The German case may also be special because of the constitutional aspects of the debate, which limit the overall options of the legislator and make any reform a risky business. The Federal Constitutional Court is therefore a powerful veto player, and supporters of income splitting will call on the Court to measure any reform against the standards of the Constitution. Notwithstanding these risks, Germany could and should embrace any possibilities for abolishing indirect gender discrimination within its taxation system.

REFERENCES

Althammer, J (2000) *Ökonomische Theorie der Familienpolitik* (Heidelberg, Physica-Verlag).

Apps, P (1981) *A Theory of Inequality and Taxation* (Cambridge, Cambridge University Press).

Bach, S and Buslei, H (2003) 'Fiskalische Wirkungen einer Reform der Ehegattenbesteuerung' 22 *Wochenbericht des DIW Berlin* 345–60.

Baclet, A, Dell, F and Wrohlich, K (2005) 'Income Taxation and Household Size: Would French Family Splitting Make German Families Better Off?' IZA Discussion Paper no 1894.

Beblo, M, Beninger, D and Laisney, F (2004) 'Besteuerung von Familien: Ökomomische Wirkungen der Reformalternativen Individualbesteuerung und Familiensplitting' in J Althammer and U Klammer (eds), *Ehe und Familie in der Steuerrechts und Sozialordnung* (Tübingen, Mohr Siebeck) 93–114.

Berghahn, S (2004) 'Ist die Institution Ehe eine Gleichstellungsbarriere im Geschlechterverhältnis in Deutschland?' in M Oppen and D Simon (eds), *Verharrender Wandel: Institutionen und Geschlechterverhältnisse* (Berlin, Edition Sigma) 99–138.

Daly, M (2000) *The Gender Division of Welfare: The Impact of the German and British Welfare States* (Cambridge, Cambridge University Press).

Dingeldey, I (2001) 'European Tax Systems and Their Impact on Family Employment Patterns' 30 *Journal of Social Policy* 653–72.

Dorbritz, R, Höhn, C and Naderi, R (2005) *The Demographic Future of Europe: Facts, Figures, Policies—Results of the Population Policy Acceptance Study* (Stuttgart/Wiesbaden, Federal Institute for Population Research at the Federal Statistical Office/ Robert Bosch Foundation). Available at: www.bosch-stiftung.de/content/language1/downloads/PPAS_en.pdf.

Dressel, C (2005) 'Erwebstätigkeit' in Bundesministerium für Familie, Senioren, Frauen und Jugend (ed), *Gender Daten Report* (Berlin, Bundesministerium für Familie, Senioren, Frauen und Jugend).

Färber, C, Spangenberg, U and Stiegler, B (2008) *Umsteuern Gute Gründe für ein Ende des Ehegattensplittings* (Bonn, wiso direkt Analysen zur Wirtschafts—und Sozialpolitik, Friedrich-Ebert-Stiftung). Available at: library.fes.de/pdf-files/wiso/05586.pdf.

Gottfried, P and Witczak, D (2006) *Das Ehegattensplitting: Expertise für das Kompetenzzentrum für familienbezogene Leistungen im Bundesministerium für Familie, Senioren, Frauen und Jugend* (Berlin, BMFSFJ). Available at: www.bmfsfj.de/bmfsfj/generator/RedaktionBMFSFJ/Abteilung2/Pdf-Anlagen/splitting-expertise,property=pdf,bereich=,sprache=de,rwb=true.pdf.

Gröschner, R (2004) 'Art. 6 GG' in H Dreier (ed), *Grundgesetz Kommentar, Band 1 Art. -19* (Tübingen, Mohr Siebeck).

Gustafsson, S(1992) 'Separate Taxation and Married Women's Labor Supply: A Comparison of West Germany and Sweden' 5 *Journal of Population Economics* 61–85.

Joosten, A (1990) Die Frau, das *'segenspendende Herz der Familie': Familienpolitik als Frauenpolitik in der Ära Adenauer* (Pfaffenweiler, Centaurus-Verlagsgesellschaft).

Kirchhof, P (2000) 'Ehe- und familiengerechte Gestaltung der Einkommensteuer' *Neue Juristische Wochenschrift* 2792–95.

—— (2003) 'Die Einkommensbesteuerung von Ehegatten während des Zusammenlebens und im Falle von Trennung und Scheidung' 44 *Familie, Partnerschaft, Recht* 387–90.

LaLumia, S (2008) 'The Effects of Joint Taxation of Married Couples on Labor Supply and Non-wage Income' 92 *Journal of Public Economics* 1698–719.

Leuthold, JH (1984) 'Income Splitting and Women's Labor Force Participation' 38 *Industrial and Labor Relations Review* 98–105.

Lewis, J (2001) 'The Decline of the Male Breadwinner Model: Implications for Work and Care' 8 *Social Politics* 152–69.

Lewis, J and Ostner, I (1994) *Gender and the Evolution of European Social Policies* Arbeitspapier no 4 (Bremen, Zentrum für Sozialpolitik der Universität Bremen).
Lietmeyer, V (1998) 'Ehegattensplitting –Zankapfel der Steuerpolitik' 45 *Deutsche Steuer-Zeitung* 849–911.
Lucke, D (1996) *Recht ohne Geschlecht? Zu einer Rechtssoziologie der Geschlechterverhältnisse* (Pfaffenweiler, Centaurus-Verlagsgesellschaft).
Ludwig-Mayerhofer, W (2007) 'Geldarrangements von Paaren: Ein internationaler und zeitlicher Vergleich auf der Grundlage der ISSP-Befragungen von 1994 und 2002' in S Berghahn (ed), *Unterhalt und Existenzsicherung: Recht und Wirklichkeit in Deutschland* (Baden-Baden, Nomos Verlag) 231–47.
Niehuss, M (2001) *Familie, Frau und Gesellschaft: Studien zur Strukturgeschichte der Familie in Westdeutschland* 1945–1960 (Göttingen: Vandenhoeck & Ruprecht).
Orloff, A (1993) 'Gender and the Social Rights of Citizenship: The Comparative Analysis of Gender Relations and Welfare States' 58 *American Sociological Review* 303–28.
Rosenfeld, RA, Trappe, H and Gornick, JC (2004) 'Gender and Work in Germany: Before and After Reunification' 30 *Annual Review of Sociology* 103–24.
Rüling, A and Kassner, K (2007) *Familienpolitik aus der Gleichstellungsperspektive: Ein europäischer Vergleich* (Berlin, Friedrich-Ebert-Stiftung).
Sacksofsky, U (2000) 'Steuerung der Familie durch Steuern' 44 *Neue Juristische Wochenschrift* 1896–1903.
Sainsbury, D (ed) (1994) *Gendering Welfare States* (London, Sage Publications).
Seel, B (2007) 'Einführung' in B Seel (ed), *Ehegattensplitting und Familienpolitik* (Wiesbaden, Deutscher Universitäts-Verlag) 1–6.
Spangenberg, U (2005) *Neuorientierung der Ehebesteuerung: Ehegattensplitting und Lohnsteuerverfahren* (Düsseldorf, Hans-Böckler-Stiftung).
—— (2007) 'Ehe-interne Verteilung von Einkommen: Recht und Realität' in B Seel (ed), *Ehegattensplitting und Familienpolitik* (Wiesbaden, Deutscher Universitäts-Verlag).
—— (2008) '50 Jahre Ehegattensplitting! Gute Gründe für eine Reform der Besteuerung der Ehe' 30 *Streit Feministische Rechtszeitschrift* 161–67.
Steiner, V and Wrohlich, K (2006) 'Familiensplitting begünstigt einkommensstarke Familien, geringe Auswirkungen auf das Arbeitsangebot' 31 *Wochenbericht des DIW Berlin* 441–49.
Vogler, C (2005) 'Cohabiting Couples: Rethinking Money in the Household at the Beginning of the Twenty First Century' 53 *The Sociological Review* 1–27.
Vollmer, F (1998) *Das Ehegattensplitting: Eine verfassungsrechtliche Untersuchung der Einkommensbesteuerung von Eheleuten* (Baden-Baden, Nomos Verlag).
Wagenhals, G (2007) 'Auswirkungen einer Reform des Ehegattensplittings' in B Seel (ed), *Ehegattensplitting und Familienpolitik* (Wiesbaden, Deutscher Universitäts-Verlag) 239–60.

Part IV

Savings, Wealth and Capital Gains

12

Income Splitting and Gender Equality: The Case for Incentivizing Intra-household Wealth Transfers

LISA PHILIPPS*

IN THIS CHAPTER I examine the problem of income splitting under an individual tax unit and Canadian legal developments that have expanded the scope for such tax planning by spouses. Income splitting poses a dilemma for tax policy analysts concerned with gender equality because, left unchecked, it opens a back door to joint taxation, with its troubling impact on labour-market incentives for secondary earners, who are mainly women. Yet ignoring intra-familial transfers in order to prevent income splitting may disrespect women's individual agency over property to which they hold legal title, and it may close off a potential source of economic power for those who do the bulk of the unpaid work in a household. This tax policy dilemma engages fundamental, normative debates about the meaning of gender equality and whether it is possible to enhance women's access to markets while also valuing and compensating their unpaid contributions.

A way through this dilemma is to differentiate between forms of income splitting that enhance the economic autonomy of a lower-earning spouse and those that entail no meaningful sharing of economic power but merely reduce tax for the transferor. The key problem with recent Canadian changes is that they confer the tax benefits of income splitting without any requirement that the transferor share the underlying income or assets with the lower-income partner. While this form of tax planning should be aggressively constrained, a gender-equality case can be made for more liberal treatment of genuine

* I am grateful to Kim Brooks, Jonathan Kesselman, and participants in the May 2009 workshop on *Challenging Gender Inequality in Tax Policy Making* for helpful comments on earlier drafts of this chapter. I thank Roni Hoffman for excellent research assistance. The work has been supported by a Social Sciences and Humanities Research Council of Canada Standard Research Grant and by the International Institute for the Sociology of Law in Onati, Spain.

intra-household transfers. (For an analysis of the tax/benefit implications of redistribution of personal income within both heterosexual and gay/lesbian households, see Warman and Woolley, chapter nine this volume.)

A number of objections may likely be made to this proposal to differentiate between good and bad forms of income splitting. In particular, feminist tax scholars may be concerned that tolerating any income splitting at all will reinforce women's financial dependency on male partners and discourage them from pursuing their own market incomes. In responding to this concern, I argue that reducing labour-market barriers should be one objective but not the exclusive focus of tax reform from a gender-equality perspective. Drawing on feminist scholarship outside the tax field, I suggest that fiscal policy should also be crafted with a view to enhancing the autonomy of those who invest their energies in providing unpaid care. Designing rules about income splitting that encourage genuine redistribution of control over household resources would contribute modestly toward meeting this goal, at least for women with relatively affluent partners. However, I recommend that this be complemented with other tax and spending reforms that would offset the erosion of revenues resulting from income splitting, provide caregivers with access to alternative sources of public support and fund childcare and other programmes that reduce the costs to women of entering the paid workforce.

THE DILEMMA OF INCOME SPLITTING: THE CANADIAN EXAMPLE

The policy challenge of income splitting is closely related to a country's choice of tax unit. Since the adoption of its first federal income tax in 1917, Canada has always defined the taxpayer as the individual or corporate 'person' (Income Tax Act: section 2). The individual unit has been extensively eroded over time by family-related concessions and by the use of a joint unit for purposes of tax-delivered benefits (Lahey 2005: 74–76; Law Commission of Canada 2001: 72–89). However, it has survived as a basic structural feature of Canadian income tax despite repeated challenges by supporters of joint marital or familial taxation (Lahey 2000: 40–44). In the 1960s, both the Royal Commission on Taxation (better known as the 'Carter Commission') and the Royal Commission on the Status of Women recommended a switch to family unit taxation (Royal Commission on the Status of Women in Canada 1970; Royal Commission on Taxation 1966). In the 1990s, social conservative advocacy groups and politicians lobbied for various forms of tax relief for single-earner couples with children, including a wholesale shift to joint filing (Philipps 2002: 64–70). Among the stated reasons that policy makers have given for rejecting such proposals and for maintaining the individual tax unit is the unfairness and negative labour-market incentives of joint taxation for women as secondary earners (Benson 1969; House of Commons Standing Committee on Finance 1999).

Academic opinion in both Canada and the United States has largely validated this judgement. Many scholars have concluded that joint taxation tends to discourage women from entering the paid workforce or from spending more time on paid labour because it raises the marginal tax rate on a couple's lower-earning partner, usually a woman whose employment is socially constructed as more discretionary than the man's (see, for example, Blumberg 1971; Brooks 1996; Lahey 1995; McCaffery 1992). In addition, tax scholars have criticized the propensity of joint taxation to reward couples with a traditional gendered division of labour with a 'marriage bonus', whereas two-earner couples may suffer a 'marriage penalty', depending on their relative earnings and the size of tax brackets for couples as compared with singles (Brown 1997; Forman 1996; Kesselman 2008: 8). Administratively, joint filing can also result in 'innocent spouses' being stuck with tax liability for household income over which they have no legal control (Kahng 2004; McMahon 2010: 40–41). In addition, a joint unit privileges couples over singles and privileges some personal relationships over others that do not enjoy the same degree of legal recognition because, for example, they are not conjugal or are not heterosexual (Brooks 1996: 63; Infanti 2009). For all these reasons, tax policy analysts interested in questions of gender equality have overwhelmingly argued against joint taxation.

Unfortunately, choosing an individual unit does not necessarily resolve the concerns raised by joint taxation. All countries adopting individual taxation must contend with the incentives it creates for income splitting, which not only erodes revenues, but creates some of the very same problems more often associated with joint taxation. Tax policy makers in both Canada and the UK, for instance, have waged lengthy battles to design effective anti-avoidance rules to prevent forms of income splitting deemed unacceptable (Donnelly, Magee and Young 2000; McMahon 2010: 33–36; Tillotson 2009). In Canada the principal strategy has been to ignore certain intra-familial property transfers for tax purposes by attributing passive income back to the transferor (Income Tax Act: sections 74.1–74.5). These so-called attribution rules have never been more than partial, as they explicitly tolerate some forms of tax planning.[1] Moreover, it has not been easy to enforce the spirit of the attribution rules through the courts in the face of tax planning arrangements designed to circumvent them.

Perhaps the widest loophole was opened by the Supreme Court of Canada when it upheld a so-called dividend-sprinkling arrangement, whereby a

[1] Eg, capital gains can be split with minor children; passive income can be shifted to children once they reach 18 years of age; passive income may not be attributed if a spouse or child paid fair market value consideration for an underlying property; and spousal registered retirement savings plans (RRSPs) may be used to split income between spouses.

spouse received special non-voting shares on incorporation of a family holding company (Duff 1999; *Neuman v Minister of National Revenue* 1998). Although the husband controlled the corporation through his ownership of the voting shares and influenced the distribution of dividends, the Court refused to apply the attribution rules on the basis that the corporation was a separate person and the husband was never entitled to the dividends that the board of directors had declared on his wife's shares. In response to this decision, the government introduced a 'kiddie tax', which imposes the highest marginal rate on private corporation dividends received by an individual who is under 18 throughout the taxation year (Income Tax Act: section 120.4). However, because it applied only to minors, this reform still permitted spousal dividend sprinkling, now a popular method of income splitting for those with significant income-generating assets and access to expert planning advice.[2]

The election in 2006 of a Conservative minority government has reignited the public debate over income splitting, as there is significant support for income splitting among Conservatives. This support is reflected in the party's official Policy Declaration, which states:

> We support the elimination of all tax disadvantages for families and those who care for children at home. It recognizes the economic value of stay at home parents, and supports the introduction of tax fairness measures such as income splitting for couples with children.
>
> (Conservative Party of Canada 2008a: 7)

This resolution has not yet been adopted as government policy, perhaps because doing so would be costly. According to one estimate, the Canadian government would lose over $2 billion per year if it extended income splitting to all couples with children—and almost $5 billion if it did so for all couples (Library of Parliament 2007: 5). However, the 2006 Budget took a first step towards permitting more income splitting by allowing taxpayers to report up to one-half of their private pension income on their spouse's or common-law partner's tax return (Income Tax Act: section 60.03). This is unprecedented; Canadian taxpayers have never before been permitted to engage in this form of income splitting, which is only notional, because it is purely a function of how tax returns are filled out. Previously, income splitting had always required a transfer or other restructuring of legal title to property or income. Pension income splitting can now be accomplished without any change of legal control over the actual pension income, not even to the extent necessary to cover the spouse's additional tax liability (Woolley 2007).

The pension income splitting rules are as close to a joint return as has ever been possible in Canada. Any employment or other income earned by the

[2] A similar arrangement has been upheld judicially in the UK. See *Jones v Garnett* [2007] UKHL 35, discussed in McMahon (2010) 34–35.

spouse will be stacked on top of the pension income reported on her return, creating the same type of market barrier as a joint unit.[3] The provisions also allow tax to be levied on so-called 'innocent spouses' who have no legal right to demand a share of the underlying income, despite having signed a joint election form that results in a 'deemed' receipt (Income Tax Act: section 60.03(2)). Although the measure currently applies to only one source of income (and only to pensioners over 55), it established a precedent. Indeed, in their 2008 re-election campaign, the Conservatives proposed to extend this model of income splitting to all sources of income for families in which one spouse works less than full time in order to care for a child or an adult with a disability (Conservative Party of Canada 2008b: 8).[4]

Following their re-election with another minority, the Conservative government created a new Tax Free Savings Account (TFSA), which also has an income-splitting component (Income Tax Act: section 146.2). Taxpayers may make non-deductible contributions of up to $5000 per annum to a TFSA, with no limit on total contributions. Investment income and capital gains earned on contributions are tax exempt, as are all withdrawals from the account. Most importantly for present purposes, gifts to a spouse or common-law partner that are used to fund a TFSA are exempt from the attribution rules (Income Tax Act: section 74.5(12)(c)). This concession effectively provides one-earner couples with access to two TFSAs, provided they have the means to save more than $5000 each year. However, unlike the pension income splitting rules, it is conditioned on a legal transfer of funds to the spouse or partner.

Reaction to these developments by feminist scholars and gender-equality advocates has been strongly negative (see House of Commons Standing Committee on the Status of Women 2008). For example, a coalition of activists and academics (including the author) working with the Canadian Feminist Alliance for International Action (FAFIA) called for the repeal of the pension income splitting rules and opposed their extension to more couples for the following reasons:

- — The tax savings will be received mainly by higher-income men.
- — Income splitting discourages women's paid workforce participation by increasing the tax rate on any income earned in the market.
- — Income splitting biases the tax code in favour of couples with very unequal incomes and against other family forms, including single parents, unattached individuals and couples with more equal incomes.

3 The legislation does not require spouse who is the 'pension transferee' to be a pensioner, of pensionable age, or retired from the labour force: Income Tax Act: s 60.03(1).

4 At the time of writing, the Conservative government had not yet moved to implement this promise.

- Dependent spouses/common-law partners receive no direct benefit, and in fact will suffer additional burdens, because they are liable for the tax but have no legal entitlement to the underlying income.
- The gradual extension of income splitting to cover all couples would be so costly as to preclude more effective and equitable programs to support families and caregivers.

(Canadian Feminist Alliance for International Action undated: 11; see also Weir 2007; Woolley 2007).

Notably, these points overlap substantially with the criticisms usually levelled against joint filing. Canadian economist Jonathan Kesselman has made similar arguments regarding why either joint taxation or full splitting of employment income would be unfair to two-earner couples and would reduce women's labour supply in ways harmful to their full equality (2008: 25–34). Similarly, in the United States, Lawrence Zelenak has argued in favour of an individual unit but has opposed the idea of recognizing inter-spousal assignments of earned income under such a system because it would recreate the labour-market disincentive of joint taxation since, as he points out, 'the wife's income will still be stacked on top of the husband's, and she will be discouraged from working' (1994: 380). I argue in the balance of this chapter that concerns about discouraging women's paid work through income splitting are valid but should be tempered by equally valid concerns about the need to encourage intra-household redistribution and to give unpaid caregivers greater control over household economic resources.

The strong feminist opposition to recent tax reforms in Canada should be understood in context as a reaction to the specific forms of income splitting being promoted by the Conservative government, which is perceived generally as hostile to equality norms. This image was reinforced by several high-profile spending cuts and other policy moves targeting gender equality programmes, as reviewed by Lahey in chapter one of this volume (see also Brodie and Bakker 2008). In other contexts, tax scholars have sometimes argued that income splitting may be quite consistent with gender-equality goals. This perspective is elaborated below, with a view to developing a feminist approach that distinguishes the most harmful forms of income splitting from those which could be desirable if combined with other tax and spending reforms that enhance women's economic autonomy.

WHAT INCOME SPLITTING RULES WOULD BEST PROMOTE GENDER EQUALITY?

A gender equality case can be made for allowing some types of income splitting between conjugal partners, specifically where there is an actual transfer of legal and beneficial title to property or income. However, several concerns and caveats attend even this preferred form of income splitting. While the basic analysis presented here could apply to any country that taxes conjugal partners as individuals, I concretize the arguments by describing specific reform proposals for Canada. The discussion will be organized around three claims that are typically made to support the argument for allowing more income splitting on gender equality grounds: (1) that such a system would encourage more equal sharing of economic resources between men and women; (2) that it would respect women's agency as property owners; and (3) that it would recognize women's unpaid contributions to household welfare. The analysis is predicated on the assertion that gender equality is no less legitimate a measure for evaluating tax policy than are the more familiar criteria of vertical and horizontal equity among different groups defined by income level, non-discretionary needs or choice of economic activity (*cf* Zelenak 1994: 380, 385). However, tax policy can address itself to gender equality only if rules are designed with an awareness of intra-household impacts and of the relative treatment of paid and unpaid economic activities undertaken by partners in a marriage or common-law relationship (both of which are recognized in Canadian tax law as discussed in chapter nine by Warman and Woolley).

Incentivizing Intra-Household Redistribution

Commentators have asserted that the Canadian attribution rules, which ignore inter-spousal gifts and even some fair market value sales for income tax purposes, have 'the effect of discouraging husbands from transferring family property to their wives during marriage and thus achieving a more equitable distribution of wealth' (Brooks 1996: 74; see also Kesselman 2008: 24). Conversely, it has been suggested that 'when tax liability follows legal ownership of incomes and property, individual taxation of people in relationships promotes economic sharing' (Lahey 2005: 26; see also Gann 1980: 50–51; Zelenak 1994: 384–87). Claire Young recommended that empirical research be undertaken in Canada to assess whether repealing the attribution rules would actually result in more asset transfers from men to women (2000: 45, 48–49). Since then, a UK study has found evidence of just such an effect (Stephens and Ward-Batts 2004). The UK switched from joint to individual taxation in 1990 and allowed inter-spousal transfers without any attribution of income from the transferred property. Stephens and Ward-Batts examined the relative shares of investment income reported by higher and lower-income spouses before and after the reform and found 'strong evidence that households did indeed take advantage of this opportunity for tax avoidance through income shifting', though most households did not exploit its full potential (2004: 2005–06). In addition, economist Herbert Schuetze found evidence that self-employed men in Canada are more likely than their counterparts in the US to allocate salary, wages or profits to their wives for income tax purposes, providing further empirical support for the view that income splitting incentives impact on the distribution of ownership rights within households (2006).

However, income splitting can promote this behavioural response only if it is conditioned on a transfer of legal and beneficial title to wealth or income. Joint tax provisions which presume that household income is shared have the opposite effect: 'Giving people who do not share incomes or property the tax benefit of presumed sharing eliminates any incentive they might otherwise have to share' (Lahey 2005: 26). As Woolley stated, in discussing the recent Canadian developments, '*[n]ominal* or *notional* splitting of pension income ... discourages real transfers of ownership and control' (2007: 613). These comments highlight the crucial distinctions between income splitting that is based on actual sharing of control over resources, versus that which is based on a reallocation of income for tax purposes only. While the first is potentially gender equalizing, the second merely ratifies existing distributions of economic power within households. Kesselman has argued that the notional pension income splitting rules may in fact result in a more equitable gender distribution of resources because the partner with the lower tax rate must give consent before pension income can be shifted to her return, and this should increase her power to bargain for a share of the income (2008: 22). However, with this approach the onus rests entirely on the financially dependent spouse to wrest control over household resources through a process of private bargaining in which power differentials of many kinds can still be expected to shape the outcome. At best, one could imagine a savvy and relatively empowered spouse insisting on enough income to cover the additional tax liability as well as a portion of the higher after-tax income obtained through income splitting. By comparison, making income splitting conditional on a transfer of title to income or assets would create a stronger incentive for richer spouses to share ownership, likely increasing the transferee's economic power and security over the longer term.

If Canadian tax policy makers sought to incentivize intra-household transfers, they would therefore have to repeal *both* the notional pension income-splitting rules and the attribution rules that ignore real transactions between spouses. One caveat is that in order to avoid attribution of future income, the property transfer itself should be taxed on a current basis so that any accrued gain is realized in the hands of the transferor spouse. This would not only limit the revenue loss from allowing more income splitting; it would also reinforce the incentive for sharing ownership within marriage by encouraging property-owning spouses to transfer appreciating assets early, before significant gains had accrued.

Respecting Women's Agency

A second argument in favour of recognizing genuine inter-spousal transfers is the need to respect women's agency as legal rights holders. Ignoring these transactions seems inconsistent with the basic principle of individual taxation—that people should be taxed on income which they legally control, and it 'fails to recognize the autonomy of the spouse receiving the property (usually the wife)' (Brooks 1996: 74; see also Duff 1999: 379). Similarly, Lahey comments that women are too often treated as mere puppets in tax planning transactions (2000: 119).

A common objection to this view is that inter-spousal transfers may be purely formalistic, reflecting no change in de facto decision-making power. This concern must also underpin the argument that income splitting reduces the progressivity of the tax system, as this assumes the income really belongs to the transferor in some economic sense despite legal title being held by the transferee. One way to address the issue of informal control would be to enact administrative and anti-avoidance rules that established criteria for ascertaining whether the transferee was the true owner of the transferred property (Lahey 2000: 119; Philipps 2002). It would be important to require spouses to submit some form of written evidence of their contractual arrangements with their tax returns (Gann 1980: 63). This would serve to alert tax authorities to cases where the legal validity of a transfer might be questionable, and would also make it more difficult for a transferor to deny the transaction later, for example on relationship breakdown.

In addition, there are many precedents within tax systems worldwide of rules that look beyond the form of a transaction to assess its economic substance. In Canada, for example, control of a corporation for some purposes is defined not only by the traditional de jure test of majority ownership of voting shares, but by a de facto test that considers whether a person exercises control 'directly or indirectly in any manner whatever' over the corporation (Income Tax Act*:* section 256(5.1)). De facto control can include a situation where a single creditor is allowed to withdraw all the corporation's financing by demanding repayment of a loan on short notice (Canada Revenue Agency 2001: paragraphs 19–23). Another rule that could be adapted to apply to inter-spousal transfers is the provision that denies the charitable donation credit for so-called 'loanback' arrangements, where a donor uses any property of a charitable entity within five years after making a donation to that charity (Income Tax Act: section118.1(16)). This provision applies, for instance, if a private foundation lends money back to a donor, even if the loan is at a market rate of interest. In addition, Canada already has a rule that prevents income splitting through revocable trusts, which are defined very broadly (Income Tax Act: section 75(2)). If the trust property may revert to the settlor at any future time, or if the settlor has any right to determine or even consent to distributions of trust property to others, then all the income and capital gains realized by the trust are attributed back to the settlor.[5] These examples show that for many purposes, Canadian tax policy makers have been prepared to distinguish substantive changes of ownership from those that are merely superficial tax avoidance devices. It would not be desirable or workable for tax authorities to question a spousal transfer on the basis of purely informal agreements between the parties to spend or invest the funds in particular ways. But if a transferor reserves legally enforceable rights to get the property back or consent to how it is used, he or she should also be required to pay tax on the income.

Kesselman objects that such anti-avoidance rules would be costly and intrusive to apply in the case of inter-spousal transfers (2008: 24; see also McMahon 2010: 33–37) However, this criticism could be directed toward any anti-avoidance rule that employed broad standards such as 'reasonableness' which require interpretation, rather than bright line tests. Such standards constitute an essential tool for reducing avoidance precisely because they inject some flexibility to deal with new and unforeseen transactions, and create some uncertainty as to how far the rules may be stretched by tax planners (Edgar 2008: 874; Royal Commission on Taxation 1966: 552–67). Anti-avoidance rules thus serve as deterrents to aggressive tax planning, even in cases where they are not directly applied or enforced by revenue authorities.

Absent some form of blatant retention of de facto control over the use of income or assets, transfers of legal and beneficial title should be treated as tax effective on the basis that transferees are rational agents with the capacity to exercise their legal rights directly or through the process of bargaining with a spouse over consumption decisions. Such a system would be similar to the UK rule which treats inter-spousal gifts of income producing property as fully effective for tax purposes, provided they are outright gifts in form and substance. That principle has now been extended judicially to apply to the payment of spousal wages and dividends by a family corporation.

Empirical evidence supports the view that women tend to enjoy greater power over household financial decisions and feel less guilt about spending money when they have a stream of income that is legally their own (Burton, Phipps and Woolley 2007; Kornhauser 1993: 80–91). The studies emphasize that couples are extremely diverse in terms of the extent to which they share decision-making power about how income will be spent, managerial responsibility for banking and the actual consumption of income. However, Kornhauser concluded after reviewing her own and other empirical studies on intra-household financial management that '[d]espite the presence of joint

[5] I disagree with Zelenak's argument that all transfers to a spouse via a trust should be treated as ineffective for tax purposes (1994: 387). Such a blanket rule would risk unfair exclusion of spousal trusts established purely for non-tax reasons, such as a desire to protect assets from either spouse's commercial creditors.

accounts and a belief in resource sharing, control of the money generally still resides with the earner' (1993: 90). If the income is derived from property the title-holding spouse can exert control over both the income stream and the underlying asset, further increasing her chances of financial autonomy. As Zelenak argues, 'owners of wealth can always determine how to employ that wealth. Even if ... owners cede some control over the consumption of their income by marrying, they still have control over the source of the income (as well as control over whether to stay married)' (1994: 357).

Even in cases where a transfer of title does not alter substantive power relations within a relationship, legal ownership may become more important on relationship breakdown. Canadian family law provides for property equalization on divorce but formal rights are often difficult for a non-titled spouse to enforce in practice for a host of reasons—including lack of access to costly legal advice or to courts in order to establish or enforce a claim; the difficulty of tracing assets that may be owned outside the country; pressures to trade child custody for a lesser share of property; the exclusion of some intangibles like professional degrees and licences from what is considered divisible property; and the legal uncertainty surrounding others such as unvested pension plan rights (Bala 1989; Grassby 2004; Langer 1994; Poirier and Boudreau 1992; Law Commission of Ontario 2008). Moreover, statutory property equalization regimes do not apply to common-law partners in most provinces, making title even more important in determining the post-relationship distribution of assets for these couples (Law Commission of Ontario 2008: 39; Mossman 2008). Thus, encouraging intra-household transfers promotes the long-term financial security of a lesser-earning spouse or partner, even where the transferor continues to exercise a degree of informal influence over the use of property or income while the relationship subsists.

Valuing Women's Unpaid Labour

An argument frequently advanced to justify income splitting is that it recognizes the value of women's unpaid contributions. In considering this claim, it is worth distinguishing between unpaid caregiving for children or other dependants on the one hand and, on the other, unpaid work that is done informally within family businesses or to assist employees. Elsewhere I have described this latter form of activity as 'unpaid market labour' because it contributes directly to the generation of market income (Philipps 2008a, 2008b). I argue below that while Canadian tax rules should make it easier to deduct amounts paid to compensate a family member for informal assistance in a business or job, using income splitting as a means of compensating unpaid caregivers is more problematic from a gender-equality perspective.

With respect to unpaid market labour, many sociological studies have documented the roles that family members play in the operation of small businesses and professional firms and in directly assisting with employment duties of their spouses or other relatives (reviewed in Philipps 2008a: 92–98). Spouses may perform tasks that are easily recognizable as a contribution to business operations or management or to the fulfilment of the other spouse's employment obligations. A spouse may also serve in a capacity such as social host or community ambassador for an organization that is owned by or employs the other spouse. One scholar has used the term 'two-person career' to describe middle class jobs in which spousal participation is expected or desired in order to generate goodwill, develop commercial relationships or simply provide backup for the paid worker (Papanek 1973). Recent studies suggest that the flexibilization of labour markets and working practices and the rise of self-employment and micro-businesses have ensured ongoing and perhaps rising demand for this unpaid market labour within many families (see, for example, Baines et al 2002; Baines and Wheelock 1998; Danes and Olsen 2003; Eardley and Cordon 1996: 111; Rowe and Hong 2000). While more empirical research is required to determine the full extent of unpaid market labour contributed to different economies, I have argued that existing evidence is sufficient to justify the assumption that most paid workers rely to some degree on this form of direct support for their market activities (Philipps 2008a: 101).

Anti-avoidance rules designed to prevent income splitting may actually discourage payment of an informal family assistant for her or his services. For example, historically, Canadian income tax legislation imposed a presumption that spouses were not business partners for tax purposes (Income Tax Act: section 74(5); Philipps 2008a: 77). While this rule was repealed in 1979, revenue administrators and courts remained sceptical in some cases towards claims that spouses had a commercial partnership, even in the face of evidence of a wife's extensive involvement in a business (see, for example, *Cullen v Canada* 1985; *Kuchirka (M) v Canada* 1991; *Sedelnick Estate v Minister of National Revenue* 1986). It is particularly difficult under Canadian law for an employee (as opposed to a business proprietor) to deduct wages or fees paid to a spouse who assists in their work. Such costs may be deducted only by an employee who is 'required by the contract of employment' to hire and pay an assistant (Income Tax Act: section 8(1)(i)(iii)). Thus, even where there is clear factual evidence that a spouse has rendered valuable services to assist his or her employee-spouse in performing job duties and even when the employer knew of and permitted this arrangement, any compensation paid to the spouse is non-deductible unless mandated by the employee's contract. Revenue authorities have stated that, as a matter of administrative policy this condition will 'ordinarily' require an express term in a written employment contract, but that it may also be satisfied 'where the taxpayer can establish that it was tacitly understood by both parties (the taxpayer and the employer) that such payment was to be made by the taxpayer and was, in fact, necessary under the circumstances to fulfil the duties of the employment' (Canada Revenue Agency 1994: paragraph 1). However, it is not clear what will suffice as evidence of such a tacit understanding.

The courts have taken different views of this question. In one recent case, the Tax Court of Canada held that a branch manager for investment advisor Merrill Lynch could not deduct a salary paid to his wife, as his written contract of employment was silent on the need for an assistant, though the employer had signed a separate form confirming that an assistant was required (*Morgan v Canada* 2007; see also *Prince v Canada* 2000). The Court held that, even if a contractual term had been established, the wife's salary of $35,000 in one year and $52,000 in another was unreasonably high, as some of her time billed was spent attending social functions, particularly in the month of December. The decision clearly reflects a concern about tax avoidance:

> I have no doubt that Ms Morgan did some useful work for her husband during the two years under appeal, but it appears that the amounts that she invoiced and was paid were driven at least as much by income-splitting objectives as by any contractual arrangement.
> (paragraph 10)

Other judges have more easily accepted that spousal assistance may be tacitly necessary in order for an employee to carry out his or her job successfully, despite the lack of any reference to this need in the formal contract of employment. A good example is *Schnurr v R* (2004), where the Court allowed the taxpayer to deduct a $30,000 salary paid to his wife for secretarial and client relations work, including making contacts in the community to generate clients for her investment advisor husband (see also *Longtin v R* 2006). Yet even the most liberal interpretation of the statutory rule does not permit the deduction of payments to a spouse who is participating in the work purely because the employee finds this helpful or efficient as a means of carrying out the job—or needs help to deal with a heavy workload (see, for example, *Sauvé v R* 2007; *Emery v Canada* 2004).

The unfairness of this regime is highlighted by the fact that business proprietors have a much broader scope for deducting wages or fees paid to family members. These expenses may be deducted just like any others that are incurred 'for the purpose of earning income' from the business, subject to a reasonableness test (Income Tax Act: sections 9(1), 18(1)(a), 67). The courts have also conferred significant discretion on business owners in setting the amount of family salaries, which need not always be limited to the market rate for an equivalent non-family employee (*Cie Idéal Body v R* 1989; *Maduke Foods Ltd v R* 1989). While the current rules for business owners may be too lax, they do encourage the redistribution of profits to spouses and other relatives involved with the business, especially by male business owners. In a study comparing US and Canadian couples, Schuetze found evidence that self-employed men in Canada were significantly more likely than their US counterparts to deduct amounts for wages or salary paid to wives (2006). While Schuetze makes the point that a system of individual taxation may result in revenue leakage through illegal (ie, fraudulent) income splitting, his data could also be interpreted to suggest that Canada's individual unit encourages more men to pay their wives for the work they contribute to family run enterprises. I argue that whatever regime applies to the self-employed for this purpose should also apply to employees whose spouses help them carry out job duties (*cf* Kesselman 2008: 28). Indeed, it is questionable whether one should even describe commercially reasonable compensation of a family assistant as 'income splitting', as this suggests a gratuitous payment purely driven by tax-avoidance motives.[6] While there may be a tax incentive for an individual to employ their spouse, this alone does not negate the income-earning purpose of the arrangement or the value of the services provided.

A possible criticism of my proposal is that it would encourage women to work for their husbands instead of seeking independent employment. However, a spouse's involvement in the work of a primary breadwinner should not be regarded stereotypically as merely a form of subjugation or gender oppression. For some women at some times, collaboration in a family enterprise may provide better opportunities and work–life balance, and indeed more economic power, than the regular labour market (Philipps 2008a). Neither, however, should such arrangements be romanticized as somehow free of the conflicting interests and hierarchies of family life. Household inequalities are reinforced by a tax regime that discourages fair compensation of spouses for their informal market work by denying deductibility for tax purposes. Liberalizing the rules would not only encourage redistribution of control over market income within households, but would help to de-gender market work symbolically by acknowledging that it is frequently produced through the joint labour of spouses.

Using income splitting as a mechanism to recognize the value of unpaid caregiving is more problematic. For instance, some commentators have suggested allowing taxpayers to deduct actual payments to a spouse who is providing unpaid care to dependants (Duff 1999: 73–74) or simply extending the notional pension income splitting rules to all couples (Mintz 2008: 17). While some such proposals openly promote a patriarchal model of the family with more sharply defined gender roles (for example, Szabo 1997), others present it as a route to greater equality within relationships. Undoubtedly, the failure of public policy to value the work of caregivers is significantly

[6] Thanks to Kim Brooks for this point.

linked to women's ongoing economic inequality. Yet I would argue that promoting more income splitting of any kind is a problematic strategy for addressing this issue. When a spouse directly assists an employee or entrepreneur to produce income, these are market-oriented services that primarily benefit the individual income earner. By contrast, unpaid caregiving provides more significant benefits to society at large. Inter-spousal transfers cannot be the main way of recognizing these contributions because that would leave primary caregivers dependent on the goodwill of individual breadwinners. Rather, a system of refundable tax credits or other state transfers is needed to increase the autonomy of primary caregivers by providing an alternate source of economic security. In Canada, such a system could be financed by repealing the spousal credit and other dependency credits delivered to primary earners and discussed by Warman and Woolley in chapter nine, this volume, and replacing them with a refundable credit paid directly to caregivers (Law Commission of Canada 2001: 73). This approach would have the advantage of reaching single caregivers and those living in lower-income households, who receive little or no benefit from income splitting, or indeed those whose affluent spouses are not interested in intra-household redistribution.

Some feminist tax scholars have objected to caregiver subsidies, even if delivered directly to the intended beneficiaries, because they strengthen the already significant incentives for many women to engage in unpaid rather than paid work (see, for example, Lahey 2005: 41–42). This view is consistent with the literature reviewed earlier in this chapter on the choice of tax unit, in which the overriding concern has been to reduce barriers to women's paid labour.

Strategies to demarginalize caregiving work have received far less attention within tax scholarship. While improving women's labour-market opportunities is obviously a crucial dimension of gender-equality struggles, feminist scholars working outside the tax field have increasingly argued that this needs to be tempered with efforts to value caregiver work and to assign it more equally to men and women. Joan Williams, for example, has discussed the failure of a 'full commodification' strategy, focused single-mindedly on equalizing employment opportunities, to achieve gender-equality goals (Williams 2000: 40–48). Among other problems, she points out that this strategy glosses over the discrimination and poor working conditions that many women face in the labour market and the relative satisfaction and solidarity they may derive from their family work, a perspective that has been voiced especially by many women of colour and working-class women. Similarly, Nancy Fraser has argued that a 'universal breadwinner' model of gender equality that values labour market access above all else fails to address the problem that women continue to do the bulk of unpaid household work, even when they are employed full time (1997: 41–68). If feminist tax scholars do not directly address the need to value unpaid caregiving, they risk ceding this ground to a social conservative movement that has a clearly defined politics of promoting one-earner families (Luxton and Vosko 1998: 52).

Biases in taxation and other biases against women's paid labour do need to be addressed. However, these barriers should be tackled more directly through tax reforms aimed at lowering the cost of entering paid work and reducing the fiscal burden on secondary earners. Providing better access to substitute care services is obviously a central requirement, whether through tax measures or direct programming. Lahey has outlined a comprehensive set of recommendations for reducing the high marginal tax rates experienced by secondary earners in Canada, including a possible earned income tax credit or, alternatively, full deductibility for the costs of earning employment or business income (2005; see also Kesselman 2008). These could be implemented alongside refundable caregiver credits to neutralize any tax bias in favour of household production.

REAL INCOME SPLITTING

This chapter has offered a feminist intervention in the debate over income splitting by couples, a topic that is perennially troublesome for countries that treat individuals as separate taxpayers. It has highlighted the confusion that arises when the term 'income splitting' is used to describe both real and notional transactions between conjugal partners. I argue that differentiating these phenomena is the key to articulating a tax policy solution that coheres with gender-equality goals. That solution, I propose, is to recognize real income-splitting transactions more readily for tax purposes while eliminating notional income splitting rules in tax legislation. The practical implication of these principles will vary from country to country, depending on the details of their existing tax regimes.

As demonstrated in this chapter, no single tax reform can achieve significant progress toward gender equality in isolation, because women comprise a highly diverse group and because taxes interact with transfers and other policies, and with informal norms that influence behaviour in markets and families. In the Canadian context, however, I suggest the following set of complementary reforms: (1) repealing the pension income splitting rules; (2) repealing the attribution rules, subject to anti-avoidance provisions designed to catch transfers that have no economic substance and subject to the transferor realizing any accrued gains at the time of transfer; (3) replacing spousal dependency credits with a new refundable credit or transfer for caregivers who individually have low incomes; and (4) creating new tax or direct-spending measures to reduce the fiscal and other cost barriers that discourage secondary earners from undertaking paid labour.

REFERENCES

Baines, S et al (2002) 'A Household-Based Approach to the Small Business Family' in D Fletcher (ed), *Understanding the Small Family Business* (London, Routledge).

Baines S and Wheelock, J (1998) 'Reinventing Traditional Solutions: Job Creation, Gender and the Micro-Business Household' 12 *Work, Employment & Society* 579.

Bala, N (1989) 'Recognizing Spousal Contributions to the Acquisition of Degrees, Licenses and Other Career Assets: Toward Compensatory Support' 8 *Canadian Journal of Family Law* 23.

Benson, EJ (1969) *Proposals for Tax Reform* (Ottawa, Queen's Printer).

Blumberg, G (1971) 'Sexism in the Code: A Comparative Study of Income Taxation of Working Wives and Mothers' 21 *Buffalo Law Review* 49.

Brodie, J and Bakker, I (2008) *Where Are the Women? Gender Equity, Budgets and Canadian Public Policy* (Ottawa, Canadian Centre for Policy Alternatives).

Brooks, N (1996) 'The Irrelevance of Conjugal Relationships in Assessing Tax Liability' in J Head and R Krever (eds), *Tax Units and the Tax Rate Scale* (Burwood, Victoria, The Australian Tax Research Foundation).

Brown, DA (1997) 'Race, Class, and Gender Essentialism in Tax Literature: The Joint Return' 54(4) *Washington and Lee Law Review* 1469.

Burton P, Phipps, S and Woolley, F (2007) 'Inequality within the Household Reconsidered' in S Jenkins and J Micklewright (eds), *Inequality and Poverty Re-Examined* (Oxford, Oxford University Press).

Canada Revenue Agency (26 August 1994) *Interpretation Bulletin IT-352R2: Employee's Expenses, Including Work Space in Home Expenses.*

—— (14 August 2001) *Interpretation Bulletin IT-64R4: Corporations: Association and Control.*

Canadian Feminist Alliance for International Action (undated) *Gender-Responsive Budgeting and Upholding Canada's International Human Rights Commitments Essential in a Weakened Economy: 2009 Pre-Budget Submission of FAFIA.* Available at: osgoode.yorku.ca/osgmedia.nsf/0/DF7C8633F3187F3E85257560005718B5/$FILE/FAFIA_Submission_2009_Pre-Budget_Consultations.pdf.

Conservative Party of Canada (2008a) Policy Declaration. Available at: www.conservative.ca/media/2008-PolicyDeclaration-e.pdf.

—— (2008b) *True North Strong and Free: Stephen Harper's Plan for Canadians.* Available at www.conservative.ca/media/20081007-Platform-e.pdf.

Danes, S and Olson, P (2003) 'Women's Role Involvement in Family Businesses, Business Tensions, and Business Success' 16 *Family Business Review* 53.

Donnelly, M, Magee, J and Young, A (2000) 'Income Splitting and the New Kiddie Tax: Major Changes for Minor Children' 48 *Canadian Tax Journal* 978.

Duff, D (1999) 'Neuman and Beyond: Income Splitting, Tax Avoidance, and Statutory Interpretation in the Supreme Court of Canada' 32 *Canadian Business Law Journal* 345.Eardley, T and Cordon, A (1996) *Low Income Self-Employment* (Aldershot, Avebury).

Edgar, T (2008) 'Building a Better GAAR' 27 *Virginia Tax Review* 833.

Forman, J (1996) 'What Can Be Done About Marriage Penalties?' 30 *Family Law Quarterly* 1.

Fraser, N (1997) *Justice Interruptus: Critical Reflections on the 'Postsocialist' Condition* (New York, Routledge).
Gann, P (1980) 'Abandoning Marital Status as a Factor in Allocating Income Tax Burdens' 59 *Texas Law Review* 1.
Grassby, M (2004) 'Two Income Couples: Presumption of Need for the Lower Income Spouse' 20 *Canadian Journal of Family Law* 321.
House of Commons Standing Committee on Finance (1999) *For the Benefit of the Children: Improving Tax Fairness*, Nineteenth Report of the Standing Committee on Finance, Sub-Committee on Tax Equity for Canadian Families with Dependent Children (Ottawa, Queen's Printer).
House of Commons Standing Committee on the Status of Women (2008) *Towards Gender Responsive Budgeting: Rising to the Challenge of Achieving Gender Equality* (Ottawa, House of Commons Canada). Available at: www.parl.gc.ca.
Infanti, A (2009) 'Decentralizing Family: An Inclusive Proposal for Individual Tax Filing' (draft on file with author).
Kahng, L (2004) 'Innocent Spouses: A Critique of the New Tax Laws Governing Joint and Several Tax Liability' 49 *Villanova Law Review* 261.
Kesselman, J (2008) *Income Splitting and Joint Taxation of Couples: What's Fair?* (Montreal, Institute for Research on Public Policy). Available at: www.irpp.org/fasttrak/index.htm.
Kornhauser, M (1993) 'Love, Money, and the IRS: Family, Income-Sharing, and the Joint Income Tax Return' 45 *Hastings Law Journal* 63.
Lahey, KA (1995) *Women and Employment: Removing Fiscal Barriers to Women's Labour Force Participation* (Ottawa, Status of Women Canada).
—— (2000) *The Benefit/Penalty Unit in Income Tax Policy: Diversity and Reform.* Study prepared for the Law Commission of Canada. Available at: dalspace1.library.dal.ca/dspace/handle/10222/10400?show=full.
—— (2005) *Women and Employment: Removing Fiscal Barriers to Women's Labour Force Participation* (Ottawa, Status of Women Canada).
Langer, R (1994) 'Post Marital Support Discourse, Discretion, and Male Dominance' 12 *Canadian Journal of Family Law* 67.
Law Commission of Canada (2001) *Beyond Conjugality: Recognizing and Supporting Close Personal Adult Relationships* (Ottawa, Minister of Public Works and Government Services).
Law Commission of Ontario (2008) *Division of Pensions Upon Marriage Breakdown* (Toronto, Law Commission of Ontario). Available at: www.lco-cdo.org.
Library of Parliament (2007) *Income Splitting: A Brief Overview* (Ottawa, Parliamentary Information and Research Service).
Luxton, M and Vosko, L (1998) 'Where Women's Efforts Count: The 1996 Census Campaign and 'Family Politics' in Canada 1980–1995' 56 *Studies in Political Economy* 49.
McCaffery, E (1992) 'Taxation and the Family: A Fresh Look at Behavioral Gender Biases in the Tax Code' 40 *University of California at Los Angeles Law Review* 983.
McMahon, SH (2010) 'London Calling: Does the UK's Experience with Individual Taxation Clash with the US's Expectations?' *St. Louis University Law Journal* (forthcoming).
Mintz, J (2008) 'Taxing Families: Does the System Need an Overhaul?' (Spring/Summer) *IMFC Review* 15.

Mossman, M (2008) 'Equity and "Family" Relationships: Cohabitation and Constructive Trusts' in M Gillen and F Woodman (eds), *The Law of Trusts: A Contextual Approach* 2nd edn (Toronto, Emond Montgomery) 775.
Papanek, H (1973) 'Men, Women and Work: Reflections on the Two-Person Career' 78 *American Journal of Sociology* 852.
Philipps, L (2002) 'Cracking the Conjugal Myths: What does it mean for the Attribution Rules?' 50 *Canadian Tax Journal* 1031.
—— (2008a) 'Helping Out in the Family Firm: The Legal Treatment of Unpaid Market Labor' 23 *Wisconsin Journal of Law, Gender & Society* 65.
—— (2008b) 'Silent Partners: The Role of Unpaid Market Labor in Families' 14 *Feminist Economics* 37.
Poirier, D and Boudreau, M (1992) 'Formal Versus Real Equality in Separation Agreements in New Brunswick' 10 *Canadian Journal of Family Law* 239.
Rowe, B and Hong, G (2000) 'The Role of Wives in Family Businesses: The Paid and Unpaid Work of Women' 13 *Family Business Review* 1.
Royal Commission on the Status of Women in Canada (1970) *Report of the Royal Commission on the Status of Women in Canada* (Ottawa, Information Canada).
Royal Commission on Taxation (1966) *Report of the Royal Commission on Taxation* (Ottawa, Queen's Printer).
Stephens M and Ward-Batts, J (2004) 'The Impact of Separate Taxation on the Intra-Household Allocation of Assets: Evidence from the UK' 88 *Journal of Public Economics* 1989.
Szabo, P (1997) *Strong Families ... Make A Strong Country* (Ottawa, House of Commons, Office of Paul Szabo MP).
Schuetze, H (2006) 'Income Splitting Among the Self-Employed' 39 *Canadian Journal of Economics* 1195.
Tillotson, S (2009) 'The Family as Tax Dodge: Partnership, Individuality, and Gender in the Personal Income Tax Act, 1942 to 1970' 90(3) *The Canadian Historical Review* 391.
Weir, E (2007) *Splitting All Income Would Worsen, Not Lessen Inequality* (Ottawa, Canadian Centre for Policy Alternatives). Available at: www.policyalternatives.ca.
Williams, J (2000) *Unbending Gender: Why Work and Family Conflict and What to Do About It* (New York, Oxford University Press.
Woolley, F (2007) 'Liability without Control: The Curious Case of Pension Income Splitting' 55 *Canadian Tax Journal* 603.
Young, C (2000) *What's Sex Got To Do With It? Tax and the 'Family'* (Ottawa, Law Commission of Canada).
Zelenak, L (1994) 'Marriage and the Income Tax Act' 67 *Southern California Law Review* 339.

Cases

Cie Idéal Body v R [1989] 2 CTC 187; 89 DTC 5344 (Federal Court Trial Division).
Cullen v Canada [1985] 2 CTC 2059; 85 DTC 409 (Tax Court of Canada).
Emery v Canada [2004] 1 CTC 2480; 2003 DTC 4034 (Tax Court of Canada).

Kuchirka (M) v Canada [1991] 1 CTC 339; 91 DTC 5156 (Federal Court Trial Division).
Longtin v R [2006] 5 CTC 2323, 2006 DTC 3254 (Tax Court of Canada).
Maduke Foods Ltd v R [1989] 2 CTC 284; 89 DTC 5458 (Federal Court Trial Division).
Morgan v Canada [2008] 1 CTC 2516; 2007 DTC 1360 (Tax Court of Canada).
Neuman v Minister of National Revenue [1998] 3 CTC 177; 98 DTC 6297; [1998] 1 SCR 770, 225 (Supreme Court of Canada).
Prince v Canada [2000] CarswellNat 1650; 2000 DTC 3629 (Tax Court of Canada).
Sauvé v R [2007] 1 CTC 2295; 2006 DTC 3671 (Tax Court of Canada).
Schnurr v R [2005] 1 CTC 2213; 2004 DTC 3531 (Tax Court of Canada).
Sedelnick Estate v Minister of National Revenue [1986] 2 CTC 2102; 86 DTC 1563 (Tax Court of Canada).

Legislation

Income Tax Act, RSC 1985, c1 (5th supp), as am.

13

Indirect Discrimination in Tax Law: The Case of Tax Deductions for Contributions to Employer-provided Pension Plans in Germany

ULRIKE SPANGENBERG*

THE RELIEF AND incentive structures inherent in German tax laws are rife with gender inequalities.[1] These inequalities are linked to the different socio-economic positions of men and women—in particular, their different positions in the labour market and their income levels. Using the example of tax deductibility of contributions to employer-provided pension plans, this chapter presents the legal implications of the disparate impacts that these tax deductions have on men and women. The example is especially interesting, since Germany, like many other countries, is relying increasingly on capital-based pensions as an alternative or supplement to statutory pensions financed in a 'pay-as-you-go' fashion.

In the United States and in Canada, scholars have analysed and illustrated the disparate gender and racial impacts of tax regulations.[2] These studies typically include proposals for changes in tax policy to avoid such discriminations. However, a topic less frequently considered is this: at what point do laws with differing gender impacts actually become unlawful, ie, at what

* I want to thank the editors for inviting me to the workshop at the Onati International Institute for the Sociology of Law. It has been very inspirational and a great experience to discuss issues of gender and tax policy in such an international and knowledgeable context. Thanks to all the participants, who made helpful comments on the draft of this chapter. My special thanks go to Christian Boulanger and Bridget Crawford, who made the publication of this chapter possible.

[1] The chapter is limited to the discussion of gender as a dimension of differentiation between women and men, without discussing other dimensions of discrimination, such as race or age. If the problem of interwoven discriminations (intersectionality) is taken seriously, the evaluation of indirect discrimination in tax law becomes much more complex than discussed below (see McCall 2005).

[2] The impact of tax deductions for pension plans has been discussed by Brown 2004, 2007; Young 2000 and Donnelly 1993.

point do tax regulations violate laws made to prohibit discrimination? This chapter refines the concept of indirect discrimination in tax law in order to develop a standard for evaluating the different impacts of tax regulations on men and women. Such a standard is relevant not only to court decisions, but to the 'legal impact assessment' required by recent German legislation.[3] This chapter frames the discussion, makes suggestions and outlines questions that must be raised in working toward a standard for evaluating indirect discrimination in tax law.

The chapter begins with a description of the German pension system and tax regulations governing employer-provided pension plans. The gender impacts of laws governing tax-deductible contributions to employer-provided pension plans are then examined, through a description of their distributional impact, the incentive structures they establish for the creation of retirement income and their long-term consequences for men and women. The concept of tax equity and its relationship to indirect gender discrimination is then explored. The chapter ends with a discussion of specific problems encountered in determining the scope of comparisons needed to demonstrate the negative impacts of tax deductions on gender equality. This discussion also considers rationalizations that could potentially be offered to justify these negative impacts.

TAX REGULATIONS GOVERNING EMPLOYER-PROVIDED PENSION PLANS

The German pension system consists of the statutory pension system and supplementary employer-provided and private pension plans. Most employees are members of the statutory pension system, since it is mandatory for the majority of German employees to make social security contributions. The only employees not included in the statutory pension system are those who are not subject to social security contributions, since their income exceeds the social security contribution ceiling. Also, employees in short-term or in marginally paid occupations, known as *geringfuegige Beschaeftigung* (limited occupations) are not obliged to make social security contributions.[4] The statutory pension system is financed largely on a pay-as-you-go basis, though it is supplemented by the state with tax-financed funds to account for workforce absences necessitated by childcare. The amount of retirement income obtained from the statutory pension system depends on the level

[3] §§ 2, 44 GGO (Internal Rules of Procedures for the German Federal Ministries); see also Baer and Lewalter 2007.

[4] The social security contribution ceiling for 2009 is a monthly income of €5400 (Germany/West) and €4550 (Germany/East). Employees above that threshold, self-employed individuals and employees in limited occupations may insure themselves voluntarily. Civil servants are also not included in the statutory pension system.

of employment income, the length of time during which an employee pays into the system and the current annuity value at the time the payment is made.[5]

In the past, employer-provided, capital-based pension plans were available mainly to high-income or highly qualified employees (experts or management), as they were not part of the statutory pension system (see Leiber 2005). However, employer-provided pension plans became more important as a supplementary retirement provision for all employees when tax deductions for pension plans were extended in 2002 and 2005.[6] These new tax regulations were accompanied by a lowering of the annuity value for statutory pensions, which will result in lower payouts in the future. Several different tax deductions can be used by employers and employees for employer-provided pension plans, with some variations, depending on whether the employer or a third party provides the plan.

As an example demonstrating the gender inequalities inherent in tax deductions, I will discuss the regulation allowing employees to deduct either employer-financed or self-financed contributions to an employer-provided pension plan from the tax base. This kind of tax deduction is restricted to pension plans provided by a third party, such as the *Pensionskassen*, the *Pensionsfonds* and the *Direktversicherung*.[7] The allowable annual amount of the tax deduction is currently limited to a maximum of about €4400 but might be extended through other annual tax deductions for the same pension plan or through another type of employer-provided pension plan, such as the *Unterstuetzungskassen* or the *Direktzusagen*.[8] Employers are still not required to make contributions for all employees, and they may choose to contribute only to some categories of employees. However, since 2002 employees subject to social security contributions are entitled to contribute up to approximately €2600 of their pre-tax wages to employer-provided pension plans, and they can force the employer to provide a pension plan.[9] The income earned by funds saved in pension plans is not taxed until it is later paid out as retirement income.[10]

In addition to tax deductions for employer-provided pension plans, other tax deductions are permitted, including deductions for supplementary private pension plans and fringe benefits for individuals on lower incomes

[5] For gender implications of the statutory pension system and a review of the pension reforms of 2001, see Leitner 2003 and Fuchsloch 2004 .

[6] Altersvermögensgesetz (Act concerning the Taxation of Future Senior Citizens' Financial AssetsBGBl. I 2001, 1310ff; Alterseinkünftegesetz (Retirement Income Act), BGBl. I 2004, 1427ff.

[7] § 3 No 63 EStG. The *Pensionfonds,* the *Pensionskassen* and the *Direktversicherungen* differ especially in the return assumption and risk coverage.

[8] The *Direktzusagen* and the *Unterstuetzungskassen* are not provided by a third party, but the employer.

[9] § 1a BetrAVG (Employers Retirement Benefits Act).

[10] § 22a EStG.

(known as *Riester-Rente*).[11] Employees making social security contributions may opt for the *Riester-Rente*, but very few do so.[12] All these tax deductions usually require employment or, in the case of deductions for supplementary private pension plans, employment where contributions to social security is a condition of employment.

DISTRIBUTION EFFECTS OF TAX DEDUCTIONS

In income tax law, gender-differentiated impacts likely result from unequal distribution of income and property, gender-related employment and labour market structures and gender roles within the family unit. It is difficult to determine exact impacts because almost no German tax statistics are disaggregated by gender. However, general studies about employer-provided pension plans, as well as statistics about employment and labour market patterns, do shed light on gender-differentiated impacts in income tax law. Women seem to receive lower or no tax relief for contributions made to employer-provided pension plans, due to gender-related barriers to entry, working patterns and income differences. Furthermore, the tax deductions might—as a long-term result—intensify gender differences in retirement income.

The disparities in distribution of tax deductions for contributions to employer-provided pension plans between women and men result from gender-related barriers to entry, since certain groups are not legally entitled to tax deductions and certain employees participate in the activities associated with tax deductions to a lesser extent than others—or not at all. German studies show that female employees made tax-deductible contributions to pension plans at a lower rate than male employees did (see Figure 1). This is especially true for the *Pensionsfonds*, which, due to different regulations about how the assets may be invested, can yield a much higher return than other forms of employer-provided pension plans such as the *Pensionskassen* and the *Direktversicherungen*. The *Pensionsfonds* seem to be used as a secondary form of investment and require a high level of income that women might not have as often as men.

Overall, women, participating in pension plans in Germany do make tax-deductible contributions to employer-provided pension plans at a fairly high rate. In the case of the *Pensionsfonds*, they even do so at a higher percentage than men (see Figure 2). However, the lower number of female employees

[11] §§ 10a, 79ff EStG.

[12] The reason might be that the *Riester-Rente* may also be used to make contributions to a private pension plan as a supplement to an employer-provided pension plan. Besides, contributions to employer-provided pension plans reduce the pre-tax income, which is the basis for calculating the social security contributions. The conversion of pre-tax wages therefore decreases the social security contributions for the employees, whereas *Riester* does not.

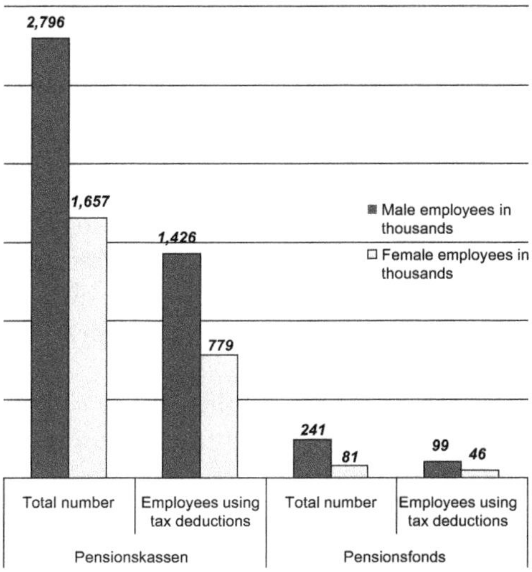

Figure 1: Number of Employees subject to Social Security Contributions in general and those who used Tax Deductions for Contributions to Pension Plans taken from Pre-tax Wages in 2007 (TNS Infratest Sozialforschung, 2008: Table 8-2c, 9-2b)[13]

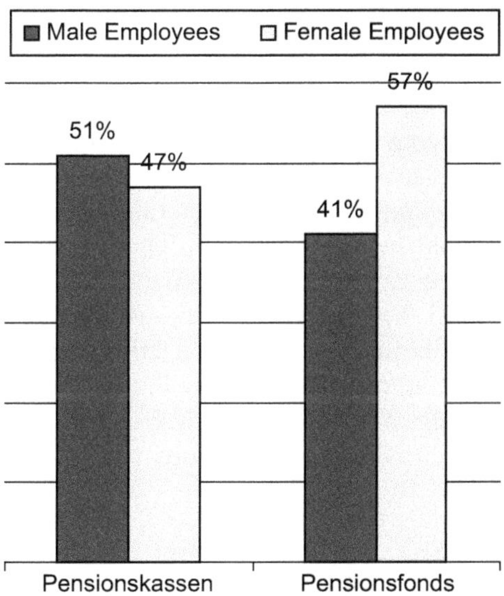

Figure 2: Percentage of Employees subject to Social Security Contributions who used Tax Deductions for Contributions to Pension Plans taken from Pre-tax Wages in 2007 (TNS Infratest Sozialforschung, 2008: Table 8-2c, 9-2b)

[13] Note that the numbers in the figures are only a fraction of employees with employer-provided pensions plans. German statistics do not provide gender disaggregated information about employees using tax deductions in other types of employer-provided pension plans.

compared with the number of male employees in Figure 1 indicate that women have fewer opportunities to contribute to employer-provided pension plans and therefore fewer opportunities to benefit from tax-deductions for pension plans.

The difference in the proportion of women and men participating in employer-provided pension plans is attributable to gendered patterns of employment and the structure of the labour market itself. Women are less frequently employed than men and therefore they often neither participate in employer-provided pension plans, nor are they eligible for tax deductions for contributions to those plans. Women also often work in employment for limited amounts of time or in marginally paid work (limited occupations) (see Bothfeld et al 2005: 133ff). These employees are often not included in employer-provided pension plans.[14] In addition, the adoption of employer-provided pension plans varies with the type of industry and the size of the company. In industries where women outnumber men—such as the service industry and social services fewer companies offer pension plans. In contrast, in the production industries, where men outnumber women, pension plans are offered more frequently. Furthermore, more often than not, women work in smaller firms with up to five employees. These small firms offer employer-provided pension plans less often than do bigger companies with 50 or more employees (Bothfeld et al 2005: 167ff; TNS Infratest Sozialforschung 2008: 33ff).

Tax-related disadvantages also result from the different amounts of contributions made to employer-provided pension plans. Gender-disaggregated statistics showing amounts of tax deductions made in relation to employer-provided pension plans do not exist in Germany.[15] So the amounts presented in Figure 3 show only contributions taken from pre-tax income and financed by the employee. These contributions represent only a fraction of the contributions that are potentially tax deductible, and contributions paid by the employer—usually in favour of male-dominated groups (see Blaufus and Ortlieb 2008; Leiber 2005)—are not included. But even the amounts shown in Figure 3 indicate that female employees' contributions are smaller than contributions made by male employees, resulting in lower tax deductions for women's employer-provided pension plans.

[14] Those employees can choose not to pay social insurance contributions. From this, it follows that they do not have a legal title to convert their pre-tax wages into pension contributions.

[15] Canadian statistics concerning contributions to pension plans claimed as tax deductions show that women's contributions are significantly less than those of men in that country as well (see Young 2000: 45ff).

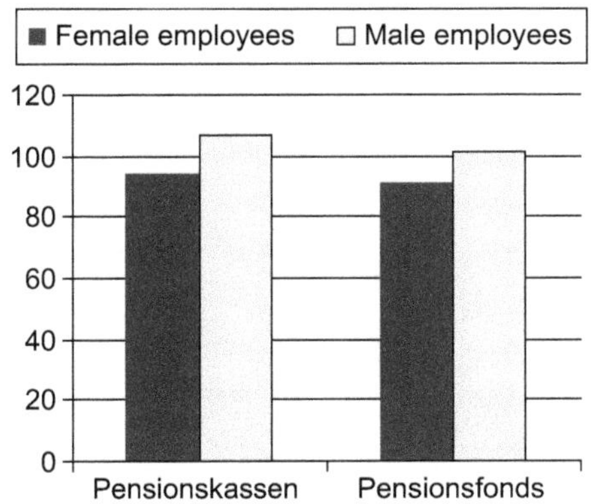

Figure 3: Amount of Contributions per month in €—taken from pre-tax wages—by type of Employer-provided Pension Plan in 2007 (TNS Infratest Sozialforschung 2008: Table 8-5c, 9-3b)

Women contribute less overall to employer-provided pension plans because contributions are often based on how much income a worker has or how many hours he or she works. Since women generally earn less than men and more often work part time (Bothfeld et al 2005), women are less likely to use the full untaxed contribution room of about €4400. Because their income is lower, the tax benefit of their deduction is also lower in a progressive tax system like the one in Germany.[16] The effects of this progressive system are mitigated because the retirement income from pensions is taxed with a progressive tax rate, resulting in a higher tax burden for higher incomes. However, the time lag between the tax relief for contributions toward pensions and the taxation of retirement income produces further financial benefits for groups with higher incomes. Unfortunately, no statistic exists to show empirical evidence of this trend, but two points support the argument. First, income is usually higher during the working and saving period than during retirement, so the tax rate on retirement income is lower (lessening the tax burden). Secondly, interest and compounding interest are not taxed during the accumulation period, so the funds accumulate at a higher rate than they would otherwise (see Dorenkamp 2001).

[16] German tax law stipulates two progression zones that increase in a linear fashion, with an initial marginal tax rate of 15% and a maximum marginal tax rate of 42%. The progression zone is followed by a proportional zone. The marginal tax rate of 42% stays constant starting with an income of €60.000 (or, for married couples, €120.000).

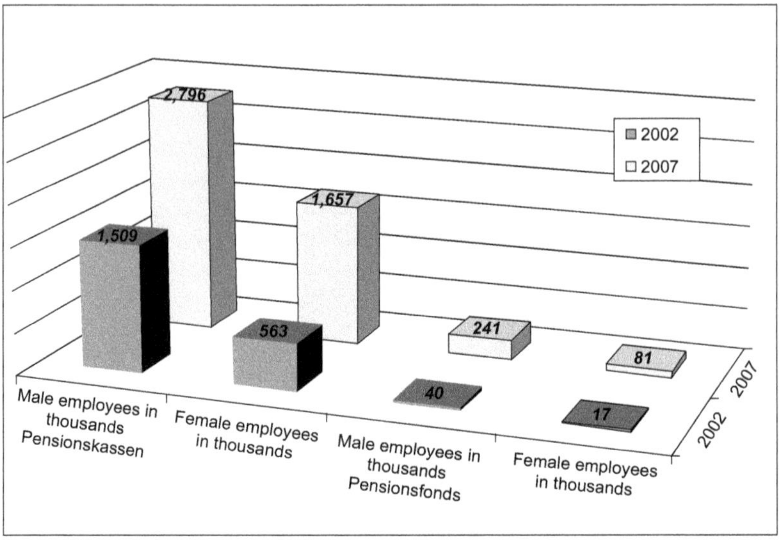

Figure 4: Private-sector Employees subject to Social Security Contributions participating in the *Pensionsfonds* and the *Pensionskassen* in 2002 and 2007 (TNS Infratest Sozialforschung 2008: Table 8-2a,c; 9-2a,b)

INCENTIVE STRUCTURES FOR THE CREATION OF RETIREMENT INCOME

Tax deductions can also provide incentives for certain behaviour.[17] In particular, tax expenditures are structured to produce particular developments, including specific types of taxpayer behaviour.[18] The intended goal of tax deductions for contributions made to employer-provided pension plans is to strengthen employer-provided pension plans and to create an incentive for the accumulation of supplemental retirement income, since the retirement income from the statutory pension system is increasingly inadequate to provide for a person's old age.[19]

[17] In Germany, the debate, concerning behaviour incentives has recently centred on the incentive effects of taxing married couples (Beblo 2007). See the contribution by Wersig (ch 11, this volume) on the taxation of marriage in Germany.

[18] Using the example of the tax deductibility of childcare costs, Fellows (1998) shows that the incentives created by the regulation affect not only taxpayers themselves, but third parties. This research demonstrates that structures of inequality cannot be analyzed adequately unless effects on the (mostly female) providers of childcare are taken into account.

[19] In German tax jurisprudence, it is debated whether the tax deductions for pension plans should be understood as social tax expenditures or as expenses that need to be deducted from the tax base in order to guarantee the principle of the ability to pay (see Tipke 2003: 756ff).

Analyses for the period 2001–07 indicate that tax deductibility has some effect on participation in employer-provided pension plans. Since the introduction of these tax deductions, the participation of both women and men increased (see Figure 4 and Table 1).

It is still true that lower numbers and a lower percentage of female employees have employer-provided pension plans than do male employees. However, since the adoption of the new tax regulations in 2002, the difference between proportions of male and female employees participating in employer-provided pension plans has decreased (see Table 1).

This general conclusion does not apply to the highly profitable *Pensionsfonds*. Here, the proportion of men has increased and the gender difference is more pronounced than is the case with the *Pensionskassen* and with employees who have employer-provided pension plans in general (see Figure 4).

Given the scarcity of the currently available research on the subject, the incentive effects of tax deductions for employer-provided pension plans can only be analyzed in a preliminary and limited fashion. However, it is evident that tax deductibility is not the only reason for increased participation in these plans. A dominating influence can especially be attributed to the legal title to pension plan contributions via deferred compensation as well as instruments of employee participation to push employers to provide pension plans (see Riedmüller and Willert 2008: 56; BMAS 2005: 189f).

LONG-TERM CONSEQUENCES OF LAWS GOVERNING PENSION PLANS

Tax incentives are not ends in themselves, but rather means for achieving long-term results, and the purpose of allowing tax deductions for contributions to supplementary pension plans is to promote appropriate retirement incomes. In order to understand and legally assess the long-term gender impact of tax regulations, it is important to bear in mind that gender differences can also result from regulations beyond the tax system. For example, the calculation of the pension itself might add to gender differences. While rates for tax-supported private pension plans must be unisex, calculations of pension benefits from employer-provided pension plans might still be based on higher life expectancies for women and therefore decrease payments for women (see Blaufus and Ortlieb 2008: 308). Even though the calculation of contributions and benefits of pension plans are private law issues, as long as the government supports this kind of pension plan through the tax system, discrimination is to be ascribed to the state.

The outcomes of tax regulations might not only reflect, but reinforce or increase gender differences in the labour market, economic developments or even social values. Young (1997; 2000) for instance, shows the privatizing

Table 1: Employees subject to social security contributions in the private sector at large and those with employer-provided pension plans in 2001 and 2007 (TNS Infratest Sozialforschung 2008: Tab. 2-3a)

	December 2001			December 2007		
	Men	Women	Proportion	Men	Women	Proportion
Private-sector employees subject to social security contributions (million)	14.9	9.2	62 : 38	14.5	9.2	61 : 39
Employees with employer-provided pension plans (million)	5.7	3	71 : 29	7.8	4.5	64 : 36
Employees with employer-provided pension plans (%)	39%	33%		54%	48%	

effect of deductions for supplementary pension plans, increasing women's dependence on their spouses and decreasing their freedom of choice. In addition, tax deductions can reinforce heteronormativity when same-sex partners are not eligible for benefits from their partners' pension plans but heterosexual spouses are eligible for these benefits.[20]

Since the new tax regulations were established only recently—in 2002—there is not enough data available to estimate either the amount of entitlements or the future retirement income that will derive from employer-provided pension plans that have been supported by the new tax regulations. It is also currently impossible to assess statistically whether the private or employer-provided pension plans can (or will, in fact) fill the gaps in statutory pensions. So far, statistics suggest significant gender differences in anticipated retirement income from employer-provided pension plans as compared with statutory pension plans (BMAS 2008: Annex, Table BC 25; TNS Infratest Sozialforschung 2005: 88).

TAX EQUITY AND INDIRECT GENDER DISCRIMINATION IN GERMANY

In German tax law, the gender impacts of taxation are largely ignored, as legal scholars in Germany and abroad have focused on the principle of 'ability to pay' as a key component of fairness in a tax system. According to the German income tax law, an individual's available income from employment dictates his or her ability to pay. The purpose of using this concept is to create equal distribution of the so-called 'impact of the tax burden' (Birk 2010: 55). However, the concept of 'impact of the tax burden' is misleading because it does not take into account real economic or financial effects or tax incentives. Rather, according to this concept, fairness is determined by equal treatment of available income. The theory behind the concept is that those who have the same ability to pay should be taxed equally (Birk 2010: 55). But note that equal treatment in this context means formal equality, not substantive equality or equality of opportunity (see also Infanti 2008: 3).

Furthermore, the ability to pay is not only a constitutional given standard of comparison, but has to be substantiated in many respects. For example, in order to accurately measure ability to pay, tax law takes into account mandatory expenses, which diminish taxable income and are usually deducted from the tax base. Mandatory expenses consist of expenses that must be paid to earn an income, but in Germany, mandatory expenses also encompass a minimum level of support for an individual and his or her family, as well as alimony payments made to a former spouse. It is

[20] For a discussion of tax disadvantages encountered by same-sex partners in the United States, see Infanti, ch 8 this volume.

important to note that, in order to determine what expenses are mandatory, certain criterions have to be selected and such criterions might contain normative assumptions that create gender differences. For example, in German tax law childcare expenses are considered to be only partly work-related and partly private. Therefore, they are only partially deductible from gross income as mandatory expenses. Labelling childcare expenses as 'not work-related' and thus not essentially mandatory is rooted in the distinction between the public and private spheres. For tax purposes in Germany and elsewhere (for example, the United States) childcare is still considered to be part of the 'private sphere' (and thus the responsibility of women, who do not work and do not pay taxes) (see Fellows 1998).[21]

Conversations about equity in taxation not only fail to take into account gender-related socio-economic differences among taxpayers. Similarly, these conversations ignore the differences in behavioural incentives that are the product of gender roles. When tax laws are motivated primarily by economic or social goals, but not necessarily by revenue goals, as is the case, for example, with tax incentives for employment close to home, the impact of tax deductions might be taken into account in evaluating the law's efficiency (see Tipke and Lang 2010: paragraph 19, no 76). However, the legality (or illegality) of tax law does not usually hinge on whether it has a different impact on women and men.

PROHIBITION OF INDIRECT DISCRIMINATION IN TAX LAW

The principle of tax equity in Germany derives from article 3, section 1 of the German Constitution, which contains the general principle of equality. According to this principle, similarly situated cases must be treated similarly as long as there is no justification for dissimilar treatment. The standard of comparison in the context of taxation is the ability to pay (see Tipke and Lang 2010: para 4, no 81ff.).

At the same time, the remaining two sections of article 3 forbid discrimination based on gender, age, national origin or disability. The Federal Constitutional Court has confirmed that, at least in the case of gender, both direct discrimination (disparate treatment) (ie, tax regulations explicitly different for men and women) and indirect discrimination (disparate impact) are prohibited. The only exception to this prohibition occurs in cases where the disadvantage is justified on grounds—not related to gender—that outweigh the discriminatory effect (see BVerfGE 121, 241 (255ff.); 113,

[21] Without doubt, there is room for debate about the extent to which these expenses should be tax deductible. In view of the financial benefits, it could be argued that full deductibility of childcare expenses would unfairly favour high-income earners over low-income earners, thus creating class or racial differences.

1 (15f.)).[22] According to the jurisprudence of the Constitutional Court, discriminatory effects include negative employment incentives for women, financial disadvantages or lost benefits, that follow from different socio-economic positions of men and women (see BVerfGE 121, 241 (255f.); 113, 1 (16ff), 6, 55 (82)). Thus, tax incentives, tax benefits and tax burdens that indirectly discriminate against women or men are illegal unless their benefit is greater than the harm they perpetrate.

The prohibition against indirect discrimination refers to an actual quantitative and qualitative impact on social life, as opposed to the idea of formal equal treatment of people who have equal ability to pay. But note, that the principle of equality found in article 3, sections 2 and 3 of the German Constitution confines the legal assessment of tax regulations, including the principle of the ability to pay, which is derived only from the general principle of equality contained in article 3, section 1. Substantiations of the concept of the ability to pay, such as the definition of mandatory expenses, must therefore recognize and avoid gender disadvantages as far as possible (see BVerfG 121, 243 (261)). The legislator continues to determine the details of the tax design. However, in order to minimize the indirect discriminatory effects of regulations, the legislator must identify and evaluate the effects of income tax by using data or prognoses and balance discriminatory effects against other objects of legal protection. By requiring this minimum standard, gender equality in tax law requires impact assessments analogous to the ecological audits that are used in environmental law (Mueckenberger et al 2007: 82ff).

Proof of indirect discrimination usually requires statistical data differentiated by gender and other structural categorizations, relevant to show societal inequalities. However, in Germany, statistical data concerning income tax is predominantly collected and analyzed without even applying gender-based categories. Similarly, data regarding the effects of tax deductions on employer-provided pension plans is questionable at best. Certainly, one could argue that the legislature is legally obliged to collect such data in order to avoid discrimination. What then is the consequence of missing data if retroactive data collections are not possible or not available (for example, the missing statistics regarding the intended effect of tax deductions for employer-provided pension plans)? If data shortcomings can justify the lack of attention paid to discriminatory effects of tax norms, the constitutional prohibition of indirect discrimination would be meaningless in tax law—especially when complex interactions with other (tax) regulations are

[22] The prohibition of indirect discrimination is accepted for disability, but in the constitutional law scholarship, it is still disputed for other dimensions such as race or origin. However, since 2006, sub-constitutional law (the General Equal Treatment Act) stipulates the prohibition of indirect discrimination on the grounds of race, ethnicity, gender, religion, conviction, age or sexual identity.

concerned, making it difficult to prove disadvantages. A possible solution to this problem is to ease the requirements to prove gender disadvantages. For example, the General Equal Treatment Act (AGG), implemented 2006 in accordance with European legal directives, accepts a prima facie case as proof of discriminatory effects, shifting the burden of proof back to the respondent.[23] Hence, the lack of sufficient statistics to prove a contrary impact goes to the expense of the government.

APPLYING THE CONCEPT OF INDIRECT DISCRIMINATION IN TAX LAW

As noted above, a tax regulation does not comply with the prohibition of indirect discrimination if it imposes a burden or a disadvantage that cannot be justified on grounds that clearly outweigh the discriminatory effect. In this context, a number of questions can be raised in applying the concept of indirect discrimination in tax law, but of these, only two issues will be discussed here: the scope of the comparisons to be made in order to demonstrate the disadvantageous impact of tax deductions and reasons that might justify financial disadvantages.

Choosing the Right Group

Equality or discrimination analysis requires comparison between groups of people. As a rule, these groups are formed based on the target group or the scope of the regulation in question (Bieback 1997: 85; Fuchsloch 1995: 159ff).[24] But what is the right target group or the right scope? Employees legally eligible for tax deductions based on employer-provided pension plans, employees actually claiming deductions, employees at large, taxpayers or everyone? The scope of tax deductions concerning indirect gender discrimination is not as easily defined as in cases of indirect discrimination regarding terms of employment or wage discrimination. Terms of employment or wage regulations are usually limited to employees who belong to a certain company or who work under a particular trade union agreement. In addition, the definition of the target group or the scope of a regulation created by the legislature can draw distinctions between groups, thereby creating disadvantages.

Looking at some of the data described earlier, it becomes apparent that tax deductions for employer-provided pension plans create very different

[23] § 22 AGG; see, among others Council Directive 2000/43/EC of 29 June 2000 implementing the principle of equal treatment between persons irrespective of racial or ethnic origin, at 21.

[24] For a different opinion, see Wisskirchen 1994: 83.

gender disadvantages, depending on the choice of comparison groups. The following are some examples:

1. Comparing female and male employees participating in employer-provided pension plans demonstrates that contributions made by women are lower than the contributions made by men. This results in a lower amount of tax deductions and diminishes the resulting tax relief (Figure 3). The same comparison group, differentiated according to type of pension plan (the *Pensionskassen* or the *Pensionsfonds*), also shows gender differences in the percentage of employees subject to social security contributions who used tax deductions to pension plans taken from pre-tax wages (Figure 2).
2. By comparing employees legally eligible for tax deductions for contributions made to employer-provided pension plans (employees at large) and employees actually participating, it becomes clear that the number and percentage of female participants in employer-provided pension plans—compared with female employees legally eligible—is less than the number and percentage of male participants (Table 1).
3. In a different scenario, it would be possible to create a category of women and men who are capable of gainful employment or who are actually in need of provisions for retirement income but who are not legally eligible for tax deductions for employer-provided pension plans because they do not pay taxes (or, in the case of private pension plans, because they do not make contributions to social security). This category would show even more significant gender differences in the use of, and access to, employer-provided or private pension plans.

These examples show that the definition of the target group or the legislature's intended scope of tax regulations may already create distinctions, limiting the legal or 'actual' access of certain groups and resulting in different kinds of disadvantages. Limiting the indirect discrimination analysis to comparisons within a specific target group or within the legislation's intended scope excludes certain groups and prevents the examination of a number of problems of equal access to tax deductions. It also does not comply with the judgment of the Federal Constitutional Court whereby the negative impact of a regulation does not depend on the intention of the legislator (for example, BVerfGE 114, 357 (364)). The prohibition of indirect discrimination is supposed to prevent disadvantageous gender impacts of tax regulations. In order to determine a disadvantage, comparison groups therefore have to be formed on the base of the outcomes of tax regulations.

Reasons Justifying Financial Disadvantages

Not every disadvantage is to be judged as indirect discrimination, but it might be justified with proper reasons. In the context of the labour market, German jurisprudence has developed categories for those justifications (see Wisskirchen 1994: 113ff). However, the categories cannot be fully transferred to tax law because, as a rule, they are related to the economic and entrepreneurial interests of the employer. In tax law, other interests and objectives related to the purpose of tax regulations need to be taken into consideration.

One could argue that the gender impact of tax deductions for employer-provided pension plans (for example, the different levels of deductions due to gender differences in income or working patterns) is justified because the tax law simply parallels differences in employment. In case law, differing levels of pension plan contributions, which were based on the level of income or hours of work, have been upheld as legal (for example, German Federal Labour Court 3 AZR 149/94, AP 1995, § 2 BeschFG 1985; European Court of Justice C-4/02 und C-5/02 *Schoenheit v Frankfurt/M* and *Becker v Hessen*).

However, it is not valid to use these reasons to justify disadvantages in tax law—at least not when they are used in such a general sense. Tax law often relates to social, economic or legal policies, but differences or disadvantages in the employment sector or other societal realms do not allow tax regulations to reproduce, reinforce or even increase those gender differences. Prohibiting indirect discrimination in tax law tackles tax-related disadvantages that reinforce or extend beyond existing employment disadvantages. Therefore, the stated reasons used to justify differing levels of contributions to employer-provided pension plans for men and women are not simply to be transferred to justify tax disadvantages. The discriminatory impact in question is the tax relief allotted by the state and not the contribution financed by the employer. Employment-related benefits and tax deductions usually have different aims and might therefore be justified for different reasons. Contributions to employer-provided pension plans are a wage substitute or supplement, meaning that differences in the amount can be justified by work performance, relating to hours of work as much as to a wage itself (for example, Federal Labour Court 3 AZR 695/92; AP 1994, § 1 BetrAVG; 3 AZR 149/94, AP 1995, § 2 BeschFG 1985). By contrast, the tax deductibility of contributions to employer-provided pensions simply reduces the pre-tax income (and therefore limiting the tax payable) without even adding the tax relief to the pension plan savings. It is primarily an incentive to sign up for this kind of pension scheme and there is no reason why the number of working hours should justify different tax incentives.

In the context of German and European jurisprudence, a balancing or proportionality test is applied to determine whether gender-related disadvantages are to be justified (see BVerfGE 113, 1 (20); European Court of Justice C-170/84 *Bilka*). According to this test, where there is a discriminatory impact, there must be a legitimate purpose if the regulation is to be upheld. Furthermore, the measures taken to achieve this aim must be effective, necessary and the purpose compared to the discriminatory impact proportionate. In tax law, the purposes of tax regulations differ.

The main purpose of taxation is to raise revenue to be spent on government programmes. In order to justify the imposition of taxes those tax regulations have to comply with the principle of the ability to pay. Since the ability to pay is confined by the prohibition of indirect discrimination, the criteria selected to substantiate the principle of the ability to pay must comply with the requirements of the proportionality test. By requiring the legislator to justify the gender impact of tax regulations, the prohibition of indirect discrimination modifies the meaning of tax equity.

Increasingly, the tax system is not only being used to raise revenue, but to achieve other goals, such as the promotion of employment or other social or economic purposes. In German tax law, tax deduction for employer-provided pension plans have been predominately discussed as tax expenditures, aiming at the strengthening of employer provided pension plans. In case of gender disadvantages resulting from tax expenditures, the intended purpose also must comply with the requirements of the proportionality principle. For example, the high contribution limit of about €4400 and the deduction of contributions to employer-provided pension plans from the tax base are effective in order to create an incentive for the accumulation of supplemental retirement income. But there are alternative regulations equally effective and less discriminatory for women, such as reducing the contribution room, deducting the contributions from the tax liability or using supplementary transfers increasing retirement income savings for low-income groups.

The proportionality test also works for the limited access to pension plans, resulting in fewer opportunities for women to benefit from tax deductions for employer-provided pension plans. As described earlier, tax incentives for contributions to employer-provided pension plans may have significantly reduced the differences between the numbers of male and female employees participating in those plans. Measures that aim to reduce gender-based differences might be considered as a purpose to justify discriminatory effects.[25] But tax incentives alone are not an effective instrument to fully abolish the different pension plan participation of male and female employees. As noted earlier, the legal title to pension plan contributions via deferred compensation, as well as instruments of employee participation to push employers to provide pension plans, have a dominating influence on the growing number of employees participating in employer-provided pension plans. In small companies and in industries where women outnumber men, instruments of employee participation very often do not exist. Furthermore, the legal title to pension plan contributions via deferred compensation is limited to employees subject to social security contributions, and therefore not effective for limited occupations, dominated by women. More effective instruments to ensure

[25] In order to justify unequal distribution effects, the draft of a new law must demonstrate an intention to reduce gender differences (see BVerfG 122, 210 (232)). *Ex-ante* justification would force the legislator to deal with the impact of a tax norm and allow other—less discriminatory—alternatives to be developed, before the new law coming into effect.

a supplemental retirement income of men and women would be pension plans that are independent of branch of trade or the adoption of obligatory employer-provided pension plans. In order to avoid indirect discrimination the legislator has to ensure that male and female employees have the same actual opportunities to participate in employer provided tax deductions.

Even then, the problem remains that tax deductions for employer-provided pension plans are limited to employees. Just as the statutory pensions system, the promotion of employer-provided pension plans through the tax systems does not acknowledge unpaid work, mostly provided by women. The choice of the purpose or the goal of a certain tax regulation lies within the manoeuvring abilities of the legislator. Goals, such as the strengthening of employer-provided pension plans are shaped by gender relations. Within the proportionality test, this problem can only be discussed as part of the consideration, whether the intended purpose is proportionate to the discriminatory impact. But note, that there are very few standards and the consideration very much depends on the political weight gender equality has in society. A much stronger instrument to promote an equal distribution of (tax) expenditures in consideration of public goals is the instrument of 'gender budgeting'.

REFERENCES

Baer, S and Lewalter, S (2007) 'Zielgruppendifferenzierte Gesetzesfolgenabschätzung. Ein Aspekt des Gender Mainstreaming und ein Beitrag zu "better governance"' 3 *DÖV* 195–202.

Beblo, M (2007) 'Die Wirkungsweise des Ehegattensplittings bei kollektiver Entscheidungsfindung im Haushalt' in B Seel (ed), *Ehegattensplitting und Familienpolitik* (Wiesbaden, Deutscher Universitätsverlag) 269–94.

Bieback, KJ (1997) *Die mittelbare Diskriminierung wegen des Geschlechts: ihre Grundlagen im Recht der EU und ihre Auswirkungen auf das Sozialrecht der Mitgliedstaaten* (Baden-Baden, Nomos-Verlag).

Birk, D (2010) *Steuerrecht* (Heidelberg, CF Müller Verlag).

Blaufus, K and Ortlieb, R (2008) 'Betriebliche Zusatzleistungen: Analyse und Gestaltungsmöglichkeiten am Beispiel der betrieblichen Altersversorgung' in G Krell (ed), *Chancengleichheit durch Personalpolitik* (Wiesbaden, Gabler Verlag) 305–16.

BMAS (Federal Ministry of Employment and Social Affairs) (2005) *Alterssicherungsbericht 2005*. Available at: www.bmas.de/portal/9292/alterssicherungsbericht__2005.html.

—— (2008) *Alterssicherungsbericht 2008*. Available at: www.bmas.de/coremedia/generator/29492/2008__11__19__alterssicherungsbericht.html.

Bothfeld, S, Klammer, U, Klenner, C, Leiber, S, Thiel, A and Ziegler, A (eds) (2005) *Frauendatenreport 2005* (Berlin, Ed Sigma).

Brown, DA (2004) 'Pensions, Risk and Race' 61 *Washington and Lee Law Review* 1501–39.

—— (2007) 'Pensions and Risk Aversion: The Influence of Race, Ethnicity, and Class on Investor Behavior' 11 *Lewis and Clark Law Review* 385–406.

Donnelly, M (1993) 'The Disparate Effect of Pension Reform on Women' 6 *Canadian Journal of Women and the Law* 419–54.

Dorenkamp, C (2001) 'Die nachgelagerte Besteuerung der sog. Riester-Rente—einkommensteuerrechtlich ein großer Wurf, zumindest für den Regelfall. Eine Analyse der §§ 10a, 22 Nr. 5 sowie des XI. EStG-Abschnitts' 3 *Steuern und Wirtschaft* 253–70.

Fellows, ML (1998) 'Rocking the Tax Code: A Case Study of the Tax Treatment of Work-Related Child-Care Expenditures' 10 *Yale Journal of Law and Feminism* 307–96.

Fuchsloch, C (1995) *Das Verbot der mittelbaren Geschlechtsdiskriminierung Ableitung, Analyse und exemplarische Anwendung auf staatliche Berufsausbildu ngsförderung* (Baden-Baden, Nomos-Verlag).

—— (2004) 'Moderne und geschlechtergerechte Anforderungen an eine Alterssicherung' in M Koreuber and U Mager (eds), *Recht und Geschlecht. Zwischen Gleichberechtigung, Gleichstellung und Differenz* (Baden-Baden, Nomos).

Infanti, AC (2008) 'Tax Equity' University of Pittsburgh Legal Studies Research Paper no 2007-01 *Buffalo Law Review*.

Leiber, S (2005) 'Formen und Verbreitung der betrieblichen Altersvorsorge—eine Zwischenbilanz' 6 *WSI-Mitteilungen* 314–21.

Leitner, S (2003) 'Wenn ich einmal alt bin. Alterssicherung von Frauen nach der Rentenreform 2001' in B Wrede (ed), *Geld und Geschlecht. Tabus, Paradoxien, Ideologien* (Opladen, Leske und Budrich).

McCall, L (2005) 'Managing the Complexity of Intersectionality' 30 *Journal of Women in Culture and Society* 1771–1800.

Mueckenberger, U, Spangenberg, U and Warncke, K (2007) *Familienfoerderung und Gender Mainstreaming im Steuerrecht* (Baden-Baden, Nomos-Verlag).

Riedmüller, B and Willert M (2008) *Die Zukunft der Alterssicherung. Analyse und Dokumentation der Datengrundlagen aktueller Rentenpolitik*. Available at: www.boeckler.de/pdf_fof/S-2008-90-4-1.pdf.

Tipke, K (2003) *Die Steuerrechtsordnung 2. Steuerrechtfertigungstheorie, Anwendung auf alle Steuerarten, sachgerechtes Steuersystem* (Köln, Verlag Dr Otto Schmidt).

Tipke, K and Lang, J (2010) *Steuerrecht* (Köln, Verlag Dr Otto Schmidt).

TNS Infratest Sozialforschung (2005) *Künftige Alterseinkommen der Arbeitnehmer mit Zusatzversorgung*. Final report. Available at: www.sozialpolitik-aktuell.de/.../kuenftige-alterseinkommen-der-arbeitnehmer-mit_20zusatzversorgung-2005.pdf.

—— (2008) Situation und Entwicklung der betrieblichen Altersversorgung in der Privatwirtschaft und im öffentlichen Dienst 2001-2007. Final report. Available at: www.bmas.de/coremedia/generator/30028/property=pdf/f384__forschungsbericht.pdf.

Wisskirchen, G (1994) *Mittelbare Diskriminierung von Frauen im Erwerbsleben. Die Rechtsprechung des Bundesarbeitsgerichts, des Europäischen Gerichtshofes und des US Supreme Court* (Berlin, Ducker und Humblot).

Young, CFL (1997) 'Public Taxes, Privatizing Effects, and Gender Equality' in SB Boyd (ed), *Challenging the Public/Private Divide: Feminism, Law, and Public Policy* (Toronto, University of Toronto Press) 307–29.

—— (2000) *Women, Tax and Social Programs: The Gendered Impact of Funding Social Programs through the Tax System* (Ottawa, Status of Women Canada). Available at: http://publications.gc.ca/pub?id=293915&sl=0.

14

Gender and Capital Gains Taxation

MARJORIE E KORNHAUSER

MOST COUNTRIES GRANT capital gains preferential treatment under their income tax laws by either excluding them from taxation or taxing them at a lower rate than wage or interest income.[1] Although this preference is not uncontroversial, few people question it on grounds of gender. Nevertheless, gender issues exist. Most obviously, men as a group benefit more from the preference than women because they generally have more capital gains than women. Moreover, a major justification for the preference is that it increases economic growth by encouraging investments. However, to the extent it does so, it can have a disparate impact on men and women because economic growth can affect men and women differently. More subtle gender differences also exist. Empirical evidence suggests that attitudes and behaviours regarding financial decisions—including capital gains—are gendered. Women, for example, being more risk averse than men, may have fewer capital gains because they invest in fewer risky assets, which are the types of assets that produce the biggest capital gains. Risk aversion could produce this result even if men and women value economic growth equally, but it is possible that women do not value economic growth per se as highly as men do. They might value economic security and steady income more than men and therefore might prefer less volatile investments that produce ordinary income—such

[1] The United States is no exception. In 1921, only months after the US Supreme Court declared that capital gains were taxable income, Congress for the first time accorded such gains preferential treatment (see *Merchants' Loan & Trust Co v Smietanka* 255 US 509 (1921)). The Revenue Act of 1921 provided for a maximum tax rate of 12½% and also enacted various non-recognition provisions such as the one for exchange of like kind property (now § 1031). Comprehensive tax reform in 1986 eliminated the preferential rate, since the top tax rates were generally lowered to 28%—the former capital gains rate—but certain exclusions and deferrals remained. The preferential rate returned when Congress increased tax rates. Some countries do not tax capital gains at all, but the number of such jurisdictions is much smaller than it used to be. See n 5 and accompanying text (below) for a very brief discussion of a few of the rationales for capital gains treatment.

as certificates of deposits—to riskier investments, which would produce capital gains.[2]

This chapter explores the relationship between gender and capital gains taxation, an analysis that has generally been absent from debates about capital gains. It briefly examines disparate impacts due to disparities in economic situations, but it concentrates on differences in attitudes and behaviours relative to capital gains. The chapter's limited space permits only an introduction; a fuller discussion awaits not only more space, but more data.

The chapter is structured as follows. First, it briefly addresses two preliminary issues regarding gender—the difference between sex and gender, and the problem of gender essentialism. Next, it presents—again briefly—some basic data regarding economic disparities between men and women that might create different preferences regarding tax policy.

Gender differences are then examined in the context of worldviews, attitudes and financial behaviour. Gender and worldviews are first discussed in a general way, followed by a summary of some empirical evidence regarding specific attitudes and behaviours involved in financial decisions, such as risk and competitiveness. The chapter asserts that although worldviews and gendered attitudes both affect financial decision-making behaviours, the individual influence of each factor is difficult to determine. Since women are more associated with one worldview and men with another, there is a tendency to conflate the two factors into one gendered account of difference. Consequently, although gender differences play an important role in financial decision making, this conflation overemphasizes that role.

The preferential tax treatment of capital gains is then considered in light of the previous discussion. While recognizing that a limited capital gains preference may be merited to counterbalance tax provisions that discourage risk taking, it suggests the current preference is too strong. Not only does preferential treatment ignore those investors who prefer less risk taking and more stability, but in addition, the current degree of preference may contribute to unhealthy amounts of speculation, which contribute to financial busts such as occurred in the current economic crisis.

SEX AND GENDER, AND GENDER ESSENTIALISM

Any discussion of gender differences encounters two major issues, which can be noted only briefly in this chapter. The first issue is the relationship between sex and gender. The two are interrelated but not identical concepts, as sex is biological and gender is sociological. Many abilities and personality traits are associated with a particular sex and defined in gender terms

[2] See also ch 3 in this volume (Stewart) for a discussion of how women in Australia benefit less than men from capital gains tax concessions.

as either masculine or feminine. Scientific ability, for example, is often identified with males and as a masculine trait, with some people claiming that men as a group are innately more skilled at science than women. Assertiveness is labelled a masculine trait, whereas passivity is considered a feminine one. Nevertheless, genetic females—even 'feminine' women—have some masculine traits, while men have feminine traits.

Considerable debate exists as to the role nature (sex) and nurture (gender) play in creating these differences between men and women. For example, opportunities, societal expectations and innate aptitude all influence the different degrees of scientific achievement that women and men evidence. Demographic factors also affect traits that some think of as inherently male or female. Younger, more educated women tend to be more assertive than older, less educated women, for instance.

The complex relationship between gender and sex makes it difficult to understand certain phenomena, such as apparent sex-based differences in abilities (for example, mathematical skill), personality traits (for example, risk adversity) or behaviour (for example, financial decisions). Nevertheless, understanding the relative importance of nature and nurture in affecting behaviour is necessary not only to determine whether differences exist, but to identify their causes, the desirability of altering the differences, the ability to do so and the methods of accomplishing change.

Despite the importance of differentiating between sex and gender, many studies use the terms interchangeably. This imprecision inevitably skews results, complicates the interpretations of the results and contributes to inaccurate conclusions (Childs 2006; Meier-Pesti and Penz 2008). Since many of the studies discussed in this chapter do not differentiate between sex and gender, it is frequently impossible to distinguish between the two. Consequently, out of necessity, the two terms are sometimes used interchangeably in this chapter as well.

The second issue is 'gender essentialism'. To overgeneralize a concept that is itself considered by some to be an overgeneralization, gender essentialism universalizes women. According to this principle, the mere fact of being a woman influences every woman in the same way. In a sense, this is a specific example of the sex-gender confusion: the assumption that all women are alike in a fundamental way conflates sex and gender. However, women's experiences, confirmed by statistical data, reveal that sex is only one of various demographic factors that shape people's attitudes and behaviours (Brown 2007).

Gender essentialism assumes that sex trumps other demographic factors such as age, race, class, education, ethnicity, health, marital status and the presence of children. In reality, however, these other factors also play a significant role in determining attitudes and behaviour. For instance, a low-income, southern, rural, white, American-born-and-raised woman who dropped out of high school differs in many significant respects from a high-income, college-educated, white, American-born-and-raised woman living in New York City, let alone a high-income, college-educated Indian woman raised in Mumbai and living in California. Studies are mixed. Some have found that when controlling for demographic factors such as income, age, class, education and race, at least some gender differences disappear as did a recent study regarding wealth (Warren 2006). In contrast, other studies do not deny the importance of these other demographic factors but hold that sex by itself still creates distinctions between men and women (Huddy, Cassese and Lizotte 2008; Swers 2002). For example, one study found that gender differences are greater in wealthier countries and in countries where there is greater gender equality (Feng and Seasholes 2008; Schmitt et al 2008). The authors suggest that one possible explanation for this phenomenon is that as equality between the sexes improves in a society, innate differences have more opportunity to flourish.

Most financial studies that consider the issue find significant sex/gender differences. Men and women have different actual financial positions, and they have different attitudes regarding finances. It is not clear, however, whether these differences are a result of sex, gender, a combination of the two or flaws in the study designs themselves. Financial decisions are complicated; they are not one-time events but take place over years, so that prior decisions influence later decisions and all are affected by actual present conditions and by future uncertainties of life.

ECONOMIC DISPARITIES BETWEEN MEN AND WOMEN

Statistical differences exist between men and women regarding basic economic status. For example, in the United States and many other countries most studies find that men, as a group, have more income than women, even though the gap has narrowed in recent years (Deere and Doss 2006; Yamoskowki and Keister 2006). Although there are fewer studies regarding wealth, the data that does exist indicates that men as a group are also generally wealthier than women. Older women's wealth is frequently the result of inheritance.

Although men as a group have more income and wealth than women as a group, the intersection of sex with other demographic factors creates wide variations within subgroups. White males in the United States earn more than black males, for example, and intersectionality creates similarities between subgroups that cross sex lines. The composition of financial assets held by black males, for example, more closely resembles that of white females than that of white males (Moran and Whitford 1996: 764–69).

Studies differ as to whether economic gender gaps exist after controlling for demographics. Yet even when a study reveals no gap, a gap may still exit. The authors of one study, which found no gender wealth gap between young men and young women, suggest this result might simply indicate that the gap does not emerge until later in life (Schmidt and Sevak 2006: 162). When studies do show gender wealth-income gaps even after controlling for some demographic variables, it is unclear whether the cause is sex, gender, other demographic factors or a combination of these. For example, a number of studies have found that gender differences in negotiating skill, desire and/or personality traits explain part of the earnings gap between men and women (Mueller and Plug 2006). The underlying cause of those differences, however, remains uncertain.

Economic conditions also affect men and women differently. For example, in recent years, American women's wages grew at a faster pace than men's wages (Autor, Katz and Kearney 2008: 302–04) but as a group, women still earn less than men. During the current recession in the United States, men are losing jobs faster than women, largely because the most hard-hit industries, such as the car industry, are male dominated (Belkin 2009).[3] At the same time, since women work part-time more than men, and since they hold fewer high-tech, financial and executive jobs, they are less likely to benefit from the extreme upside of booms. Even high-earning women may benefit less than high- earning men because of glass ceilings and also because women often are hired for high executive jobs when the company is already failing (Thompson 2008).

Leaving aside, for the moment, the issue of how women invest money, women are less likely to have capital gains income than men.[4] This occurs because high-income, wealthy individuals receive the bulk of capital gains income (Hungerford 2009) and women—as previously noted—generally have less income and wealth than men. Moreover, women are less likely to receive job compensation in the form of capital gains income than men. The jobs that produce capital gains as part of their compensation packages—such as entrepreneurial, high-tech, financial and CEO positions—are still largely male dominated. Hedge fund and private equity managers, for example, whose enormous fees have been taxed at capital gains rates, are predominantly male (McGee 2008).

Again, although the facts are clear, the causes are not. Do women work part-time by choice or out of necessity? Do men dominate hedge funds

[3] In April 2009, unemployment rates rose 7.1% for adult women and 9.4% for men (Bureau of Labor, 'The Employment Situation: April 2009'). Available at: www.bls.gov/news.release/pdf/empsit.pdf.

[4] Statistics in several countries indicate that women do, in fact, receive far less capital gains income than men. For instance, Canadian statistics for 2006, the last available year, indicate that in all age groups except 20–25, men have more capital gains than women (Final Basic Table 4: All Returns by Age and Sex, All Canada. Available at: www.cra-arc.gc.ca/gncy/stts/gb06/pst/fnl/html/tbl4-eng.html). Data in Spain similarly shows men with more capital gains income than women (de Villota Gil-Escoín, Ferrari Herrero and Sahagún Blanco 2008).

because of their greater abilities and interests in the area or because of societal forces? To what degree is biology or society the cause of the differences? Without weighing in on the question of causation, the rest of this chapter will examine the concept of worldviews (or cultural cognitions) that appear to be related to gender differences regarding attitudes about capital gains. These attitudes, in turn, affect both ultimate holdings of wealth and the ways in which the wealth is used.

THE INTERPLAY OF SEX/GENDER, WORLDVIEWS, ATTITUDES AND FINANCIAL BEHAVIOUR

Worldviews: Individualism versus Connectedness

Worldviews (or cultural cognitions) shape a person's attitudes, beliefs, perceptions and behaviours, including those involving financial decisions. Involving both cognitive and affective processes, worldviews allow people to respond quickly to the otherwise overwhelming amount of stimuli that bombard them daily. They create general 'rules of thumb' that allow individuals to efficiently acquire, store, organize and retrieve knowledge; they influence the perception of new data (including financial data) and an individual's reactions to it, often at a subconscious level (Kahan, Hoffman and Braman 2009).

Paired worldviews are situated on a spectrum, with opposing outlooks at each end. There are two major continua: egalitarian-hierarchist and individualist-communitarian. Although one end of a worldview spectrum generally dominates in an individual, a person may also have traits characteristic of the other view. An egalitarian, for instance, may have some hierarchist views. Moreover, certain worldviews on different spectra tend to go together. Egalitarians, for example, are often communitarians.

Nations, like individuals, may be dominated by one worldview or another. Scandinavian countries, for instance, are more communitarian and egalitarian than individualistic and hierarchist. Americans, on the other hand, are stereotypically viewed as individualists, but in fact, Americans demonstrate that people exhibit both attributes of the continuum of a worldview. For example, the United States Constitution was established, as its preamble proclaims, not only to secure liberty (an individualist value) but to promote the general welfare (a communitarian value). The quintessential American belief in equality of opportunity also rests on both views. It is individualist in promoting each individual's agency—his or her capacity to achieve a personal goal; it is communitarian, however, in recognizing that the community (and government) must bear some responsibility for ensuring that each person has adequate means (health, education, food, etc) to take advantage of opportunities. Although there is disagreement about the amount of responsibility the community must assume, there is agreement that some level is necessary. Otherwise, there is no level playing field, and no true equality of opportunity exists.[5]

Since worldviews influence people's attitudes, beliefs and actions, they also affect financial decisions. At a general level, individualists—who value autonomy, self-reliance and individual responsibility—might be more willing to engage in risky financial behaviour in order to provide for their welfare than communitarians would be, since communitarians are more oriented towards cooperation and emphasize joint obligations for societal needs such as health and education. Hierarchists might be more willing to engage in risky behaviour to achieve greater gains that would establish and/or confirm their place in the hierarchy than egalitarians, who are less concerned with this issue. An egalitarian, however, might be more willing to engage in a financially risky decision if the desired outcome would promote equality by spreading benefits to numerous people, rather than to just one individual.

People tend to perceive and value traits and behaviours that fit their worldviews, although they often do so at a subconscious level. For example, they generally minimize risk when a policy or action harmonizes with their worldview (Kahan 2008). Consistent with this phenomenon, one study found that communitarian (labelled 'solidaristic' in the study) and egalitarian-oriented individuals were more concerned with environmental risks such as global warming and pollution than were individualistic, hierarchist individuals (Kahan et al 2006: 1086).

Logically, attitudes and behaviours regarding financial risk would show similar divisions. Individualists, who value industriousness and economic growth as steps towards self-sufficiency would have a different view of financial risk taking from communitarians, who are more concerned with the group as a whole than with individual achievement. Because they value the results of financial risk taking, individualists might either underestimate the amount of risk involved in a particular financial decision, or they might estimate the risk accurately but believe the goal (self-sufficiency) justified the risk. Valuing risk more, individualists would then engage in it more. Furthermore, they would also be more likely to support a tax policy that favoured capital gains.

Although most people have elements of both individualist and communitarian worldviews, individualist ones—as discussed later—are often deemed to be masculine and the communitarian ones are considered to be feminine.

[5] See also ch 1 by Lahey for a discussion of the effects of community property systems on equality between men and women in terms of income tax.

Sex/Gender and the Financial Constellation

Sex and gender—like other demographic factors—influence a number of attitudes and behaviours connected with financial decisions, which this chapter calls, collectively, the 'financial constellation'. Risk, competitiveness and confidence are the most prominent factors, with risk being the factor most investigated in studies to date. Studies generally show that, across cultures, women are more risk averse than men. According to some studies, differences regarding risk actually increase as gender equality in the society as a whole improves (Schmitt et al 2008).

There are many kinds of risk, however, and while studies overwhelmingly find that women are more risk averse in terms of physical or life-threatening risks, the evidence regarding financial risk is more mixed. Nevertheless, numerous studies conclude that women are more risk averse than men in financial situations as well. Different attitudes regarding financial risk taking translate into different behaviour. For example, wealthy women hold a smaller percentage of their assets in closely held businesses, and women generally hold less common stock than men do (Barber and Odean 2001: 275; Raub 2004).

Several systemic factors contribute to the mixed empirical findings. The design of the study, for example, can skew results. So, too, can the differences between laboratory and real-world environments (Antonovics, Arcidiacono and Walsh 2009). The complicated—and only partially understood—nature of financial decisions (as discussed later) further confuses matters. Additionally, the failure of studies to differentiate between gender and sex plays a role in the mixed results.

Some studies find few, if any, differences between men and women regarding financial decisions once the study controls for appropriate factors such as age and education (Kruse and Thompson 2003). This failure to find any differences suggests that existing differences are not biologically (sex) based but instead are sociologically mediated gender differences. Most Western cultures, for example, view risk taking as a 'masculine' trait. Cultural changes, however, could alter this view. Indeed, one recent study of college students found that gendered differences disappeared as women acquired education and engaged in the market because the women then acquired more masculine traits and became less risk-averse (Meier-Pesti and Penz 2008: 190–91). Nevertheless, other studies contradict this result and find that differences between men and women remain even among relatively homogeneous populations such as college students (for example, Charness and Gneezy 2007). The persistence of female risk adversity may indicate that biologically based sex is implicated, but this is not necessarily the case, as other possible explanations exist. For example, the persistence of the difference may simply indicate either that the financial decision-making process is not yet fully understood and/or that studies need further refinement to tease out gender differences that may disappear as individual and societal circumstances change.

Mixed findings may also occur because studies do not properly account for various other factors connected with risk. Recently, however, studies have begun to deconstruct the components of risk that can affect behaviour, such as different perceptions and evaluations of the kind (and amount) of risk. One study, for instance, found that women and men assign different weights to the possibility of gains or losses (Fehr-Duda, de Gennaro and Schubert 2006). Another one found significant gender differences in perceptions, depending on whether negative consequences would occur, as well as whether the participant was likely to enjoy the possible gains from successfully engaging in the risky behaviour. This study also found that women were more likely than men to engage in a risky behaviour if they believed a small cost might produce a large gain. The authors suggested two possible reasons for this: women's 'greater investment in producing offspring physically, and women's greater responsibility for taking care of children' (Harris and Jenkins 2006: 60). Interestingly, this last hypothesis meshes extremely well with a communitarian view. As researchers continue to tease out the different strands of risk, study results may show more consistent results.

Yet another cause of the mixed results regarding sex/gender and financial decisions is that risk—complicated though it is by itself—is not the sole trait affecting financial decisions. Research is just beginning to tease out the components of the 'financial constellation' that closely interact with risk taking. Results so far suggest that the components of this constellation, such as competitiveness and confidence, also correlate with gender. For example, some studies indicate that women are not only less competitive than men, but that they perform better in non-competitive situations than in competitive ones (for example, Fellner and Maciejovsky 2007; Niederle and Vesterlund 2007). Men tend to be more confident than women, and they are frequently overconfident when 'masculine' behaviours are involved. Overconfidence, for example, may be the critical factor causing men to engage in more frequent securities trading than women (for example, Heminway 2008). The general cognitive phenomenon of framing, or how an issue is presented, also appears to affect men and women differently when financial decisions are being made (for example, Agnew et al 2008).

Some observers recently suggested that sex/gender may be both a cause of—and a cure for—the over-speculation that contributed to the world's current financial disaster. The financial world is a heavily male world. Referring to recent studies concerning the effects of testosterone on risk taking, confidence and competitiveness, some commentators have noted that in the testosterone-laden, male-dominated atmosphere of the stock market, male traders became both overconfident and overcompetitive.

Consequently, they engaged in inappropriately risky behaviour. Increasing the numbers of women traders and CEOs, the commentators claimed, could 'tame' these excesses and lead to wiser financial investments (Thomson and Graham 2005; De Vita 2008; Dobrzynski 2008; Kristof 2009). However, it may be too simplistic to say that overly speculative attitudes are caused by sex/gender alone. A worldview analysis provides additional insights.

Gender, the Financial Constellation and Worldviews: A Tentative Analysis

Although many studies find that men and women differ—to a statistically significant degree—in their financial attitudes and behaviours, the causes of these differences—as previously shown—are not clear. The fact that some differences disappear when important variables such as age and education are controlled suggests that socially mediated gendered traits, rather than biological sex traits, account for some of the differences. To the extent that differences remain, it is possible that biological sex traits are involved as well as gendered traits.

It is also possible, however, that worldviews are a major variant, since they affect a person's perceptions, attitudes and beliefs, including those connected with financial decisions. Indeed, a recent study found that although gender and race were factors, worldviews accounted for a significant portion of differing risk perception when 'cultural' identity was threatened (Kahan et al, 2007). Thus, for example, it found that individualistic and hierarchist people discounted claims of environmental risks because such risks would justify governmental regulations that would contradict their belief in individualistic effort, the free market and their competency. Egalitarians and communitarians, however, did not discount such claims.

Worldviews can similarly affect financial risk and financial decisions generally because worldviews influence people's personal goals and hence their definitions of success. These differences logically could lead to differences regarding the financial constellation of attitudes and behaviours. For example, communitarians—concerned about their responsibilities to others—might be less competitive, less interested in acquiring personal wealth and more interested in helping others obtain basic necessities. Consequently, they might prefer to invest the wealth they do have in less risky assets in order to produce a steady return and therefore to ensure that there is income to provide for their needs and those of others. Communitarians also might be more likely to spend the capital itself to achieve these results, leaving them with less wealth. A communitarian view might also influence other traits connected to risk. Communitarians, for instance, might be less competitive than individualists, and this fact would temper impulses to (over)invest in risky assets in the hopes of besting others.

More women than men have a communitarian worldview as their dominant view. This fact undoubtedly explains—at least partially—why American society, like other Western societies, considers many communitarian values feminine. The 'web of care' feminine viewpoint posited by Carol Gilligan and others, for instance, is essentially a communitarian one (Gilligan 1982). A great deal of empirical evidence about women's political and economic attitudes and behaviours supports it. Politically, for example, women generally are more concerned about poverty, social welfare, education and maintaining a safety net, whereas men are more concerned with the economy (Childs 2008: 25–34; Huddy, Cassese and Lizotte 2008: 38–40; Miller 2008).

Women's greater tendency to be communitarians may partially explain many gender gaps, including the differences between men and women regarding financial attitudes and behaviours. Numerous studies indicate that women use their income differently from men, and evidence increasingly shows that they also use their wealth differently (Doss, Grown and Deere 2008: 5). These gendered patterns are consistent with a communitarian sense of connectedness and appear to reflect women's greater role in caring for others in the household. In general, women spend more on health and household-related items, especially child-related items such as childcare, food, clothing and education (Conley and Ryvicker 2004: 42, 51–53; Doss, Grown and Deere 2008). Other studies reveal different gifting patterns, suggesting that women may be more altruistic than men (Andreoni, Brown and Rischall 2003; Burton, Phipps and Woolley 2007; Kamas, Preston and Baum 2008). One study found, for example, that retired women were more likely than retired men to give gifts to friends and relatives; others found that women were more likely to give to charity (though they give smaller amounts) and more likely to donate money for health and education. A view of women being more communitarian than men is also consistent with a recent study that found that women are more likely to choose annuities than men are (Agnew et al 2008). This result held true even when controlling for risk and financial literacy. Women's webs of care and sense of connectedness might lead more women to put a priority on ensuring that they have a steady income to provide for their basic needs (and to support those relying on them). This priority could influence women to prefer conservative but steady investments such as annuities, rather than riskier, but possibly more productive, investments.

REDUCING CAPITAL GAINS PREFERENTIAL TREATMENT: A BALANCED APPROACH

United States tax laws, like those in many countries, grant preferential income tax treatment for capital gains for both economic and non-economic reasons. Economic rationales include encouraging investments, compensating for nominal gains caused by inflation, mitigating increased taxes caused by the 'bunching effect' (taxing gain accrued over many years in one year can push the taxpayer into a higher marginal bracket) and alleviating the 'lock-in' effect[6] that inhibits individuals from selling assets in order to avoid the consequent taxable gain. Probably the most important non-economic justification for the capital gains preference is an underlying admiration for confident, successful, self-sufficient people and for the type of entrepreneurial, risk-taking behaviour they engage in (which produces capital gain). American culture, with its strongly individualist worldview places particular value on such traits and behaviours.

Despite these positive rationales for favouring capital gains, both economic and non-economic arguments exist for opposing a capital gains preference. One economic reason for abolishing the preference is that, like any tax preference, it can distort economic behaviour. Favourable treatment encourages overinvestment in assets that yield capital gains as opposed to ordinary income from normal business activities or other investments. The preference can also encourage too much speculative activity, and this can contribute to gyrating economic cycles.

One important non-economic reason for opposing a capital gains preference is its disparate effect on men and women. Men generally benefit more from preferential capital gains treatment than women do because they receive more capital income. There are two primary reasons for this. First, men as a group have more income and wealth than women, especially at the top levels, where most of the capital gains occur. Secondly, holding wealth and income constant, men's investment portfolios generally contain riskier assets, which produce more capital gains than women's portfolios do.

It is not yet fully clear why capital gains disparities exist between men and women, since demographic factors such as income, wealth and education account for only part of the disparity. Two 'prime suspects' for the differences are gender/sex and worldviews. These two factors are intertwined because societies generally identify communitarian attitudes as feminine, and, in fact, more women than men tend to be communitarian.

Different worldviews—rather than gender per se—may account for many of the observed differences. People with individualist views, for example, might tend to be more competitive than communitarians and to value the accumulation of personal wealth as an indicator of valued traits such as self-reliance and industriousness. Communitarians, in contrast, might tend

[6] The lock-in effect occurs because gains on property that have accrued over many years are not treated as income for tax purposes until they are 'realized'—that is, until the property is disposed of. If a large amount of income results from the sale of property, the seller's income may move into a higher income tax bracket, but even if this is not the case, there will still be a large tax. The threat of that tax can cause the taxpayer to refrain from selling an asset that she or he would otherwise sell.

to be less competitive and more risk averse than individualists. They might also be more willing to sacrifice some of their own individual economic gain in favour of greater security and equality for themselves, those who depend on them and even the wider community. Logically, therefore, communitarians might prefer investments with more certain—albeit lower—returns than higher-yield but riskier investments. Alternatively, communitarians might have similar portfolios to those held by individualists, but the portfolios might be smaller (and so yield fewer capital gains) because communitarians amassed less wealth as a result of spending more current income and/or capital on others. The perceived gender bias evidenced in some studies may result from the fact that women tend to be more communitarian and less individualist than men.

Theoretically, different worldviews align more naturally with different tax treatments of investments. Individualists would tend to favour preferential capital gains treatment, not only because such a preference would be in their self-interest (because they have investments that would produce capital gains) but because the preference would be congruent with their moral values of industry, competition, self-reliance and economic growth. Communitarians, on the other hand, might favour preferential treatment for lower-risk, lower-yield investments, not simply because those assets are their preferred type of investment, but because such a preference would be congruent with their moral values of providing care. Low risk investments are more likely to preserve capital and provide some degree of guaranteed income. Such capital and income would fund a safety net and be readily available to smooth out lumpy consumption. In fact, communitarians might oppose capital gains preferences on the grounds that such a preference encourages speculation that could put at risk capital that might be needed for leaner times.

In reality, gender, worldviews and actual life conditions interact to create contradictory attitudes toward capital gains. For example, although women are generally more risk averse (gender) and have more communitarian values (worldview), they also generally have less income/wealth than men as well as longer life expectancy than men (life conditions). Consequently, for self-interested reasons, women might favour capital gains (despite the greater risk) because of the need to build a larger nest out of fewer sticks. On the other hand, they might object to a capital gains preference because their ability to accumulate wealth is more limited than men's and their need for current income greater. A communitarian might favour some preferred capital gains treatment but not others. For example, she might support capital gains treatment for specific items that support a communitarian view rather than a broader, more general preference. In the United States, for example, women might support § 121 that excludes from income a certain amount of capital gain from sale of a personal residence on the grounds that it facilitates the provision of shelter (specifically home-ownership), but, at the same time, she might oppose the preference for gains from stock. She might favour the exclusion of insurance proceeds or of some gifts and inheritances but oppose the preferential treatment of income from stock (dividends) especially since interest income from conservative investments such as bonds and savings account, for example, is not preferred. On balance, however, it seems likely that a communitarian worldview and gendered attitudes regarding financial decisions are more likely to contradict a desire for favoured capital gains treatment and more likely to lead women to support preferential treatment for items that strengthen the safety net (such as life insurance proceeds and retirement income).[7] At the least, the countervailing factors may lead to a more balanced treatment of different types of investments.

A more balanced treatment may be the appropriate one. It may even be exactly what the United States needs. American tax laws, like those of many countries, contain some provisions that align more closely with individualist worldviews (such as small business incentives and capital gains preferences) and some that are more consistent with communitarian ones (pension and educational preferences, for example). Both types of provisions have proliferated greatly in recent years, but those favouring capital gains have expanded dramatically. Rates have been both lowered (or, in some instances, eliminated) and extended to cover more types of income, such as dividends. Some preferential treatment may be good because it encourages necessary risk taking or compensates for economic distortions such as the lock-in effect, but—as the current financial crisis indicates—excessive risk taking can have disastrous consequences. Americans already admire risk taking and commonly regard entrepreneurs as the embodiment of the nation's individualist spirit of self-reliance. According to this view, entrepreneurs 'who know the rules of the world and the laws of God ... are the heroes of economic life' (Gilder 1984: 19). Consequently, a tax policy heavily tilted towards capital gains, together with greatly deregulated markets, may stimulate behaviour that already needs no encouragement and can transform wise investors into reckless speculators. Cutting back on those preferences would help restrain such speculation while at the same time reducing gender and/or worldview biases created by capital gains preferences.

[7] Although this suggests that women legislators would be less likely to vote for preferential capital gains treatment, that might not happen for a variety of reasons. Women legislators, for example, might be disproportionately individualist, or party affiliation might trump worldview. Thus, in the United States, where the Republican Party is more individualist than the Democratic Party, a Republican communitarian congresswoman might vote for capital gains preferences out of party loyalty. Similarly, the arcane, technical nature of tax might obscure the connection between the tax preference and a woman legislator's worldview. Although studies indicate that women legislators vote for direct spending to improve welfare and the safety net (see the main text, below), they might vote against safety net tax preferences—for the same reasons that they might vote for capital gains preferences (party affiliation, etc) or simply because the connection between the tax provision and their view is not so obvious. Although these complications would make the results of an empirical study of women legislators' voting preferences on these matters inconclusive, such a study would still be of value.

REFERENCES

Agnew, J, Anderson, L, Gerlach, J and Szykman, L (2008) 'Who Chooses Annuities? An Experimental Investigation of the Role of Gender, Framing, and Defaults' 98 *American Economic Review* 418.

Andreoni, J, Brown, E and Rischall, I (2003) 'Charitable Giving by Married Couples: Who Decides and Why does it Matter?' 38 *The Journal of Human Resources* 111.

Antonovics, K, Arcidiacono, P and Walsh, R (2009) 'The Effects of Gender Interactions in the Lab and in the Field' 91 *The Review of Economics and Statistics* 152.

Autor, D, Katz, L and Kearney, M (2008) 'Trends in US Wage Inequality: Revising the Revisionists' 90 *Review of Economics and Statistics* 300.

Barber, B and Odean, T (2001) 'Boys Will Be Boys: Gender, Overconfidence and Common Stock Investment' 116 *Quarterly Journal of Economics* 261.

Belkin, L (2009) 'The New Gender Gap' *New York Times Magazine* (4 October) 11.

Boushey, H (2009) 'Infographic: The Importance of Women Breadwinners' American Center for Progress. Available at: www.americanprogress.org/issues/2009/04/women_breadwinners.html.

Brown, DA (2007) 'Pensions and Risk Aversion: The Influence of Race, Ethnicity, and Class on Investor Behavior' 11 *Lewis and Clark Law Review* 385.

Bureau of Labor Statistics (2009) 'Household Data: Annual Averages, Table 11' 56 *Employment & Earnings Online* 196, 212. Available at: www.bls.gov/opub/ee/home.htm.

Burton, P, Phipps, S and Woolley, F (2007) 'Inequality within the Household Reconsidered' in S Jenkins and J Micklewright (eds), *Inequality and Poverty Re-Examined* (Oxford, Oxford University Press).

Charness, G and Gneezy, U (2007) 'Strong Evidence for Gender Differences in Investment'. Available at: ssrn.com/abstract=648735.

Childs, S (2006) 'The Complicated Relationship between Sex, Gender, and the Substantive Representation of Women' 13 *European Journal of Women's Studies* 7.

—— (2008) *Women and British Party Politics: Descriptive, Substantive and Symbolic Representation* (New York, Routledge).

Conley, D and Ryvicker, M (2004) 'The Price of Female Headship: Gender, Inheritance, and Wealth Accumulation in the United States' 13 *Journal of Income Distribution* 41.

Cooper, M (2008) 'The Inequality of Security: Winners and Losers in the Risk Society' 6 *Human Relations* 1229.

Deere, CD and Doss, C (2006) 'The Gender Asset Gap: What do we Know and Why does it Matter?' 12 *Feminist Economics* 1.

De Vita, E (2008) 'Let Women Tame the Macho Excess' *Management Today* (1 December) 51.

Dobrzynski, J (2008) 'Maybe the Meltdown's a Guy Thing' *New York Times* (16 November) Wk 5.

Doss, C, Grown, C and Deere, CD (2008) 'Gender and Asset Ownership: A Guide to Collecting Individual-Level Data' World Bank Policy Research Working Paper Series. Available at: ssrn.com/abstract=1260131.

Fehr-Duda, H, de Gennaro, M and Schubert, R (2006) 'Gender, Financial Risk, and Probability Weights' 60 *Theory and Decision* 283.
Fellner, G and Maciejovsky, B (2007) 'Risk Attitude and Market Behavior: Evidence from Experimental Asset Markets' 28 *Journal of Economic Psychology* 338–50.
Feng, L and Seasholes, M (2008) 'Individual Investors and Gender Similarities in an Emerging Stock Market' 16 *Pacific-Basin Financial Journal* 44.
Gilder, G (1984) *The Spirit of Enterprise* (New York, Simon and Schuster).
Gilliam, J, Goetz, J and Hampton, V (2008) 'Spousal Differences in Financial Risk Tolerance' 19 *Financial Counseling and Planning* 3.
Gilligan, C (1982) *In a Different Voice: Psychological Theory and Women's Development* (Cambridge, Harvard University Press).
Harris, C and Jenkins, M (2006) 'Gender Differences in Risk Assessment: Why do Women take Fewer Risks than Men?' 1 *Judgment and Decision Making* 48.
Heminway, J (2008) 'Female Investors and Securities Fraud: Is the Reasonable Investor a Woman?' 15 *William and Mary Journal of Women and the Law* 102.
Huddy, L, Cassese, E and Lizotte, M (2008) 'Gender, Public Opinion, and Political Reasoning' in C Wolbrecht, K Beckwith and L Baldez (eds), *Political Women and American Democracy* (Cambridge, Cambridge University Press).
Hungerford, T (2009) *Economic Effects of Capital Gains Taxation* (Washington, DC, Congressional Research Service).
Kahan, DM (2008) 'Cultural Cognition as a Conception of the Cultural Theory of Risk'. Available at: ssrn.com/abstract=1123807.
Kahan, DM, Braman, D, Gastil, J, Slovic, P and Mertz, CK (2007) 'Culture and Identity-Protective Cognition: Explaining the White Male Effect in Risk Perception' 4 *Journal of Empirical Legal Studies* 465.
Kahan, DM, Hoffman, D and Braman, D (2009) 'Whose Eyes are you going to Believe? Scott v Harris and the Perils of Cognitive Illiberalism' 122 *Harvard Law Review* 837.
Kahan, DM, Slovic P, Braman, D and Gastil, J (2006) 'Fear of Democracy: A Cultural Evaluation of Sunstein on Risk' 119 *Harvard Law Review* 1071.
Kamas, L, Preston, A and Baum, S (2008) 'Altruism in Individual and Joint-Giving Decisions: What's Gender got to do with it?' 14 *Feminist Economics* 23.
Kristof, N (2009) 'Mistresses of the Universe' *New York Times* (8 February) Wk 12.
Kruse, J and Thompson, M (2003) 'Valuing Low Probability Risk: Survey and Experimental Evidence' 50 *Journal of Economic Behavior and Organization* 495.
McGee, S (2008) 'Hedge Fund Women'. Available at: www.forbes.com/2008/04/29/hedge-executive-travel-forbeslife-cz_0429hedgefund.html.
Meier-Pesti, K and Penz, E (2008) 'Sex or Gender? Expanding the Sex-Based View by Introducing Masculinity and Femininity as Predictors of Financial Risk Taking' 29 *Journal of Economic Psychology* 180.
Miller, G (2008) 'Women's Suffrage, Political Responsiveness, and Child Survival in American History' 123 *Quarterly Journal of Economics* 1287.
Moran, BI and Whitford, WC (1996) 'A Black Critique of the Internal Revenue Code' 4 *Wisconsin Law Review* 751.
Mueller, G and Plug, E (2006) 'Estimating the Effect of Personality on Male and Female Earnings' 60 *Industrial and Labor Relations Review* 3.
Niederle, M and Vesterlund, L (2007) 'Do Women Shy away from Competition? Do Men Compete too Much?' 122 *Quarterly Journal of Economics* 1067.

Raub, B (2004) 'Personal Wealth' 28 *Statistics of Income Bulletin* 282. Available at: www.irs.gov/pub/irs-soi/08fallbul.pdf.
Schmidt, L and Sevak, P (2006) 'Gender, Marriage, and Asset Accumulation in the United States' 12 *Feminist Economics* 139.
Schmitt, D, Realo, A, Voracek, M and Allik, J (2008) 'Why Can't a Man be more like a Woman? Sex Differences in Big Five Personality Traits across 55 Cultures' 1 *Journal of Personality and Social Psychology* 168.
Swers, M (2002) *The Difference Women Make: The Policy Impact of Women in Congress* (Chicago, University Chicago Press).
Thompson, C (2008) 'Women in Power are set up to Fail' *New York Times Magazine* (12 December). Available at: www.nytimes.com/2008/12/14/magazine/14Ideas-section4B-t-006.html.
Thomson, P and Graham J (2005) *A Woman's Place is in the Boardroom: The Business Case* (New York, Palgrave Macmillan).
Villota Gil-Escoín, P, Ferrari Herrero, I and Sahagún Blanco, C (2008) 'El Impuesto sobre la Renta de las Personas Físicas en Castilla y León desde la perspective de género: Una propuesta a favor de las mujeres asalariadas' *Premio Colección de Estudios del Consejo Económico y Social de Castilla y León*, 2nd edn. Available at: isadoraduncan.es/files/File/Colecc08.pdf.
Warren, T (2006) 'Moving beyond the Gender Wealth Gap: On Gender, Class, Ethnicity, and Wealth: Inequalities in the United Kingdom' 12 *Feminist Economics* 195.
Yamoskowki, A and Keister, L (2006) 'The Wealth of Single Women: Marital Status and Parenthood in the Asset Accumulation of Young Baby Boomers in the United States' 12 *Feminist Economics* 167.

Index

www.ingramcontent.com/pod-product-compliance
Ingram Content Group UK Ltd.
Pitfield, Milton Keynes, MK11 3LW, UK
UKHW020241290926
15470UKWH00002B/659

9 781849 461238